I0878542

The American and British Debate over Equality, 1776–1920

The AMERICAN and BRITISH DEBATE OVER EQUALITY 1776–1920

JAMES L. HUSTON

LOUISIANA STATE UNIVERSITY PRESS BATON ROUGE

Published by Louisiana State University Press
Copyright © 2017 by Louisiana State University Press
All rights reserved
Manufactured in the United States of America
First printing

Designer: Barbara Neely Bourgoyne
Typeface: Ingeborg
Printer and binder: Maple Press (*digital*)

Library of Congress Cataloging-in-Publication Data are available at the Library of Congress.
978-0-8071-6744-1 (cloth : alk. paper) — 978-0-8071-6745-8 (pdf) — 978-0-8071-6746-5 (epub)

The paper in this book meets the guidelines for permanence and durability of the Committee on Production Guidelines for Book Longevity of the Council on Library Resources. ♾

Equality is the life-blood of American society.

—Frances and Teresa Pulszky, *White, Red, Black,* II:249 (1853)

[The United States] makes no invidious distinctions; there is no partiality—no respect of persons. Its spirit and genius are those of perfect political and civil equality. It creates no dukes, marquises, earls, or lords; there are no aristocracy,—no hereditary rights,—no hereditary honours and privileges. The whole nation is politically a level mass, without any nobles or local magnates either to check or to head public opinion.

—James Phillippo, *The United States and Cuba,* 57 (1857)

One sentence in the Declaration is worth repeating, not only annually, but daily:—We hold these truths to be self-evident, that *all men are created equal;* that they are endowed by their Creator with certain *inalienable rights;* that amongst these are life, *liberty,* and the pursuit of happiness.

—Archibald Prentice, *A Tour in the United States,* 6th ed., 111 (1848)

CONTENTS

PREFACE

All authors have stories about how they came to write on certain subjects, interesting little tales of libraries, historical societies, treasures never before consulted, and oddities of discovery. I have mine. The genesis of this book, which I had never planned to write, came from strange experiences and directions, and I shall take a few pages to narrate them.

As my abiding interest for over forty years of research and writing has been political economy and sectional antagonism in the two decades before the Civil War, I decided to explore the possibilities of agricultural differences being the foundation for antebellum sectional hostility. That interest led to my book *The British Gentry, the Southern Planter, and the Northern Family Farmer: Agriculture and Sectional Antagonism in North America* (Louisiana State University Press, 2015). The subject took me to times far earlier than 1840 and to Great Britain in search of understanding the evolution of American agricultural development. Rather late in the research, after I had actually visited all the repositories necessary to make conclusions, I remembered that foreign travelers, mainly British, had visited the United States in the nineteenth century and I probably should consult them. Quite frankly, this was almost a research methodology afterthought. My initial skepticism about the use of travel accounts was based on my earlier impression that these visitors were people obsessed with the practice of American democracy. Moreover, historical research has been governed by the description of the United States by one person in particular: Alexis de Tocqueville. Tocqueville's *Democracy in America* has become a standard text and a standard topic for explication, and most of his analysis had little to do with agriculture (but, surprisingly, more than I originally thought). I soon found out that there were loads of interesting commentaries on American agriculture by these travelers, and the sources became fundamental to my work. As is my custom, I took the occasion to peruse the works for more than agriculture—and, to be honest, more than the usual grumping about mass politics—and found there a deep and abiding discussion of equality, what it meant, and how equality shaped American lives—and for some, how it was denied. That was a starting point for a reassessment of how historians have presented the nineteenth-century American idea of equality and its operation, and especially its comparison to inequality—the comparison, often ignored by historians, being supplied by the same British travelers.

Several personal incidents, but one in particular, convinced me that an article or short book on the subject was not only useful for historical understanding of the American past but had a poignant relevance to modern debates in the twenty-first century. In 2009 I was part of a roughly twenty-member committee assigned to winnow down candidates for the position of Dean of Arts and Sciences at Oklahoma State University. Interviews were arranged, and several candidates were brought to campus. One was a political scientist. So the committee sat at a long oval table and asked the usual questions, and the discussion wandered off onto various topics. At one point, the applicant exclaimed, for some reason I cannot remember, that "No one believes in equality any more in academia, except for historians." The eyes turned to me, and I blurted out something to the effect, "It comes from the heart," thumping my chest with my fist. A little laughter ensued, but I went no further in explanation. I was dumbfounded by the assertion. I had just read ample primary sources on the battle between equality and inequality between nineteenth-century Americans and Britishers and had written a one-hundred-page monster article that required considerable revision. All the stories just crashed around in my head, and I knew if I started talking I would keep talking for the next five or six days. But that day I did not have my wits about me. When the mind is filled with too much detail, the tongue gets tied in knots.

Yet the candidate's assertion has not been an isolated incident. Statements about the uselessness and folly of equality have reverberated in endless forums in the late twentieth century and the early twenty-first. It is time to remind ourselves of not just a heritage seemingly forgotten, but the realities that equality and inequality produced in the nineteenth century—

and why all of western Europe finally shed its hallucinations about the glories of inequality and opted for the morally correct and realistic vistas of equality in the mid- and late twentieth century.

The reason that this debate over equality and inequality is being presented in a book format—besides the fact that no historian has even covered the subject before—and not in article form derives from an unwelcome realization about the tendencies within the academic historical community. Certain types of investigations and conclusions are welcome, others are not. The writing on the American colonies and states prior to 1950 had its celebratory quality, and the parts that were not laudatory—such as slavery and conflicts with Native Americans—were seen as temporary aberrations of the main American patterns of equality, democracy, and liberty. After 1960, the aberrations started to become the dominant themes of American history, and equality, democracy, and liberty were seen as the actual aberrations. Slavery, Jim Crow, and continued racism has been a mainstay of the American experience; the treatment of Native Americans has been revealed to have been one of almost unrelieved gory brutality. The inequality of women has been a lasting tale, and immigrants from countries outside of western Europe have suffered discrimination and limited opportunities. A work, such as mine, rediscovering equality in the American past is not welcome. To explain how equality operated in this mass of inequality takes far more time and pages than journal editors are willing to permit. Just to presage matters somewhat, the answer lies in the difference between equality and diversity; equality within a homogeneous ethnic group was clearly understandable for people two and three hundred years ago, and it is sometimes difficult for modern Americans to remember that the doctrine of inequality was applied to people of the same ethnic group who resided in one nation. Equality across ethnic groups, a partial definition of diversity, was not recognized by previous generations and is clearly a late twentieth-century concept.

The limitations of the American idea of equality in the nineteenth century are clear enough to people in the twenty-first century, but what has been missed is that the American concept of equality was a direct challenge, clothed in befuddling universalist language, to the British and European idea of inequality.[1] This was more than an exchange of letters and treatises, more than a theoretical debate among intellectuals. It turned on observable patterns of behavior. Over time, one saw the behavioral virtues of equality, while the drawbacks of inequality became more and more prominent. This book seeks to recapture that discovery to remind Americans that this is their heritage, and it is one that if given up will lead right back to the injuries that inequality inflicted on the majority of people in Europe. The resurgence of the conservative movement in the United States has led to an unusual emphasis placed on the functioning of the economy, economic growth, and the benefits of a free market, a market that rewards certain kinds of inequality extremely well while punishing other types of inequality with a sickening ferocity. This has led its propagandists to virtually declare that the real genius of the American "system" was not political or social but economic; it was the creation of a free market. The free market drew Europeans and then other ethnic groups to the United States. My own reflection is that such a claim is false; the free market in the form of high wages was an important factor in the reasons for migrating to the United States, but the grand allure was the fact of legal and general social equality—of life in a land where deference did not rule, where no person had to admit others were superior, where one was not constantly humiliated by customs reinforcing the sense of inferiority.

The reviewer of this manuscript argued that it was the duty of the author to tell his audience at the start his position on the equality/inequality debate, presumably so that readers could detect biases in the presentation of evidence. In subservience to the suggestion, I will offer my opinions, some that arrived due to my own reflection and inclinations, some from various outside readings, and some from the research I have done for this book. I am distinctly on the egalitarian side of the debate. (1) It is my own personal observation that the differences between people are not profound. I have known some of the stupidest of people and some of the most brilliant; and yet they all perform on a scale that marks them members of the human species decidedly different from any other species. But humans constantly make distinctions among themselves and constantly elevate molehills of differences into mountains of separation (as a historian, one sees this all the time in various scholars trying to distinguish their research from that of others). We can allow that there are differences among people, but those differences can in no manner justify the way the "market" rewards those differences. (2) In dealing with other people, I find that the assumption of equality operates far more fairly and effectively than an assumption of inequality. Treating people as equals leads to harmonious exchanges, while assertions of superiority engender animosity and strife. (3) As an observation learned from the research that informs this book, egalitarianism tends to increase everyone's desire to foster their talents, whereas inequality tends to suppress them. As will become apparent, visitors to the United States ascribed the boisterous activity among the population in North America not to unusual amounts of greed or a damaged morality but to the fact that so few suffered from a haunting sense of inferiority derived from an inegalitarianism which stifled talent and optimism. (4) Inequality creates a damaged society, and when the inequality becomes extreme the dominant faction has to resort to brute force to continue to exist. A society is generally harmonious and civilized when its members believe in the justness of its arrangements. In strict operational terms, and not delving into mystical qualities of *mentalité,* what the preceding sentence means is that people obey the laws of their society not out of fear of the consequences of transgression but out of the justness of their operation. Great inequality erodes obedience to law, and as portions of the society become less obedient, the benefactors of inequality are confronted with a torturous choice: either alleviate the inequality by some measure of redistribution or egalitarian behavior, or increase the police power of the state to enforce compliance with the laws. For those of the conservative persuasion, this presents the contradictory course of arguing for the minimal state and lavishing praise on inequality but recognizing that the only means of maintaining the inequality is by creating a powerful state that could then turn on the people who profit from inequality.[2]

I extend my gratitude to Matt Mancini of Saint Louis University for his suggestions about improving the manuscript. The staff at Louisiana State University, as always, improved the book immensely; my thanks go to executive editor Rand Dotson, managing editor Lee C. Sioles, publicist Jennifer Keegan, and manuscript editor Gary Von Euer. As always, my greatest appreciation has to be bestowed upon my technical writer wife, Kathy, for her editing suggestions. Finally, I bless my cats who for reasons unknown largely did not trample my keypad as I was writing this book. However, any errors in grammar, endnotes, bibliography, or citations can be ascribed to them.

The American and British Debate over Equality, 1776–1920

INTRODUCTION

A Word Lost in a Definitional Fog

Today the US public is drowning in publications about the rise of economic inequality. One of the more potent tomes on rising inequality is Thomas Piketty's work, *Capital in the Twenty-First Century* (2014). Piketty established that the United States now possesses the most inegalitarian wealth and income distribution of the Western nations: the highest 10 percent of wealth-holders possess 75 percent of the wealth, more than the top 10 percent controlled before the stock market crash of 1929. In his summation about the income and wealth of the highest 1 percent and even the highest 0.1 percent of the population, Piketty, an economist with broad interests in the arts and social sciences, decided that the usual "sterile debate about merit and wealth," or the entrepreneurial argument for inequality, "cannot justify all inequalities of wealth." Wealth and income concentrations have gone beyond "reasonable limits" and, indeed, beyond "any possible rational justification in terms of social utility."[1]

ECONOMISTS AND POLITICAL PHILOSOPHERS ON EQUALITY

Piketty's book, which had a considerable impact on the reading public, is hardly unusual. It is perhaps the most sophisticated and detailed analysis of the historic distribution of wealth over western Europe and the United States. Yet an explosion of books detailing the growth of economic inequality began in the 1980s. Early works came from authors such as Nan Maxwell, Frank Levy, Lars Osberg, and Peter Danziger and Peter Gottschalk. The publication of works decrying the growth of inequality accelerated after the great recession in 2008–2010 to the point that former secretary of labor Robert Reich starred in a movie entitled *Inequality for All.*[2] At the same time, some political scientists feared that the disparity in income distribution was undermining the democratic process.[3] All one has to do is go to the Amazon website and type in either "equality" or "inequality" in the search device to see hundreds of books printed in the last two decades on the topic.

The debate about equality and inequality has taken some interesting twists and turns over several centuries, but the recent quarrel—in academia, not in the political world—can be said to have commenced with the work of moral and political philosopher John Rawls, who in 1971 published *A Theory of Justice.* When he wrote, the nation was still arguing over the extent of poverty and the need for government programs such as President Lyndon B. Johnson's War on Poverty. Rawls argued for two principles to govern society: a liberty principle and a "difference" principle. The difference principle justified a redistribution of goods to achieve a "just" society.[4]

The question of equality and fairness then became a rage within the academic community. When the nonsocialist Rawls justified some sort of income and wealth redistribution, he waved a red flag that brought out the bulls of opposition. His work immediately drew a response from political philosophers enmeshed in individualism and from economists who looked upon market determinations of worth as the equivalent to the ten commandments. The most famous response to Rawls was penned by Robert Nozick, whose work *Anarchy, State, and Utopia* became a sensation by defending the individualist philosophy of John Locke and inequality (the famous means by which he did so was the "Wilt Chamberlain" illustration, to show that people of their own free accord made Chamberlain rich—they paid money to see him play basketball—and that no injustice was inflicted on anyone as a result). In the 1970s, debates over equality and inequality became frequent.[5]

In the battle over equality, those praising inequality increasingly came from a microeconomic perspective. That is, many of these inegalitarians were taught the economic principles of the individual, the firm, and the market; microeconomics explicitly assumes individualism in all economic activities. The leaders of this group of economists came from the University of Chicago, and indeed the economic libertarian perspective has been labeled the Chicago School of political economy; its most visible figures were

Milton Friedman, George J. Stigler, and Gary Becker. In their vast output of writings they drove home one basic point: inequality in talents and in rewards was absolutely essential to economic improvement, and the way that inequality was best expressed was through individual liberty in the marketplace with no distortions imposed by governmental regulations.[6] The embrace of inequality was so extreme that Nobel Prize winner Friedrich Von Hayek doubted the principle of equality of opportunity.[7]

The microeconomists have in many ways triumphed over other intellectual strands that have supported inequality and individual liberty. Indeed, Tibor Machan, a philosopher, decries the subservience to economists on the question of the philosophical defense of freedom because the economists have essentially written moral principles out of the defense of capitalism in favor of utility and pragmatism; he calls economics "an imperial discipline." It is generally now considered that economics is one of the two "imperialist disciplines" because of its effort to belittle any approach to human life that is not based on the theories of individualism and markets (the other imperialist discipline is considered to be sociology.)[8] Nonetheless, one interesting component of the attack on equality has come from political science, and more pointedly from political philosophy. Various writers have justified inequality on political grounds: it is best to leave the individual with the maximum amount of liberty to steer his or her way through life without government coercion, whereas to obtain more income equality, government coercion would be absolutely necessary.[9]

Defending inequality has led to one obvious political result: a denunciation of the political system of democracy. Because libertarians and conservatives in general argue that inequality in economic condition is natural, they have reason to doubt the superiority of the political system of democracy. Democracy assumes an equality among the citizenry in political affairs, and that assumption irks libertarians and conservatives. Thus one obtains a sustained attack on democratic procedures from libertarians and conservatives because they deny that the majority has a right to overrule the minority in economic matters, especially in the distribution of economic rewards.[10]

Justifications for constructing a more egalitarian society came from political philosophers and economists, but events overran those of egalitarian sentiments and generated a rethinking of certain basic ideas, especially the worth of "equality" in human life. Besides the economic difficulties in the US domestic economy in the 1970s, emigres from eastern Europe told disturbing stories of their communist regimes. Then in 1989 popular uprisings occurred—not against capitalism, as Marxists had predicted, but against communism, which Marxists had not predicted. The communist regimes in central and eastern Europe crashed, and two years later the Soviet Union itself was no more. In the face of this collapse, the extreme political Left of Europe withered and disappeared. As David Miller, a leftist political philosopher, wrote, socialism is no longer "an unsullied ideal."[11] Gerald Cohen, a prominent defender of Marxist theory, admitted that Marxism had the ideals of equality, community, and self-realization, but he had never defended them theoretically but only assumed that everyone intuitively knew their truth content. And the pillar of the means of explaining exploitation, the labor theory of value, was discarded. By 1999 the political philosopher Thomas Nagel could write, "I assume no one believes in the labor theory of value any more."[12]

Among political philosophers the scramble was on to justify wealth and income redistribution for the purpose of creating a better community, for, as Ronald Dworkin put it, no government is "legitimate" that does not show "equal concern for the fate of all those citizens over whom it claims dominion."[13] The difficulties with the capitalist framework were laid out: much wealth distribution had to do with initial position and inheritance, advantages of family, the disassociation between merit and reward, and talent originating from a biological lottery and not from individual work effort.[14] For the political philosophers who believe in egalitarianism and schemes of redistribution, the pressing question became, as Amartya Sen famously asked, "equality of *what*?"[15] In other words, what quality of society required correction so that fairness (also known as "social justice") could become its hallmark. So began a search in the 1980s for what had to be redistributed or rearranged, but the search was conducted within an individualist framework. David Miller argued for market socialism, that is, keeping a market mechanism for consumption of goods but having the firms involved in production socialized. John Rawls had contended for supplying all citizens with primary goods and opting for the distribution that maximized the position of those earning the lowest income (the difference principle). Dworkin advocated an initial redistribution of resources, Amartya Sen wanted society to compensate for individual capabilities, and Richard J. Arnesen called for equal access of opportunity to welfare, while G. A. Cohen stressed access to advantages. A particular group, since named Luck Egalitarians, argued on the basis of a strict reading of John Locke that goods should be redistributed to offset advantages that had been given by birth, circumstance, and happenstance.[16]

Because of the collapse of communism, numerous authors grappled with the general ideal of "equality"—why it was a valued goal and how it could be morally defended. In other words, what was worthwhile about the social goal of achieving equality? Ronald Dworkin began the introduction to his 2000 book *Sovereign Virtue* with the question, "Does Equality Matter?" Recognizing the surge in conservatism in western Europe and America, he proclaimed that "equality is the endangered species of political ideals." Defining what equality entailed became a major undertaking. For practical political scientists engaged in conducting surveys and predicting election outcomes, *equality* was too ambiguous a term for defining, and the ideal "continues to bedevil our civic life." In 1985, Sidney Verba and Gary Orren were exasperated about "this endless debate on equality" and concluded that the "essential ambiguity of the concept endures." The possible meanings of equality were the following: equality before the law, equality of initial conditions, equality of rights, equality of opportunity, equality of resources, and an equality of all people in moral judgment.[17]

The conservative/libertarian position just cuts through the ambiguities, rejects equality altogether, and embraces inequality. In the case of Melvin E. Bradford, a literary critic who wrote about, in his estimation, Abraham Lincoln's fallacious and duplicitous ideas, there was no such thing as a conservative who believed in any idea of equality whatsoever—in the law, in opportunity, in moral standing, or in any other way. He wrote that equality in any form "is the antonym of every legitimate conservative principle."[18]

THE UNITED STATES AND THE QUESTION OF EQUALITY

When Piketty wrote his 2014 treatise on the new heights of inequality, he made it a point to stress that the early United States (c. 1800) was more egalitarian in wealth and income distribution than the west European nations; it was equivalent then in income and wealth distribution to Sweden's present-day (2012) distribution. Piketty noted that in the United States there was a "nostalgia" about its egalitarian past which helped to explain the near-panic he sensed among various American writers on the subject.[19]

The problem in one sense was Thomas Jefferson's Declaration of Independence and the short but potent words: "We hold these truths to be self-evident: That all men are created equal; that they are endowed by their Creator with certain unalienable rights; that among these are life, liberty, and the pursuit of happiness." Here was the bold assertion of equality, and no one in the Continental Congress bothered to question, comment on, or alter the language. A year before his death, Jefferson wrote about his word choice that he did not seek "to find out new principles, or new arguments, never before thought of, . . . but to place before mankind the common sense of the subject."[20] Historian Pauline Meier agrees with Jefferson: his formulation was "absolutely conventional among Americans of his time."[21]

But what exactly did the word *equality* in the Declaration mean? While debates over the operative definition of equality continued throughout the nineteenth century, sometimes with great heat, people held the general opinion that the United States was unique among nations in the Western world, and usually among all the nations in the world, because it alone proclaimed the equality of men. Its political form took obvious shape in the arrival of democratic politics during the presidency of Andrew Jackson, and French aristocrat Alexis de Tocqueville in 1835 proclaimed it the salient feature of American civilization. In the first sentence of his classic work, *Democracy in America,* he said that when in the United States, nothing "struck me more forcefully than the equality of conditions," and, as equality and democracy marched hand in hand, he investigated the new republic to foresee the fate of the monarchies and aristocracies of western Europe.[22] For decades into the twentieth century, even in the face of some angry dissenters, equality became the hallmark of the United States and was celebrated every July 4.

The celebration did not last much beyond 1945, if even that long. In politics, there had been throughout the first half of the twentieth century an unease about the growing plutocracy in the country. But the widespread emergence of the denial that equality characterized American life probably came during the Civil Rights Movement in the 1950s and 1960s. This development was only partly connected to wealth and distribution: it was more about the subjugation of non-Caucasian ethnic groups. White American treatment of African Americans had been anything but equal. Then came with it social movements seeking full citizenship rights and opportunities for Native Americans, American women, American Hispanics, and other ethnic minorities. These arguments about "equality" took a poststructural turn as numerous writers forsook economic equality, or at least lessened its salience, to advocate a social acceptance of various groups and accord them equal treatment—what is today termed "diversity" or multiculturalism among religious, ethnic, and gender groups. Those of a Marxist perspective were not happy with this new direction in intellectual life.[23]

Nonetheless, the work of New Left historians, commencing in the 1960s, constituted an intense criticism of the economic experience of American workers and a castigation of those who hoarded mountains of dollars. Coupling this economic analysis with the cultural analysis of whites' treatment of nonwhite ethnic groups, historians came to rebuke utterly the interpretation that "equality" had ever been a central feature of the American experience and postulated instead that inequality had been the rule. By the beginning of the second decade of the twenty-first century, the connection between the words "equality" and the "United States" was wholly severed, and in its place has come the nearly unconquerable pairing between the words "inequality" and the "United States."[24]

Yet for Americans saddled with the heritage of the Declaration of Independence, jettisoning the ideal of "equality" is a bitter pill to swallow, regardless of economic logic, rationalism, or any other way to delegitimize the idea. In 1959 David S. Lovejoy wrote in the *William and Mary Quarterly,* "Equality has become a fundamental principle of American democracy. Although we are frequently reminded that Americans fail to practice altogether what they preach, still, the concept of equality is as much a part of the democratic ideal as manhood suffrage and public education." One may rant and rave as much as one likes about the impracticality and the harmful effects of equality, yet as political philosopher Larry Temkin has written, "Equality . . . [remains] among the most potent of human ideals."[25]

POLITICAL PHILOSOPHY AND THE MERITS OF EQUALITY

Because of the Soviet meltdown and the economic failures of the socialist experiments in eastern Europe, the communitarian dreams once dominant in leftist political writings have all but vanished. Instead, nearly all political philosophers agree that some inequality in social and economic life is justified and practical. Ultimately, the new goal for a just society has become decidedly individualistic: a just society allows individuals to develop their talents, and talents—no matter how acquired—are not equally distributed. The point of departure for egalitarians, however, is the extent of the inequality.

Political philosophers can come to no agreement on a positive definition for the term *equality,* but they actually do agree about its opposite: inequality. Three fundamental positions exist. First, humans have to live in groups, and so measures have to be taken to make group existence harmonious and "civilized." Second, inequality makes a group's existence perilous and violent. According to political philosopher Michael Walzer, "The aim of political egalitarianism is a society free from domination. This is the lively hope named by the word *equality;* no more bowing and scraping, fawning and toadying; no more fearful trembling; no more high-and-mightiness; no more masters, no more slaves. It is not a hope for the elimination of differences; we don't all have to be the same or have the same amounts of the same things." The problem, says Samuel Sheffler, another political philosopher, is that inequality breeds hierarchies, and "the resulting patterns of deference and privilege exert a stifling effect on human freedom and inhibit the possibilities of human exchange; . . . they distort people's attitudes toward themselves . . . [and encourage] an insidious sense of superiority in others." A third position is propounded by political philosopher Frank Lovett. Rather than explicitly offer a definition for "equality," he asserts that societies should seek to avoid the outcome of inequality—domination. Domination results from people being dependent on others, the inability to escape the condition, imbalances of power, and the arbitrariness in some people's capacity to wield power for their own gratification. If such factors leading the few to dominate the many are reduced, then one obtains "human-flourishing" and people achieve self-respect, security, freedom of expression, and nonexploitive positions in the economy. He notes that on the economic side of life, poverty is a condition of severe inequality that leads to domination, and that therefore some (undetermined) amount of basic income is required for everyone. Overall, Lovett actually defines equality by the absence of domination, and the absence of domination leads to human flourishing.[26]

HISTORY AND THE DEBATE OVER EQUALITY

Within this immense philosophical debate is the absence of one set of facts—the historical record. G. A. Cohen makes it plain: philosophers seek transcendent truths that are not confined by historical epochs.[27] But history has indeed a highly germane record for this discourse. When the United States formed in 1776, its Declaration argued for some sort of equality, however poorly defined, and placed itself in opposition to the European societies formed precisely on the idea of inequality—monarchy and aristocracy. The situation was momentarily obfuscated by the French Revolution and its aftermath, but it was clear that in the Anglo-American world a mighty breach had occurred: the former colonists operated on some notion of equality while the former mother country, Great Britain, openly embraced inequality. For a century and a half after 1776, Americans and Britons conducted on the literary battlefield a conflict over which ideal, equality or inequality, best suited the human condition. This debate occurred because a plentitude of British travelers came to North America between 1790 and 1920. Such persons saw the principle of equality operating in rural America and on the family farm—they obviously did not see it in the slave states nor really in the urban metropolises of the republic. It is the comparison that these sojourners made between egalitarian northern rural America with inegalitarian Great Britain (and western Europe) that should attract our attention, even though the travelers had next to no conception of the ideal of ethnic diversity.[28]

But in a practical, experiential sense, these travelers laid bare the results of a society based on egalitarian principles versus one based on inegalitarian principles. Most of the present-day debate about equality versus inequality is theoretical and ideological, having no basis in human experience. But the arguments for and against equality by European and British travelers were not metaphysical: they recorded and commented upon the actual outcomes of a system of equality with the outcomes of a system of inequality. It is the practical, not theoretical, quality of this debate that is important for Americans in the twenty-first century. Here they can find the actual results: the merits of equality and the vices of inequality. Laying bare this comparison is the purpose of this book.

1

THE TRUMPET SOUNDETH FOR EQUALITY

The Enlightenment and the American Revolution

The idea of equality has had a strange history. Until the eighteenth century in Europe, philosophers recognized a notion of human equality based on all people belonging to the same species and facing the same fate (death and then judgment by the deity), but in regard to earthly affairs and especially political affairs, inequality was everywhere the standard in theory and practice. The breaking point came in the Enlightenment when the gross inequalities of material life came under attack. The diatribes against the artificiality of European monarchs, aristocrats, and court life flowed across the Atlantic and affected the thinking of the individuals who would lead the American Revolution. That thinking became enshrined in the Declaration of Independence, and before long the American republic became not only an experiment in republicanism but also in egalitarianism. But the Americans also inherited another feature of the Enlightenment: though it was easy to describe inequality, it was less easy to define equality. In the end, what survived was only an imprecise idea of equality; precision was much greater when it came to inequality.

THE LONG WESTERN EUROPEAN TRADITION OF INEQUALITY

When today one hears about the traditions of western European civilization, it is seldom mentioned that this tradition included a distinct defense of inequality as being the appropriate political and social standard for any society to function rationally. The celebrated philosophers, Aristotle and Plato, in the fifth and fourth centuries BCE, rationalized inequality for

Greek society, explicitly denouncing democracy in political affairs. When Christianity came to Europe in the form of the Catholic Church, its structure mirrored the social orders of monarchy, aristocracy, and commons (i.e., the pope, archbishops, and finally the laity). The prominent theologian St. Augustine accepted inequality in the political and economic world, even though in the spiritual world all were equal in the eyes of God. Martin Luther, during the Protestant Reformation, distinctly favored strong government in the hands of the few, although John Calvin added doctrines that could nourish an idea of some earthly equality. The Italian city-states had philosophers who wrote about republican equality, but their equality was limited to citizens engaged in public affairs and did not rule out slavery or aristocracy as being part of society. From 600 BCE to about 1500 CE, the standard for Europe was inequality in religion, politics, and society; the sanctioning of equality for humans was strictly limited to the dead.[1]

THE ENLIGHTENMENT AND EQUALITY

The first breach in the domination of the ideal of inequality as the guide for western European life arose with the intellectual movement known as the Enlightenment, which commenced with the scientific revolution of the seventeenth century that allowed individuals the possibility of breaking away from religion as a means to explain the physical world.[2] The catchphrases of the Enlightenment were logic, reason, and nature. Its enemies became superstition, religion in general, and finally the political establishment of Europe. However, there were (as there always are) complications. Scholar Jonathan Israel divides the Enlightenment philosophers into radicals, moderates, and actually, Anglo-Americans. The radical Enlightenment arose out of the Dutch republican experiment and ultimately stressed equality and democracy. Moderate Enlightenment thinkers, including Voltaire, were not convinced of the superiority of the ideals of equality and democracy, and wanted to reform society (that is, make it more rational) by educating people and convincing princes of the merit of Enlightenment principles. The Anglo-American Enlightenment was different because of Isaac Newton and John Locke; rather than attack mysticism and religion, they argued for the supremacy of Christian teaching, making the English Enlightenment much more traditional than the thinking on the continent. Intellectual historian Ellen M. Wood questions some of these generalizations, arguing instead that the centralized nature of England allowed a different kind of political philosophy to appear (basically, Locke on property, progress, and representative government), while France, because of its peculiar civil service and its political failure to centralize, came to trumpet democracy and equality, as seen in the first stages of the French Revolution.[3]

Scholars have not accorded "equality" a prominent element in their writings on the Enlightenment. For example, Peter Gay, one of the Enlightenment's premiere historians, did not bother to investigate the philosophical discussion about the subject. The governing scholarly disposition seems to be that the Enlightenment thinkers were largely elitists, and most feared the masses and distrusted giving them power. In political terms, equality implied democracy, and democracy, while it might be legitimated as a branch of government, was never to be allowed to be government's only mechanism. Nonetheless, outright expressions favorable to equality arose during the eighteenth century and were probably made possible by the intellectual disillusionment with monarchs and aristocrats. The simple truth was that it was *theoretically* true that if one could find a person of outstanding wisdom and virtue, that person as king would produce a golden age for his people. And if aristocracies could indeed be composed of the "best" people, who also had virtue and wisdom, then local government would be superb and the people would obtain perfect justice. But after several centuries of rule by monarchs and aristocrats, virtue and wisdom among them was undetectable; they ruled ruthlessly, engaged in war, and plundered their people. They ruled by passion, and their passions reflected their intentions to gratify their self-interests by violently imposing their will on others. One of the ways that equality (and democracy) came to be acceptable to philosophers was the realization of the utter failure of monarchy and aristocracy to live up to their theoretical pretensions; the gap between reality and theory had become too wide to be bridged.[4]

The idea of equality probably received its greatest impetus from the English Civil War when the Levellers (1647–1648) argued for an expanded suffrage, a natural equality, and, in the work of James Harrington, a limitation on great estates. The Levellers lost, but the idea of human equality then sprang up in some unlikely places. Thomas Hobbes began his treatise *Leviathan* by postulating that all men were born equal, and one did not much differ in talent from another. But to get out of the destructive chaos of life in the jungle, humans gave up their natural equality by consenting to government by kings. John Locke did not accept the alienation of natural rights in the manner of Hobbes (that is, purchasing security and stability by selling their equality), and instead insisted that not only were men born equal (in the state of nature) but they kept their natural rights to life, liberty, and property when they consented to form governments—and governments could not trespass those natural rights without inciting, justifiably, rebellion. To some extent, Hobbes, and by that route Locke, were influenced by the writings of Baruch Spinoza (1632–1677), who argued that people never gave up their natural equality.[5]

By the mid-eighteenth century, advocates for human equality became more outspoken. Locke had compromised human equality by letting property rights and inheritance trump other rights—ultimately he defended the great landed gentry—but others became more assertive that the aristocrats and monarchs had gone too far in plundering their people and living in ostentatious and unjustifiable luxury. Francis Hutcheson (1694–1746), the founder of the Scottish Common Sense school, believed in natural equality in the enjoyment of civil rights and attacked all forms of slavery; he criticized Locke's origin of property rights and justified the limitation of property aggregations—that is, he theoretically accepted some sort of "agrarian" law. Claude Helv'tius and d'Holbach attacked the existing social order and its superficiality. When Guillaume Thomas Raynal as general editor put together the *Historie Philosophique* (six volumes, 1770), it included a diatribe by Diderot against European imperialism, a denunciation of the extremes of wealth and poverty in Europe, and a declaration of universal human rights. The triumph of the principle of equality was fully expressed by Condorcet in 1795, an equality that embraced women as well as non-Europeans.[6] Some of this writing may have set the stage for Jean Jacques Rousseau and his insistence that the invention of private property was the source of human inequality. Rousseau eventually drifted away from most Enlightenment philosophers in his creation of the "general will" to guide society, a belief that the common citizens would reach a unanimous consensus about proper institutions and policies. Most Enlightenment writers insisted on freedom of expression and not the potential censorship arising from a consensus imposed by the masses.[7]

Among scholars of the Enlightenment, Jonathan Israel is one of the few who investigated the subject of equality, and he produced a chapter on the topic. He concluded that the radicals desired equality before the law

(Spinoza) and held the aristocracy in contempt for its privileges; he summarized that radicals held that all humans had a "moral equivalence" that each member of a society had to acknowledge, and that only among equals would one obtain the "reciprocity" of relationships that constituted a good society. And Israel noted that nowhere in the Western world save for the United States after 1776 and France after 1789 did equality before the law exist.[8] For a standard by which one might compare European Enlightenment ideas about equality with those of the American Revolution, one could take the entry of "Egalité" from the *Encyclopédie,* volume 5, 1755, by Chevalier de Jaucourt. He stated that all men were naturally equal by having a common humanity, and any social inequality that did exist did not exempt any person from "treating their fellow beings as the natural equals they are." Obviously, slavery was a violation of natural law and rights. However, equality among men did not mean an absolute equality; what was meant was "*natural equality*" because people have different conditions, abilities, and distinctions; "*natural* or *moral equality* is not opposed to these."[9]

Why did some Enlightenment philosophers come to advocate an idea of human equality and argue its practical implementation as a social standard for European societies? The answer has to lie in their observation of the wreckage that inequality—i.e., aristocracy and monarchy—made of the societies in which they lived. Monarchs generally ruled politics, but aristocrats ruled society. The aristocrats obtained privileges; on the continent, they escaped taxation; everywhere, the sons of aristocrats became the officeholders in government and the officers in the military. Europe had a divided justice: one set of rules and punishments for the nobility, another set for commoners. In England only the aristocracy could openly bear arms. All common people had to bow and scrape before their superiors; their persons were not to be touched; in England, the aristocrats demanded a deference that was extreme. And then there was the disparity in wealth and landholdings. A considerable peasant proprietorship existed in most of the European nations, but nevertheless the great estates of the aristocracy contained the bulk of the land. In England, the peasantry and yeomen were disappearing as the aristocrats and gentry consolidated land ownership among themselves. In France, the peasants were taxed to the breaking point in order to allow the aristocracy to live in luxury at Versailles and to support a large bureaucracy. In England, the landed magnates in the eighteenth century exhibited their wealth by building astounding country estates, buying up blocks of London real estate, and wallowing in ostentatious leisure. And everyone, especially the few Americans who traveled overseas, noticed the misery of the common people.[10]

Given the social and economic divisions in England and the rest of Europe, it was hardly any wonder that a reaction to such chasms emerged. Aristocratic inequality almost naturally evoked a desire among many for its opposite, democratic equality. This polarity also explains the amorphous definition of *equality*: many writers could be quite explicit about what they disliked about aristocratic inequality, but negatives added together could not build a positive and exact definition of equality.

THE DECLARATION OF INDEPENDENCE

The first paragraph of the Declaration of Independence trumpeted the Americans' intention to break free of the British Empire. The second paragraph encapsulated the principles that the Americans hoped would become the foundation of their nation:

> We hold these truths to be self-evident: That all men are created equal; that they are endowed by their Creator with certain unalienable rights; that among these are life, liberty, and the pursuit of happiness; that, to secure these rights, governments are instituted among men, deriving their just powers from the consent of the governed; that whenever any form of government becomes destructive of these ends, it is the right of the people to alter or to abolish it, and to institute new government, laying its foundation on such principles, and organizing its powers in such form, as to them shall seem most likely to effect their safety and happiness. Prudence, indeed, will dictate that governments long established should not be changed for light and transient causes; and accordingly all experience hath shown that mankind are more disposed to suffer, while evils are sufferable, than to right themselves by abolishing the forms to which they are accustomed. But when a long train of abuses and usurpations, pursuing invariably the same object, evinces a design to reduce them under absolute despotism, it is their right, it is their duty, to throw off such government, and to provide new guards for their future security. Such has been the patient sufferance of these colonies; and such is now the necessity which constrains them to alter their former systems of government. The history of the present King of Great Britain is a history of repeated injuries and usurpations, all having in direct object the establishment of an absolute tyranny over these states. To prove this, let facts be submitted to a candid world.

Immediately following these principles came a list of actions that Jefferson and members of the Continental Congress believed proved the intent of the British realm to impose despotism upon the American colonies. Most people have lingered over and debated the inordinately long first sentence in the second paragraph, in which Jefferson seemed to derive ideas of natural law, philosopher John Locke's listing of human rights as life, liberty, and property, the justice of revolution/rebellion, and the recognition that governments rested on the consent of the people and not on the caprice and power of a king or aristocracy. Although it is not much commented on, the fourth sentence of the second paragraph yields a stunning summary of why most populations have accepted rule by the governing clique, even though that rule exhibited unfairness and injustice.

Ever since 1776, writers have immediately seized on the phrase "all men are created equal" and wondered how the Continental Congress could have approved such an assertion.[11] Colonial America did not have the aristocratic order everywhere found in Europe, but it certainly had inequality. The Virginia planters acted as a gentry, deference was a hallmark of the society, the urban poor lived in misery in the American port cities, some merchants were extremely wealthy, women were strictly subordinate to men, colonists coveted the land of the tribes of North America and had no compunction about killing Native Americans when they resisted encroachment, and, most obviously, slavery existed everywhere in the colonies and composed a major part of the population in the colonies (states) beneath the Mason-Dixon line.[12] Because of these blatant inequalities, the Declaration made no sense as a declaration for egalitarianism. Thus it has become commonplace among historians to assert that the congressmen who voted to adopt the Declaration must have had a restricted sense of equality, such as citizen equality before the law, equality in the sense of belonging to the same species and the same gender, equality in the chances for improving their condition without being hindered by government favoritism, and equality restricted to members of their own ethnicity. Michal Jan Rozbicki argues that the protesters of British policy only meant liberty for themselves, not the rest of society, and the equality they wanted was an equality between themselves and the English gentry. The congressmen could not have meant equality in talents or in possessions.[13] Rather, many scholars insist that liberty was far more revered than equality, a position that favors a decidedly conservative reading of the purposes of the revolutionary founders.[14]

INTERPRETATION OF THE DECLARATION

Scholars continue to struggle with the influences acting on the American revolutionaries to find the meaning of such phrases as "all men are created equal." For example, John Locke's role in shaping the minds of the revolutionaries has become a bone of contention. Earlier scholars had little doubt about Locke's influence, as Jefferson's phrasing is almost exactly that of Locke's except for the substitution of the phrase "pursuit of happiness" for the word "property." Locke is currently seen as one of the earliest modern philosophers because his ideas proved congenial to individualism and capitalism—thereby establishing that Locke's philosophy justified inequality, not equality. The most powerful refutation of the Lockean dominance over the mental world of mid-eighteenth-century colonials came from John G. Pocock, who situated American political expressions in the civic humanism of Renaissance Florence. This interpretation became known as republicanism, and its basic vocabulary included the terms *republic, corruption, virtue, independence,* and *landed property.* Equality became an equality of citizens who owned landed property and thus exhibited economic independence from others; it was also widely believed that a republic required a broad distribution of wealth among its citizens. There were problems with this equality as, first, it did not embrace all the population in the polity, and second, slavery was permissible (as in the examples of Athens and Sparta). Allied to the interpretation of republicanism was a stress, first promoted by Bernard Bailyn, upon a group of dissident English writers in the early eighteenth century—namely, John Trenchard and William Gordon, Catherine Macaulay, James Harrington (actually, in the English Civil War), and James Burgh. These writers stressed the evils of government consolidation, reacted angrily to "capitalist" advances (especially in banking), lauded life on the independent country estate, and warned of "corruption" via the monarch's and his prime minister's abilities to reward stalwart supporters of the ministry's plans by giving offices and favors. Added to the country ideology of the anti-Whig writers and the civic humanism of the Italian city-states was the spread in the mid-eighteenth century of the Scottish "common sense" philosophy stressing the innate moral abilities of humans in choosing paths that created social harmony. The Common Sense school had problems with some assertions of Locke, and its historians have suggested a non-Lockean outlook among American revolutionary leaders. All three of these major schools also commonly stressed one other feature of American life: community bonds held people together, and a fully developed individualism, such as existed in the mid-nineteenth century, was not to be found. Rather, many terms, such as *liberty,* had to be understood as indicating the liberty of a community rather than of an individual.[15]

These views have had a marked influence on how the idea of "equality" was understood at the time of the Revolution. Two examples are revealing. All sorts of writers have trouble believing that Virginia slaveholders and great landholders could issue a statement about "all men are created equal" without chortling at the unreality of it. Michal J. Rozbicki, for example, notes (as do all students of the prerevolutionary Virginia elite) that the leaders of Virginia craved to be members of the English gentry and desired to worm their way eventually into the aristocracy. They were stunned, however, by the English elite's rejection of their claims to gentility. What the colonial elite meant in the Declaration was that American leaders were socially equal to the leaders in Great Britain.[16] Another example comes from Barry Shain, who took seriously Stephen A. Douglas's claim that Abraham Lincoln misconstrued the intention of the second paragraph of the Declaration. In a debate with William Seward in the US Senate on February 29, 1860, Douglas declared, "I hold that the Declaration of Independence was only referring to the white man—to the governing race of this country." Shain concluded that Douglas was right. Late eighteenth-century Americans only held one individual right beyond question, Shain asserts, and that was freedom of conscience; other than that, Americans meant most often community rights, or the rights of communities to detail the freedoms and duties of their members. Slaves were not considered members of any American community.[17]

There are limitations to how far one can take these arguments. Almost every philosopher since the Greeks has argued that communities define individual freedoms—a position acceptable to modern-day libertarians (who call the definitions the rules of the game). The revolutionaries did conceive of individual rights, and there were distinctly two of them, not one: the right to individual freedom of conscience, and the right of the individual to be protected in property legally acquired, which is to say the individual's right to private property. Because of the debate between British officials and American leaders over taxation after 1764, which Americans interpreted as an attack on their property ownership, the American written protests were heavily freighted with property rights arguments. The leaders made it clear: they were talking about individual rights to property, not the community's right to property. There is a real problem with interpreting documents of the revolutionary era by insisting on this community-individualist dichotomy. If the revolutionaries wanted to mean community rights, they could have plainly written such. For instance, here is one example from Trenchard and Gordon in 1721, two of the writers most beloved, we are told, by the American revolutionaries:

> By Liberty, I understand the Power which every Man has over his own Actions, and his Right to enjoy the Fruit of his Labour, Art, and Industry, as far as by it he hurts not the Society, or any Members of it, by taking from any Member, or by hindering him from enjoying what he himself enjoys. The Fruits of a Man's honest Industry are the just Rewards of it, ascertained to him by natural and eternal Equity, as is his Title to use them in the Manner which he thinks fit: And thus, with the above Limitations, every Man is sole Lord and Arbiter of his own private Actions and Property.—A Character of which no Man living can divest him but by Usurpation, or his own Consent.

This passage is obviously about an individual's right to property earned by labor. And Trenchard and Gordon's works are filled with a version of Locke's labor theory of property. The same view was propounded endlessly by the American revolutionaries.[18]

In the case of the Declaration itself and Jefferson's meaning in the phrase "all men are created equal" and possessed of the unalienable rights to "life, liberty, and the pursuit of happiness," there is a more direct way to evaluate the breadth of intended universalism and whether African Americans were excluded or not. Congress excised Jefferson's paragraph dealing with slavery because slaveholders preferred not to address the subject. The paragraph so deleted read:

> He has waged cruel war against human nature itself, violating it's [*sic*] most sacred right of life & liberty in the persons of a distant people who never offended him, captivating & carrying them to slavery in another hemisphere, or to incur miserable death in their transportation thither. This piratical warfare, the opprobrium of infidel powers, is the warfare of the Christian king of Great Britain. [*sic*] determined to keep open a market where MEN should be bought & sold, he has prostituted his negative for suppressing every legislative attempt to prohibit or restrain this execrable commerce [determining to keep

> open a market where MEN should be bought and sold—crossed out] and that this assemblage of horrors might want no fact of distinguished die, he is now exciting those very people to rise in arms against us, and to purchase that liberty of which he has deprived them, by murdering the people upon whom he also obtruded them &. [*sic*] thus paying off former crimes which he urges them to commit against the lives of another[.]

This uncharacteristically poorly phrased paragraph obviously had two purposes. First, it blamed the existence of American slavery on the monarch of Great Britain—a feeble rationalization—and, second, it listed among the king's outrages toward the colonies the attempt (by Lord Dunmore) to entice the slaves to enlist in the British campaign to snuff out the rebellion. Regardless of the purposes, the phrasing indicates that indeed Jefferson included Africans in the universe of humans who had rights to life, liberty, and probably property. Jefferson's belief that Africans were inferior members of the human family is well known, as he wrote as much in his *Notes on the State of Virginia,* and his negative view of the attributes of Africans increased as he grew older. Nonetheless, it is not a far-fetched proposition that Jefferson, as an intellectual who put himself in the company of European Enlightenment philosophers, was willing to include Africans in the phrase "all men are created equal."[19]

INTERPRETATIONS OF CHANGE AND EQUALITY DURING THE REVOLUTION

The reputation of the American Revolution for instigating fundamental change has its advocates and its detractors. The Americans never had a formal aristocracy, and so they did not undergo the class upheaval that France would during its revolution; rather, the prerevolutionary ruling groups continued to be the ruling groups (at least for a time) after 1776. Contemporary American writers stressed the division of the people into the "natural aristocracy" and the masses; they hoped that voters would have the common sense to elect natural aristocrats to office. Democracy was not implemented—indeed, it was generally feared—although suffrage requirements were generally lowered, while the fate of women in some ways became worse. Above all, slavery continued to exist. Then in the late 1780s came the reaction, the adoption of the Constitution, which most have seen as an attempt to stifle democratic advances.[20] Other scholars see the

Revolution as breaking down hierarchy, opening opportunity, and extending the area of democracy.[21]

Current historians have found a host of topics central to the Revolution, but often the subject of equality is not included. The current trend is to assert that Jefferson's second paragraph in the Declaration was largely ignored and forgotten for decades and that the major reason why that section is so celebrated today is that Abraham Lincoln in the Gettysburg Address made "scripture" of the phrase "all men are created equal."[22] Perhaps Lincoln made the phrasing of the Declaration more vital in the mental life of Americans after 1863, but the discussion of equality and what it meant was widespread after 1776, and Gordon Wood's treatment of the topic is essentially correct.[23] At the time of the Revolution, the phrasing of equality by Virginian George Mason in the Virginia Declaration of the Rights of Citizens became more copied in state constitutions than the phrasings in the Declaration of Independence, but the essential idea of equality being the hallmark of a republic was omnipresent.[24] Because almost all political scientists then and now agree that the political system of democracy necessarily requires citizen equality, the vast political discourse in the early United States in the 1780s over fear of or desire for democracy evoked explicitly or implicitly the subject of equality.[25]

THE PROBLEM OF LIBERTY VS. EQUALITY IN THE REVOLUTIONARY ERA

Part of the conundrum surrounding the American Revolution is the struggle to determine whether the revolutionaries touted individualism or community, or, in more understandable terms, liberty or equality. This division had (and has) strong ideological characteristics. Liberty has long been associated with aristocracy, antidemocracy, and hostility to anything smacking of egalitarianism—the conservative position. Outside of a dismissal of the average person's ability to discern truth, those favoring liberty dread the possibility of the person of genius being circumscribed by the low standards and traditionalism of the masses. For conservatives, the American Revolution was about removing the fetters of feudalism and allowing individuals to exercise their creativity—if they had any, and only the few did. The egalitarian tradition emphasizes the common humanity all share, and the rules about life, because they are made by governments, affect all, and should be determined by all. They tend to think of the gifted few as exploiting the many, not aiding them. In any event, those who sit on the left portion of the political spectrum tend towards egalitarianism and community.[26]

The difficulty with this dichotomy between liberty and equality is that historical contexts change, and when they do the possibilities of one era get lost in the search for novel solutions to the problems of a new era. In the particular case of the late eighteenth and early nineteenth centuries, liberty and equality did not necessarily follow separate paths. They certainly would in the late nineteenth and early twentieth centuries when economic development, technology, and population growth would redefine how liberty and equality could operate. But in the decades after the American Revolution and before industrialization, large population growth, and especially technological change, one could quite easily see how individual liberty could lead to general social and economic equality. The key to understanding the convergence is to acknowledge how aristocracy was the source of inequality.

In the European world of 1750, aristocracy (and monarchy) reigned, and its hallmark—blatantly trumpeted—was inequality. This inequality had many aspects, but the one that stood out—and has been the concern of historians now for decades—was economic. In the eighteenth century, European economic inequality had three visible manifestations. The first was slavery, primarily in the sugar plantations of the West Indies but also in the tobacco and rice plantations of the British North American colonies. Slaves in large numbers per plantation labored to produce products, they received little of the value of the goods they produced, and the rewards went to a single person, the slave master; thus one obtained the many poor and the few rich. The second institutional arrangement producing economic inequality was the estate agriculture of the British gentry and aristocracy, in full operation by the first decades of the eighteenth century. The British gentry and aristocracy nearly monopolized the arable land of the realm, they found tenant farmers to manage production on their hundreds and thousands of acres, and to perform the actual work the tenant farmers employed large numbers of agricultural laborers at miserable wages. Again, a large number received little value for their labor, while a few—some tenants and the landowners—accumulated fortunes, thus producing the few rich and the many poor. The third method of generating economic inequality was taxation, and the extreme example of that process was France. The French monarchs tried to control the nobility by collecting them at Versailles and giving them lavish living arrangements; to get the money to do so, the monarchs taxed the French peasants to the point of starvation. Again, the many were made miserable so a few could live in material splendor.[27]

In each of the three methods of producing economic inequality, a damaged community of commoners was constructed (slaves, agricultural laborers, and peasants) in order to give a few aristocrats and landowners magnificent lifestyles. Laws were the means of making the damaged community: slavery by a legal code; propertyless peasants by the large landed estate (monopolization of land) via the laws of entail, primogeniture, and strict settlement; and impoverished peasants by class-biased taxation. It makes a certain amount of sense given the conditions surrounding economic inequality at that time to argue that a complete individualism—i.e., individual liberty, coupled with equality before the law—would result in an appropriate equality of economic condition; it would not be one that was mathematically equal, but one that was socially *acceptable* in that inequality due to unequal talents would exist but the extremes of wealth and poverty so visible in the aristocratic world would be lopped off. A pure equality would not exist but *equitability* would, as each individual reaped only the fruits of his or her individual labor. Behind this projection was the belief that differences in talent among people were not great, and that if a person were limited to the rewards from his or her exertions only, then the amount of wealth compiled would be limited. Hence, society obtained a distribution of income that was workable in the sense that there would be no open discontent because some felt cheated of their appropriate rewards.[28]

THE FOUNDERS AND ANTIARISTOCRACY

Thomas Jefferson witnessed the effects of aristocracy, unequal laws, and land monopoly in creating the few rich and many poor. His comments are commonplace among Jefferson scholars. While in Paris, and writing to Madison about the problems of Shays' Rebellion and the security of property, Jefferson reacted by stressing the abysmal state of French society: common people lived under "governments of force. . . . To have an idea of the curse of existence under these last, they must be seen. It is a government of wolves over sheep." Another time he wrote that French society was divided into two parts, the few and the many: "every man here must be either the hammer or the anvil." He told Madison in 1785 in response to his worries over paper money legislation, "I am conscious that an equal division of property is impracticable. But the consequences of this enormous inequality producing so much misery to the bulk of mankind, legislators cannot invent too many devices for subdividing property." By reflection and experience, Jefferson tried to go in the opposite direction from the European aristocracy.[29]

The context of economic life at this time also needs to be factored into this analysis. If land were divided into small farms, owned and operated only by families, then individualism would yield equality. The disparity in social condition among European rural people stemmed from the disparity in land ownership. Even in eighteenth-century manufacturing, the scale of enterprise was small, the modal business form was the artisanal shop, and so long as that condition continued, egalitarianism could be the primary characteristic there. Beyond the great estates of the gentry and nobility, the other location of inequality was the city, and probably trade and shipbuilding were the endeavors where great wealth was rising and where the number of miserably paid workers was increasing. But at this moment in the eighteenth century, the factory was yet to be born and technological change had not altered the usual means of earning a living. Technological change becomes a vital factor in producing inequality because it allows people with the right types of talent to augment their incomes far above the average. But in 1750 or in 1780 these forces for individual wealth augmentation were future developments. For the rural economy of the eighteenth century, a belief that a proper land distribution and equal rights before the law would produce an egalitarian income distribution made sense to those in that era.

While many during the Revolution held these ideas about obtaining a distribution of income that evoked social harmony, others did not. James Madison, who occupied a middle ground on the subject of the existence of the poor and the rich, thought population growth was a powerful creator of inequality. Nonetheless, he admitted that when "Government assumes a freer aspect, and the laws favor a subdivision of property," the less-well-off would benefit. John Adams of Massachusetts found the argument unconvincing. Perhaps because he worked in Boston and saw how commerce piled up wealth for its practitioners, he stressed the role of the family in producing winners and losers in society, and he firmly believed that a "natural aristocracy" of talent existed that would earn great wealth. "After all, as long as property exists, it will accumulate in individuals and families. As long as marriage exists, knowledge, property, and influence will accumulate in families." Thus nothing would stop a growing gap in wealth-holding among citizens: "I repeat it, so sure as the idea and existence of *property* is admitted and established in society, accumulations of it will be made; the snow-ball will grow as it rolls."[30]

By the 1780s, American leaders often put their ruminations about a proper distribution of wealth aside because they saw threats in politics and society that threatened the sanctity of property rights, which for those with extensive property holdings overrode the general republican belief that republics required an even distribution of wealth. A great source of concern for the leadership was the paper money legislation coming out of the popular branch of state legislatures. In the movements of distressed people, as in Shays' Rebellion, the upper classes grew fearful of the democratic tendency among the common people because it portended an attack on wealth-holders.[31]

THE PRINCIPLES OF ARISTOCRACY LEADING TO AN INEGALITARIAN SOCIETY

If revolutionary leaders fumbled around trying to find the practical means of promoting the correct property distribution in a republic, they had fewer problems about pinpointing the sources of inequality of property in Europe. They attacked the hereditary principle; it was the special privileges of inheritance that over time produced families of great wealth and left the masses with so little. Thomas Paine pointed out the problem of hereditary government in 1776 in *Common Sense* when he described the hereditary succession of kings as an "evil," and then in 1792 in his *Rights of Man,* he simply declared that "all hereditary government is in its nature tyranny."[32] Societies based on hereditary principles produced aristocracies, and aristocracies in turn required "an inequality of rights." To maintain that inequality, aristocracies needed an "unnatural, unequal, and unjust state of social order, and social rights."[33] During and after the Revolution, writers of all political shades attacked the artificiality of an elite that ruled because of inheritance; this was embedded in the phrase "we suffer no hereditary offices or titles."[34] In the *Federalist Papers,* James Madison even wrote (issue 43) that one of the purposes of a new central government was to ensure states remained republican by preventing "aristocratic or monarchical innovations."[35]

While there was general agreement among revolutionaries that government should not foster an aristocracy by unjust laws and privileges, there was a divide over whether wealth in and of itself produced an aristocracy, whether wealth enabled the favored few to obtain more advantages than other members of the community. This division was clearest in the debates over ratification of the Constitution when the Anti-Federalists argued that a new, powerful government could abet the wealthy, thereby aiding the formation of an aristocracy, whereas Federalists insisted that an aristocracy existed by nature and all that could be done was to ensure it did not obtain any advantages other than those nature had given.[36] The Anti-Federalists were decidedly more fearful of an aristocracy, but they testified as well to the impact of hereditary practices upon accumulation. John F. Mercer forcefully wrote, "Where *wealth* is hereditary, *power* is hereditary, for *wealth* is *power*—Titles are of very little, or no consequence—the *rich* are *nobility,* and the *poor plebians* [*sic*] in all countries." While thus fluctuating between the principles of simple possession of wealth and the passage of wealth over time (inheritance), Mercer nonetheless declared that in the world "hereditary wealth [is] the only universally pervading principle and characteristic." Anti-Federalists seemed to agree that natural talents and simple luck created the wealthy, who then became an aristocracy, but it was the duty of a free government to stop hereditary aristocracy "by the equality of the laws, and . . . the frequency of elections." It was when governments assisted the few that aristocracy resulted.[37]

Families in North America, however, were not denied power over time, although the formal titles and legislative privileges were prohibited. John Adams insisted on the influence of families over time, although he was rebuked by others, including his cousin Samuel Adams. Thomas Jefferson appeared to be in the forefront of those attacking family dominance in political affairs, but Virginia at the time, as well as afterwards, hardly seemed the state destined to forgo the importance of family power.[38]

The North American attack on the hereditary principle, in theory if less so in practice, was buttressed by the individualism that marked the revolutionary era. "Every man occupied that rank only," wrote David Ramsey in his history of the Revolution, "which his own industry or that of his near ancestors, had procured him"; a person rose in property holdings and social esteem by "personal talents." Success, in short, was achieved due to individual abilities and talents—not simply because a person was born into the right family. Or, to put the matter forthrightly, a person might exhibit brilliance in some activity, but there was absolutely no guarantee that his or her progeny would. Talent was not an inherited trait. One of the ways American revolutionaries testified to the vacuity of the idea of inherited abilities was their commentary on European nobility. Even John Adams, convinced as he was of the importance of family connections in Massachusetts, wrote about the Polish nobility that "magnificence is the foible of the nobility, and they sacrifice all things to luxury," and that such traits were true for all aristocracies.[39]

It is in this context that one can grasp an experiential quality to the words *virtue* and *luxury* so bandied about by the American revolutionaries.[40] Undoubtedly the revolutionary leaders extracted meanings for the two words from republican treatises of ancient and medieval times, but the existing situation in which they found themselves starkly revealed the absurd luxury of British and European aristocrats and their unwillingness to give up any self-interest and pleasure—that is, to show virtue. It was logical that fear of luxury and a desire to elevate virtue resulted from observing the antics of aristocrats across the Atlantic.

Coming out of the analysis of aristocracy was a realization that one of the props to the aristocratic order was some form of government-induced monopoly. The clearest example of monopoly was monopoly of the land, extreme in the case of England but observable elsewhere as well. The anti-monopoly impulse became a part of the American Revolution, though there were those who argued that in certain cases a monopoly could be useful in attracting capital for large-scale projects. Nonetheless, the animosity to monopolies was a strident theme in the Revolution and its aftermath. Thomas Jefferson was upset that the draft of the Constitution did not have a "restriction against monopolies." Later, in an attack on banking companies, a writer showed the evils of monopolies by referring to the activities of the East India Company. One writer wrote that "monopolizers . . . are our worst oppressors," while even conservatives like John Adams and James Wilson denounced monopolies and their effects.[41]

Just as the American revolutionaries attacked the monopolistic props that supported aristocracy, they also fired broadsides against aristocratic leisure. Supposedly, leisure—to be precise, the release of an individual from doing manual or even mental labor necessary to earn a comfortable material existence—enabled the aristocracy to pursue the arts, to become expert in political affairs, and to cultivate civilized behaviors. According to Benjamin Franklin, what the aristocracy actually did was to engraft two opinions on the people: "one, that useful labor is dishonorable; the other, that families may be perpetuated with estates." He denounced the attitudes that European aristocrats passed to their progeny; because sons had no role in actually obtaining wealth and honor, their receiving it without work makes "them proud, disdaining to be employed in useful arts." John Adams gave the same advice to son John Quincy about the effect of riches on the sons of the wealthy: "they pass their lives in idleness, or in dishonorable occupations—mere burdens [on] human society, mere cumberers of the ground." Many revolutionaries commented that it was unjust for a few to live without labor while the many toiled to no advantage for themselves. Jefferson was pleased that in the United States those "who can live without labor, either manual or professional, being few, and of moderate wealth," could not reduce the means of subsistence among the masses, for the masses in the United States lived far better than their counterparts in Europe.[42]

Americans also noted the tie between aristocratic privileges and England's established church, the Church of England. In religious circles, the Church of England became another political arm of the aristocracy to keep the people in their place without dissent. Among skeptical Americans, the Church of England was a machine for manufacturing positions for displaced sons of the aristocracy. John Adams feared that "if Parliament can erect dioceses and appoint Bishops, they may introduce the whole hierarchy, establish tythes, forbid marriages and funerals, establish religion, forbid dissenters, make schism heresy, impose penalties extending to life and limb, as well as to liberty and property." The fear of the tithe was no small matter. Internal pressures were pushing Americans to declare for liberty of conscience and separation of church and state, most likely to ensure that no American denomination could oppress the other denominations, but the aristocratic control and manipulations of an established church were not overlooked.[43]

Given this dissection of aristocracy and its foundational principle of inequality, it is no wonder that the Americans, in their quest for equality (as understood in the late eighteenth century), sought to destroy the two major roots of it in North America before it became too powerful: monopoly of the land and the passage of the estate to an heir. The result was the widespread attack on the British laws of primogeniture (all property went to the first son) and entail (the estate was to be kept intact for centuries).

Actually, Britain had already removed the practice of entail, replacing it with the practice known as "strict settlement." Moreover, the Americans did not intrude too far into the realm of choice of the individual testator. The abolition of entail and primogeniture only worked for intestate property—property that the deceased had not provided for in a last will and testament. The practice in North America was partible inheritance, in which property was divided among the sons and daughters (and not equally), and most believed the custom did not need to be reinforced by legislation. The number of revolutionary leaders who believed this action vital to the founding of a nonaristocratic republic is impressive. The states passed such laws almost immediately once the Revolution began. Although historians have expressed skepticism about the impact of the abolition of primogeniture and entail, the revolutionaries were most proud of it and continually listed it as one of their achievements; they expected it to relieve the country of a formal aristocracy for centuries.[44]

The revolutionary leaders' understanding of how aristocratic institutions resulted in inequality provided the framework for how to construct an egalitarian, or simply an equitable, society: remove the aristocratic devices. So the momentum released by the Revolution took the form of an antimonopoly crusade, elimination of entail and primogeniture, a prohibition of titles, a reduction of government favoritism to certain individuals, an opening of politics to the citizenry, and ultimately, separation of church and state (religious freedom). These were all negative actions in the sense that these were rules, laws, and practices to be prohibited. But in one area the Revolution produced a positive role for government: provision of education.

Leaders emphasized education because they also took note of one other aspect of aristocracy: besides creating the obnoxious wealthy, the system also produced the stupid masses. One of the striking features of the European poor was their ignorance. Trenchard and Gordon (1720) made the case for how aristocratic institutions debased the generality of people mentally: "Poverty dejects the Mind, fashions it to Slavery, and renders it unequal to any generous Undertaking, and incapable of opposing any bold Usurpation."[45] Using an allusion to becoming enslaved by political despotism, Trenchard and Gordon made explicit the connection between the political system and the mental state of the citizenry: "People who live in Freedom will think with Freedom; but when the Mind is enslaved by Fear, and the Body by Chains, Inquiry and Study will be at an End."[46]

This effect was not lost on American colonials. When Jefferson was ambassador to France in the 1780s, he found that European higher education taught students to appreciate luxury and to denigrate working people. He championed a public education system for Virginia—not enacted—and of course later became the founding father of the University of Virginia. When exchanging views over containment of the "unnatural" aristocracy with John Adams in 1813, Jefferson listed the ways he stamped out the "pseudo-aristocracy" by outlawing entails and primogeniture, allowing religious freedom, and eventually by establishing "freedom of the mind" by ending the "aristocracy of the clergy" and obtaining a "diffusion of knowledge" by establishing a system of public education.[47] Madison came to agree with Jefferson, while John Adams at the outset of the Revolution was convinced that the schooling conducted by local communities in Massachusetts, and New England generally, had produced an informed public that could well comprehend political problems and make intelligent decisions. However, he did note the importance of the "liberal arts" obtained from university education that enabled citizens to be wise in their political decisions, and observed that only rich people obtained such education, not "laborers, husbandmen, mechanics, and merchants in general." This latter point was the aristocratic justification for denying voting rights to the masses of people and keeping the vote restricted to the aristocracy or at least to those of considerable property.[48] The course of American education would have a strange road to travel, pushed by varying motivations of creating economic opportunity, imposing a moral code, teaching lower-class children obedience to superiors, and inculcating in youth the responsibilities of citizens in a republic. Nevertheless, tax-supported school systems became a standard and were, in the transatlantic perspective, an antiaristocratic endeavor.[49]

THE EMERGING FACE OF AMERICAN EQUALITY

Gordon Wood has written that out of the Revolution came an "explosion of energy," and that energy originated in the idea of equality sweeping the land. This is an accurate interpretation, and its rhetorical manifestation took the form of social mobility exclamations. This was more than merely a bourgeois battle cry of opportunity for the lower classes (for whom the pronouncement was further made that if they could not take advantage of opportunities, the problem lay within themselves); it was the obvious result of removing aristocratic impositions on the mass of citizens—the people could now acquire property instead of having everything leeched away in tithes, taxes, and rents. Thus Samuel Bryan, an Anti-Federalist, could write that in the American states there was "a happy equality and independency" that pervaded the land, "as the field to fame and riches is open to all, it stimulates universal exertion and exhibits a lively picture of emulation, industry and happiness." Some of the former would-be American gentry of the 1760s and 1770s were upset at the sudden emergence of political and economic activity among the lower and middle orders of American society, but that such social turmoil would happen—something so foreign to the ordered agrarian society of aristocracy—was predictable with the removal of aristocratic restraints on behavior.[50]

THE SPECIAL CASE OF SLAVERY

There could be no hiding from the fact that the egalitarian melody ringing throughout the land during the American Revolution became discordant when the subject of slavery was addressed. Slavery simply contradicted all the major themes of independence, representative government, fruitful labor, liberty, and equality that flowed out of the mouths of leaders during the revolutionary era. A few insisted that enslaved Africans belonged to the category of servants in the household and that slavery was therefore a private, not a public, practice. The rhetorical fear about being enslaved that the revolutionaries constantly pronounced was a fear of enslavement by governmental institutions, an enslavement that was totally unlike the arrangements of the household.[51]

Yet the inconsistency—for some, the blatant hypocrisy—of having the word *equality* issue from the mouths of slaveholders was so overwhelming that commentators then and now have assumed that at the least, the revolutionaries were conditional about who was allowed in the realm of egalitarianism.[52] The means of escape from the obloquy that contemporaries heaped upon the revolutionaries for slaveholding has already been discussed in connection with the Declaration of Independence: the signers really meant American leaders were equal to the British gentry; the signers believed in equality of communities and not necessarily individuals, they blamed slavery on the Crown, they were arguing only about slavery to civil institutions and not about slavery in private households, and they made a plea for equality only for those of European descent. Working against all these rationales was the quick development of an antislavery sentiment above the Mason-Dixon line and the appearance of written protests about the existence of the institution. St. George Tucker defended Virginians from the opprobrium of having slavery and freedom-shriekers at the same time. In 1788, a contributor to the Philadelphia *American Museum,* probably an African American, chided the Americans for revolting against Great Britain on the principle that all men were equal while indulging in slaveholding. Tom Paine early declared against slavery, and Abigail Adams made barbed comments about slavery that she lacerated her husband John with.[53]

Moreover, in the revolutionary period—extending it to 1790 or so—many individuals were directly connecting the practice of slavery to aristocracy. James Madison, who harbored fears about emancipation, nonetheless knew that the effect of slaveholding on the political apparatus was aristocratic. For Madison, aristocracy flowed from a concentration of wealth, whereas republicanism—or increasingly, democracy—originated in an equal distribution. "In proportion as slavery prevails in a State, the Government, however democratic in name, must be aristocratic in fact. The power lies in a part instead of the whole; in the hands of property, not of numbers"; and hence the southern states "are . . . aristocracies." The lower class of the southern states, in their poverty and ignorance, resembled the lower class in aristocracies. John Adams wrote that southerners "have large plantations of slaves, and the common people among them are very ignorant and very poor." During the Massachusetts debates over ratification of the Constitution, James Winthrop argued against a union with the slaveholding states because Massachusetts was so different from them; those states had an unequal wealth distribution, slavery, and "the ignorance and poverty of the lower classes," all of which were unlike the "small and nearly equal estates," "equality of rights," and education of the people in New England. Another Anti-Federalist, Cato, also harped on the aristocratic character of the southern states. There, one obtained "a passion for aristocratic distinctions, where slavery is encouraged, and liberty of course, less respected, and protected." Southerners did not know "what it is to acquire property by their own toil" and lacked the northern people's "freedom, independence, industry, equality, and frugality." Contemporary historian Mercy Warren of Massachusetts admonished readers that slavery brought into practice "aristocratic principles," and thus one obtained a different idea of liberty:

not liberty "from a sense of the common rights of man, as from their own feelings of superiority."[54]

One may say that many revolutionaries understood that a grave flaw in the American pronouncement of equality was the existence of slavery. Moreover, as innumerable historians have pointed out, class tensions between small landowners and great landowners existed, a class system had already developed in American cities, and a stark division between those who labored manually and those who labored mentally was apparent. Some of the tensions between classes and occupations could be explained away as the result of natural talent and a relaxed idea of equality (not exact, but including a broad distribution of property among most citizens), but slavery and especially racial slavery could not be so easily rationalized. Although the "scientific" explanation of race awaited the middle of the nineteenth century, Euro-Americans were already behaving on its premises, not only towards Africans but also towards Native Americans. So how can the idea of universal male equality be reconciled with the actual condition of racial prejudice, which took the form of wars with Native Americans and enslavement of Africans?

The most obvious answer is that it cannot be reconciled, that in terms of behavior Euro-Americans pronounced inequality on the ethnic groups whose skin pigmentation was non-European. They understood their failings and lived with them when it came to egalitarian principles. However, there is one way to illuminate the Euro-Americans' restricted idea of equality. The people of Europe held no idea of the diversity that now exists in the twenty-first century. Equality for them may have meant all men were equal (the vote for women would come one and one-half centuries later) in the homogeneous ethnic community to which they belonged, but different ethnic groups may have been unequal in their talents and abilities when compared to each other.

Below is the solitary table that will be presented in this work. It takes information from the *World Almanac and Book of Facts* for 2009; it is a yearly publication that gives information about news, governments, and national economies, focusing primarily on the United States; the factual information is several years old. In this publication, there is a listing of the nations and, among the other information, the ethnic divisions within them. So in about 2007, the ethnic division for these western and central European countries was as given in the table.

Table 1: Ethnic Divisions within Selected European Nations, c. 2007

Nation	*Ethnic Divisions*
United Kingdom	White, 92% (English 77%, Scottish 8%, Welsh, 5%, Northern Irish, 3%), Black 2%, Indian 2%
France	Celtic and Latin with Teutonic, Slavic, North African, Indochinese, Basque
Spain	Mixed Mediterranean and Nordic
Portugal	Homogeneous Mediterranean
Belgium	Flemish 58%, Walloon 31%
Luxembourg	Luxembourger 63%, Portuguese 13%, French 5%, Italian 4%, German 2%
Sweden	Swedes with Finnish and Sami minorities
Finland	Finn 93%, Swede 6%
Norway	Norwegian (including Sami)
Denmark	Scandinavian, Inuit, Faroese, German, Turkish, Iranian, Somali
Germany	German 92%, Turkish 2%
Italy	Italian (including small clusters of German, French, Slovene, Greek)
Switzerland	German 65%, French 18%, Italian 10%
Poland	Polish 97%
Russia	Russian 80%, Tatar 4%

Source: From *World Almanac and Book of Facts, 2009* (Pleasantville, NY: Reader's Digest Co., 2009). According to *World Almanac and Book of Facts, 2004* (Pleasantville, NY: Reader's Digest Co., 2004), Sweden's ethnicities were Swedish 89%, Finn 2%, and Sami 9%.

These figures are correct roughly 250 years after the American Revolution, and in these figures one reads that almost each European country is essentially ethnically homogeneous. They must have been even more homogeneous in the eighteenth century. The essential referent that these people, except for aristocrats and probably scientists, must have had was their own ethnic group. Each nation-state was supposed to be composed of one ethnicity. This belief was put into print by Anthony Trollope, the nineteenth-century English novelist, who toured the United States at the outbreak of the Civil War in 1861. He held, as did many Europeans, that the United States was destined to break apart simply because it was too big; the bigness brought about ethnic diversity, which was poison for a harmonious nation-state. Europeans believed that the ethnic stock should be "homogeneous" in order for a people "to live together as one nation."[55]

Alexis de Tocqueville also testified to the validity of the idea that the standard for a nation-state's society was a homogeneous ethnic group. In volume I, part II, chapter 10, he discussed the "three races" inhabiting the United States. In his analysis he penned the line, "The people who have spread across this territory are not, *as in Europe, all offspring of a single family*" (emphasis added). Again, to cite Tocqueville:

> In the past there existed among us great inequalities whose origins lay solely in legislation. What could be more fictitious than a purely legal inferiority? What more contrary to man's instincts than permanent differences established between obviously similar people! Yet these differences persisted for centuries. . . . [Given the inability of aristocrats to yield their unequal positons to those of similar ethnicity] I despair of seeing the disappearance of an aristocracy founded on visible and imperishable signs [of ethnic differences].[56]

Woodrow Wilson gave famous affirmation to the concept of one people abiding together in one state in his vision for post–World War I Europe. The squabbling ethnic groups of western Europe should be permitted "national self-determination"—that is, each separate ethnicity should be given its own nation-state. Such a vision is an utter rejection of the diversity standard erected in the late twentieth century. Equality among diverse ethnic groups in one nation is indeed a late twentieth-century concept that has few roots in the western European past.

But in the eighteenth century, equality was nowhere the standard for a nation's political and social system even though the nation had a people who were ethnically homogeneous. Rather, the standard for any homogeneous ethnic group was inequality. The application of equality and inequality to the system of a state was parochial: it was meant to apply to the homogeneous ethnic group that composed a nation. Thus when individuals did argue for a "universal" equality of mankind in the last part of the eighteenth century, the unspoken understanding was that the idea of equality applied to people in a homogeneous ethnic community, of one type of people in each nation-state. That condition still enabled some to argue that inequality in abilities and intelligence might be evident when some communities were compared to others.

Because the revolutionaries were descended from Europeans, they took this idea of ethnic homogeneity with them. Therefore, they could argue for universal equality within a single ethnic group, conceived of as the dominant element in a nation-state, and still acknowledge inequalities when different ethnic groups were compared with one another. The logical extension of this understanding, however, leads directly to an inequality among different ethnic groups within a nation. It was and became a justification of "separate but equal," of the practice of Jim Crow segregation that appeared formally in the United States in the 1880s and 1890s.

Whatever confusions surrounded the Americans' definition of equality, others took it seriously and reacted once the Napoleonic Wars were over. Historians, who erected their own standards of what equality should have been, could easily denounce any pretensions the Americans in the nineteenth century had of being an egalitarian society, but eighteenth- and nineteenth-century Europeans did not. It is their printed commentary about the virtues of equality and the vices of inequality that has a power to instruct us about our own contemporary situation. The first enemy that egalitarianism faced was the practice and ideal of inequality within a homogeneous ethnic community. The challenge of defeating the doctrines and practices of inequality that were imposed on people from different ethnic communities was to come much later.

In one of the issues of the *American Museum,* a contributor named Russel wrote an article entitled "On Aristocracy." In it he penned the line, Nature "appears to be a decided democrat, and one of the greatest levelers known to us."[57] Now that statement was one major gauntlet thrown in the face of aristocracy. The British aristocrats did not like being slapped in the face so belligerently. They accepted the challenge and the duel began.

2

THE FORTRESS

The Defense of Inequality, 1750–1820

Americans in 1776 were alone in the Western world in their adoption of an ideal of equality. The upper classes of western Europe in the middle of the eighteenth century unabashedly embraced inequality because inequality was the hearthstone of aristocracy, and western Europe ran on the principles of monarchy and aristocracy. Therefore the justification of aristocracy both as a political system and as a social system was intimately bound together with inequality. The principles buttressing aristocracy and inequality had been shaped for nearly two millennia, so that by 1750 the arguments had assumed a standard form.

Principle One. Nature had made men unequal. This precept stemmed from the obviously different talents and interests that people displayed, and the talents were given by an original power over which no person had control. The ancients had a somewhat cosmic idea of nature, and it would not achieve the status of natural law until it was delineated by Francisco Suárez and Spanish legal theorists in the sixteenth century. However, it appeared early in the writings of Plato and Aristotle, who openly sided with an aristocratic form of government (meaning rule by the best) and the exclusion of common people—small farmers, ship carpenters, herdsmen, and urban workers. The justification was straightforward: these people did not have the mental capacity for understanding complicated political problems and for leading the polis in the direction of philosophical discovery—discovering truths—that was the special destiny of humankind and what made humans different from the other animals on the earth. The stress on aristocracy as the true guide for a society also emanated from the Roman Republic. Cicero denounced the influence of plebeians and demanded that the "republic" remain true to its legal principles, which largely meant giving dominance to the aristocracy.[1]

Principle 2. The Divinity decreed that human society be ordered and that a few should rule. The role of the Greek and Roman Gods in blessing a system of aristocracy is unclear, but such is not the case with Christianity. The stark division evidently commenced with St. Augustine of Hippo, who argued that because of the fall of Adam and the reality of original sin dominating the human species, mankind was doomed to live in sin and depravity in this world, though in the eternal city of paradise all ills would vanish. Because of the capacity for sin, Augustine insisted that people required government by the best people, an aristocracy, in order to suppress wantonness. The Roman Catholic Church indeed duplicated the ordered society that Augustine felt was necessary for the secular world, as the church structure had for its head a pope, like a king, and archbishops, like an aristocracy, and then a chain of officials finally reaching down to the laity. About eleven hundred years later, the Protestant Reformation began a change in the theological doctrines and liturgical practices of Christianity but did not disturb the idea of an ordered political community. Martin Luther was exacting in his demand that people obey the laws of princes, and he supported the authorities in suppressing peasant revolts. England turned away from the Catholic Church under Henry VIII but not from its hierarchical structure; even after the Elizabethan settlement in the late sixteenth century, the structure of the Anglican Church replicated almost exactly the structure of the Catholic Church. The dissident groups of Puritans did receive from John Calvin a theory of resistance to the state, but except for the Pilgrims and Congregationalists, most of the dissident Puritans, such as the Presbyterians, had a structure of power for their denominations in which approved doctrines and procedures came from the leaders of the church and were then passed down to the underlings to be implemented and obeyed. The connection between church hierarchy and state hierarchy received its broadest affirmation in the divine right of kings: that secular authority was given to a king by the divinity.[2]

Both principles 1 and 2 underscore an important feature of the rationales for monarchy and aristocracy in terms of equality and inequality. Writers were consistently able to argue for a general equality among all humans when humans were considered as a species, but in the practical management of affairs small differences among people made for monumental differences in results. In religion, equality before God was asserted, but the sinfulness of humans made inequality the standard for the rule of people. In one way or another, an equality of all people as ordained by nature or by God could be affirmed, but then inequality in secular activity rendered the necessary guide. It seems that until the eighteenth century, equality was always confined to an area that never intruded on the actual inequality that governed most people's lives.[3]

Principle 3. In order to advance the human species in its quest for truth and to understand human relationships properly so the right governmental policies were implemented, rulers needed leisure time. Leisure was defined as time not needed to acquire subsistence; subsistence had to be assured to rulers so that they could focus on state problems and study, acquire information, and obtain education. More specifically, it excluded all those who labored manually to obtain their daily bread, raiment, and shelter. Socrates, in the voice of Plato, made this argument against Athenian democracy, as did Aristotle. Government required a ruling group that did not have to labor to survive; such a group was deemed an aristocracy. This idea of leisure remained a pillar of justification for the existence of an aristocracy even into the twentieth century.[4]

Principle 4. An aristocracy must possess wealth, a wealth greatly exceeding that of the average citizen. This principle is a derivative of the necessity of leisure for the ruling group. The only way to obtain the leisure necessary to acquire knowledge and to reflect on universal truths was to have subsistence assured. That condition was satisfied if a person had wealth. The wealth in most societies prior to 1600 was landed wealth, and the means of obtaining the wealth that yielded subsistence was to have others till the fields either as day laborers or tenants. The other avenue to wealth was taxation; government taxed commoners—most frequently peasants, small landholders, urban workers, and businesspeople—to provide income for the ruling group. But the basic proposition was clear: the common people had to sacrifice some of the fruits of their labors to the ruling group for the ruling group to gain the subsistence that freed them from work and enabled them to engage in intellectual pursuits afforded by leisure time. And here leisure time does not mean sport or games or anything of that sort; the reference is time given to study and becoming enlightened about universal truths and appropriate governmental policies.

Prior to 1600, most writers on aristocracy dealt with politics and the necessity of obtaining wise persons to guide a society, a condition that called for an aristocracy and that rejected the participation of commoners. A further rationalization for the establishment of aristocracy was to act as a brake on the designs of the monarch. In principle, kings obtained their license to govern from God, but on occasion God chose a dud or at least one who decided not to obey biblical commandments, and so some check was necessary to make sure that such monarchs did not ruin a kingdom. Later Montesquieu would justify the inclusion of a branch of government that represented commoners, as was the case with Parliament in England, so all three branches—monarchy, aristocracy, and democracy—could check the injurious potential each had separately.[5]

The fusion of the aristocratic practice of government rule with economic dominance raises some awkward questions seldom answered by the ancients or the moderns. It seems that in Europe until 1600 aristocracies always had wealth, and in fact had monumental amounts of it. They leeched the wealth from commoners and thereby inspired peasant and urban revolts that plagued the ancient and medieval worlds. How did they obtain that wealth? According to Benjamin Franklin, they stole it by conquest. The aristocracy did have a military justification for their existence, and one conjectures that military conquests led to the acquisition of landed wealth as well as to the accretion of slaves. In any event, from the beginning, wealth and aristocracy marched together as a blatantly observable fact, a fact far more obvious than any involving the search for scientific knowledge, universal truths, or wise governmental policies. What republicans would later call "virtue"—the characteristic of a citizen who in matters of public policy placed the general welfare above his or her self-interest—was not especially observable in the behavior of the aristocracy. The often unstated but most pressing reason for aristocratic control of politics was the aristocrats' obsession with preserving their wealth and possibly extending it. By controlling the government apparatus, aristocrats ensured that government could not intrude upon their holdings. And there was the matter of taxation. By controlling government, aristocrats could ensure that tax policies injured commoners and not themselves, and they could reject anything like an excessive land tax that would harm them. So control of politics was intimately connected with wealth, and as the aristocrats were generally a wealthy element in society, they naturally became wrapped up in politics. This connection was made most obvious by the Roman Republic's creation of the modern-day idea of individual property and by Cicero's denunciation of schemes designed to have the government donate property to impoverished citizens (actually, soldiers) to alleviate plebeian unrest.[6]

Within the ancient concept of aristocracy was an additional idea that persisted until the first part of the twentieth century: the wealth to be owned was property in land. The reasons for elevating land ownership above other forms of wealth had to do with stability, presence, and longevity—and perhaps a demonstration of obvious mastery over others. Land did not change over the years and seemed a part of the natural world; by owning it, one had a continuous presence in the community; and one's ownership of land was not likely to be of brief duration. Finally, the aristocrat owned the land and obtained his standard of living from its productions, but he or she did not do the farming personally. The manual labor of the farm was relegated to peasants, day laborers, tenants, or serfs. Thus the aristocrat could oversee operations and exude his superiority over commoners in a visible manner. Until industrialization in the late eighteenth century, the other means of acquiring wealth was commerce. Trade, however, involved long-distance transactions, the value of the property in goods could fluctuate wildly, one could by one or two bad decisions lose everything, and commerce had none of the visible mastery over others that landownership had. Moreover, merchants violated the principle of leisure. Because merchants had to attend to details, even though the details involved mental and not manual labor, they did not have the kind of leisure prized by political philosophers. Thus land ownership for the aristocracy had a status that superseded all other kinds of wealth-holding—at least as long as an adequate income was derived from it.[7]

Certain questions about wealth-holding, leisure, and aristocracy never were answered. One may admit that some leisure time was necessary to study political problems or to educate oneself about universal truths, but no one determined how much wealth was necessary to obtain that leisure. Even within the Catholic Church, it was possible to obtain the time necessary for education by becoming a monk or a nun and yet never obtain a position of wealth. Few, or perhaps none, ever addressed the question of when wealth inhibited the acquisition of truth, or when excessive wealth was more of a problem than a blessing.[8]

Principle 5. Heredity and family lineage trump all other aspects of social life. The economic principle of aristocracy is inherited wealth, and thus an inequality created ages ago could be perpetuated over time. How inheritance got so wrapped up in the justification of a ruling class's ability to govern with wisdom and justice is something of a mystery. Part of the reason probably lies in the simple fact that family was such a basic institution of early societies. Another part of the answer may be that for the founders of great wealth, inheritance to sons (and maybe later daughters in the modern period) was a surrogate for immortality, a condition mortals may yearn for but can never achieve. Tocqueville said the desire for family wealth across the centuries was a case of "egotistical illusion." He continued, "a person may seek to perpetuate and immortalize himself, in his posterity."[9] A practical reason for reliance on heredity is that rich aristocrats could afford to educate their sons in private academies and so enhance the opportunity that the progeny would acquire knowledge and wisdom; commoners had no school except the one of hard knocks. Aristotle believed that inherited wealth improved a person's outlook for humanist studies because he then avoided becoming dominated by an acquisitive personality.[10]

Inheritance became the center of aristocratic reality and kept the system alive, and aristocrats realized it. Others came to question how virtue, wisdom, and knowledge became transmitted to aristocratic youth. Rather, the youth could learn other ways to enjoy leisure instead of reading and studying.[11] In later periods, inheritance would be questioned both as an economic practice and an intellectual activity. A great entrepreneur may have skills and personality traits that enable him or her to amass a fortune; but the sons and daughters of such people most often do not exhibit the same traits. As for intellectual capacity being passed along from parents to progeny, simply let it be noted that there are no parent-child pairs who have won Nobel Prizes in chemistry, physics, medicine, literature, or economics.

Of the centuries over which inequality has ruled Europe, one constant has appeared: to justify whatever economic or political system was in operation, the justifiers always argued that the elite deserved their wealth and possessions, and that the commonality had neither the talent nor the virtue to merit more than a bare material subsistence.

ARISTOCRACY AND INEQUALITY AT THE TIME OF THE AMERICAN REVOLUTION

The world in which the American republic was born was an aristocratic world full of inegalitarian rhetoric. The special case for the Americans was the British aristocracy because the people of the American nation, regardless of European migrants from Germany, Switzerland, France, Spain, and Sweden, retained English habits and patterns of thought. The number of aristocrats in England varied, but by 1800 there were probably 270 peers. They were the great landholders but not the only ones. Large landowners might not possess aristocratic titles, but they could nonetheless own thousands of acres. About 15,000 families in 1790 could be considered gentry—people who lived on rents from their land—and of these, about 400 could be considered the high gentry who earned over £10,000 per year. By 1790 the domination of the gentry over agricultural England (and Great Britain) was almost complete. They owned probably 80 percent of the arable land, the peasantry had been transformed into a rural proletariat, and actual farming was done by wage laborers who were managed by tenants.[12] All now concede that the great landowners controlled the politics of England and Great Britain from the Glorious Revolution until the 1880s.[13]

The British aristocracy, however, had differences from their mainland European counterparts. As large as were the estates of some British landed magnates, the greatest ones were in Hungary and Poland. Most European aristocrats escaped taxes, as the monarchs gave them tax exemptions to win their assent to kingly rule. However, the tension between kings and aristocrats continued on the continent, whereas the battle between them had been settled in England in favor of the great landed families. In France, the aristocrats had special courts for alleged illegal activity, and they were forbidden by law to engage in retail trade or certain professions, or to labor with their hands. None of these advantages were given to British aristocrats who, on paper at least, had to obey the king's law and pay taxes; the strictures against the trade and professions were accomplished primarily by the desire to maintain social status. One of the most important differences between the British aristocracy and their counterparts in the rest of Europe were the numbers. By 1900, England had only 520 peers. The number of aristocrats elsewhere was, in the eighteenth century, 500,000 in Russia, 410,000 in Hungary, over 700,000 in Poland, 722,000 in Spain, and 350,000 in France. The reason for the disparity was the inheritance laws; England passed the title and entire estate to the eldest male whereas elsewhere in Europe partible inheritance ruled and all the sons partook of the title.[14]

The degree to which class dominated Great Britain in the eighteenth century remains for some a controversy. England had more social mobility than did continental European nations, although it seems to have existed primarily in small towns and urban areas, not in the countryside where the landlords were extending their ownership of the land. Unlike Europe, the idea of "English liberties" had permeated all of society, and the English aristocracy generally acknowledged the "liberties" of others. Social customs allowed for some interplay among the income groups, and some historians assert class lines were not strongly drawn. But the more recent scholarship insists that, in the words of Roy Porter, English society was "unashamedly inegalitarian, hierarchical, hereditary, and privileged."[15]

Of the primary traits of the English aristocracy, the first was ownership of land. Ownership of land had a prestige that trumped all other possessions, and to obtain social status wealthy merchants and later industrialists sacrificed some of their fortunes to obtain land for the sole sake of being able to enter higher social circles. Then, the key to the peerage was to have the land held within the family for centuries and, if at all possible, to increase the size of the holdings.[16] The means of holding an estate together over the centuries were the inheritance laws. G. E. Mingay related that in maintaining the position of the aristocracy and gentry, inheritance and marriage were "the most prominent factors," while a nineteenth-century writer of English landed society remarked, "The English aristocracy looked upon entails and primogeniture as the last and strongest bulwark of their power and existence." Passing the estate to the eldest son (primogeniture) remained a standard procedure, but the old practice of entail—by last testament insisting that the estate be kept intact for centuries—had been outlawed in the days of the Tudor monarchs. However, it was then replaced by the "strict settlement," by which an agreement was made by grandfather, father, and son, when the son came of legal age, to keep the estate together. However, at that point it was possible to break the agreement and to sell portions of the estate. But the inheritance practices of England, all agreed, produced the unified and small aristocracy that ruled that island for centuries.[17]

Tightly bound with the ideal and the reality of family as the crucial institution of the aristocracy was the power distribution within the family, and that was irredeemably patriarchal. The father ran the household, and all others were dependents—inferiors to be exact. The inferiors included women, children, servants, and in the colonies, slaves. Prior to 1700, the law gave heads of households the right to inflict physical punishment on the dependents. However, in the eighteenth century, violence against servants had to be abandoned as servants increasingly fought back, and the courts no longer legitimized the rights of heads of households to resort to violence against other adults. Much of the ideal of inequality derived from the practice of patriarchy, as it approved the division of the family into units inferior to the father and gave one member the responsibility of overseeing the behavior of the others. Of course, the Anglican Church approved family government under these premises and found appropriate biblical strictures to lend it divine authority. For the aristocracy, the principle of patriarchy supposedly extended outward to the rest of society in the form of assistance (noblesse oblige) to the needy.[18]

The aristocracy and gentry exercised immense political power in England until the 1880s. The aristocrats owned the House of Lords, of course, which was not rendered impotent until 1911. But voting privileges until the Reform Act of 1832 were restricted to those who owned land (the 40-acre freehold), and even after the Reform Acts of 1832 and 1866–1867, the great landed families continued to control the British government. In the eighteenth century, it was reputed that thirty-one families supplied one-fourth of the members of the House of Commons. The purpose was to protect the laws of property. From the time of the Roman Republic, the idea was that the existence of private property was the key to civilization, and that only those who possessed property should make rules about its disposition, including taxation. On the national level, there was no dispute about the ability of the aristocracy to protect its exalted position and its material holdings.[19]

The great landowners also had almost total control of local government. Most aristocrats accepted the rule of Parliament, especially once they obtained ascendency over the monarch in the Glorious Revolution of 1688–1689, and wanted law and order in the countryside. They also wanted to be the kingpins in terms of selection of officeholders and church officials to make sure decisions reflected their ideas. During the rule of the later Stuarts, the office of lord-lieutenant became the means by which the aristocrats obtained their dominance in the countryside. The local aristocracy nominated local officials, particularly the justices of the peace, and the monarch then appointed them. They also had their say in the parish vestries, overseers of the poor, and church wardens. They chose lesser gentry or yeomen (if any were available) and generally controlled the county clerks and road surveyors. The only popularly elected official was the coroner.

David Eastwood argues that the landholders had a "virtual monopoly" on local offices, and part of the attitude of the landholders was that anything smacking of democracy had to be suppressed and that only landholders had the virtue necessary for ruling. One of the ways the battle between monarchs and aristocrats ended in England was by allowing the aristocrats to run the counties to their own satisfaction but always within the laws of the national government (at first the king's law but later Parliament's law).[20]

Another institution controlled by the aristocracy was the Church of England, the Anglican Church. The purpose of the Anglican Church was to provide charity when needed but primarily to teach doctrines to the mass of people extolling hierarchy and aristocratic control of society; their main function was to indoctrinate the masses with obedience to authority. The gentry and aristocracy kept the vestries under their control and dominated the selection of clergy. The Church of England was an established church that in the eighteenth century and much of the nineteenth ran on public funding; membership in the church was necessary for political office. Even though toleration of nonconformist sects came with the Glorious Revolution, the ideal of a homogeneous religious culture fit the aristocratic order well and was thus considered part of the aristocratic establishment.[21]

A practical matter was involved in the aristocratic/gentry control of politics and religion. These families contained more than one son, and fathers wanted their progeny to have some decent future. Thus, the other sons of the nobility could find places as government bureaucrats, church officials, and officers in the military.[22] In addition, the aristocracy controlled the game laws of England, making sure that woodland animals were not killed by tenants, workers, and villagers; these animals were to be the sport of the aristocratic hunting parties. The game laws inspired a great deal of rural resentment against the peers. Because of rural resentment, it was the law in England that only the aristocracy could have weapons on their person.[23]

Since the middle of the sixteenth century, English aristocrats and gentry lived by the creed that a gentleman was a man of leisure who did no manual labor and, overall, as little of any other kind of labor as possible. The upbringing involved an education in the liberal arts, by a tutor in youth or a finishing school and then matriculation to Oxford or Cambridge. Such education was meant to put polish on young aristocrats and gentry. From it as well came the cultivation of manners and control of passions—that is, a civilized life. In that civilized life, the behavior of the aristocrat was to serve as a model for the commoners to emulate. However, education was not a gift that manual laborers required. The aristocrats and gentry held education was wasted on the masses and represented nothing more than a senseless tax; common laborers would remain common laborers—for example, ploughmen in the fields—and education would only ruin them. The only source of schooling for commoners was what the Church would provide in Sunday schools and some parish schools. Basically, the aristocracy and the gentry scoffed at the need of an educated public.[24]

The leisure the aristocrats enjoyed enabled them to claim two special political values. The first was virtue—the ability to be dispassionate and disinterested about any subject—and thus be able to judge policies for the general welfare objectively. Virtue was lauded by political writers, but the aristocracy's exhibition of virtue was not exhilarating, and it was partly because the elite became so passionate for the wrong causes that aristocracy fell into disfavor.[25] The second political value prized by the aristocracy was liberty—that is, liberty for themselves. For others they believed in order and stability, but the aristocrat should speak and act with perfect freedom.[26] It was their elevation of liberty that set the aristocracy against the system of democracy, because aristocrats bristled at the thought of a majority telling them how to behave or having the power to make aristocrats censor themselves. Throughout the nineteenth century, not to mention earlier times, aristocrats believed democracy equaled enforced conformity whereas liberty connoted aristocracy and freedom of action.[27]

The great aristocrats maintained a retinue of servants that numbered between twenty-five and fifty, considerably down from the hundreds whom aristocrats employed in earlier centuries. The masters rigidly enforced hierarchy. Jean Hecht wrote that servants in the seventeenth century were "expected to abandon all thought of maintaining a private life" and were on call at all times, day or night; they were taught to "know [their] place" and to maintain a "deferential manner." In the eighteenth century, the masters and servants became physically separated, the servants living in basements and eating at separate dining tables. An older custom in the countryside of landlords eating at the same table with farm laborers (called servants) disappeared. The servants who manned carriages and served at special occasions had special uniforms and were called "liveried servants"; and aristocrats and gentry used their servants as part of a show of wealth. Servants offered some resistance to their servitude, but often it was viewed as a means of social mobility. Servants often identified with their masters; they jostled with other servants over who occupied superior positions.[28]

All historians agree that England, and then Great Britain, was a deferential society; the nonaristocratic social orders deferred and did not contest social, economic, and political rule by the aristocracy. However, the deference was excessive and pervasive. It evolved into a number of social customs that amounted to daily rituals that inferiors were always expected to obey. In the presence of nobility, commoners took off their hats and looked downward. Commoners never affronted nobility with a direct gaze. It was taboo for commoners to touch nobility; a physical contact was only permitted when first initiated by the aristocrat and never by a commoner. In many ways, the normal customs of everyday interactions between nobles and the rest of society had a resemblance to servitude. One difference is worth mentioning: deference in London and the industrial cities was breaking down, as a more democratic spirit marked the lower classes. In the countryside, deference could be utterly stifling.[29] For this reason, people located the democratic spirit in England in the cities, the conservative spirit in the countryside.

Theoretically, education and leisure enabled the aristocracy and gentry to preside over society and offer a model of appropriate behavior, while their learning and knowledge would guide government into adopting wise policies. Reality was something else. They were magnificently wealthy. In the eighteenth century, they set a standard for high living by buying blocks of London real estate, by constructing huge mansions, and by garnishing their country homes with extensive gardens. They kept kennels of hounds for hunting, and even closed off areas for "deer parks," places where the great landlords could hunt deer. Sexual restraint was never one of their characteristics; according to O. D. Lillibridge, Lord Herford in his sixties went "travelling about with a company of prostitutes who formed his principal society, and by whom he was surrounded up to the moment of his death."[30] Aristocrats spent months in London going to plays and parties, showing off their wealth in as splendid a manner as possible. Then if London became boring, they turned, as J. H. Plumb has written, to "the hounds, and the horses, the women and the gaming tables."[31] The life of leisure was capable of extreme abuse.[32]

Behind the show of wealth was a purpose. Class tensions existed in England and could explode in violence. The aristocracy sat atop a society with monstrously skewed wealth-holdings to their favor, and poverty since the sixteenth century had been the fate of at least one-half the kingdom.[33] The fear of the mob was palpable because England did not have an extensive police force, especially in the countryside. As G. E. Mingay has written, "the remedy of the property-less and unenfranchised was to riot." Class tensions were shown in allowing only the aristocracy to arm itself: "In London a duke dare not walk alone through the streets in his usual dress."[34] English deference was inculcated by the shock-and-awe tactics of the aristocracy. By flaunting wealth, by donning regalia, by having parades and fashionable parties, and by displaying manners, the aristocracy wrought order and emulation from the rest of English society.[35]

The separation of the nobility from the untitled British population rested on a cavernous divide in wealth and income, especially in rural England. The land had about 286,000 farms, probably 100,000 owned by "yeoman" farmers. Fifteen thousand farms belonged to the gentry and aristocracy, who owned about 80 percent of the arable land, and the rest were operated by tenant farmers, as the word usage in England, different from the United States, was to call a tenant a farmer. In comparison to the landowners and tenants, Great Britain in 1851 had 1,461,000 male farmworkers and 225,000 female farmworkers. British agriculture since the early eighteenth century was characterized by a tremendously lopsided land distribution; it was a land of a few landowners and a massive number of farm laborers. And the wage earned by farm laborers was nearly the lowest of all categories of wage workers.[36]

The luxurious lifestyle of the British nobility rested entirely on the immiseration of the agricultural laborers, a well-known fact in the nineteenth century. The strangulation of independent farmers and the peasantry to obtain the excessive concentration of ownership by the gentry and aristocracy produced, in historian Robert Allen's words, a landed society in which "the landlord's mansion was lavish, the [tenant] farmer's house modest, the laborer's cottage a hovel." In the nineteenth century, Theodore Parker said about rural England that it "is the paradise of the rich, the purgatory of the wise, and the hell of the poor."[37] Laurence Stone wrote about seventeenth-century England that the landed elite at best accepted "the grinding poverty of the lower classes as part of the natural order of things." As one poet wrote,

> The rich man in his castle, /the poor man at his gate,/
> God made them high or lowly,/ and ordered their estate.

John Wesley had said that the imbalances had to be accepted: "Suppose the rich grind the face of the poor, what remedy against such oppression can be found in a Christian country?" Misery for the bulk of humankind was the natural and divine order of things.[38]

All the elements that composed the aristocracy pointed to one absolute truth: in human affairs, inequality ruled. This was the creed of the ruling group of England, of the aristocracy and the great gentry. It would be pronounced vehemently starting in 1790 and reiterated by English writers and aristocrats for almost all of the nineteenth century. It was their national anthem.[39]

The Americans doubted that aristocrats had a vaunted mental superiority and rejected the usefulness of either monarchs or aristocrats as rulers and social superiors, although they could see their importance in being symbols of authority to the lower class. American "conservatives" at the time of the Revolution could be defined by their rigid and unyielding belief in the sanctity of property rights, their desire to limit the suffrage, and their fear of the mob. Generally, they loved order and obedience to the law; they tended to have strict views on the importance of religion. While they had a foul taste of aristocracy because of their colonial experience with Great Britain, they nonetheless believed in a "natural aristocracy," one that should lead the country. The major debate concerning the natural aristocracy was whether that natural elite was revealed by education and refinement or business success. For many American conservatives, the word *equality* held no attractions and was almost anathema. Nonetheless, the example of Great Britain's aristocracy coexisting with its wretched masses was an outcome to be avoided, not emulated.[40]

Both in the United States and Great Britain, the French Revolution became an argument in favor of inequality. The touchstone phrases of the French Revolution—liberty, equality, and fraternity—became synonymous with guillotining the best people, mass murder, war, standardization of bureaucratic rules, elimination of heritage, repudiation of Christianity, intolerance for any but the approved ideological standards, and a state that devolved into tyranny. It certainly was true that the French revolutionaries veered into disastrous courses and that all sorts of ills came from too strong an ideological fervor, but the root causes of the upheaval still remained immoral and unconscionable: an elite that lived on crushing others, a mass of peasant farmers ruined by taxes, and an inequality in government favoritism that was morally unsupportable. In the United States, the reaction to the French Revolution became apocalyptic in the minds of the Federalist Party and those of strong religious sentiments, so much so that such people were ready to cast off important elements of their republic to save property owners from the mobocratic madness of democracy and equality.[41]

The French Revolution, the wars that followed, and the reign of Napoleon nearly axed the European aristocracy. Titled individuals continued, but the laws that Napoleon imposed ended the inequalities by which aristocrats earned money, the land systems were freed from feudal dues, and equality before the law was established.[42] That is, except in England. The aristocratic tree there was spared the French axe, and the British aristocracy retained its political and economic eminence. It also retained all the centuries-long justification for aristocracy based on the inequality of mankind. The spokesperson for aristocracy's cause became Edmund Burke.

Edmund Burke remains a difficult person to describe adequately in terms of ideology. He was no absolute rearguard philosopher of a medieval society, he accepted some change, he had a notion of fairness in dealings with others, and as a youthful member of the House of Commons he attacked British policies on a number of fronts, not the least being the handling of North American affairs. Ultimately, however, he becomes the father of modern conservatism—and modern in the American sense means the twentieth century. Actually, in the last part of the eighteenth century and the whole of the nineteenth century Burke was not that important to Americans. There was a reason for that delay in the American appreciation of Burke: the United States needed large structures in the economy to evoke an ideology to protect those structures, and that time came in the early and mid-twentieth century.[43] Burke ultimately defended the great landowners of England, the large-scale economic operators of his time. That defense of bigness and all it implied had an imperfect fit with twentieth-century corporate America, but the fit was close enough.

Burke reacted to the French Revolution in his great work, *Reflections on the Revolution in France* (1790), a response to the laudatory pamphlets on the Revolution by Tom Paine and Richard Price. The main gist of Burke's understanding of politics and society was that societies were not created by reason or rational models but by traditions built up over centuries. People lived their lives and understood their situations by reference to these traditions; the traditions brought forth order, harmony, and a constraint on bestial passions. Change should come to all societies, but the change had to be governed by the cadence of the past. This was his major denunciation of the French Revolution: by forcing upon the society a philosopher's ideal of the good, people lost their traditions of restraint and respect. They then were open to all types of murderous activity and injustice.[44]

Burke's relationship to the British aristocracy was an odd one, but the specific elements of his program buttressed their position.[45] First, the principle of human life was inequality, not equality. Second, the ideas of Locke and Hobbes—not to mention Rousseau—about a state of nature and natural rights, were rubbish. Property rights were established by human convention, by the necessities of society over time; but Burke did agree with Locke and Hobbes about the importance of the protection of the rights of property and of inheritance, and the injustice of any attempted redistribution of property. The political corollary to his ideas about ownership was that only the propertied should govern. Human life also needed to be guided by churches for at least the practical reason of keeping the lower classes in place but also because spirituality was an enduring aspect of the species. While Burke advocated toleration, he favored an established church. He did believe rulers required a life of leisure, and he advocated the political value of liberty—liberty being defined as the space people could operate in once the necessary restraints were established. Some people had to be deprived of liberty because of their nature and lack of self-restraint. He held that the upper class by demonstrating decorum and taste would lead the masses into civilized behavior. Burke probably did not like the individualism and economic liberalism arising in Europe and North America, but many of his views supported the new economic order. As for the wrenching poverty in which most western Europeans found themselves, Burke felt it was regrettable and unfortunate, but there was nothing to be done about it—no changes to be made—because it was part of the natural order. These ideas could only end in one conclusion: equality and democracy were not only impossible and unattainable, they were dangerous apparitions of unsound minds—they were folly. C. B. Macpherson may have been slightly parsimonious in his description of Burke's ideas but he was generally on the mark: Burke had a "darker undemocratic side" composed of beliefs in hierarchy, prescription, inherited rights, the rule of customs and prejudices, and a society embodying a divinely ordained order.[46]

Burke rather repackaged the age-old justification of inequality and its political offspring, aristocracy. This was not the path that the nineteenth-century American republic was going to take. And because the ethnic compositions of the United States and Great Britain were so similar, the fact that one branch of the ethnicity stood for equality and the other branch for inequality meant a raging debate was bound to ensue. And it did.

3

THE DUEL BEGINS

THE BRITISH TRAVELER TO AMERICA IN THE NINETEENTH CENTURY

The Europeans who came to see the American republican experiment in the nineteenth century, mostly British citizens, have been studied for decades, and their views have informed innumerable histories. Because a number crisscrossed New York, local and state histories of the Empire State have used their observations.[1] Foreign visitors commented extensively on slavery, and students of abolitionism have long investigated the transatlantic connection.[2] And the whole topic is dominated by Alexis de Tocqueville, whose masterpiece, *Democracy in America,* continually inspires rumination and commentary.[3]

In the nineteenth century there were probably over 150 books published about the United States by foreign travelers. They had various purposes. Some came to deflate the idea of democracy and reassure home readers that aristocracy remained the ideal condition for society and government; others were radicals or near-radicals who wanted to reveal the possibilities of society other than rule by an elite. Some evidently knew there was a reading public in England and elsewhere in Europe interested in the transatlantic nation, and writing about a visit to North America was a way to make money. Decades ago historians listed these people and provided a glimpse into their political and social background, the most important of them being Allan Nevins, Jane Mesick, and Max Berger.[4] Nevins provided a framework that remains useful. English commentary about the American republic was hostile after the War of 1812 until about 1840. Although he did not say so, Great Britain was so absorbed with battling the ideas of the French Revolution, and then Napoleon, that its government and people had little inclination or incentive to cast a positive judgment upon American political evolution. Because the Americans effectively sided with the French by declaring war on Britain in 1812, the British were hardly in a mood to give the young nation any benefit of a doubt concerning its social or political ideals. Postwar adjustment to peace after 1815 created a crisis in English rural society, as returning soldiers overwhelmed the population, employment was scarce, and crop prices dropped precipitously. Tenant farmers could hardly make ends meet, and the farmworkers were close to starvation, producing the riots of "Captain Swing" and the Luddites. In response to those conditions, the expanse of land in North America looked promising, and certain founders of settlements, such as George Flower and Morris Birkbeck, published glowing portraits of life in the backwoods of America. To counter the favorable depiction, and stop the feared outflow of England's agriculturists, numerous other writers—like Henry Fearon and William Faux—derided life in the American republic.[5]

Britain was the last stalwart bastion of the principles of aristocracy because Napoleon had rooted out most of Europe's feudal system and thereby injured the aristocracy's economic position. Within England, popular movements by 1832 led to a demand for suffrage extension, in effect seeking more democracy in the land of aristocracy. That put the Britishers who opposed suffrage extension, the Tories, in a foul mood and they took out some of their frustrations on the democratic republic. This included the well-known writers Basil Hall, Captain Marryat, and Thomas Hamilton, but the most notorious was Frances Trollope, whose depiction of the crude customs and bad manners of the Americans left a distaste among US citizens for British travelers that lasted decades. After 1840, criticism of the United States became more temperate, and as the republic grew in territorial size, population, and economic strength, the British travelers found more to appreciate and even celebrate, although they were always confounded by the presence of southern slavery. After the triumph of the North in the Civil War, British opinion of the United States became more favorable, and writers emphasized the similarities between the two nations.[6]

Several authors have amply described the content of these British travel accounts. They cover American eating habits, table manners, modes of transport, treatment of servants and the lower class, the existence of classes, educational facilities, charitable institutions, and technological development. Much of the attention has been on politics and the British perception of how democracy functioned. Interpretations have varied on the degree of difference between Great Britain and the United States, because so much in their institutional makeup was identical. More often than not, the fact of industrial development and the rise of great wealth has overshadowed any other aspect of the relationship, yielding the interpretation that the two nations were basically similar.[7]

Neither the egalitarian creed of the Declaration of Independence nor the fight between its principles and those of aristocracy have been stressed in these works. This will be the vantage point of the following pages, seeing the British travelers as a way of understanding the contest between the principles of equality and inequality. This struggle was foretold when Jefferson penned that famous line, "We hold these truths to be self-evident: That all men are created equal." The American republic would be founded on the principle of equality, however undefined that principle was. England, especially after the struggle with revolutionary France and its motto of "Liberty, Equality, Fraternity," stood foursquare for aristocracy and inequality as the only means of ordering society and giving it stability and harmony. The British and American principles were opposites. And the British travelers wasted no time in letting the rest of the world know it.

REACTING TO THE DECLARATION OF INDEPENDENCE

Some historians believe that the idea that "all men are created equal" was a phrase in the Declaration that most Americans shrugged off until Abraham Lincoln made it gospel in the Gettysburg Address.[8] Such was not the case with British visitors. They referenced the Declaration often and commented on its salience: equality was to be the foundation of the American republic, so its founding document declared, and the Declaration should be judged on whether or not the nation lived up to its professions.

As soon as the international waters calmed down after 1815, Britons started investigating the social and political institutions of the United States. In 1818, John Palmer went through Cincinnati, and on July 4 he recorded that the celebrants there read the Declaration aloud. Two years later, Daniel Blowe, providing a geography of the unknown continent, remarked on the oddity of slavery in the United States: "If there be an object truly ridiculous in nature, it is an American patriot, signing resolutions of independency with the one hand, and with the other brandishing a whip over his affrighted slave." William H. Blane decided that the previous ancient republics had been different from the United States, and to make his point he quoted the preamble to the Declaration. When hearing the debate over Missouri's entrance to the Union, the hostile writer C. H. Wilson snidely remarked, "Does such decision bespeak despotism or republicanism, as the first article of their boasted charter of Independence runs thus:—'*God created all men free.*'" Charles Dickens also commented on the hypocrisy of having a national creed of equality while permitting slaveholding. Adlard Welby started his treatise on the English settlements in North America with the line, "Ever since the period of our war with North America, which ended in the independence of the United States, the attention of Europe has been intensely drawn to that portion of the globe; and many Philanthropists have entertained sanguine hopes that the Declaration of Independence was the commencement of a new era of radical improvement to mankind—that the old Governments of the world, full of abuses, and unable to stand before the light of the new Republic, must soon fall before it."[9] He asserted with some glee that such hopes had been dashed.

Harriet Martineau did not disparage the Declaration, but rather said that the American "experiment" showed that mankind was capable of self-government and that governance based on the principle "that all men are created equal" was possible. By the 1840s others issued favorable pronouncements on the idea of equality. Sarah M. Maury claimed that she published the Declaration of Independence, the US Constitution, and Washington's Farewell Address because they had not been printed before in England. Archibald Prentice, an Anti-Corn-Law Leaguer, recounted a reading of the Declaration in Saratoga, New York: "One sentence in the Declaration is worth repeating, not only annually, but daily:—"we hold these truths to be self-evident, that *all men are created equal.*" Another writer quoted a Briton who told a New Yorker about British philanthropists and the desire for an open society; if done rightly, then all would receive "the truth of that mighty principle on which her Constitution is founded, 'All men are created *equal,* and are endowed by the Creator with certain *inalienable rights—life, liberty,* and the *pursuit of happiness.*'" The English Methodist Frederick Jobson journeyed to the United States in the mid-1850s, and while noting all the defects of New York City, he remarked about human interactions that "In this, as in other things, an Englishman finds he is in a republican land, where all men are declared to be equal."[10] One vacationer, Charles R. Weld, related that he saw the Declaration of Independence, housed in a glass case in Washington, DC, in the early 1850s, and called it "one of the most important [documents] in the world."[11]

Other writers were far more hostile. One said that the idea that "*all men* are created *equal*" was a "sham." Another witnessed a July 4 celebration in New York City and was annoyed at its anti-British sentiments, while another stated that "of all the follies practised in that country, those of the fourth of July are supreme," as the "bombast and rhodomontade . . . would outface an Irish mob orator." As late as 1861, one sojourner riding a railroad was impressed how the people were "fully impregnated" with Jefferson and the Declaration's statement "that all men are created equal."[12] David W. Mitchell in 1862 pointed to what was wrong in the political edifice of the United States: "The task of the good citizens of that country is a difficult one: . . . to purify and organize its suffrage, and to erase from its Declaration of Independence that great French fallacy, . . . the text of Yankee abolitionism—the alleged truth, the palpable untruth, 'that all men are created equal.'"[13]

But of course the opening wedge for anyone seeking to establish the hypocrisy of the American egalitarian creed and to discredit everything about the United States was the existence of slavery. Jefferson, the Declaration, and slavery were all linked together to show how meaningless the idea of American equality was. George Featherstonhaugh spent two pages denouncing Jefferson and shortly thereafter spoke of being revolted by a coffle of slaves being herded toward the Mississippi River; the Africans were "driven by white men, with liberty and equality in their mouths." The agricultural observer Patrick Shirreff was a little kinder, calling slavery "an anomaly" in the land of freedom, while James Stuart found the anomaly more incongruous: "The existence of slavery in its most hideous form, in a country of absolute freedom in most respects, is one of those extraordinary anomalies for which it is impossible to account." William Ouseley held that slavery throughout the country should have been ended "one instant after the declaration of independence." Charles Dickens also noted the inconsistency between slavery and the creed that all men were created equal.[14] But the most vituperative depiction of the hypocrisy of the Americans came from a Mrs. Felton in 1838: the United States should erect a statue of "a man, wearing the cap of liberty, and holding a slave whip in his right hand, while his left displays the 'Declaration of Independence'"; his "right foot . . . resting [upon] the naked back of a prostrate negro.—With this motto: 'All men are born free and equal.'"[15]

THE BRITISH ECONOMIC ANALYSIS OF AMERICAN EQUALITY

Few British sojourners to the United States came without preconceptions of what the nation and its fate must be. Those tired of exclusive government and a pampered nobility liked the republic; those who admired aristocracy and order did not. There were a great number who rejected the United States on the basis of politics.[16] And more than a few discarded the notion that the republic was the land of economic equality. "But the truth of it is," wrote James Stirling in a blistering attack on slavery in 1857, "that there is no equality in America, except as to the elective franchise; and this is perhaps the worst equality they could have." More incisive—and in accord with modern historical analysis—was Thomas Hamilton in 1834: "It is the fashion to call the United States the land of liberty and equality. If the term equality be understood simply as implying, that there exists no privileged order in America, the assertion, though not strictly true, may pass. In any wider acceptation it is mere nonsense." He added that he never heard an American woman utter the phrase that all men were created equal.[17]

The British detractors of American equality and democracy did not convince many people that their observations were unbiased. Michael Chevalier, a Frenchman visiting the republic in the late 1830s, commented acidly on the British disdain for American democracy: "It does not belong to the most complete aristocracy in Europe, the English aristocracy, to sit in judgment on a democracy." Most admitted that Tocqueville had it right: except for slavery and the treatment of Native Americans, the United States had a considerable element of equality in its economic life.[18] That observation came from a standard realization: the United States had neither the wretched poverty nor the magnificent wealthy of Europe, but it did have classes. Thomas Cooper in the 1790s made a statement that British visitors to the republic would reaffirm for decades: "There are no men of great rank, nor many of great riches. Nor have the rich there the power of oppressing the less rich, for poverty, such as in Great Britain, is almost unknown. Nor are their streets crouded [*sic*] with beggars. . . . You see no where in America the disgusting and melancholy contrast, so common in Europe, of vice, and filth, . . . and wretchedness in the immediate neighbourhood of the most wanton extravagance, and the most useless and luxurious parade." One testimony to northern egalitarianism came from a surprising source: the son of the proslavery extremist Edmund Ruffin. In 1829, Ruffin's son traveled to Connecticut and liked the society there: "You do not see here such very rich men or such poor ones, but all seem to have enough to support them[selves]. Here the carpenter if he is honest is as much respected as the merchants."[19]

Of all the scribbling about North America done by British writers, the one constant in terms of social class was the lack of a pauper element. Pauperism was extensive in Great Britain and Europe, and even before the American Revolution, Americans traveling abroad were appalled at its extent. The absence of pauperism was "particularly striking to the English," wrote Sarah Maury in 1848, and while she saw poor people they were, unlike paupers, not "hopeless." This observation was so commonplace that A. M. Maxwell could pen (1841) that "Also, I will again re-echo the assertion that I have never seen a beggar nor a drunken man." (Others would contest this note about a lack of drunkenness.)[20] But almost no one said there was no poverty. When Charles Lyell visited Baltimore, he noted, "we were reminded for the first time of the poorer inhabitants of a large European city." Everyone noticed poverty in American cities, and the Five Points slum of New York City became famous. As early as 1819, one observer said that poverty was a condition of all cities in all places at all times—something a person expected: "There are doubtless poor in New-York, as there must be in all cities."[21]

Where the British found equality was in the countryside of the northern states. In a stark and breathtaking contrast to England, the North was a land of small farmers who worked the land themselves. Tenancy was not unknown but it was a minor aspect of northern agriculture. Most people owned the land in lots of 80 to 120 acres. These areas were, according to Michael Chevalier, the "truly democratic republics," and the residents were "an essentially farming population" formed "on equality and the subdivision of property." Harriet Martineau said that the scenes of "universal presence of competence" exhilarated her. Going through Massachusetts, C. D. Arfwedson, in comparing the American rural landscape to the English, wrote, "it is peculiarly gratifying to witness, instead of gorgeous palaces by the side of poor huts, a row of neat country homes, inhabited by independent farmers." As his carriage was moving through the countryside, an accompanying Swedish servant girl asked, "where [do] the peasantry live in this country?" W. E. Baxter, Member of Parliament, in 1855 penned an intriguing remark about New Hampshire: "Nowhere in the world will the stranger find a more thriving, comfortable, and independent, a better educated, or a more moral and religious peasant proprietary, than inhabit this New England district." Patrick Shirreff in 1835 observed that in America "the soil is chiefly cultivated by its owner."[22]

The owner-occupier farmer, more often called the yeoman farmer, was something of a paradox in the aristocratic sense of inequality. In the nineteenth century, the people who actually farmed the land did severe manual labor: digging, hauling, lifting, hoeing, and shoveling. This was sweated labor. Therefore, the American farmer could not be considered dignified and elevated. Yet the farmer was a property owner and over the course of the nineteenth century was lionized in American rhetoric. He was not so exhorted in British rhetoric, where the highest accolades went to the gentry, who lived without labor. Alexis de Tocqueville picked this up. In a land without aristocracy, "the idea of work as a necessary, natural, and respectable condition of humanity is therefore evident wherever one looks." But what aristocracies hold "in contempt is not precisely work but work for profit. Work is glorious when inspired by ambition or pure virtue." The yeoman farmers of the North became the vast middling element in American society that Europeans marveled at; they also were the basis in the 1840s and 1850s for the free-labor exhortations of the Free Soilers and Republicans.[23]

Another class that the British travelers noted were mechanics, artisans, and day workers in cities and factories. The general impression was that such wage earners fared considerably better than their English and European counterparts. Tocqueville ascribed the result to high wages. This condition he thought inherent in any democratic form of society because the only way for these people, who were voters, to approve the social system they functioned in was to obtain a comfortable subsistence, and the only means of doing so was to have high wages. The economic conditions in Europe, including England, depressed wages, turning wage earners into enemies of the social system—but the lack of voting rights saved society from a proletarian demand to redistribute wealth. Tocqueville's depiction of high wages has not earned him any honors among modern historians, but his observations about high wages were not uncommon, although many saw the beginning of a class battle over wealth. Among the travelers there was some debate as to whether high wages were due to republican institutions or the existence of an abundance of land.[24]

Finally, the sojourners took on the question of the existence of an American aristocracy. On this subject they divided. First, everyone agreed that the United States had classes and that, just as there were some poor, there were the wealthy who presided over society. As John Palmer stated in 1818, "Wealth carries great influence in the States, as well as elsewhere, and generally entitles a man respectable." By the 1850s, Isabella Bird found that New York City and Boston housed class differences as strong as those in Great Britain. She said New York had its exclusive "charmed circles" and its upper class was equal to the best upper class in England.[25] But a wealthy class did not constitute an aristocracy in the opinion of some. For Tocqueville, there simply was no monopoly of the soil, which was vital for an aristocracy to take root. For Alexander Mackay in 1849, the Americans had grown up amidst too much democratic sentiment for the populace to bear an aristocracy, and wealth was too impermanent within families to create a stable leisure class.[26]

"There is," wrote Godfrey Vigne, a supporter of the aristocratic model, "as I have before remarked, an aristocracy in every city in the Union." Numbers of British visitors were willing to relax some standards to assert the existence in the United States of an aristocracy—an upper class that ruled government and society. Alexander Mackay admitted that millionaires had aristocratic leanings and "would have no objection to the establishment of a different order of things," though the democratic spirit remained staunch. Mrs. Matilda Houstoun found that many Americans did not consider aristocracy a degraded form of government, and that they actually respected titles. Besides the rich in Boston, New York, Philadelphia, and Baltimore, English visitors noted one other group that seemed to have the aristocratic bearing: southern planters were "nearly in the situation of the English country gentlemen, whose character in many respects they resemble."[27]

Foreign visitors thus made many speculations and assertions about the direction of the American republic. For those who came after 1830, they encountered the first explosion of Jacksonian democracy, the battles against large institutions such as the Second Bank of the United States, ear-splitting orations about the rights of the people versus the incursions of the rich, and working-class movements in the cities calling for a better distribution of wealth. Some assigned such activities, regardless of their wisdom, to the commotions of an open political system with no endangerment to permanent institutions, while others saw the harbingers of the apocalypse. The foreign travelers, though, were certainly correct that there were Americans who moaned over the extension of the suffrage to the unpropertied, who lived only to despise the Democratic Party, and whose main worry was that somehow the masses threatened property rights. Americans who went overseas, as few as there were, often found aristocratic society hypnotic in its attractions. These people held "equality" in contempt. How many of these traveling Americans wanted an actual aristocracy with hereditary power, or the social misery that went along with the societies over which aristocrats ruled, is dubious. At the least they wanted the old republican faith: property qualifications to vote and hold office, and leadership coming from the most qualified. Nonetheless, even the conservative parties, such as the Whigs, had to shy away from exhibiting too much of an inegalitarian attitude.[28]

THE MEANING OF NINETEENTH-CENTURY ARISTOCRACY

In their description of American democracy and equality, the foreign visitors upheld the standard of aristocracy for comparison. That comparison held some frightening concepts about property, coercion, and government. The Americans were well aware of the economic props necessary for aristocracy to operate—the British travelers told them about these props all the time.

Many British visitors were offended by the antiaristocratic oratory of politicians and others, and such wayfarers came to the conclusion that Americans had no realistic idea of life in Great Britain. Edward Sullivan in 1852 thought that small-town American newspapers were run by dolts who "delight to describe [England] as a bloodstained country, where an iron-heeled aristocracy is continually trampling up to their knees in the life-blood of a crushed peasantry." Alexander Mackay believed the Americans overemphasized the power of the aristocrats and did not understand that their real importance lay in establishing decorum and style: "The time was in England when Marquis, Earl, and Viscount indicated something more than mere arbitrary social rank." Another stated that Americans thought the aristocracy browbeat the masses into subservience, that the people were "mere serfs . . . compelled to bow down to the dust when we meet a lordling and to submit to Queen Victoria's will without a murmur." D. R. Thomason added, "Americans generally, really know as little what British monarchy is, as the people of England know of American republicanism."[29]

In defense of aristocracy, the British travelers referred to the importance of limiting the power of the monarch, thereby erecting a barrier to despotism and establishing the principle of liberty.[30] However, they tended more to elaborate the social traits an aristocracy bestowed upon its people. The visitors made it clear: aristocrats absolutely did not work. Thomas Grattan, a British consul who had worked in Boston and who loved to point out the juvenile qualities of American society, remarked that "In England there are thousands who never think of making money, who, born to a certain inheritance, are satisfied to . . . earn so much a year. . . . In America there are no such persons." Basil Hall summarized this point by saying no one in the United States knew how to spend money "like a gentleman." Francis and Theresa Pulszky wrote that European aristocrats believed that "any other employment than war or government is . . . unbecoming."[31]

Money from inheritance enabled the aristocracy (and gentry) to live without labor, and that meant such people had leisure. All Americans worked and had no leisure. The result was the lack of refinement, of the arts, and of gracious manners. Tocqueville was insistent on this aspect of aristocracy: it was the aristocracy that kept intellectual life alive. Thomas Hamilton, a severe 1830s critic of American life, offered the age-old adage—used by Plato and Aristotle—that "the man whose whole energies are required for the supply of his bodily wants" cannot be raised to an equality of knowledge with those who have greater wealth and time to bestow on its acquisition. Thus, as Basil Hall summarized, America was suitable for "hard-working labourers; but it is quite another affair [for] ladies and gentlemen, accustomed to the comforts of civilized life."[32]

Beyond the arts, literature, and the sciences, aristocrats gave the proper "tone" to society. According to Edmund Burke, whom the semi-Chartist Robert W. Russell quoted, "it is necessary to maintain a pampered class by legislative enactment" for the people to emulate. An editorial in the London *Atlas* stated that the British aristocracy was not a closed circle, and that it gave people incentive to join the ranks of the nobility by excelling in business and the arts. The aristocracy also provided an example of correct moral principles for the masses to follow.[33]

Some visitors had less complimentary statements about the British aristocracy. One of the daintiest came from Mrs. Houstoun, who said of the Americans that, with "all their faults," they at least "are not *bores*." She made that statement because she found that England had become a land of bores, presumably due to the aristocracy, because original thought was being squashed out. Others tackled the idea that the aristocrats served as models for the common people. Because of the aristocrats' insistence on recognition of rank and deference, they robbed the people of "all sense of personal dignity, and [they] become cringing and servile." That attribute was agreed upon by William Ouseley, who said aristocratic ostentation invoked "an abject worship of rank and wealth that debases the lower orders." As for elevating the arts and stimulating intellectual creation, the critic Harriet Martineau blamed the European aristocracy for creating the blank mental state of the people of Europe, for producing the "brutal ignorance" of the masses.[34]

But ultimately the main attribute of British aristocracy the travelers testified to was the concentration of property in families over time. European aristocracy had suffered economic blows from Napoleon's laws, but not the British aristocracy; as the Pulszkys said, "it is fully understood that the English aristocracy is peculiar to the English, . . . [and its] landed property, does not, and cannot exist anywhere on the continent."[35] The English aristocracy was built on property, and most emphatically on landed property. Writers gave no room for misunderstanding: aristocracy required great wealth; and from that wealth came income, the income taken from those who performed manual labor on their property. The social display of aristocratic wealth and income yielded national splendor and magnificence. Thomas Grattan left no wiggle room about the economic foundation of British aristocracy: "Aristocracies are built on the indestructible rights of property." Thus, the "few must always be rich; the poor are the many." Equality would therefore never produce greatness—splendor and magnificence—because equality halted the creation of the few rich and the many poor.[36] James Johnston in the 1840s summarized the difference between Britain and America: the difference of "the Anglo-Saxon race on the opposite sides of the Atlantic is this: on the one side the masses rule, and property pays; on the other side property rules, and the masses pay. The paradise of the poor man is on the one side of the water, and that of the rich on the other."[37] Aristocrats monopolized the offices of government, the military, and the church; the government collected taxes from commoners, while the progeny of aristocrats relaxed in "leisure." It was this association between aristocracy and monopoly that led Michael Chevalier in the 1830s to notice that in the United States the two words, *aristocracy* and *monopoly,* "carry real opprobrium" and the phrase "NO MONOPOLY" moved the masses.[38] Many of course referenced the misery of the English working class, but for the aristocracy the sufferings of the lower orders were simply a part of the natural order.[39]

Into this discussion of the aristocracy's ownership of property and family wealth ineluctably entered the laws of inheritance, primogeniture, and entail. British wayfarers to the United States equated aristocracy with inheritance, and the laws that, in their estimation, gave aristocracy its preeminent position were entail and primogeniture, although the word *entail* was probably used as a shorthand for strict settlement. Any number of writers ascribed equality in North America to the practice of partible inheritance and the abolition of entail and primogeniture. As a sort of summary of how critics viewed the operation of inheritance practices in Britain, William Mackenzie in 1833 wrote, "the emigrant farmer in the United States has not inflicted on him the pain of seeing the hardy and laborious farm-servant toiling from generation to generation in hopeless poverty and privation, his ill-rewarded industry serving only to increase the countless luxuries of the drones of [the] community," a condition wrought by the unnatural laws of "entail, half-blood, and primogeniture." Tocqueville thought an American aristocracy might have arisen if landed property "had been capable of transmission from father to son," but partible inheritance ruined that possibility. The result has been, penned another, that "property becomes more equalized."[40]

A few writers even ascribed the condition of Virginia to the failure of its leaders to maintain the laws of entail and primogeniture. By the 1820s, the ruined plantations of the Virginia Tidewater were well known, and almost every sojourner talked about the region's dilapidated condition. Somewhere the institution of slavery interjected itself on the topic, but often they referred to the lack of inheritance to stimulate families to take care of the land. Charles Murray in 1854 said Virginia had manor houses that were "good [and] substantial" when built when primogeniture was the practice, but they fell apart because partible inheritance enticed the children to flee the state. (The idea was that if the estate fell to one person, that person would have remained and kept the property in good shape; but as the property was to be divided among the children and transformed into small parcels, it made more sense to migrate away to find fresher land and in larger amounts.) The agricultural reporter Robert Russell used the absence of primogeniture and entail to explain why slavery did not develop in the North: without large farms, which one got with primogeniture and entail, slavery could not exist. A side effect, however, was to make farmers "expansive [and] more aggressive" in their movement westward. But nearly all visitors agreed that entail and primogeniture were not laws suited for a republic.[41]

Some writers offered an extended analysis of the laws of inheritance. Godfrey Vigne, who was a critic of equality and an ardent supporter of the aristocratic ideal, said American ideas about British inheritance laws were exaggerated and incorrect. The reality was that an estate could not be rendered inalienable for more than one generation. The estate could be kept together after the owner's death for twenty-one years, but then the father and son had to make a new agreement to keep the estate together for the next generation. If the father died without the agreement, the land could be sold. He then noted, as would others, that American law did not stop transmission of an estate to a single son, and most English inheritance practices could be employed in the United States if citizens so desired; it simply was not the custom of the people.[42]

The differences between the systems of equality and inequality in regard to inheritance were frankly stated, and they led the Americans to celebrate labor as a path to advancement, whereas in aristocratic circles the path to status was family, not labor. Inheritance stood as a repudiation of Locke's labor theory of property (though he bizarrely managed to approve inherited estates). A contributor to the *New York Farmer* put the difference on the role of birth this way: "In a republican and in every free government, where merit, and not favor, is the ladder by which we mount to preferment, 'virtue alone is true nobility.'" Harriet Martineau caught the idea by labeling the United States as a land of labor, which virtually all sojourners agreed to. Hereditary preferment was an escape from labor and, the Americans would insist, from real contribution to society. In a purported conversation, Francis J. Grund recorded one American replying to a would-be aristocrat, "I do not see of what use hereditary privileges could be to us, except to make the proud prouder, and the rich more influential, than they already are. . . . We are essentially an industrious people . . . and nothing promotes industry so much as to let all men start fair and even[.]"[43] The United States was following the path of individualism, and individuals were to establish their merit by their own activity, not by relying upon their family's past merits; the British example stressed the family to the point where the individual did not matter. As Francis and Theresa Pulszky wrote, England had "reverence for social rank and station without regard to the individual who holds them."[44]

The British defended inequality. Lord Brougham, supposedly a spokesman for the English middle class, dismissed ideas of equality: "The notion of equality, or anything approaching to equality, among the different members of any community, is altogether wild and fantastic." He recounted the advantages of inheritance, of having gifted and informed legislators, and the importance of social deference. Isaac Holmes in 1823 had a more picturesque reason why some called for equality and how limited the call was: "We may speak in favour of equality; but the fact is, that nearly all who advocate this doctrine wish to reduce every one to the equality of themselves; but they by no means wish to raise those who are below or beneath them to their own level." George Lewis was disgusted by "the political dogma prevailing in America . . . that 'all men are equal.'" Scholars have been so focused on Tocqueville's description of American equality, and on criticizing him for it, that they have scarcely noticed that everyone else was saying nearly the same thing.[45]

Not everyone was certain about the future of equality in the United States, but a few were: aristocracy would eventually come to rule the North American continent. Tocqueville famously declared it might arise out of manufacturing. Others were more general. Aristocracy grew out of wealth. They knew its future location, although perhaps not the exact economic mechanism. Godfrey Vigne said it would grow up in the cities, and eventually families would move to keep their wealth centralized. As well, the country over time would fill up with population, and a desperate mass of impoverished citizens would emerge. Cries for a redistribution of property would fill the land, and the wealth-holders would have to exclude them from politics. That is when all the ingredients would be set for a group of families to rule the nation, for the foundation of an American aristocracy. He was not alone in foretelling this outcome.[46]

AMERICANS AND THE SHRIEK OF EQUALITY

In numerous ways many white male Americans celebrated their equality and democracy, particularly in respect to the situation in Europe and especially England. One example is a story that circulated among some of the agricultural journals in the middle of the century. An American was at a party at Cambridgeshire, England, and was doing well with the ladies. So some young lords enticed him into a game: he was asked a question and he was to give a "Solomon's answer," the best answer being awarded with the crown of the wisest. The question was, "you have no court standard for the manners of a gentleman," so what is the best school to learn politeness? The answer allegedly given was: Niagara Falls, which "teaches humility to the proudest, and human nothingness to the vainest" and makes man acknowledge "that God only is Lord, we feel that Men are our equals. A true Christian is always polite."[47]

When the British visitors picked up the American scream of equality and tied it to Jefferson's wording in the Declaration, they may have done so by a prior reading of the essential documents, but probably they learned about American faith in equality by simply observing American political habits. Among Jacksonian Democrats, reference to equality and to Jefferson was commonplace. They frequently charged that in America, the two political parties had distinctly different foundations: "The one, the advocates of the rights of the People; the other, the advocates of the privileges of Property."[48]

Democrats often used Jefferson's phrasing in his first inaugural address when he claimed the United States stood for a strict equality of citizens, but there were some interesting uses by Democrats of Jefferson's second paragraph in the Declaration, many of them stemming from the early debate over slavery's potential expansion to the west. Martin Van Buren in his letter to a Convention of New York City, wrote the line that the founders were not "insensible to the apparent inconsistency between the perpetuation of slavery in the United States, and the principles of the Revolution, as delineated in the Declaration of Independence." Thus Van Buren put the fountain of principles guiding the United States in the Declaration, not the Constitution, even though the Democrats never wavered from a strict division of sovereignty between the states and the federal government. At the Pennsylvania state Democratic convention of 1849, the administration Democrat Jehu Glancy Jones gave a July 4 oration in which he said the Democrats were attempting to put into practice the ideas of Jefferson, that "all men be FREE and Equal." At a Bangor, Maine, meeting of Independent Democrats in 1846, the attendees resolved in favor of a strict adherence to the doctrine of "equal and exact justice to all men," called for all citizens to be true to Jefferson's hopes for the nation, and insisted that "human slavery is grossly inconsistent with the principle embodied in the Declaration of Independence, and the spirit of our Republican institutions." In 1848, the Democratic paper (later to be Republican) the *Weekly Wisconsin* insisted that the core of the Democratic Party was the ideal of "Equality," and that "equality of rights and privileges . . . is *the* essence of democracy itself."[49]

There are two fascinating examples of Democrats using the idea of equality and the Declaration. The first was by the "hunker" Buchanan Democrat Daniel S. Dickinson of New York, who at a special mass meeting gave a speech calling for unionist sentiment after John Brown's raid on Harpers Ferry. In this speech, he interestingly mixed equality with acceptance of slavery in the southern states:

> The great chart of Democracy may be read in the Declaration of Independence; its guiding star is the Constitution; its strong and radical analysis exposes and casts off error, and its grand and majestic conservatism forms a barrier against which the waves of falsehood and fanaticism may dash in vain for ages. Its "irrepressible conflict" is a conflict for freedom, equality, and the rights of man, against falsehood, favoritism, and privilege; for complete equality of political rights between persons, and for that equality of right between sovereign States which the spirit of the compact suggested and the provisions of the Constitution guaranteed.[50]

While Dickinson interestingly mixed the Declaration with the Constitution, he nonetheless saw, as did most Democrats, that Jefferson's Declaration had been the ideological star illuminating the path for the nation's future.

The second expression came from Edwin M. Stanton, and was less a comment on Jefferson than it was a denunciation of any sympathy for aristocratic institutions. Very unusual for Anglo-Saxon writers on the French Revolution, Stanton found a justification for the French upheaval in the crimes the aristocracy committed against the people, and he inveighed against the way historians had written about the past. After reading Arnold's history of Rome, he commented,

> Most of our histories have been written by aristocrats, and are mere lying apologies for aristocracy, its wicked frauds and bloody crimes in all governments and in every age. Agrarian & Jacobin, have become words of uttermost reproach because unjust privilege was struck at;—but the world sickens with horror at a few spurts of aristocrat[ic] blood.[51]

Republicans in the antebellum decade continually referred to the Declaration and its focus on equality as the road the United States had to travel. Abraham Lincoln even gave a preview to his Gettysburg Address in his eulogy on Henry Clay in 1852. Discussing Clay's view of the slavery issue, Lincoln was shocked to find that in St. Louis the idea of inequality, so prevalent in South Carolina and in the speeches of John C. Calhoun, had taken root. A clergyman had declared that "free" and "equal" were not terms used in the Bible. Lincoln proclaimed that the nation had to be appalled about those who ridicule "the white man's charter of freedom—the declaration that 'all men are created free and equal.'" Likewise, the debate over Indiana representative John Petitt's assertion that the Declaration was a "lie" provoked strong rebukes. In 1857 the *Toledo Blade* complained about the Dred Scott decision. The nation had to restrict slavery's expansion to guarantee the hopes of the revolutionary generation: "We do not see how the idea of equality and liberty, set forth in the Declaration of Independence, and repeated in the Preamble to the Constitution, could be carried out by stronger guarantees." In Republican state and county conventions, equality and the Declaration were often part of the resolutions.[52]

While the pro-aristocracy British travelers extolled the luxurious lifestyle of the aristocrats and their contribution to the arts and social refinement—acknowledged by a number of Americans—others in the United States focused on the immense property holdings of the aristocracy, which permitted this ostentatious show of wealth; the property ownership of the aristocracy was well known to the American reading public, as was the disastrous European distribution of wealth and income. The *Milwaukee Weekly Wisconsin* printed a typical editorial about England: "Enormous Wealth and Grinding Poverty," and the source of the evil was "*class legislation.*" American journals published figures on the monstrous revenues of the aristocracy and detailed some of the holdings. The Duke of Sutherland had 96,000 acres, the Duke of Richmond had 340,000 acres; the Earl of Lonsdale controlled 8 seats in Parliament, the Duke of Norfolk's park in Sussex was 15 miles in circuit. The Earl of Holkam, Mr. Coke of Norfolk, had an estate of 3,500 acres enclosed by a brick wall extending for 10 miles; it had an artificial lake plus a private woods. At the same time, the misery of the farmworker was well documented. According to one writer, R. Wheateley, the farmworkers politically were "white trash[;] they are but tools of the lords of the lash, who monopolize the soil."[53]

Americans had their own problems to quarrel about, and so they did not spend vast amounts of energy criticizing the British aristocracy, but nonetheless the Americans lived in a world where aristocrats held real power and, in the case of Great Britain, enormous power. Any number of Americans, but especially Yankees, derided the idea and practice of aristocracy. Wrote Theodore Parker to Samuel J. May, "We admit no hereditary claim to political or ecclesiastical honor: we will not tolerate the idea that a man can be born a *noble,* or a king, and in virtue of the accident of birth be entitled to rank and power irrespective of his merits and the consent of the people." Another abolitionist wrote, "In all ages men have worshipped power, and have assumed that the conferring of a title made men noble. . . . The nobility could look disdainfully down upon the multitude, regarding them of inferior make, with the taint of low condition in their blood." James Boardman, writing in the 1830s, affirmed the existence of the horror Americans held for kings and all those of "artificial and unnatural elevation of rank," and held that the Americans' distaste for aristocracy "cannot be conceived by those who have not resided in this country." As for primogeniture and entail, the visitor James D. Lang said all those laws accomplished was to enable a few families to live "in heartless extravagance and dissipation"; he believed the wider distribution of wealth arising from abolishing primogeniture and entail produced the beneficial effect of elevating the "general morality of the country."[54]

James Fennimore Cooper also defended American equality, though meekly comparing it to others, by writing a book on the subject in 1838. He admitted many of the problems foreigners found in the republic, often connected to politics and majority rule, but his defense of American life was made by contrasting it to conditions under the European aristocracy. He agreed that the Declaration could not be taken literally, and he forthrightly stated that property ownership was not and never could be made equal among the inhabitants. Yet the essence of the nation was the rejection of the European idea of caste and hierarchy: the purpose of the United States "is to set up new and juster notions of natural rights than those which existed previously, by asserting, in substance, that God has not instituted political inequalities, as was pretended by the advocates of the Jus Divinun, and that men possessed a full and natural authority to form such social institutions as best suited their necessities." The history of aristocracy, he claimed, showed that the aristocracy did not rule for the general welfare but instead governed to slake their own thirst for pecuniary betterment; they "perverted" the use of government "to their sole advantage."[55]

British critics of American equality were certain that the nation was careening into an "agrarian" moment, when the masses would demand a division of the rich person's property—the inherent flaw in a society that used the political system of democracy. The Americans continuously denounced agrarian laws and emphasized that no law could ever impose equality of material possessions among the citizenry because of—at the least—inequality of talents and intelligence. But their insistence on civil equality and no monopoly did have an economic component. The cure for Europe's social woes of wealth division was the ending of aristocratic class privilege; when all were equal politically, then all obtained the just fruits of their labor and the distribution of income settled into a pattern acceptable to all income groups. People were then lifted above subsistence and put into competence. The path for Europe to take to escape revolution and to install social justice was laid out by James K. Paulding, writing from Hyde Park, New York to, of all people, John C. Calhoun.

> The extreme Radical Democrat of Europe is a very different Person from the sober Democrat of the United States. . . . One is destructive, the other conservative. . . . The great grievances of Europe are a surplus population, a heavy load of Debt leading to burdensome Taxation, and an unequal division of Property, which while it enables a few to revel in luxury, entails on the masses a load of hopeless poverty, approaching almost to absolute destitution. Hence, in my opinion, all effectual relief in that quarter must be based on a new division of Property, either brought about by the slow and salutary operation of wholesome regulations depriving the few of monopoly, and giving the many an opportunity for honest acquisition untrammeled by artificial restraints, or by a violent revolution. [No simple change to a republican form of government can relieve the masses.][56]

Inequality thus produced economic damage to the generality of mankind. But it did more. The creation of orders, of a hereditary nobility, sapped the essence of humanity out of the citizenry. It was the social behavior of Americans without aristocracy, as much as if not more than economic equality, that caught the eyes of European sojourners, and taught how the practice of inequality could rot a society from the inside.

4

EQUALITY, MANNERS, AND CIVILITY

Scholarly attention has often been directed toward foreign visitors' views of American politics and the functioning of democracy, a topic to be discussed later, but in the midst of a welter of other subjects, these wayfarers wrote incessantly about the differences between American social interaction and British social interaction; the subject rises like a mountain range above the other points they discussed. The difference in the way people treated each other in daily life caught the attention of almost every traveler. And they themselves ascribed these contrasting patterns to the systems of equality and inequality. In one sense, they were using a framework of class: the system of aristocracy demanded one behavioral pattern, while the system of nonaristocracy required another pattern.

Much of the attention given to these sojourners involves the sarcastic reports they made about the primitive quality of early American life. Pigs were the essential garbage system of early cities, the weather was unbearable, the eating habits of the Americans were monstrous, and the citizens of the republic were always bustling about to make money. They seemingly cared little for the arts and literature. The sojourners' accounts make for fun reading, and some of the incidents are remarkable in their own right. But attention to the picturesque and humorous misses the point: throughout the nineteenth century, these commentators were assessing the differences, the advantages and disadvantages, of a system of equality of citizens versus a system of inequality characterized by graded ranks.[1] Everything they witnessed was put into that analytical perspective. And while their barbs or compliments were aimed at the United States, because they constantly were running a contrast (usually with Great Britain), their writings also tell as much about how social interactions were conducted in England and Europe.

Part of the difficulty in deriving generalizations from visitors' observations of the early United States was that individuals carried a set of prejudices and saw sometimes exactly what they wanted to see. They often reported something out of the normal. What was very normal they often did not report. Moreover, they all carried with them political biases that sorted out their experiences as ones worthy or unworthy of publishing. Nonetheless, given all the problems of according these travelers any objectivity, their accounts all have a central tendency—no matter if they were Tory, high or low aristocrat, Chartist, Whig, middle-class, or Anti-Corn-Law Leaguer—in that they all saw the system of equality producing a more civil society in which people of all income levels treated each other with more courtesy, directness, and respect than did the system of inequality in England. Excepting Euro-American treatment of Africans, Native Americans, and the Irish, the United States had more civil harmony than Great Britain and the other nations of Europe.[2]

GENERAL MANNERS, DEFERENCE, AND INDEPENDENCE

Foreigners who wrote about American manners and habits and published in the 1830s frequently had little good to say about the republic. Those authors—Frederick Marryat, Frances Trollope, Basil Hall, and Thomas Hamilton—castigated the nation for its primitive, uncouth, and unrefined state. Even in the 1830s, however, their conclusions were contested. Then, in the 1840s, with the usual number of disputes among authors, the overall assessment changed to one more favorably disposed to the activity of the Americans. The problems were duly noted, the infancy of the country stressed, but a recognition, sometimes begrudgingly given, emerged that the differences between the United States and Great Britain seemed natural and understandable. Moreover, due to the geographical growth of the country and its economic strength, many started to take pride in what they considered an "Anglo-Saxon" achievement. However, the point is that authors in the 1840s and 1850s explicitly rejected the findings of Trollope, Marryat, Hall, and Hamilton.[3]

On the question of interaction among Americans of all income classes, the voyagers were in agreement: deference as they knew it in England did not exist in the United States. Alexis de Tocqueville universalized the idea of democracy (and hence equality) on citizenship exchanges versus what occurred in an aristocracy. In aristocracies, people become more attached to one another (or may become so) because servants and clients rely on masters and patrons, so the bond between them might be stronger—but the price to be paid was deference in manners. In democracies, like the United States, the bonding did not appear—but then neither did the deference. Instead equality made "their habitual relations easier." Aristocracy, and the particular problems the English had mating it with some social mobility, made people of great stature more reserved, but in the United States the manners of the people were "natural, frank, and open."[4]

Whether or not Tocqueville's generalization holds, hordes of foreign visitors attested to deference's absence in the republic of equality. In some of the earliest writings after the Revolution, the end of deference was noted. Richard Parkinson, an agriculturalist who worked for George Washington, said farming on a large scale with free workers was impossible in the nation because "the idea of liberty and equality there destroys all the rights of the master, and every man does as he likes." In his work on the geography of the North American continent, Daniel Blowe remarked that "A native free-born American knows no superior on earth." Writers made the individualism of the Americans explicit. Ebenezer Davies, an abolitionist and nonconformist minister from the West Indies, visited North America in the mid-1840s, and celebrated its religious equality and the way people treated each other: "This is the genius of America. You meet it everywhere. Man is Man (except his skin be black), and he expects to be treated as such. Respect to superiors is not among the maxims of our Transatlantic brethren." Later he went to Lane Seminary in Cincinnati and "nothing struck me more than the feeling of equality that seemed to subsist between students and professors," the students having a bearing that seemed to say "'I am as good a man as you are.'" Joseph J. Gurney recorded his shock at the presumptions of equality by everyone he met: "This independence—this practical oblivion of all distinctions of class—although strange to my former habits, was far less offensive to me than I expected."[5]

David W. Mitchell was a ten-year visitor to the United States who left in 1861 and then published a memoir of his experiences. He did not particularly like slavery, but he had absorbed enough racism to accept the institution for Africans; he did not like democratic government as practiced in the

United States, and he found the Declaration of Independence full of French buffoonery. But the practice of equality did make a difference in social intercourse. "The American," he wrote, "has more tact and considerateness in manner, and in expressing himself, than Englishmen in general." Some dispute this, but "the free and straight forward, unceremonious manner in which superiors and inferiors—a mistress and her housemaid, an overlooker and his labourers, for instance—address each other, are proofs enough of what is said here." Then he added a sentence that tells as much, if not more, about social practices in England as in America: while Americans knew their class situation and status, "none expect from others such a show of deference as is very common in England." Another added that the US people had a "very imperfect assertion of man's dignity and equality," but "it is better than the stolid subservience of the [English] lower classes."[6]

In his summation of what transpired in the republic, John Bristed argued that the United States was a land of the middle, for its people "exhibit a *medium* of manners, between the rude vulgarity of the lower orders, and the artificial refinement of the higher classes in Europe." Natural equality was impossible and talents would create economic gradations among the citizenry, but equality in politics, religion, and law cut off the extremes of European life and thus made for a more courteous people. Thus visitors found that the "equal air of demeanor and manner . . . surprises Europeans who [have] been accustomed to the insolence of wealth and power on one hand, and to the servility of pauperism and dependence on the other." The European upper classes put on a show of ostentation and power to awe the other classes. When one American interviewed Richard Cobden, the English politician told him to read the English country newspapers "most of which were half-filled up in describing the dresses worn by the nobility upon public occasions. . . . I replied that I had not been able to look into one of them without being sickened to nausea."[7]

Somewhat interestingly, and contrary to the views of most economic historians in the twentieth century, foreign visitors constantly found that the reason for the lack of a desperate working class was high American wages. Because wages were high, working-class Americans, though almost always at the bottom of the American income scale, still had some comfortable conditions, and in many instances could save and eventually obtain independence. But attention should be focused less on what such visitors said about American workers than about the condition of British and other

European workers. James Phillippo wrote in 1857 that while Americans had prospects because they expected to capture the rewards of industry, "A kind of caste exists in England, in consequence of which a labourer or artisan can scarcely ever hope to rise to the rank of a master." About the same time, John Oldmixon said that the workers in the world all moaned about how "the monotony of willing hard work eats into and puts out any little *mind* they may possess."[8] It was the extremes of inequality that produced haughtiness and submissiveness; in a middling society—that is, one of practical equality—with the extremes excised, then the haughtiness and submissiveness disappeared and one obtained cordial social interactions between different income groups.

FARM SERVANTS AND DOMESTIC SERVANTS

Servants earned a special consideration in most accounts of the developing United States. The subject of servants has two particular categories. First, aristocracies used all types of servants for their domestic activities: cooking, cleaning, taking care of animals, driving carriages, and serving at public functions. In the English tradition, however, farmworkers were considered servants in the early modern period; they lived in the home of yeoman farmers and were sheltered and fed. Farming in Great Britain then evolved by the early eighteenth century into a system in which land was owned by the aristocracy and gentry, who contracted with tenants to cultivate the fields, and the tenant farmers then hired wage workers to do the actual manual labor of farming, the tenant farmers becoming more the managers of labor rather than cultivators themselves. At the time of the founding of the republic, the English term for a farm laborer was a servant. These two separate conditions then informed the somewhat different ways that the topic of servants in America was handled.[9]

In the matter of farm servants, North America—Canada included—was an unwelcome shock to British tenant farmers and gentry. They could not obtain farm servants at all. Elias Fordham in the second decade of the nineteenth century reported that people on the farm "all work, and there are not half so many labourers for hire, as there are farmers. The former live with their employers, and are their equals." The gentry and aristocratic landowners in North America would fail because, William Faux found out in a conversation, "if they come to America, [they by themselves] must drive [their] own carts, wagons, and ploughs into the field and to market, and work here as hard as labourers work there." This observation continued into the mid-nineteenth century. Robert W. Russell, the near-Chartist, saw the plentitude of American family farms and remarked that the "American farmer is generally a labourer on his own farm, with no other assistance than those of his own family and a little occasional help from his neighbours. . . . His life is one of ease and independence, not luxury." John Oldmixon in 1855 told Englishmen that only those accustomed to manual labor—not aristocrats, not gentry, and not tenant farmers—should migrate to America: "farming is impossible except to the labourer; hiring servants to work soon ruins those of being gentlemen farmers! There is—and can be—no exception to this rule."[10]

The reality of equality became fundamental to the relations between farm laborers and farm owners in North America. Due to high wages and the availability of land, or so at least foreign visitors theorized, the farm laborer soon saved enough to purchase his own farm. The social mobility that existed in America was mobility from propertylessness to farm ownership—it was a rural phenomenon, much less an urban one. Britons immediately remarked on the widespread ownership of American farms. Excepting southern plantations, the travelers found the United States a land of small farmers, of owner-occupiers.[11] The celebration of the climb to farm property ownership led to everyone singing hosannas about the act of labor, and this gave a decided coloration to travel literature. William Hancock in 1860 wrote that the "motto of the republic might very well be, 'respect for labor.'" This sentiment was echoed continuously from the time of the Revolution to the Civil War. These exaltations were the American response to the European praise of aristocratic leisure—the two ideas, labor and leisure, were direct opposites, and by inference so were the societies.[12]

Because of the reality that labor was scarce for farm work and that farmworkers did climb a ladder to farm ownership, equality became a common social condition in the rural North. Foreign observers noted with surprise the equality between farm owner and farmworker in one particular: farmers and workers ate together at the same table, a custom that had died out in England by 1800, if not earlier. The expression used in the Ohio Western Reserve was, "if a man is good enough to work for me, he is good enough to eat with me." At the Birkbeck settlement in Illinois, it was noted that the owners (Flower and Birkbeck) ate with their servants. Adam Hodgson admitted that he had trouble eating with "labourers in their shirt-sleeves; but that family, and those labourers, appeared as cordial, obliging, and accommodating, as those with whom I have ventured to compare them." As Richard Flower admitted, servants were the epitome of the "equality problem."[13]

DOMESTIC SERVANTS AND EQUALITY

Alexis de Tocqueville gave an elaborate explanation of servants and their relation to masters in France, the United States, and England. First, the French invented the word *lackey* to describe domestic servants as the lowest of the low—it was a mean word: "the poor man is trained from infancy with the idea of being subject to command." Ultimately the domestic servant came to identify himself with his master and his master's interests, as the two were frozen in place eternally. As to the differences among nationalities, the English held the reputation for having the "bond of domestic service [drawn] tightest," while the French were generally known for being polite and lax in relations between aristocrats and servants; the Americans held a middle ground in relations between masters and servants.[14]

Commentary about domestic servants in America from the beginning stressed how servitude was disrespected by Euro-Americans. Elkanah Watson, writing after the Revolution, laid out the essential position of the republic. He said the English servant was "generally an ignorant and servile being, who has no aspiration beyond his present dependent condition." That could not serve the goal of the Revolution in which all men were equal. In the United States, servants had a consciousness that independence was not beyond their grasp; thus the usefulness of a servant was impaired but the damage "cannot be deprecated, whilst it adds to his [the servant's] self-respect as a man." For a counterpoint, consider the words of Basil Hall, a severe critic of American customs, on the benefits of servitude. First, the wealthy were heavily inconvenienced by the lack of servants in America. Second, servants in England formed a class happy to be servants, and they shared in the honor bestowed upon their masters; servants found enjoyment in being servants. But in North America, there was "a deep-rooted, but surely very idle, prejudice against this description of labour" which he believed was perhaps caused by the institution of slavery.[15]

Everyone reported on the servant problem in North America, and nearly all ascribed it to the doctrine of equality that permeated everything. William

Priest in 1802 recorded that the republic was not the place to find good servants; for whites, the words *master, mistress,* and *servant* had been expunged from the dialect. And if one grumbled about the service being given, the maid "will leave you at a moment's warning." He concluded, "This is one of the natural consequences of liberty and equality."[16] Isaac Holmes, who had many compliments to give to the young nation, nonetheless realized that English people were not ready for the "degree of freedom which the servants and lower orders assume in America." In 1827, a German noble heard the sea of complaints about American servants and their notions of "equality": "Of this insolence of servants I saw daily examples." The abolitionist J. J. Gurney thought that American women lost their beauty early in life because wives did not have servant women to do chores. Europeans found that servants in America by the 1840s tended to be African slaves or Irish.[17] William Kingdom warned British readers not to abuse waiters or other employees at hotels or inns or they would have insults fired right back at them.[18]

Perhaps the most famous diatribe against American manners and servant attitudes came from the sarcastic pen of Frances Trollope, who lived several years in Cincinnati with her husband. As a person accustomed to a high standard of living, she expected to have a servant maid do the household chores. She noted that it was almost "treason" to call a "free citizen a *servant.*" She could not command servant girls twenty-four hours of the day, the girls talked freely, and they acted independently. Frances Trollope was not used to such behavior from the lower class. Later in her work on the deplorable manners of the Americans, she said American women looked so old by age thirty because they did not have servant help. As revealing, she gave the aristocratic explanation of why servitude was a good practice for poor people: girls who were not servants "have not that natural and reasonable dependence on the richest classes." In short, society was better off having the poor learn to obey the commands of superiors than to be independent in their actions.[19]

An interesting spinoff of the Revolution, probably not at all contemplated by the leaders of the Continental Congress, was a revision of the language. The word *servant* was replaced by the word *help,* an alteration noted by numerous visitors. Daniel Blowe in 1820 explained the reason for the linguistic change: "There is no such relation as *master and servant* in any part of the Union: indeed the name is not permitted:—'*help*' is the designation of one who receives wages for service." The idea of help indicated an equality; one was not being commanded to do something, but was willing to help someone in the accomplishment of a task. Thus the ideal of equality even invaded the choice of words in the early republic.[20]

Evidently many British wayfarers to the United States took servants with them. It would be interesting if those servants had written about their impressions of the United States and the independence of the servants in the republic, but evidently none did so.[21] But for English servants, experiencing the relationship between employer and employee in North America must have been quite a shock if the reactions of their masters were any faithful indicator.

COURTESY, MERIT, AND THE LOWER CLASS

Some foreign visitors to the antebellum United States insisted that the Americans were a crude, intrusive people who did not know polite manners and appropriate ways of conducting themselves in the company of others. Godfrey Vigne, for example, said in 1833 that the people in the republic had "no standard for manners" because their democratic politics taught them to be boisterous and offensive. Adlard Welby in 1821 offered the opinion that the independence given to every member of society produced incivility. And, of course, the standard work for the exhibition of American crudeness was Frances Trollope's *Domestic Manners of the Americans.*[22]

Exactly what behaviors Europeans were referring to is sometimes problematic. Many of the scribblers expected a repetition of European elite courtesies and, finding they were absent, were outraged at some American behaviors. Most others, however, had a different perspective. Tocqueville had theorized that American manners had to adjust itself to the condition of equality, and thus one could not have interchanges that Euorpean nobility demanded, ones that called for deference between master and servant, between aristocrat and commoner. Thus Americans had manners that were "natural, frank, and open," unlike the reserve of the British people. William Blane noted in the 1820s that in the backwoods, people treated others as equals and had a tangible civility, an observation confirmed by several others. Indeed, Elias Fordham said that among the backwoodsmen, he witnessed "more genuine kindness and politeness . . . than among any set of people, I have yet seen in America." In his 1818 book, John Palmer gave an idea of the "republican simplicity" that ruled social interactions: Major-General Isaac Worrell, "a soldier of the Revolution, living in the vicinity, called at the tavern for a glass, he was accosted by his former title by several farmers and tradesmen, assembled under the tavern portico, and conversed with them quite at his ease"; Palmer then noted that Worrell "drives his own wagon."[23]

Those visitors who came in the late antebellum period agreed with earlier sojourners that Americans were courteous and civil. They openly wondered how Americans ever got the reputation for being rude and intrusive. An earl, George Carlisle, who ventured into the United States in 1841, wrote later that he never "encountered a single specimen either of servility or incivility of manner." Isabella Bird, who detected large class differences in the cities, nonetheless found she liked the simplicity of manners that she found.[24]

The broad civility that these adventurers discovered came, they believed, from the national ideal of equality. William Dalton, publishing his work in 1821, said all Americans had "a certain independence" that arose from the common knowledge that each "citizen is upon terms of equality with his fellows." That equality resulted in an expectation: if one was treated honorably, then the treatment was reciprocated. As Patrick Shirreff summarized, "every individual seems possessed of self-respect, and in the intercourse of life, arrogance is seldom assumed, and never submitted to." Equality meant that all classes treated each other civilly; and Shirreff thought it would be a good thing if Americans could teach manners to the "fagged and fagging youthful aristocracy of Britain."[25]

Visitors also noted that Americans did allow some to have more honor and respect than others. But it was not due to family or rank; it was due to performance. A. D. Griffiths wrote that in the United States the question is not "*What is he?* but, *what can he do?*" As Archibald Prentice wrote, although different classes mingled much more freely in America than in Europe, there was not any deference given to "wealth or rank"; rather, people who were "entitled to respect will receive it." How inequality interfered with talent and merit earning its fair place and reward came out several times. Hans Mattson, a Swedish migrant and future governor of Minnesota, remembered that he was born to a farmer, went into the army (to escape farming), but found his future stunted because "inherited names and titles" were the only routes to advancement. In his guide to Irish immigrants in 1851, John

O'Hanlon stressed that free institutions mean "that all public offices and employments, and all stations of trust and eminence are thrown open to the competition of all persons capable of obtaining them by ability, influence, and popularity . . . ," and that the abolition of "titles and rank . . . in no small degree [has worked] to produce that social equality" so renowned in the United States. Merit counted, not the actions of ancestors centuries ago.[26]

Special attention was given to the American working class, which in those days was an amalgam of some factory workers, especially the Lowell textile mill women, artisans, mechanics, and farm laborers—those who performed manual labor and who were near the bottom of the income pyramid. Foreign visitors found the working class in the United States polite and civil. They were surprised at this. The observation cut across political lines. Frederick Marryat, a confirmed Tory and denouncer of democracy, nonetheless wrote that American workers were much more civil than their British counterparts; insolence, he felt, came from recent immigrants. He decided that in a land of equality, all people had to learn to control themselves. About the same time that Marryat was visiting, Simon Ferrall also said that in manners there was no awkwardness "in the behavior of the humblest person" and that this "good conduct . . . [is] remarkable." In 1854 or so, the agricultural observer Robert Russell was in New England and had a conversation with a person whom he assumed was a "gentleman" but was just "a working mechanic." The abolitionist George Rankin, writing in 1853, was impressed: "I was very much pleased at the extreme civility with which the commonest people answer any question you may ask, though the equality which is supposed to exist out here amuses me vastly."[27]

"The indignation of the working people, in this land of equality, is really to be dreaded," remarked Isaac Holmes in his 1823 publication, and others saw work relations being leveled by the ideal of equality. Shop foremen and shop owners did not tower over employees as they did in England because Americans rejected any idea of subservience: "No workman conceives himself obliged to his employer." The Anti-Corn-Law Leaguer Archibald Prentice summarized, "Amongst the small storekeepers and working men the familiarity with persons, in the parlance of the old country, would no doubt be offensive to fastidious gentlemen who have been accustomed to a deference which is paid rather to their wealth or rank than to the man." In England, shop owners were haughty; in the United States, the workers were independent, or at least so these sojourners wrote.[28]

These visitors made broad generalizations based on a minimum of observation, and so a considerable portion of their commentary has to be taken with skepticism. What is interesting is that they all testified to the existence of a broad income spectrum among the Americans, thereby scuttling the idea that the nation had true economic equality; they saw the economic classes clearly enough but merely lopped off the extremes of high wealth and desperate poverty or pauperism that they were familiar with in Britain and the rest of Europe. Nonetheless, it is worth reflecting on their continual exploration of working-class manners and their nearly universal surprise at how polite American workers were. The explanation is of course that they were accustomed to rude behavior and sullenness—and perhaps implied violence—from workers back home, and against that background the American laborer's outward behavior seemed remarkable. And they all ascribed such politeness to the doctrine of equality and, by extrapolation, explained the rudeness of their own country's workers by the doctrine of inequality.

The economic basis for the politeness, regardless of all other considerations, was a high wage. High wages enabled workers to dream of climbing into some comfort and independence, and gave them incentive to be industrious and considerate of others. They thought they could become members of the community in good standing. This was actually captured by a writer on American farming in 1775. The ability of workers to save money from laboring and then to buy a farm was observable in New England, and the writer noted the economic effects, and by extension the social effects, of this incentive: "This great ease of gaining a farm, renders the lower class of people very industrious." Thus the advantage of life in a society formed around the ideal of equality: high wages led people to be able to achieve their modest dreams, and that ability to fulfill modest aspirations produced a civil society among all income groups. The price of a society founded on the principles of inequality was that it produced an uncivil society where social violence was a common result. Among a few travelers, the notion of why the masses had to be kept near starvation was made explicit: "Man is by nature an idle animal; and generally speaking, shrinks from labour, unless impelled by necessity." Positive incentive, it seemed, only operated for the economic elite. The few visitors who went abroad noted that European lands required a large police force to keep social violence from erupting.[29]

From these remarks on civility and the American working class, an observation can be suggested about class hostility. For decades it has been asserted that the foundation of class tension is economic, that out of this phenomenon of the few wealthy holding most of the property and the mass of workers holding little property, must come class antagonism. The ranking done in aristocracies had little to do with class animosities. Yet one can read in the comments of these travelers that the British insistence on social distance between classes, the demand of the elites to witness servility and deference from the lower classes, gave an added dimension to the role of class. The British made economic class so much worse by their system of aristocracy and deference that they nearly goaded the lower class into looking upon the upper classes with loathing and hatred. The travelers revealed how the doctrine of inequality fomented class hatred. In the United States, the same class structure arose, minus the extremes, but the class animosities of Britain did not. The presence of the ideal of equality before the law and in general appreciation of equality in humanity ruled out the legal orders and privileges of aristocracy, thereby enabling income differences to be taken with more grace, or at least with less anger. Incivility came not from economic differences alone; forced social ordering on its own engendered a class antagonism.

SPECIAL INSTANCES OF AMERICAN EQUALITY IN MANNERS

In England, gentility had a precise meaning: a person who had enough wealth to live off interest or rental income without having to resort to manual labor and thus was able to live a life of leisure. The preferred form of wealth was land, which was then rented out to tenant farmers, with the owner living off the rents. The titles of gentleman and lady, as well as the denomination of esquire, had class meanings in terms of the ability to live in leisure. Charles Lyell found the Americans had turned gentility into something else. "It appears that the spirit of social equality has left no other signification to the terms 'gentleman' and 'lady' but that of 'male and female individual.'" The *Maine Farmer* decided that "gentility, that is, politeness of manners, and easy, graceful behavior, may be cultivated in the country as well as in the city." Under equality, appellations changed.[30]

While foreign visitors noted the American boasting, the unruly children, the repulsive tobacco-spitting habits, and other behavior unbecoming to a civilized people, they also found certain social customs missing or altered because of the ideal of equality. The basic observation was that classes were not separated in America as they were in Great Britain. For example, the American practices in transportation received considerable comment. Henry Tudor was horrified in the 1830s when a coach driver decided to sit down with the ladies dressed in elegant clothes and talked to them with a "familiarity" which by his clothes he had no reason to presume. All the lowest classes, said another, presume a "complete equality" with travelers of "rank," which disgusted true gentlemen and ladies. One of the more telling incidents of the classes mixing with each other came from Robert Russell in the mid-1850s. He found "the equality which prevails among travelers who observe the ordinary courtesies is striking," and to underline the fact that all were treated equally, he was talking to some farmers when "I learned that the gentleman on my left was General Scott, the hero of the Mexican War, who was receiving no more attention than I."[31]

Hugo Reid believed that the lack of differentiated carriages and railroad cars for the different classes "showed that the 'sovereign people' were a real power in the United States and had to be attended to." And the shock of American railroad travel in antebellum times was a fright. No class differences were made; "Each car holds from thirty to fifty. There is a stove blazing hot. Except where a branch-road joins the main one, there is seldom more than one track of rails. They rush across the turnpike-road, where there is no gate, no policeman, no signal. There is painted up, 'When the bell rings, look out for the locomotive.'" Ebenezer Davies summed up: in England the "railway is haughty, exclusive, and aristocratic," while in the United States it was democratic and egalitarian.[32]

Once the railroad deposited the antebellum person in the city, horses were used to go from place to place. Within American cities, the foreign visitor saw no coachmen and liveried footmen. Matilda Houstoun said a Frenchman tried such a display in New York and was met with "ridicule and disapprobation." Another noted that in the cities, at least in the 1830s, the names on doorplates did not have "Mr." on them—not even the one for the governor of the state of New York. And during transportation and in stays at hotels in the cities, foreign travelers had to get accustomed to eating in one large dining room in which all the classes intermingled—"in true republican simplicity." Robert Baird when in Ohio disliked the common dining room: "I prefer the English system, where men are not so gregarious in their eating."[33]

A practice many travelers seized upon for elaboration was a lower-class individual removing his hat in the presence of a superior, or "doffing" the hat. Americans in the mid-nineteenth century did not take off their hats inside a house or to anyone. It was the practice of Americans wearing their hats all the time that quickly set Godfrey Vigne off on a rampage in the first few pages of his book about boorish American manners. Alfred Pairpoint saw it as well: employees would not take off their hats before their employers. "And why is this?—simply because the operatives consider themselves under no obligation to their employer, who would at once dismiss them, if they did not suit his purpose; and they deem it beneath an American to acknowledge or cringe to a superior." One assumes that the refusal of Americans to take off their headgear had little to do with notions of courtesy but was a recognition that the practice belonged to aristocratic systems trying to impose inferiority on people. The Tory Henry Tudor related his experience of being saluted by men in the fields when he was in Canada. He compared this to American behavior: "A laboring man in the States would think himself degraded, his manhood lowered, and his equality compromised, were he to notice . . . any person whatever, let his station in life be as superior to his own as it might."[34]

One of the more interesting stories of Americans and their hats came from James F. W. Johnston, who told a story about a farmer near Boston who had a farm laborer who was a good worker but who would not take his hat off when he entered the house. When the farm owner asked why he kept his hat on, the worker said, "'Well, if I have a right to, why shouldn't I?' This was a poser from one man to another where all have equal rights." When the owner asked how much money he would accept to take off his hat, the laborer said one dollar per month. The English author summarized, "So works democracy."[35]

When individuals met for the first time in England, and one presumes in Europe, the behavioral procedure was to go through introductions and not permit physical contact. By the middle of the nineteenth century at least, the American handshake was taken virtually to be a salutation of citizen equality and to be engaged in by all Americans. Thus, grasping the hand of another during an introduction was an instant behavior for American males, but it offended the British sense of personal space reserved only for those of the same class or better: "A frigid and a refined Englishman, or a polished and formal Frenchman, looks upon this as the perfection of vulgarity," wrote one. Of this custom, Matilda Houstoun decided that Americans in their introductions were "invariably and uniformly polite. In England, we are far too apt to utter in our inmost hearts, the admirable speech of the Spanish satirist—'Let me know who you are, that I may measure my civilities according to your deserts.' *Here,* a man is equally civil to the president of the country, and to the Irish *gentleman* who acts as his servant [or *help*]."[36]

Finally, the social ethos of aristocracy demanded pomp and reserve in state functions, where aristocrats, state officials, and high-ranking politicians wore uniforms, displayed medals, and were surrounded by servants. People did not physically touch one another, distance was observed unless the superior invited the inferior into contact, and the common people were excluded. This was not the custom of American democracy and equality. William H. Blane wrote that in the early 1820s he met President James Monroe on the street, later visited him at his house, and exchanged handshakes. He liked the "unaffected urbanity and politeness of the President, so entirely different from . . . a person of anything like the same importance in Europe." This certainly was "republican simplicity." The same phenomenon was observed by another Englishman, James Robertson, when he met the president, presumably Franklin Pierce, watched people arrive in carriages, and noted that some came in "homely and uncourtly garb." "And yet all were received with the same frankness and civility. The simplicity of this intercourse between the people and their first magistrate, is somewhat startling to a European, who has been accustomed to the distinctions which prevail in the old world, between class and class, to the deference which the rich exact from the poor, and the wide gulf which separates royalty from the mass of people."[37]

The most ludicrous example of the problem of appropriate clothing for political functions between republicans and aristocrats occurred in the mid-1850s when James Buchanan was ambassador to Great Britain. Queen Victoria would hold balls and the attendees were expected to dress themselves in full aristocratic regalia: medals, ribbons, swords, pistols, and uniforms. But James Buchanan had to deal with the decree of Secretary of State William Marcy that American ambassadors were only to wear typical American business attire at foreign state functions—no special uniform. It caused a minor scandal at the court of St. James. The problem was that the ambassador of the United States could be mistaken for a servant. Finally, Marcy allowed Buchanan to wear a black coat, cravat, black pantaloons, dress boots—and a sword strapped to his side: "This is to gratify those who yielded so much, and to distinguish one from the upper court servants."[38]

From these social practices and the constant comparison European visitors made between social life in the United States and in their home countries, one generalization seems to hold merit: a system of equality belittled nobody and perhaps instilled in people a sense of worth and standing that came out in the form of civility to others. The system of inequality, regardless of what its advocates hoped it evoked in the masses of people, belittled people, suppressed the people's energy, and ultimately gave birth to a resentment that found expression in incivility.

5

EDUCATION AND RELIGION

Any number of subjects leapt into the minds of European travelers as they wandered throughout the early United States, but two received special consideration. The clash between the ideals of equality and inequality found continuous expression in the differences between Europe and the United States on the matters of public education and state-supported religion. Europeans did not have the same perspective on these subjects as did contemporary Americans or current historians. It is possible to conceive of both education and religion as ways for the elites to control the masses, to indoctrinate them, to give them false ideas about their welfare, and to bring them to support the basic institutions of society and in some cases their appropriate political role.[1] All this may be true to some degree. But foreign visitors saw in American education and religion a vast liberation of the bottom layers of society, an explicit understanding that equality demanded public education and the separation of church and state. In many ways, the European sojourners found that public education in particular gave American income groups a common ground for interacting with one another.

AMERICAN PUBLIC EDUCATION

There were some detractors of American public education, but if near unanimity existed among foreign visitors on one subject, it was the excellence of the availability of common education in the United States. After finding fault with nearly everything else, it was usual to declare that the educational institutions in the United States were "the best institutions of

America." Foreigners ascribed the intelligence of the average person in the country to the educational experience. The Earl of Carlisle called the public school system in the nation "excellent." Charles Dickens took time to note the schoolhouses he saw in every village of New England, and another visitor observed that more children went to school in the United States than in any other country on earth. The minister Ebenezer Davies listed what he liked most about the United States, and, after religious equality and the voluntary principle, he singled out American general education.[2]

When Matilda Houstoun visited the United States in the late 1840s, she jotted down the condition of some New England towns. While she deplored the lack of old trees, she noted the plentitude of small farms, the ability to obtain a competence—and, for the children of farmers, the "advantage of an excellent and practical education, *free of cost.* This is a privilege to which both rich and poor are equally entitled, and its advantages are duly appreciated." A theme remarked upon time and again was the availability of education to all youth, paid by taxes. As early as 1802, William Priest remarked that the free schools in Boston "are maintained by a tax on every class of citizens, therefore education may be claimed by *all* as a *right.*" William Chambers in the 1850s wrote that in England, education was considered a charity; "here, it is a right." Observers did not shy away from giving monetary details. James Silk Buckingham said that around Boston, male teachers made $25 per month with board, female teachers $12 plus board. Chambers also noted that in Rhode Island more public money went to education than to all of civil government. Emphasis was placed on the New England schools, but travelers noted the extent of educational facilities throughout the northern states.[3]

Not all the sojourners were enthralled with American education. Thomas Hamilton witnessed the capacity for reading among Americans, but that was insufficient for true appreciation of the arts and sciences; Americans lacked the leisure to develop such sensibilities. Hugh Tremenheere went to the republic to look at the system of education there, as the voluntary efforts in England were not bearing fruit. He decided that overall, American education was thin gruel and, most importantly, lacked religious instruction. The failure of Americans to indoctrinate students with biblical passages was noted by others, and one said it was not possible to separate education and religion.[4] And, of course, many faulted the southern states for their lack of public education, customarily laying the fault on the institution of slavery.[5]

The United States was an anomaly compared to western Europe in that it established such a broad system of public-supported education, and English travelers in particular wanted to explain why. They immediately jumped at the political system of democracy. There were precious few English visitors to North America who praised democracy, and all were convinced that the aristocratic system of government in England was the superior method of providing law, order, justice, and progress. Letting the mob vote seemed the height of foolishness. Therefore, the only way to make democracy work was by educating—or, indoctrinating—the masses to obey the law and their intellectual superiors. In 1818, Obadiah Rich wrote that the United States had more education than any other nation, "where it is well understood that free institutions can be rendered secure only by the diffusion of intelligence among the citizens." James F. W. Johnston in 1851 held that in a democracy, free education was necessary to counter potential demagogues, and even Richard Cobden agreed that the "genius" of American legislation was its emphasis on education and elimination of "ignorance in the people, as [it is] the most deadly enemy of good government." Alexander Mackay in 1850 penned the line that if the American experiment in popular government worked, then it "will in [the] future chiefly owe its success" to education. On the eve of the Civil War, William S. Hancock determined that education in the republic was a good development because it offset "the growing evils of democracy."[6]

Of course, there were those who doubted that even education could overcome the evils democracy inflicted on humankind. James Stirling was a British abolitionist who traveled through the slave states and published a book in 1857 about his experience, but he had no good words to say about democratic government: "The American ballot-box riddles away the gold and retains the dirt." At a public dinner in Ohio, the agriculture reporter Robert Russell listened to the bombast of a local politician—"pompous, inflated, nonsense"—and rushed up to him to talk about the claims made. He found the speaker practical and sensible, but to get the ear of the people, he needed "inflated oratory." The reason there was so much emphasis on education was to counter such hyperbole.[7]

American education in the nineteenth century was limited and utilitarian.[8] Students did not usually receive more than six or eight weeks of schooling per year and went to school at times that did not disrupt farm work. One writer related that farmers apprenticed their youth out to other farmers for four years, and the terms of the apprenticeship demanded that one-fourth of each year be reserved for education.[9] However limited the education was, and however slanted it was toward prevailing social class orthodoxies, it nonetheless, in the estimation of British visitors, had profound effects. If modern researchers have severe doubts about the quality and quantity of American education in the early republic, their perspective is informed by post–World War II expectations. But the perspective of travelers was shaped by the mass of illiteracy in Europe, and by that standard the educational attainments of Americans were astounding.

Two general themes run throughout foreign commentary on American public education. The first was its impact on social class. Alfred Pairpoint obtained a job at Dorchester, and he noted the attendance at the public school: "I have often seen the children of wealthy merchants or traders with those of mechanics and labourers, trudging in friendly company to the same school-house, neither one nor the other dreaming of any disparity in their several conditions." Hugo Reid ascribed to education the "bright, animated intelligent" look of American workers. Archibald Prentice investigated the books of public school students in New York City, and there found students from parents who were smiths, carpenters, masons, bricklayers, and draymen. Another argued that public schools reduced the snootiness of wealthy sons while it elevated the refinement of sons of laborers. The Pulszkys visited working-class homes in Connecticut and were impressed with the reading material they found. Robert Russell agreed with these authors that public education raised the morale and social condition "of those who labour with their hands"; it was, in fact, a leveler of classes.[10] Although experiences in public schools in the nineteenth century undoubtedly varied, there may be kernels of truth in the assertion of abolitionist John F. Clarke: education taught "social equality. . . . There is no aristocracy in a public school but the natural leadership of superior ability."[11]

The second theme that resounded in their writings was that the system of aristocracy intended for the mass of people to be ignorant, and aristocrats purposefully kept education away from the common people. Robert W. Russell, a Chartist, made the charge forcefully: the Church combined with the aristocracy to deny commoners access to public education—they did not want to tax themselves, even though their wealth was so exorbitant, and thereby ruin the cheap labor they got on their landed estates. Harriet Martineau bitterly remarked about the "brutal ignorance" of paupers and serfs, all of whom were oppressed by "an aristocracy which insults humanity." Education in England was reserved for those who could afford it. Patrick Shirreff then interjected some biting comments about how social class there operated. Senior students engaged in "fagging"—turning junior students into "slaves" to serve the seniors. In a discussion about Scottish farmworkers, William Chambers told a Rhode Island audience that due to low wages, the farmworker was "*without hope.*" An American in the audience responded, "Your aristocracy, having insured the ignorance and incapacity of the peasantry, turn round and say they are unfitted to exercise any political privileges—a pretty kind of liberty, that!" And few could compare with James D. Lang in the disgust he displayed when he compared the American worker to the English. The American worker "is an intelligent man, and has got a good common education" and expects "to rise to a higher level in society than the one he occupies." The English worker was "lean, unwashed," and filled with rage. "Hope is annihilated within him from the very first"; English laborers do not attend church, and most were chartists or socialists "cherishing a deep-rooted feeling of hatred towards the higher classes of society, whom they almost uniformly regard as their oppressors."[12]

At least some Americans understood universal education as a necessary attribute of equality, while ignorance was the natural condition of the people in a system that operated on inequality. At one agricultural address in Indiana, a speaker exhorted his audience to embrace practical education and not the schooling of Greece and Rome because that "system of learning . . . is best suited to an aristocracy on one hand, and an ignorant commonality on the other—a learning that does not accord with the spirit of our times, our laws, our common equality and the genius of our institutions." Frederick Law Olmsted visited England in the early 1850s and was outraged that the aristocracy regarded "their laboring class as a permanent, providential institution, not to be improved in any way, educated, [or] to take an equal share with all Englishmen in the government of the commonwealth of England." A feminist, Hetty Lee, made the plea in 1853 that women should not only possess equality in politics (and, be it noted, equal remuneration for services of equal value) but also "equal education."[13] William Grimes, a Whig turned Republican and governor of Iowa in the late 1850s, called for a system of tax-supported public education in a list containing the usual reasons; he also added, the tax would be paid by property-holders: "It [property] has its duties, as well as its rights." Amidst the American calls for public education came an interesting dissent. The radical abolitionist of New York, Gerritt Smith, denounced public education at the Cooper Institute in 1858—saying, let self-interest govern the choice of education, a stand that befitted a total libertarian.[14]

Visitors were impressed with the level of education of the average American citizen during the days of the early republic. They were amazed at the amount of reading done by all income classes. By the 1840s and 1850s, they started to realize that this educated citizenry had portents for the future well beyond any presentist concerns. Somehow it was all connected with the health of the social welfare of the nation. In terms of social harmony, public education was acting as a common ground for the citizenry, where people from different income classes could meet, acknowledge the worth of others, and learn the manners of equality. The second had to do with international prominence, which was intimately connected to economic performance. In their own odd way, these visitors were noting that an educated working class meant productivity and growth, whereas an ignorant working class led to inertia and stagnation. This perception was growing and starting to motivate European governments to address the question of education, but it would not be until the late nineteenth century that anything was done. But the examples were already being noted. Arthur Cunynghame in 1851 remarked as an aside on how ideas and devices diffused so rapidly in the United States. He mentioned specifically a water pump—he called it a China device—that was spreading fast; he attributed that speed to the high mental abilities of average Americans that the common school system had inculcated.[15]

RELIGION, THE STATE, AND VOLUNTARY ASSOCIATION

Some of the travelers to the United States came for purely religious reasons, to see how their denominations were faring in North America, but most made some observation about religious practices in the republic. At issue was a dramatic parting of the ways: Great Britain had an established church supported by taxation, whereas the United States had no established church and its religious experience was governed by voluntary association. The British visitors were interested in seeing how well the practice of voluntarism in religion operated. More than a few believed the state had to impose religion on the people or disorder would result.

Richard Cobden wrote in an essay about the United States that "If a word be said about the well-known religious and moral character of the Americans, these worthy people will stop you with the exclamation of, 'How can there be religion or morality in a country that maintains no established church?'" Many visitors said it was not there. Henry Duhring in 1833 devoted a chapter to the subject, the title being "That the Want of an Established Church has Produced Want of Religion in the United States." Francis Wyse agreed that the Americans were immoral due to lack of an established church, while Edward Sullivan in 1852 wrote, "There being no Established Church in America dissent and unbelief flourish in their rankest growth."[16]

For others, usually belonging to a non-Anglican sect, the escape from an established church was delightful. The abolitionist nonconformist Ebenezer Davies admired the American system of religion: The "free and efficient working of the voluntary principle is the glory of America," and the voluntary principle worked best in religion. Charles Lyell noted how the different denominations were all on an equal basis, while William Kingdom pointed to words of the Constitution of Ohio that stated that all men were born free and independent, and that they had the right to worship in their own way. Mrs. Houstoun decided that the United States had "liberty of conscience in religious matters, if in nothing else." Some were perplexed about the operation of religion without state compulsion, and remarked that final judgment would have to await the passage of time.[17] There were those who openly liked the separation of church and state, but some still had criticisms.[18] In 1818 John Bristed wondered about the general American practice of excluding clergymen as legislators in their state constitutions. The antislavery, antidemocracy James Stirling found it strange that education in the United States was compulsory but not religious instruction.[19] The writers wavered in their opinions about religious instruction in the public schools. The person most pursuing the question of American public education versus British education in Anglican charity schools was Hugh S. Tremenheere, and he decided that Americans were not getting biblical instruction—but he was also convinced the British system of voluntary education was a failure. Robert Russell, however, found, as he expected to, religious views being propagated in American public schools.[20]

For those appreciative of the separation of church and state, one element about the American system of religion stood out: there was no tithe.

Especially in the years after the end of the Napoleonic Wars, English tenant farmers and farm laborers fell upon hard times. They continuously complained about rents, the poor rate, and the tithe. For nearly three decades, the great appeal of the United States to the hard-pressed agriculturists of England was an escape from poor rates and tithes. In England, William Cobbett issued publication after publication denouncing the taxes and tithes that farmers had to pay. Isaac Holmes wrote a book about the United States in 1823, and originally he intended to warn English farmers not to emigrate to the republic; but upon returning he saw the "great distresses of the British Agriculturist" and had decided emigration was a necessity because farmers were being ruined by "Taxes, tithes, and poor-rates." This was a continuous chant throughout the 1820s and 1830s. In 1841, James Silk Buckingham wrote admiringly about the condition of American agriculture that it had no tenants, no game laws, no squirearchy, and no clerical magistrates: "There being no tithes, great or small, for the support of a State clergy, all that large class of evils growing out of tithe disputes and tithe compositions are here also unheard of."[21] The difference between an established church and organization by voluntary association came home in an emphatic form to Alfred Bunn, who was touring New England. He went to a Boston church, and there donations for support of the church were made voluntarily—no tithes.[22]

Many of the travelers recorded their reactions to the practices of American churches. John Godley went to services in a western New York village and found that the "American liturgy differs but slightly from ours," the major difference being the lack of the Athanasian Creed. When Frederick Jobson was investigating American Methodism around Indianapolis, he heard one Methodist minister cry out that one could be saved by hearing the words of Jesus. Jobson remarked that there was no predestination there. George Combe gave a series of lectures on phrenology, and he found, evidently to his surprise, that the Americans asked him more questions about religion than did people back in England. As to the style of preaching, Richard Cobden when in America heard Henry Ward Beecher and formed a negative impression about the New York minister; he raised "his voice out of all proportion to the weight of the ideas it has to utter." The English abolitionist Goldwin Smith, writing immediately after the Civil War, found a connection between northern Protestantism and the egalitarian condition of life. Spared the migration of aristocrats and their laws, the northern states grew up in a true Christian spirit, establishing a "real community" and not the "spurious communities of heathen antiquity" where "oligarchical communities of masters tyrannize[d] over a people of slaves." He claimed that Christianity tends toward "as fair a distribution as may be of this world's goods" among its practitioners and "abhors at least the hideous extremes of wealth and destitution."[23]

Of the specific topics that came to the minds of the wayfarers, one was especially pursued: the effect slavery had on religious sentiment. As one would expect, given that almost all sects in Great Britain found slavery a violation of scripture, numerous travelers found the South irreligious. What surprised them was how many defended slavery on religious grounds. Even in the North, some ministers would defend slavery as an institution sanctioned by the Bible.[24]

In the comparison between the system of an established church and voluntary association, writers often related ministers' salaries. For the United States there was a considerable difference between ministers in the countryside and those in the cities. In the 1830s, William O'Bryan said the range was $200 and $1,000 per annum. Ebenezer Davies believed the range of salaries in 1849 New York City was between $1,000 and $4,000, while at about the same time John Godley put village salaries at $800 per year and town salaries at $1,500 to $2,000 per year. George Lewis reported that Princeton ministers were obtaining $2,000 to $4,000 yearly.[25] The pay of Anglican ministers did not seem to have greatly differed from the American scale; about £200 or $1,000. The difference came at the top, with the archbishops and bishops. Americans heard of bishops getting £10,000 to £20,000 (or about $50,000 to $100,000) annually and "they are astonished," calling it "oppression under the name of religion."[26]

William Dalton in 1821 said he found it odd to think that religion could thrive without state support. A number of English visitors came to the same conclusion. In 1833 Stephen Davis announced that the United States proved "that an establishment is not indispensable to secure the prosperity of religion in its outward profession, to say nothing of the internal principle, which is a totally distinct thing." Francis Hall, visiting immediately after the Napoleonic Wars, gave an economic libertarian twist to his view of an established church. Instead of obtaining increased religious devotion, one received the typical results of monopoly: "stagnation and decrement." In a free system, "competition . . . stimulates the zeal of all."[27]

In this analysis of an established church, any number of writers left little doubt that an established church was part and parcel of the aristocratic social apparatus and reflected the belief in the principle of inequality. Francis Hall explained that the doctrine of divine right marched with the establishment of monarchy and the feudal hierarchy; ultimately in Europe, the defense of aristocracy came from religion. It was the duty of the state "to support true religion," argued James F. W. Johnston, and true religion meant accepting the social classes found in aristocracies. In particular, the British established church was "in no way dependent on the people, but solely on the aristocracy."[28] The inequality principle behind aristocracy in governance was replicated in religion. As only the leisured few could make just rules for society in governance, so too were they the ones who knew best for the manual laborers in spiritual matters; moreover, religion taught the masses to obey their superiors.[29] The existence of voluntary religion in America and established religion in Great Britain set up the obvious comparison, which, as in other areas of life, revealed much about the practical outcomes of the equality principle versus the inequality principle.

British sojourners found one striking characteristic of the multitude of denominations in America: the ministers worked arduously in caring for their flocks. Robert Playfair (probably a pseudonym) remarked on how ministers had to act as a friend and adviser to church members. Moreover, their pay depended on tending to the needs of their parishioners. As Simon A. Ferrall wrote, "Ministers of religion [were] paid as they deserved." The result of paying attention to the needs of their congregations resulted perhaps in the ministers giving less learned and rehearsed sermons, but voluntary association made ministers more attentive to the personal needs of their members. The result was that religion flourished in the United States.[30]

In Great Britain, the aristocracy pushed the Anglican Church in a direction that repelled congregants, or so a number of travelers stated. By its connection with the state, the Anglican Church became a dumping ground for the sons of nobles who would never inherit the family fortune. Thus men entered the offices of the church with less than sterling religious aspirations. Sermons in England seemed dull to Robert Playfair. According to William O'Bryan, writing in the 1830s, the Anglican Church hired "reading" ministers whose only duty was to read books. He also said the bishop made ministers give only two or three sermons per year.[31] The Church was given, until 1870, the responsibility of educating commoners. Many concluded it had failed the task. Indeed, George Combe decided that the Anglican Church had allowed the English people to fall into ignorance. James D. Land, openly hostile to the impositions of the Church of England on the Presbyterians of Scotland, also found the Church guilty, along with low wages, of turning working people away from religion; most manual laborers did not attend church.[32]

Robert W. Russell, the near-Chartist visitor to the United States and a vitriolic critic of aristocracy, neatly summed up the view of the established Anglican Church among many British travelers to the American republic. "The very name of religion is made obnoxious to thousands of intelligent men by the English and Irish Church establishment," he wrote, "with its princely prelates, lords of parliament, palaces, starving curates, neglected congregations, and wealthy holders of livings, appointed by landed aristocrats."[33] Indeed, in the savage denunciation of the established church, one sees perhaps the origins of the middle-class attack on paternalism and large government. In their observations about the United States, these sojourners gave testimony to their belief that patronage in church affairs resulted in people relying on status to obtain positions of income instead of their performance: there, one obtained a useless bureaucracy; there, state funds were furnished to allow some to escape useful labor. When the system of "voluntary association" was compared to aristocratic control of churches, one obtained the ideas that would appear so prominently in laissez-faire economics. In any event, the investigation did nothing to improve the notion that the principle of inequality operated to improve the human condition.

But if the United States had achieved something significant in education and religion, its doctrine of equality utterly failed, according to these wayfarers, in one area: politics.

6

POLITICS AND EQUALITY

Democracy as Curse

Foreign visitors to the United States either quickly or eventually got to the political foundation of the republic. They handled politics in accordance with their ultimate goals: to report on daily life, to explain economic prospects, to inspect the operation of slavery, to estimate the benefits versus the costs of emigration, and in some cases purely to engage in the ideological battle of aristocracy versus democracy. Most visitors were not enthralled with the American version of democracy, although a few were. Rather, from the beginning they found that Great Britain had the stability they yearned for. George Fibbleton, alias Asa Greene, had reportedly been barber to the king, but he migrated to America because of equal rights, and in the republic the status of a barber was equal to that of a prime minister. By the end of his stay, he was disgusted with a republican form of government and "was convinced that a monarchy is the only decent sort of government." In 1845, George Lewis wrote that "We certainly have not fallen in love with the democratic idea since visiting the States," and in 1852 Edward Sullivan revealed to his reading public, "I never had the slightest *penchant* for republics; I left England strongly biassed in favour of our government and institutions, and I returned with all my predilections strengthened by a comparison with those of our cousins in the West."[1]

The dissection of the American democratic system was most memorably performed by Alexis de Tocqueville in his two-volume work, *Democracy in America,* and his understandings of American equality have guided discussion ever since. A massive literature has emerged on Tocqueville and his observations, much to the detriment of other contemporary observers.

This chapter does not seek to revamp, revise, or reiterate what others have written. But Tocqueville did not cover every topic imaginable, and there are areas of inquiry that demand further elaboration, particularly those areas most stressed by other writers. Those areas involve equality and local government, the effects of universal suffrage on talent, the actual practices of US elections, liberty, and the prospects for agrarian laws. Finally, the American response to these criticisms deserves some attention.[2]

The political gauntlet thrown down by the American Revolution was made explicit by John Bristed in 1818: the "leading characteristics" of American politics were the "extreme elevation of the democracy or popular sovereignty of the country, and the corresponding depression of its talent and property in the scale of national influence." Popular sovereignty meant the people were "*all* equal as fellow citizens," as opposed to Europe where sovereignty was placed in a prince.[3] As well as anyone, Henry Lord Brougham gave the argument for aristocracy and against democracy and equality. Equality, he wrote, was pure chimera—"altogether wild and fantastic" because it ignored "positive distinctions" between people in wealth, intelligence, and status. Attempted equality would be injurious to the "public interests" and to liberty. Politics required people of independent judgment; inferior intellects should not be given the chance to pass judgment on appropriate laws. Moreover, hereditary wealth strengthened independent judgment by augmenting character and elevating people above servility. In this viewpoint, the hereditary possession of land was crucial because it was the most stable form of property. In short, the masses had not the mental capacity for judgment, but hereditary wealth-holders did because the wealth provided the leisure time needed for cultivation of the intellect.[4] Lord Brougham's defense had a time-honored pedigree. Several others referred to the French Revolution as proof the masses could not be trusted with control of government.[5]

Inspection of governmental activity often started at the federal level, but there was considerable attention to local politics. The British voyagers were accustomed to large landholders holding offices of local government. What they found in the early republic was different. John Palmer in 1818 related to his audience that "it no doubt seems singular to the English reader, to hear of judges and captains keeping taverns &c., but it is very common in this republican country." At a pub in Philadelphia he mentioned that he was surprised that tradesmen were "so commonly entrusted with so high an office," the example being a miller serving as a judge. The reply was, "We don't know what you do in England, but here, in choosing a public officer, we look for talents, not wealth." In the courts, the English were accustomed to great pomp, ceremony, wigs, and robes; Simon Ferrall was told, "Yes, that may be quite necessary in England, in order to overawe a parcel of ignorant creatures, who have no share in making the laws; but with us, a man's a man, whether he have a silk gown on him or not." Charles Dickens thought the English system of judges might have gone too far in its elaborate trappings, but the American court proceedings were ludicrous in their folksiness. He did mention, though, that some pomp was necessary to keep the lower class civilized.[6] William Dalton recorded that he witnessed a militia in which the colonel was a blacksmith and the captain a nailsmith.[7]

One of the features of early American national life that several writers noticed was the lack of robberies and the absence of police. Even Henry Fearon, the critic of all things American, admitted that robberies were rare. Several others testified to this phenomenon.[8] To this was attached a somewhat amazed realization that the states lacked a police force. William H. Blane wrote in the1820s that "Most other governments are maintained by force," but in the United States the stranger asks, "'Where is the government? What is it? I see nothing of it.'" Three and one-half decades later James Stirling also jotted down, "In no city of the Union have I seen any appearance of an efficient, well-organized body of police." As Michael Chevalier said, "this is real self-government."[9] Part of the difference in legal outcomes attributable to the different political systems was the number of penalties for death; according to Isaac Holmes, the United States only had the death penalty for murder, whereas Great Britain listed 70 crimes punishable by death. The inference to be drawn was that the rule of aristocracy and the principle of inequality required far more lethal legal restrictions on the masses to make the aristocracy feel secure in their positions.[10]

One of the actions most eliciting condemnation from foreign travelers was the American penchant for mobs. Reports on mob activity largely arose because of antiabolitionist riots, and the riots became a powerful argument that visitors used to support aristocracy, because aristocracy guaranteed individual liberty—at least for some. However, the pro-Southern and antidemocratic writer David Mitchell told Europeans in 1862 that the idea Americans were governed by mobs was a figment of their antirepublican imaginations; the United States had "nothing . . . similar to the repressed masses of Europe, of the large cities especially."[11]

The subject of government costs and salaries attracted considerable comment. According to Tocqueville, democracies paid low salaries and operated at less cost because none of the tax revenue went to the superfluities of fashion and pomp associated with monarchy and aristocracy. He further argued that while democracies had a more enlightened public, their leaders were lesser figures.[12] Some of Tocqueville's assertions met confirmation from other travelers, some did not. Certainly the low salaries of public officials evoked surprise. A writer hostile to aristocracy, Robert W. Russell, pointed out that the chief justice of the United States Supreme Court made £1,200 per year, while county court judges in England made £1,000; a judge of the New York Supreme Court received £500. The salary of the governor of Rhode Island in the 1850s was $400 (or £80), and the governor of New York in the 1830s received $4,500 (£900). The president received a salary of $25,000 (or roughly £5,000); Queen Victoria in 1860 received from Parliament $2,000,000 per year, or £400,000. In fact, one writer said the president did not make a higher salary than the English ambassador to the United States. Because of the revenue from the Erie Canal, New Yorkers had few taxes to pay, while farmers on the county level, besides a minor tax, had to yield 18 days' labor on roads and $2 per year for schools.[13]

Whose population, the English or the American, was most taxed generated some difference in opinion. Tocqueville thought Americans were a lightly taxed people. Two individuals, writing about 1850, decided otherwise. William Brown said that when county, state, and federal taxes were combined, the Americans were as much taxed as any people, and while the salaries of officers were moderate, there were more of them. James F. W. Johnston attempted a painstaking review of taxes in New York and decided its residents were taxed as much as Great Britain's, roughly 5 percent of income.[14] Others counterargued that taxes in the United States were weighed according to the means of the individual, while in Great Britain the working classes bore the brunt of taxation. In 1823 Isaac Holmes calculated that the total amount of taxes collected in the United States is "not at present more than what is expended for the collection of taxes in Great Britain." The US press was not silent on the issue. *Niles Weekly Register* said the top sixteen government officials in the republic received in salaries about £13,000, but there were "thousands" in Great Britain who as government officials received this much. The *United States Democratic Review* figured the annual tax in the United States was $10.00 per worker, while in England it was $100.00 per worker. Overall, the advantage was probably given to the United States because the aristocracies (according to the principle of inequality) required higher incomes for government officials who were the progeny of aristocrats, special payments to keep up the royal court and its fashions, the tithe to support a state church, and money for the police to keep the disaffected from rioting.[15]

While foreign writers on society in the United States disagreed about many things, they were almost universal in their denunciation of its politics. And one thing in particular drove the criticism: universal white manhood suffrage.[16] So wrote George Featherstonhaugh about popular voting: the American "experiment," which was "founded upon a theoretical equality in the privileges of men, if it is to be judged of by the results which have already appeared, is a signal and instructive failure" because it allowed "the ignorant to govern the wise." James Stirling decided that universal manhood suffrage resulted in a leveling, and thereby lowering, of the intellect, while the pro-Confederate writer David Mitchell stated, "True, I have now no faith in democracy, nor have the people of England; nor have the people of America, as I will show. Democracy may be unavoidable—it may be necessary; but it is no remedy for any of the great evils of society."[17]

British sojourners uniformly reported that political leadership in the republic was mediocre. Politics became a popularity contest that drove out men (always men, never women) of intelligence, reflection, and experience. Thus England, by its restriction of the franchise, opened the door for the knowledgeable, who then guided the nation wisely. Because of the independence of their position, wrote Basil Hall, English statesmen legislated for all via the ideal of virtual representation—such men went beyond self-interest to consider the fates of all citizens. This was not what happened in the United States. Basically, the common people of America would not vote wealthy people into office. To that assessment, Thomas Hamilton, Isabella Bird, and Charles Lyell agreed.[18] Thus by universal male suffrage, the poorer classes selected people closer to themselves in circumstances rather than the truly rich, who were usually superior in intellect and knowledge. As the conservative Godfrey Vigne affirmed, "it must be unreasonable, that the wealthy and enlightened should be controlled by the needy."[19]

There were some interesting variations on the theme of universal manhood suffrage. Charles Lyell, in his often astute observations of the United States, believed that democracy drove out the "natural aristocracy," and so he objected to its existence. The response he got from Americans was that all systems have their evils; and for comparison, the Americans said, look at the educational system democracy had produced compared to the one the English aristocracy had (not) produced. Lyell agreed that at least for the states of Maine and Vermont, democracy had worked well. Thomas Hamilton, an inveterate foe of republican institutions, decried universal suffrage and laid the blame "unquestionably" on Thomas Jefferson, whom he then denounced for several pages. By the late antebellum period, some balance came to the conversation as seen in the writing of James Stirling. No friend of *universal* manhood suffrage, he admitted that if the only basis for voting was the possession of property, then property would rule and abuse its position. But if the basis of voting were laid entirely on population, then paupers would rule—and abuse their position. Therefore, government had to be mixed between the classes of property holders and nonpropertied citizens. England had the proper balance in the House of Lords and the House of Commons. In the United States, the balance came from a rural-urban split: the property aspect of the nation was imbedded in the northern "yeomanry" who offset the pauperism of the "larger cities and manufacturing districts" where "the proletarian populace has a dangerous predominance."[20] In 1861, Henry Ashworth decided that the controversy over universal manhood suffrage in America had been exaggerated by both its friends and foes.[21]

Closely aligned with a distrust of universal white manhood suffrage was a dislike of American political machinery. Parties in America were divided between those who feared for their wealth (the aristocracy) versus those who feared the designs of the wealthy (the democracy). Both had to vie for votes, and the party machinery that had been created was run by manipulators who demanded that people exhibit conformity to party positions and candidates. And in the oratory, one did not get reasoned argument but bombast and appeals to the passions, usually the worst passions. Robert Baird said that sagacious leaders admitted they had different views in private than they expressed in public, for they were "trammelled and gagged by considerations of policy and popularity." The party managers used trickery and deceit at elections. Instead of political discourse bringing forth the best intellects and arguments—as it was supposed to do under aristocracy—one obtained at best a stultifying mediocrity.[22]

Some did find some virtues in democratic government and electioneering. Tocqueville noticed that politics at least involved everyone, even if it left everyone unsatisfied. More important, democracies were able to learn from their own mistakes, and they tended not to concentrate wealth in a few hands as aristocracies did. Before the Reform Bill of 1832, a few realized that the United States did not have the rotten boroughs that England did, and Charles B. Johnson in 1819 reminded the reading public that, while American politics suffered from bribery and corruption, these two faults were as well "common in English elections." And hereditary rule was not particularly rational. Simon A. Ferrall was making a journey through the United States in the 1830s, noting the impact of Indian Removal on the Cherokees, when he stopped at a barroom at Mt. Pleasant, Georgia. The king had just died, and the landlord asked Ferrall how the British "elected" a king. Ferrell replied that it was not an elective office but a birthright. Nearby, a Kentuckian put a leg on a chair and said, "'Tha's a kind of unnatural.'" Then an English radical came in and a debate raged.[23] Even by 1820, the importance of elections to Americans had already become an ingrained trait and the idea of an inherited office wholly discredited.

Closely connected to the British traveler's dread of universal manhood suffrage was the legislation that would undoubtedly result from letting paupers and the unpropertied workers vote: an agrarian law. An agrarian law meant that the wealth of the rich would be confiscated by law and transferred to the impoverished. The term arose from the history of the Roman Republic, when the tribunes of the people, first Tiberius Gracchus and then Gaius Gracchus, made a plea to give free land to returning soldiers. The actual conditions of the event are instructive. Tiberius and Gaius Gracchus were *not* taking lands away from the great landowners of Rome, who controlled the Roman Senate, but wanted to reward soldiers with some of the *public* lands that Rome had obtained via conquest. The aristocrats of Rome were so infatuated with augmenting their wealth that they could not abide the idea that they were not going to get their hands on this land but it would go instead to those who had soldiered for the Roman Republic. Cicero defended this position of the Roman Senate, but he called it "liberty" and invoked the doctrine of the "sanctity of private property." The aristocracy murdered both Tiberius and Gaius Gracchus, setting the stage for Julius Caesar to end the Roman Republic and transform it into the Roman Empire with himself as emperor. But from that incident onward, the idea of taking property from the wealthiest element in society to give to the poorest has been called an agrarian law.[24]

The most vocal British critics of American manners in the 1830s also emphatically warned that the American republic was doomed to anarchy and mob rule, descending eventually into dictatorship, because universal white male suffrage would inevitably lead to the formulation of an agrarian law. Thomas Hamilton stated that he already saw the desire for redistribution of wealth in American cities; the available land in the West might delay its appearance, but the future appearance of an agrarian law was inevitable—the impoverished but voting masses would demand one. Basil Hall agreed with this prognosis. Another added that each election brought out more dissension about property, and the American republic did not have the security of property that England had; maintaining the absolute sanctity of private property could only be achieved by establishing an aristocracy and giving it supreme political power. Godfrey Vigne, along with most of these writers, agreed that in the 1830s property was so diffused in the United States that the immediate threat of agrarianism was small; it was "a mere hydra in embryo." But because of universal suffrage and the natural tendency of property to accumulate in a few hands, the hydra was bound to grow and wreak havoc on American society.[25]

Others in the same decade doubted that the Americans were headed to a social train wreck because of an agrarian law. Tocqueville saw that Americans had few complaints about property rights, and the existence of a nearly uninhabited continent meant the population would not press upon the limits of land availability for decades, perhaps even centuries. Harriet Martineau thought that fears of an agrarian law in the United States were "silly," because the country lacked the gaping disparities that characterized Europe. William Ouseley added that not only did Americans have western land in reserve, but the inheritance laws stopped the massive accumulations of landed property so visible in England. The English advocate of democracy, Robert W. Russell, dismissed ideas of agrarianism because democracy removed the principal pathways aristocrats used to aggrandize wealth; by allowing mechanics and common laborers to vote, it defended their "rights and interests." The *United States Democratic Review* in an editorial said that as long as America kept to the rule that all laborers deserved the fruits of their labor, there would be no agrarianism in the United States, and democratic politics were about making sure that all laborers received the full rewards of their work.[26]

Liberty was a keyword among the British travelers, and to this day remains a bulwark of those who complain about equality and democracy. It deserves a special place in this narrative because while other arguments against equality fall away or are demonstrated to be nonsensical, the fear that democracy and equality will crush individual liberty remains to this day a vibrant argument against equality. The nineteenth-century debate over liberty and equality offers twenty-first-century denizens some interesting vantage points about the merits of the antiegalitarian diatribes of libertarians and the superrich.

The essential fear about equality and democracy was in practical terms about the ownership of property, but its more intellectual side was its effect on human liberty. Tocqueville sounded the tocsin with his chapter 7 in volume 1, part II: "On the Omnipotence of the Majority in the United States, and its Effects," and used the phrase, uttered ever after, the "tyranny of the majority."[27] He had no lack of allies. "*Public opinion,* that hundred-headed hydra, and the tyranny of the majority, that most intolerant and bigoted of all tyrannies, rules America with a rod of iron." Another said America had "no 'liberty and equality.'" Various sojourners wrote about how Americans repressed their opinions because they might conflict with the majority. The Earl of Carlisle said everyone who visited the United States noticed this, and it even pervaded the pulpit and legal profession. Even those favorably disposed to Americans thought their proclamations of freedom "comical" because they were mental slaves to the popular will.[28]

A few offered excuses for the American tendency to crown public opinion king. John Bristed in 1818 simply noted that liberty was related to property and that liberty meant the ability of citizens to do with property as they pleased, and he further indicated that by the US Constitution and state constitutions all people "except the negro slaves" had civil and religious rights. Patrick Shirreff reminded his readers that "*Liberty and equality,* as understood in Britain, is not to be found amongst the inhabitants of the United States" because of the absence of a hereditary privileged class. He believed equality and liberty were confined in America wholly to the political realm. In contrast to other writers, Henry Wansey commented that in England, liberty was cramped by "poverty and misfortune" and "partial laws, chartered rights, appropriations, &c.," in which he indicated that *liberty* was a term that carried class biases. The Earl of Carlisle decided that the "vaunted equality" of the Americans was due to deference to custom, and the submission to popular opinion was "paralleled in many aristocratic or even despotic communities."[29]

The strength of the ideal of liberty found its advocate in John Stuart Mill, who wrote *On Liberty* in 1859. Mill, who in many ways is the father of modern libertarianism, was no fan of democracy. Mill learned of the dangers of democracy from Tocqueville, and feared that individual liberty would be lost when a country turned to universal male suffrage. He remained in the English tradition of believing an educated elite should rule, not the unlearned, unemployed, and pauperized. Politics was supposed to reflect community interests, and the majority interest in any community was the laboring interest; if that interest obtained power, it would oppress the minority interest, property holders, and others. Mill wanted a government that reflected proportionately the interests in the community, something that universal manhood suffrage destroyed. The basic fear was that majorities stopped individuals from expressing themselves freely and acting freely.[30]

Into this discussion came the idea of "constitutional liberty" and what it meant. For many British writers, liberty did not quite have its modern libertarian connotations. James Phillippo had some intriguing comments. First, the English Constitution was based on duty (feudalism) whereas the US Constitution was founded on natural rights. Therefore, liberty in the English tradition was not freedom from restraint; men might be "wisely and benevolently controlled, and yet be free." Subordination was not inconsistent with liberty. The community, in this case Parliament, defined the boundaries of liberty (and some of those boundaries could exclude entrepreneurial behavior). Thus liberty was confined to a sphere that was politically determined.[31] (Ever since John Locke, at least, the English idea about liberty in regard to property was that a "man" could do with his property anything he wished *on the condition that* the person's use of property would not injure the life, liberty, or property of another. That turns out to be a major consideration because in the twenty-first century virtually any action a person takes can have repercussions on others; just consider Joseph Schumpeter's description of capitalism as "creative destruction" in this context.)

James Stirling, the antidemocracy abolitionist, agreed with Phillippo that the American idea of liberty included too much license and not enough restraint. For Stirling, true liberty was subordination to the "universal law of justice." Under that definition, life under monarchy could have as much liberty as any other system, but also could abuse liberty as much as any other system. Democracy had the same demerits; what counted was not the form of government but obedience to justice. The same problem infested the American idea of equality. American equality focused on outward behavior instead of the inward equality "that is rooted in man's humanity." The forced equality in outward behavior thereby violated distinctions made by nature. In any event, popular sovereignty potentially violated true liberty.[32]

Michael Chevalier also commented on American liberty, though he had few of the reservations that the British travelers had. He believed there were two types of liberty: the Yankee version and the French version. The Yankee version of liberty was really conformity, and he found a stifling consensus on most things in New England (though they had wonderful schools and rewarded labor correctly). He ascribed that conformity to the long-term influence of religion, i.e., Puritanism. The French version of liberty emphasized the capacity of being different, and in that sense of liberty he found the Virginians more like the French. Interestingly, though, he ascribed the question of liberty to cultural influences, not political ones.[33]

The European travelers' commentary on liberty has at least one gaping inconsistency. Where were the historic examples of deprivation of liberty? They came from Europe's past, and Europe's past was the history of the rule of monarchs and aristocrats. Europe's story was government censorship of books, imprisonment of dissident authors, suppression of freedoms of speech and press (observable in the British government's activities against republicanism, 1790 to 1815), and persecution of religious minorities. In the matter of liberty, no traveler noted that when Europeans wanted to try out new communal arrangements—like Robert Owen at New Harmony, Indiana—they came to the United States, not to European nations; when religious groups felt persecuted, they sought refuge in the United States. No European nation had a written bill of rights like the United States. It was true that the Americans had antiabolitionist mobs; but it was also true that states and communities were trying to reduce infringements on liberty of speech and press.[34]

So why was there among European thinkers all this fear about liberty under majority rule when it was under aristocratic and monarchical rule that people's liberties were so blatantly attacked? One has the suspicion that in this discussion about liberty among the Europeans, class governed the whole perspective. The European writers on liberty trusted their own aristocratic judgment—people of reason, leisure, and disinterest—and therefore could decide how much liberty workers and others could exercise and when those liberties needed to be curtailed. But they could not trust the reverse. If the masses had power, would they treat the aristocrats the way the aristocrats treated the masses? This was not unlike the slave masters of the old South; they feared emancipation because they imagined the freed people would treat them, the former masters, the way they had treated the former slaves.

To the European denunciation of democracy and universal white manhood suffrage, the Americans had a response. They were unimpressed with the higher order of discourse conducted by the British during elections and legislation. In an 1833 article on elections under the Duke of Newcastle, taken from the *Nottingham Review,* the editor of the *Niles Weekly Register* detailed how tenants voted the way the duke wanted; when they did not, the duke turned out widows and tenants. "The preceding is a fine specimen of English 'liberty' which has been so much boasted of, for several centuries."[35]

In a more telling article, the *Michigan Farmer* related an English election speech and the audience reaction. The editor noted that in England (1852), some 5 million people were disfranchised, taxed without representation, while voting was done by the viva voce method so the landowners, i.e., the gentry and aristocracy, knew whom to oust if some voters voted wrong. The "whole race of tenant farmers" had to vote as they were told. The editor then gave an example. He asked what would be the response of American yeomen to a speech by a politician who "upon hearing some expressions of disappro bation in the crowd, exclaim[ed] with emphatic scorn, 'You are the vilest rabble I ever saw'—yet this was done by Major Beresford, a sprig of nobility, and 'not a dog moved his tongue.'" The writer then described English elections as full of uproar, bullying, violence, and blood; he summarized, "we are quite reconciled to the little improprieties which characterize ours."[36]

The abolitionist Elizur Wright was duly unimpressed with the liberty of the English press and the means of getting published in England. He was unable to get his foot in the door in any of the publishing houses. "My friends tell me that the only way to succeed is to lay patient [siege] to some of the accessible nobility and literary men who mix with that class, and get them really to work with me, & then the thing will be done." Liberty of expression, in other words, depended upon aristocratic approval.[37]

While the apprehension about majority rule and universal manhood suffrage involved the type of laws that such a system could impose on the aristocracy, the Americans were more alive to the coercive quality of aristocratic governance, hardly a glowing advertisement for liberty under systems of monarchy and aristocracy. When Lewis Cass visited France, he saw that the major difference between European nations and the United States was that in the latter, representative government fostered affection among the citizenry, whereas the former had to rule by coercion. This was "republicanism's boast": one can get thousands assembled and yet not need a military to oversee it.[38] And in fact this was one of the rationales British travelers used for exclusive aristocratic control of government: to keep the masses in their place. Godfrey Vigne wrote that the propertied needed "a sturdy armed force . . . to put down domestic commotions." William H. Blane in 1818 wrote about the difference between the ideas of American government and European government; the European view had been expressed by philosophers that "the people must be kept down, and ruled with a rod of iron, as utterly uncapable of governing themselves," that "the people are their own worst enemies." The American ideas were the opposite.[39]

And then there were the economies to be compared and contrasted. The discourse among the British travelers and writers kept referring to wisdom, knowledge, and disinterest among the aristocrats that produced just legislation. Adam Gurowski dismissed the claim immediately; aristocrats ruled in their own class interest. Even the *American Whig Review* struck at the class legislation of aristocrats. One writer asserted that wealth and luxury were not the criteria to use to judge a civilization; the true test was "the general and equable distribution of the means of external well-being, especially if this be joined with a general diffusion of the elements of useful knowledge." Americans quickly referred to the legislation that aristocrats guarded so zealously: entail, primogeniture, and the game laws. They also drew attention to aristocratic control of the government bureaucracy, church, and military, all at inflated salaries. Overall, Americans found the weight of British legislation—taxation, land laws, and appointments to government office—responsible for the horrendous amount of poverty cursing the British Isles.[40]

In 1853, a writer for the *United States Magazine and Democratic Review* got to the heart of the question of liberty and why a divergence occurred between British and American writers on the topic. This writer brought together the ideas of liberty and equality and how they were necessarily joined. Besides discussing the role of constitutions in defining the area of freedom, he or she started out by saying the first principle of American government was liberty as defined in a constitution, a condition to which they agreed by adopting the constitution. But then, the next principle was equality. Why equality? Because "without [equality] liberty is only another name for aristocracy."[41] And there the writer laid bare the essence of the problem. In the aristocratic version of liberty, the aristocrats had liberty, but no one else did unless the aristocrats decided to give liberty to them. That is how one got liberty and despotism at the same time; liberty for some, not for others. The American version was "equal liberty for all." This was not a phrase aristocrats used when they spoke of liberty; liberty was a gift only to those who could wield liberty responsibly, and, since they were the judges of that condition, it amounted to a class disposition to allow liberty only to those similar in circumstances and ideas to themselves. The American version intended that all citizens had the same rights and privileges, and the commanding condition for that equality of liberty was that those who exercised liberty recognized exactly that other people had the same rights to exercise liberty. That, of course, was the American dilemma, because Euro-Americans did not recognize the rights of non-Euro-Americans to equal liberty. From it came the obvious inequalities that foreign wayfarers elevated as the defining earmarks of American civilization.

7

AMERICAN INEQUALITIES

Foreign visitors took seriously the Declaration of Independence, American democracy, and the ideal of equality. They measured the fidelity of the nation's inhabitants to their ideal of equality by their behaviors toward others. The travelers found that Americans were appallingly guilty of infidelity. Vast areas of American life demonstrated inequality, not equality—a fact that has been the center of historical treatment of the years of the early republic for one-half century.[1] Interestingly, the foreign visitors quickly divided the United States into two halves. The northern half was the land where a semblance of equality existed, but not the southern half. The reason for the division was the existence of slavery. The travelers commented on many of the ethnicities in the United States, but African slavery stood foremost as the great hypocrisy of the republic. However, ethnicity and African slavery were not the only subjects that elicited analyses of inequality from foreigners. They noted regional disparities and especially the development of American cities. Most foreign visitors believed that slavery, though a robust economic institution in the 1850s, was not destined to last; inequality, however, would eventually be victorious in the United States because of its observable presence and growth in the cities. On the subject of inequality, industrialization did not impress visitors as much as urban areas. There the inequality was visible. In many ways, the European wayfarers pointed out the rural-urban conflict building up in the United States and determined that it was in the city where an aristocracy would come to rule the United States socially and economically—just as it was presently doing in Europe.

INEQUALITIES OF ETHNICITY

Unlike European nations, the United States did not have extreme ethnic homogenization in its national population. While Anglo-Saxons, or those of English descent, probably were the majority ethnicity, all travelers noted the existence of other national groups. Scots and Germans seemed to prosper in the United States; the English performance was more ragged, being superior in some areas, lackluster in others. By the 1850s the Irish attracted considerable attention and were deemed the least successful of the European immigrants, having only day labor jobs or being reduced to servants. Travelers, with the possible exception of Harriet Martineau, seldom had a feminist viewpoint. They largely commented on how the amount of work that American wives had to perform took away their beauty. Few argued in favor of political rights for women or for women becoming active businesspeople.[2]

European visitors did comment extensively on Native Americans, and several came to inspect Indians' customs and folkways. The attitudes of whites were recorded as entirely hostile to the tribes. John Palmer in 1819 said of Kentucky backwoodsmen that they were ready to kill Indians on sight: "they were mere dogs." Others heard stories that male Native Americans were hostile to labor, while J. J. Gurney criticized democracy as a system because "*Numbers*" [i.e., white Americans] were pushing out the Seneca nation from New York. Simon Ferrall called Euro-American treatment of Indians disgraceful, and he recorded the stealing of Lenni Lenape lands. He also said that Euro-Americans justified the theft in the name of progress, but really it was simple thievery. Charles A. Murray visited the Pawnees in the late 1830s and was shocked at their condition and their annihilation due to smallpox, but he then related that the elimination of the tribes was the result of civilization: "The onward march of the Anglo-Saxon with the rifle, and steam, and commerce in his train, will not be stayed."[3]

But when the subject was inequality, foreign travelers turned overwhelmingly to the institution of slavery to buttress their belief about the hypocrisy of the people of the United States and their creed of equality. British wayfarers had a tradition behind their attack on American slavery; abolitionism had begun in England by 1790, the British Navy had been long deployed against the African slave trade, and the British ended slavery in their Caribbean possessions by 1833. Much of their criticism came from a long-standing argument against slavery: property rights in people were inadmissible, the New Testament did not sanction slavery, slave masters virtually tortured slaves to obtain labor, slavery was an uneconomical system in which slaves did not exert themselves, whites learned to disrespect manual labor, and slavery reared an upper class that wallowed in arrogance and useless luxury. Many of the British defamers of slavery came from dissenting religious denominations and perhaps a middle-class background. Most of their commentary fits well-known descriptions of the abolitionist denunciation of the peculiar institution.[4]

Two points, however, need to be made. The British travelers, no matter their economic class background, did not use the ideals of democracy and equality to find slavery abhorrent; their antislavery convictions did not originate from a sense of egalitarianism. Second, the comment of the near-Chartist Robert W. Russell in 1848 carries some weight: to deflect attention away from the free institutions of the United States, "English aristocrats, their dupes and satellites, are always ready to point out the condition of some of the slave States, with their Lynch law, inhumanity, and immorality, and to exclaim, 'Behold the consequences of republicanism and democratic government!'"[5]

If much of the British travelers' commentary on American slavery exhibited standard antislavery viewpoints, certain themes nonetheless deserve some consideration. The first was the extent of prejudice against Africans that visitors found in the United States, North and South. Tocqueville noted it, while Alexander Mackay said the reason emancipation could not be effected was the *"antipathy of race,"* and that Europeans could hardly believe "the intensity of this feeling." Alfred Pairpoint determined that the North was rabidly racist. The critic of all things American, Henry Fearon, wrote, "The treatment of the Negroes throughout these States is as villainous as can be well imagined."[6]

Visitors recorded the ill treatment that African slaves received: the whippings, the splitting of families at the auction block, the sights of manacled slaves moving from the Border South to the Cotton South. The slaves lived in hovels and had inadequate food. On occasion they related stories of inhuman cruelty. Visitors heard tales about slave masters having sex with female slaves and then selling the resulting children in the same manner "as he would have disposed of his hogs!" Such observers frequently wrote about the degraded work habits of whites, arguing that whites refused to do the same labor as slaves. Usually these writers made explicit the hypocrisy of liberty and equality being enshrined in the United States when the practice of slavery was the epitome of tyranny and inequality. As George Featherstonhaugh wrote upon seeing a set of manacled slaves being taken down the Mississippi River, "I had never seen so revolting a sight before," and the slaves were being "driven by white men, with liberty and equality in their mouths."[7]

The relentless hostile depiction of slavery by some of these visitors obscures the somewhat concurrent view that slaves seemed to be treated rather well. Charles Lyell, no friend to the peculiar institution, nevertheless found that South Carolina slaves seemed well fed and well dressed and that they were not overworked. Charles MacKay believed slaveholders were not the monsters that abolitionists said they were, and that slaves fared better than the European lower class. Robert Playfair discovered Richmond slaves fairly treated, and he found they displayed more independence than he expected. Isaac Holmes, who wrote that "the effects of slavery are truly appalling" and that whippings certainly did occur, nonetheless noted that slaves had small gardens and poultry. Others commented that they found slaves treated decently.[8]

A few foreign sojourners ran into the proslavery argument. Their reactions were surprisingly hostile. They often couched their riposte in religious terms. Richard Flower dismissed the argument that slaves were property; instead he affirmed the belief that God had created all people as people. James Stirling, the antidemocratic British abolitionist, dissected the proslavery tracts of George Fitzhugh and Albert Bledsoe carefully, arguing that commerce had changed "civilization by force" into "civilization by contract," and added that "man, as man, is an end unto himself, and it is unjust to make him a means to the ends of another." Harriet Martineau was appalled at the proslavery defense. Thomas Grattan was particularly offended by the assertions of John C. Calhoun and George McDuffie that African slavery was necessary to ensure white equality.[9]

A central theme that runs throughout foreign observations of US slavery was their condemnation of the system, regardless of its economic or other effects: the slavery practiced by the Americans reduced people—Africans—to beasts. Michael Chevalier wrote that Americans treated slaves "as if they did not belong to the human race." John Woods saw the same thing; whites held blacks in "utmost contempt" and did not allow "them to be of the same species [as] themselves." At Charleston, the Swedish migrant Hans Mattson believed slaves "were treated like cattle in every respect," while John Godley held that whites saw blacks as "a *domestic animal*." When in Illinois, Patrick Shirreff talked to a Scottish woman, who, Shirreff recorded, justified slavery as follows: "My countrywoman smiled at my objections to the slave states, and maintained that the coloured population were not human beings, but inferior animals created for slavery."[10]

These facets of the foreign visitors' assessment of American slavery are important in connection with the trans-Atlantic debate over equality.[11] About the only time these people used the word *equality* was to show how hypocritical Americans were because of slavery, an institution founded on inequality. But the foreign travelers never used the ideal of human equality to denounce slavery, as did American abolitionists and some antislavery politicians. In fact, their understanding of slavery was shaped by their approval of inequality as practiced in aristocratic nations. Over and over, the comparison was made between the working class of Europe and American slaves, and with some frequency it was a comparison between the farm laborers of Great Britain and plantation slaves. In this comparison, the slaves came off quite well. Upon returning to Georgia from a stay in Europe, Charles Lyell wrote, "with a vivid impression on his mind of the state of peasantry there . . . [and] the difficulty of obtaining subsistence, and the small chance they [had] of bettering their lot," that he found the condition of slaves did not induce in him "lamentation[s]." Marianne Finch investigated the diets of slaves, their small gardens, and their habitations: "Nothing like the clean pretty cottages in which some of our English peasants live, but it was infinitely better than an Irish cabin . . . or many others of the homes of the labouring poor in Great Britain." William Harris labeled slavery a revolting practice, but many slaves were in a better condition than "the poor peasantry of my own country." Marshall Hall in 1854 wrote in favor of emancipation of southern slaves and held that if given "just wages" the former slaves would become "*the finest peasantry in the world*."[12] It may also be observed that though British writers denounced proslavery writing, they did not notice the odd similarity it had to the pro-aristocratic argument: both were founded on inequality, reserving political and social power for the elite, and condemning another class to poorly rewarded manual labor.

Two writers saw the class dimensions in regard to the European analysis of slavery. George Flower in 1841 argued that in America, poverty and degradation were "confined to colour," and seeing it startled the European. But England had the same poverty and degradation, only it was due to class divisions. Patrick Shirreff made the same observation. Britons writing on America focused on slavery but then ignored the sufferings existing in England. In the southern states, southerners talked of the tyranny of Europeans and the abuse of the Irish at the same time they put the lash to their slaves; in Great Britain, the British spoke of the evil of slaveholders but were insensible to the horrors visited upon the "lower orders."[13]

By putting together these British observations on American slavery—the immorality of slavery because it transformed people into beasts, the general biblical antislavery viewpoint, and the failure to use an ideal of human equality to condemn the peculiar institution—one can get a glimpse at how upper-class people could come to denounce slavery. It was not the class position which slaves occupied that bothered the foreign antislavery wanderers—it was the violence inflicted on them. None expected a social mobility that would lift slaves to a middle-class existence or higher; rather, the slaves of the South would remain in their class position as farm laborers. But the violence would be removed. The assumption that accompanied this view—sometimes mentioned, sometimes not—was that under modern conditions of commerce and a surplus population, there was no need to inflict violence to obtain cheap labor. Cheap labor was there for the taking.[14]

That so many British visitors to the United States recorded their hostility to the practice of slavery and at the same time were intensely hostile to a society founded on equality brings up an important interpretive point. A person did not at all have to believe in equality to condemn the peculiar institution. In her discussion of Frances Trollope, the author Sara Wheeler drove home this point: for Trollope slavery was a disgrace, and she "hated slavery and equality with similar passion."[15] In the voluminous writing about the Republican Party, abolitionists, and general public antislavery sentiment in the North, innumerable historians have judged Republicans and antislavery leaders insincere in their denunciations of slavery because they rejected the idea of racial equality; therefore, they had to be disguising their true motives—say, economic or political imperialism—by uttering antislavery slogans. In reality, equality did not have to be a factor at all in disliking the peculiar institution. Most British travelers denounced slavery and equality at the same time, and had no sense that they were being inconsistent. The only inconsistency they saw was a nation whose anthem was "all men are created equal" practicing racial slavery.

REGIONAL INEQUALITY

Certainly slavery and other forms of ethnic discrimination—against Native Americans and the Irish—supplied foreign travelers with a cornucopia of details to contest the American claim of egalitarianism, but it was not the only inequality that they noted and wrote about. Another theme that occupied a prominent position in the foreign travelers' observations was the inequalities by region in the United States. They of course remarked upon the developing West and its relative poverty versus the more settled areas of the East, but the great division they saw was between North and South, between the nonslaveholding states and the slaveholding states. At the same time, they testified to the aristocratic nature of the slave states.

Alexander Mackay went from the Northeast into Virginia and South Carolina, and remarked that as he did so he saw "a nearer approach to English country life then is discernible [than] in any other portion of the republic." The Earl of Carlisle saw the same thing, that it would be "uncandid to deny that the planter in the Southern States has much more in his manner and mode of intercourse that resembles the English county gentleman than in any other class of his countrymen"—this compliment in spite of his assessment that the slaveholding states stood in relation to the free states "as Ireland does to England." The key to the aristocratic nature of the South was the large plantation; it bore a resemblance to the huge landed estates of the high gentry in England. Thus Michael Chevalier wrote that the South had created "aristocratic republics, based on slavery and the accumulation of property in a few hands." By the time of the Civil War, the Confederate sympathizer William H. Russell reported that in the South "the admiration for monarchical institutions on the English model, for privileged classes, and for a landed aristocracy and gentry, is undisguised and apparently genuine."[16]

Foreign visitors placed their emphasis on the qualities of the planter class and how they matched the qualities of European, and especially English, aristocracy. The planters were the "only class who live on the labour of others, and without their own personal exertions." Important to the ideal of aristocracy was the role of leisure; the planters were "truly [a] leisure class." And William Russell then made the point: by leisure the planters have the "time to cultivate their minds, to apply themselves to politics." Russell then added that states' rights was simply a defense against democracy, and the planters had the English aristocrats' fear about a majority's ability "to demoralize and finally to absorb the minority." From the foreigners' comments, particularly in the 1850s, one comes to the conclusion that the visitors saw the planters as an aristocracy in embryo.[17]

This analysis of the southern planters then set the stage for an inequality in regions that all saw: the active nonslave North versus the indolent, sloppy but aristocratic slave-ridden South. Almost all travelers noted it, some making extensive commentary. The division of the United States into the free labor states and slave labor states did not hail from the abolitionist imagination or disappointed northern advocates of Henry Clay's American System, a set of policies designed to foster manufacturing; it was fully elaborated by the contingent of foreign visitors who wrote about the United States. And the distinctions were made early.

Any number of foreign visitors made the common remark that the United States seemed to change in character as soon as one crossed the Ohio River or went from Pennsylvania into Maryland and Virginia. Charles Lyell traveled from Connecticut to Baltimore, and in that city "we were reminded for the first time of the poorer inhabitants of a large European city." Francis Hall in 1818 offered the opinion that as soon as one went to Washington, DC, one entered the land of wretched dwellings and the "laws of humanity [were] reversed." Ebenezer Davies stated, using Tocqueville as an additional authority, that the difference between slavery and free labor could be seen by simply looking across the Ohio River.[18]

In detailing the differences between the slaveholding states and the nonslaveholding states, the foreign travelers ended up pitting New England against Virginia or South Carolina. It was not uncommon for them to ascribe the difference to the Cavaliers of the English Civil War settling the South and carrying with them the ideas of a hierarchical society ruled over by landed magnates, while Puritans settled the New England region and brought, in very infantile form, the ideas of democracy, equality, and small farms.[19] Not everything about New England drew rave reviews. The dyspeptic Thomas Hamilton summarized about the people of New England that there was "much to approve, little to admire, and nothing to love"; nature had given Yankees "double brains and half [of a] heart." His companion in issuing acerbic commentary, Frances Trollope, also knew how to backhand a compliment; she liked New Englanders but would do no business with them—they were "too smart for me." Edward Sullivan in 1852 disliked the laws of New England because they were "tyrannical old laws" descended from the Puritans. Michael Chevalier felt that New Englanders were too individualistic.[20]

But the aspects that grabbed visitors' attention were the scenery, the village life, and the general equality of condition in northern rural areas; it was also probably the case that New England had an English homogeneity in its population. The praises flowed easily and continually. Alfred Bunn initially described New England as "almost part and parcel of Old England," and Boston had "more the appearance of the best English towns than any we have visited." Charles Daubeny in 1843 when in Connecticut wrote that "one might imagine oneself in England" due to the neat villages. Charles Dickens remarked on how the towns and cities of New England reminded him of the villages of old England.[21]

More emphatic was the equality the visitors saw, which oddly redounded on the aspects of aristocratic control of the English countryside even though most of these visitors approved of the British gentry. In 1818, John Bristed made the crucial observation that in New England "property is more equally divided than in any other civilized country." That assessment was confirmed by the acerbic Thomas Hamilton: "Wealth is more equally distributed in the New England States, than perhaps in any country of the world." No grand aristocrats straddled the land, and no miserable huts of wage-earning agricultural workers marred the vista. Isabella Bird, no great friend of things American, nonetheless could write of New England, "Oh, very fair! Smiling, cultivated, and green, like England, but far happier; for slavery which disgraces the New World, and poverty which desolates the Old, are nowhere to be seen." Matilda Houstoun commented in like fashion, stating that she felt the "great charm [of] . . . the total absence of any appearance of poverty or distress." Her other journeys in Europe were filled with "the incessant calls made by the aged, the deformed, and the starving . . . ," and the contrast of those lands with the United States was "stark."[22]

One of the great inequalities in the antebellum United States derived from the comparison of slave states to free states. It was a constant in every travelogue written by foreign visitors. Moreover, most ascribed the inequality to the effects of slavery both on the African as well as on the European.

Slavery, the visitors believed, made labor dishonorable, and thus slaves, lacking any positive incentives, tried to labor as little as possible, and the white population tried not to labor at all lest they be identified with slaves. Even in 1823, Isaac Holmes could write about the impact of slavery that, besides the "miserable state of poverty" of the slaves, the "masters or employers . . . will grow arrogant, idle, and ostentatious." Harriet Martineau said the difference between the sections could be summed up in the word *labour;* in the free states "labour is more really and heartily honoured than, perhaps, in any other part of the civilized world." In the slave states, labor was "degraded." The same point was raised by her contemporary Michael Chevalier and others. The difference between the sections was summarized by James Stirling: "On the one hand you have the industrial energy and political independence of a self-governing yeomanry; on the other, the stagnation of a people, where the rich are too proud to work, and the poor too subservient to be free; while one-third of the whole population is practically reduced to the status of beasts of burden."[23]

AMERICAN CITIES

Europeans found another striking inequality in the United States: the cities. This aspect of American life needs emphasizing. Europeans found equality in the northern countryside. But they found it neither in the slaveholding states nor in northern cities. In many ways, the historical profession has not done a good job in noting this difference because its members have almost totally ignored the equality in the countryside, which became the basis of the American claim to equality and all the ramifications that came from it, and have instead dwelled on the class divisions in urban areas. Over twenty-five years ago, economic historians Jeremy Atack and Fred Bateman forthrightly declared that historians had overlooked the egalitarian nature of northern agriculture by searching for equality precisely where it did not exist: in the city and on the plantation. True as their observation was, it became one of the great interpretive lead balloons of the history profession.[24]

The urban-rural divide was no chimera of the early nineteenth-century imagination; it was very real. And it in fact demonstrated the problem the United States would have in the twentieth century. Equality operated in rural America (or the rural American North), but as the nation became more urban it became more inegalitarian—and no one knew how to infuse equality into the urban setting. The change in context, from rural nation to urban nation, meant the United States did have a tradition of equality, but the tradition had a tenuous reality for urban life.

The topic of nineteenth-century American economic equality requires a major refinement to explain why so many visitors recorded an equality that historians and economists have failed to locate—in short, why Tocqueville's early lines in *Democracy in America*—that he was "struck by the general equality of conditions" in the country—were essentially correct. From the beginning of the republic, travelers emphasized the difference between urban life and rural life. Economic inequality reigned in the cities; economic equality was found on the American (and Canadian) farm.[25]

American historians have been obsessed with the arrival of industrialization by 1860, but this was not the case with British visitors. The chief economic characteristic of the nineteenth-century United States was agriculture, and the chief economic actor was the owner-occupier. They also realized that small farmers did not become rich. The reward of farming was most commonly called a "competence." The word arises over and over again in visitors' descriptions of the well-being of American farmers. Americans earned a modest living, not a luxurious one. Harriet Martineau characterized the situation best: one element in the "exhilaration of such scenes [village life] in America was the universal presence of competence"; there were no paupers and "the farms are held in fee-simple."[26]

The pervasiveness of owner-occupiers (once called "yeomen") implied equality but of a distinct kind. One obtained a farm by working, saving money, and slowly moving from propertylessness to property ownership. Agricultural historians call this process the "agricultural ladder," whereas everyone else calls it social mobility. For Europeans coming to the United States with limited capital, the advice given was not to go into the forest or onto the prairies but to rent land, become a laborer (farm servant), or become a sharecropper. The implication was that at any time in nineteenth-century rural America, there would be some inequality: a great number of landed proprietors but also a number of tenants, farm laborers, and others who were making the climb up the property ownership ladder. But because those at the bottom of the ladder could reasonably expect to climb the ladder, the overall characteristic of rural life was egalitarian.[27]

Mobility derived from primarily two personality characteristics: industriousness and sobriety. William Thomson became a cradler for a family farm for a season: "really it was very hard work." Simon Ferrall in 1832 observed that around Cincinnati, "Farming people in Ohio work hard." But the reward for the prodigious effort was land ownership: if the family made the struggle, "in a few years, growing happy and contented, they will find it sweet to eat the bread of independence, procured by honest industry." The celebration of the climb to farm property ownership led to everyone singing hosannas about the act of labor, and this gave a decided coloration to travel literature. William Hancock in 1860 wrote that the "motto of the republic might very well be, 'Respect for labor.'" This sentiment was echoed continuously from the time of the Revolution to the Civil War. These exaltations were the American response to the European praise of aristocratic leisure—the two ideas, labor and leisure, were direct opposites, and by inference so were the societies. Advisers to would-be migrants from Europe to the United States made it clear: aristocrats, gentlemen, and tenant farmers (who only managed laborers) would fail miserably in the United States; only people accustomed to manual labor should cross the Atlantic. "It is no child's play to cut down American timber, or bring into cultivation the new land of the West," wrote one. Only those used to manual labor could survive in America; those with "*white hands*"—meaning those who did not perform manual labor—should not make the journey.[28]

The verbal crossfire comparing American rural society to British rural society involved one key component for the American egalitarian argument: the farm laborer. The base of (northern) American agriculture was family labor supplemented by the hired hand. The base of agriculture in Great Britain, the person who actually did the farming, was the wage-earning farm laborer, hired weekly. Laborers were managed by tenants who worked land that was owned by the gentry and aristocracy; the landowners did not farm, did not oversee operations, and merely collected rent, hence the appellation *rentiers*. No comparison between the two nations was more shocking, more revealing of the contrast between equality and inequality, than that between the farm laborers of Great Britain and those of America. The United States had, by the census of 1860, 2,423,895 farmers and 795,679 farmworkers; Great Britain, according to its 1851 census, had 285,936 farms (or, as a crude estimate, farmers who were the sum of landlords, tenants, and owner-occupiers) and 1.461 million in the category of "agricultural labor, farm servant, and shepherd." When one considers only those who owned land in Great Britain by excising the tenant farmers, the number of landowners drops to between 50,000 and 100,000. Thus the comparison: the propertied owner-occupier characterized American agriculture; the propertyless wage worker characterized British agriculture.[29]

Comparison of factory workers in England with those in the United States has not generated in American historians any sense of awesome material differences between the two, as the general interpretation is that misery and deprivation stalked factory workers whether in England or the United States. The same cannot be said for farmworkers, for the difference between the two groups was stark. It was also well known. British farmworkers had earned a reputation for actually living at the subsistence level and never being able to climb out of it. But the foreign traveler's characterization of the northern American farmworker was one who, depending on the author, labored two to ten years, saved some money, slowly bought land, started a family, and finally became an owner-occupier. A report by an English commission *(written in 1879)* studying the agricultural depression starting in 1874 put forth a telling summary of the key difference between Great Britain and the United States: "The farm laborer can hardly be said to exist as a distinct class in the United States, unless it be among the colored people in the Middle and Southern States." And this report was written nearly twenty years after the start of the American Civil War.[30]

Americans were aware of the extremes of wealth and poverty in rural England and of the desperation of the British farmworker. The peripatetic Frederick Law Olmsted visited England in the 1850s and took time to investigate farmworkers; he talked to one who could not read or write, did not know his age, worked for 7 *s* per week (at $0.25 per 1 shilling, $1.75 per week), had one hog, ate dry bread and cheese for supper, and had parish charity pay his rent. "The laborers in this part of England [Hereford, Monmouth, Gloucester, and Wiltshire]," he wrote, "were the most degraded, poor, stupid, brutal, and licentious that we saw in the kingdom." Olmsted implied that the English farmworker was not responsible for his own fate but was degraded by the system of farm ownership: "God keep us evermore free from a 'powerful conservative landed gentry,' a curse not unmixed with good though it be."[31]

The source that had a widespread circulation in antebellum America was Henry Colman, the editor of the respected *New England Farmer*. Colman traveled to England to report on its advanced agriculture in the 1840s and he produced a two-volume work. After spending pages on production techniques and the wealth of aristocrats, he turned to the disturbing class system of English agriculture—the three classes, lord, tenant, and laborer—that "strike a visitor from the United States with much force." He then described the miserable condition of the English farmworker; "in no case, under the best exertions," he explained, "can they make, from the wages of labor, any thing like a provision for their old age and decay." Their children were destined to live the same existence, and the fate of old age was to depend on parish charity for survival. Colman made the comparison: "With us the laborer always is, or always may be, the owner of the house in which he lives, and of as much land as he chooses to cultivate," but the English laborer "is doomed to remain in the condition in which he is born—he cannot rise above it."[32]

Both Olmsted and Colman completed the intellectual loop by explaining the difference in the fate of agricultural labor in Britain and the United States in terms of an equality/inequality analysis. At the end of his description of the English farm laborer, Olmsted related that a London minister said the poor always existed and should be served by charity rather than by legislation, for charity held the classes together whereas legislation to aid the poor was blasphemous. Wrote Olmsted, "In America we hold that a slave, a savage, a child, a maniac, and a condemned criminal, are each and all born—equally with us, with our President, or with the Queen of England, free and self-governing; that they have the same natural rights as us." Colman also responded with the creed of equality; he declared that he was strongly attached to "the great principles of universal liberty as the birthright of every man, and of social equality as conformable to nature, and the only relation in which men can stand to their Creator, or under which they would dare to approach him [*sic*]." In short, the poverty of the English agricultural worker was unnatural and due to some violation of the doctrine of equality. And neither Olmsted nor Colman was the most vociferous advocate of equality in the United States.[33]

Anthony Trollope, the son of Frances Trollope, was a novelist who journeyed to the United States in 1861 after the start of the Civil War to view its society. He largely, but not always, softened his mother's disdain. At one point he gave testimony to the impact that education and small farming was having on the personality of northerners. He met a farmer near Milwaukee and visited him and his family. He "astonishes you by the extent of his knowledge." "He is dirty and perhaps squalid," Trollope continued; "his wife is pale, and you think you see shortness of life written in the faces of all the family. But over and above it all there is an independence which sits gracefully on their shoulders, and teaches you at the first glance that the man has a right to assume himself to be your equal."[34]

This was not the analysis the foreign visitors gave of cities in the United States. The interesting facet about European commentary on American cities was that as American cities grew in size, the travelers saw urban America as a copy of urban Europe; the seeming universal generalization was that urbanization produced identical social conditions wherever it took place. As early as 1794, English immigrant Thomas Cooper noted the rural-urban difference and stated that society in Boston, New York, Philadelphia, and Baltimore was "much the same" as in Birmingham, Bristol, Liverpool, and Manchester. In 1906, over a century later, the British writer Frederic Harrison said the same thing: "American life [in the great cities] . . . is essentially the same as our own."[35]

The travelers expected large cities to contain poverty and crime. Wrote John Palmer in 1818, "In a large city there always will be poverty and prostitution: where extreme poverty exists it is in unfortunate old age, helpless women, or from idleness and drunkenness." It was in the cities that observers saw "destitute homeless wretches lying in bulks . . . about the markets of New York and Philadelphia." Isaac Holmes in 1823 gave advice to emigrants to stay away from American cities, which had social conditions not much different from those in English cities.[36]

European visitors, unless they were specifically interested in agriculture, went from city to city, or at least from city to town. They traced out an urban itinerary, and until the 1850s they found American cities dull and uninteresting—except for the disgraceful habits of the citizens. Baltimore was "aristocratic"; Robert Russell said Pittsburgh was a "dirty town" that competed with Lancashire for smoke. In 1860, William Hancock called Cincinnati "about the dullest place for a stranger to have to pass a winter in, in the Union." Frederick Marryat, no admirer of American things, called St. Louis "the nearest to the Black Hole of Calcutta of any city I have sojourned in," while another critic, Thomas Hamilton, declared in 1834, "Philadelphia is mediocrity personified in brick and mortar."[37] Charles MacKay jotted down in his travelogue that he had arrived at "the little dingy, dull city of Wheeling." William Faux declared that in Charleston the alligators and the people had about the same morals. Boston usually drew good reviews, although visitors could not decide whether it was aristocratic or republican. Boston was something of an oddity, however; it entranced visitors because it and the New England area reminded British travelers so much of old England—which certainly testified to the standard they set for judging the United States: to wit, how much it resembled England.[38] Isabella Bird decided that there was "*less* difference between Edinburgh and Boston, than between Boston and Chicago."[39]

And then there was New York City. The Atlantic voyage normally deposited European visitors in New York, and thus reactions to the city abounded in the pages of the visitors. Of the good things about New York, nearly all agreed that it lacked the paupers and beggars that plagued European cities, though everyone was noticing by the 1840s the Irish slum of Five Points. One good aspect of the city in comparison to London was that it lacked London's thick black smog. The coal used by the English for heating was bituminous while the Americans had access to the cleaner-burning anthracite. In addition, and rare among the commentaries, New York did not have the prostitutes that were so prevalent in Europe. Robert W. Russell gave more of an explanation than most. He ascribed the smaller number of prostitutes in New York—he did say there were some—to republican laws of equality, which enabled people to live decently without having to resort to criminality and bodily debasement. But in England, when a member of the upper class saw a pretty working-class woman, he swooped down and offered her a position of kept woman to take her out of her poverty.[40]

Alfred Bunn, writing in the 1850s, decided that New York City was less American than any other city in the Union because of the number of immigrants. It also housed American millionaires and was the "city on a hill" for inequality. The antislavery antidemocrat James Stirling knew that the wealthy in the cities would soon override the masses; as his example of wealth in the United States he used financial speculator Jacob Little, who bought his "lady" a lace gown for $20,000. Matilda Houstoun entitled a chapter on the city the "Aristocracy in New York," while Isabella Bird saw dwellings in the city that had "magnificence"; she said the best society in New York was equal to the best in England.[41]

That the countryside was egalitarian in America, while the city was inegalitarian, was the "exceptionalism" that distinguished American northern states from Europe. Throughout Europe, but especially in Great Britain, the great landlords ruled and flooded the land with demands for servility and obsequious behavior from the other inhabitants—and because they controlled the means of production (ownership of the earth), they typically got what they demanded. The American (and Canadian) countryside was markedly the opposite of the European countryside. The extent of family farm ownership created the ideal of American democracy and gave reality to the claim of equality, just as cities (and southern slaveholding) demonstrated the hypocrisy of the claim. Foreign visitors noted the reversal. Charles Lyell wrote that the great difference between the United States and England was that democracy drew its strength from the countryside while the cities evoked conservatism; the reverse was the case in England, where democracy resided in the cities and rank Toryism came from the rural areas. James Stirling derided universal suffrage for England because it could only produce misrule. But in the United States it could work because in the North there was "an independent, property-holding yeomanry" who served as a barrier to "proletarians" in the city. "It is only in the larger cities and manufacturing districts that the proletarian populace has a dangerous predominance."[42]

Many of the British wayfarers in the United States mapped out the future of the republic, basically outlining its declension from equality to inequality, from democracy to aristocracy. Eventually the population would swell and the population density of the country would resemble that of England. American society would then have the impoverishment of a large enough proportion of people to justify employing miserably paid workers in manufacturing. From that would come class hostility between labor and capital just as had been the case in England. And the rural population would eventually give way to a dominant urban population. While some saw industry as the route by which American inequality would grow, others argued that it was in the cities where aristocratic wealth accumulated. Soon the wealthy would have big enough hoards to start fretting over an attack by the people using universal suffrage to implement the passage of agrarian laws. Thus the rich would commence the struggle to restrict the suffrage to the propertied. And then the aristocratic emotion would take over the wealthy: they would desire to have the family preserve wealth over the generations, and so institute the laws of inheritance that would freeze the holding of wealth in a few families. The aristocracy would then become formal and subvert all the republican institutions of the United States, and equality before the law would come to an end.[43]

Let it be noted that the scenario of subverting the American Revolution was to come from a concentration of wealth; that excessive wealth would lead the people who possessed it to fear their poorer neighbors and try to eliminate them as threats to their hoards. In the end, it was not virtue that ruled the passions of the wealthiest of people, it was ownership of property.

8

DIFFERENT PATHS

The United States and Great Britain, 1865–1920

After the Civil War, the economic and social trajectories of the United States and Great Britain diverged. Increasingly Britain encountered agricultural problems, and the predominance of the aristocracy came under attack; along with this assault came a questioning of the value of inequality. The United States, however, started its path to world economic preeminence. For a time, that preeminence included both agriculture and manufacturing. As the United States lurched into industrialization, however, new social problems arose and became more obvious; class hostilities became visible. Interestingly, the foreign visitors to the nation, reduced in number, were not quite ready to admit that the American love affair with equality had outlived its time; rather, they testified to its persistence.

THE NATURE OF TOURISM

Works on the United States by European travelers would decline after the American Civil War. That fall in interest may have had something to do with the war's settling the question of the stability of republics, but much of it had to do with the nature of British adventurers going abroad. They were attracted to the new, the spectacular, the unexplored. Between 1815 and 1860, there had been a simple cadence in the itinerary of British sojourners traveling in the United States. They of course examined that anomaly of the republic, slaveholding. Some wanted to look at the international competition in agriculture and possibly in manufacturing. But the overwhelming number took a distinct route in viewing the United States. They landed in

New York City, made all kinds of observations about hotels, race, the Irish, manners, and the like; they went en masse up the Hudson River (by steamboat and later railroad) to Albany; then they followed the Mohawk Valley to Rochester; and finally they came to one of the spectacular sights of North America, Niagara Falls. A trip to the United States without seeing and then writing about Niagara Falls was simply unthinkable.[1] While the wayfarers wanted to describe the plains, the rivers, and methods of agriculture, they also made no mistake about what they were missing: "True there are in that great republic no ruins of arches, and towers, and mighty palaces, . . . no grim castles perched on rocky heights, . . . no gloomy cathedrals, or brilliant courts, or regal thrones." The travelers wanted monuments and extraordinary sights; they were accustomed to seeing them in European cities. American cities prior to the Civil War were a great disappointment. In 1832 Simon Ferrall had written there was little reason to go to the United States because there was little to see; America was "little better than a mere forest."[2]

What happened after the Civil War was that foreign attention drifted away from the American rural landscape east of the Mississippi River and went to California and the Rocky Mountains. In search of the exotic, British tourists started writing about journeys into the American Far West and then Australia. It was not that rural America was forgotten, but it was no longer a central theme in foreign visitors' writing. Increasingly the itinerary also was from one city to another in search of monuments, interesting architecture, and urban entertainments.[3]

Comments about the United States, its government, and its people changed fairly dramatically from the hostile commentary of the 1830s. The witty but cutting remarks of Frances Trollope, Frederick Marryat, Basil Hall, and others were specifically rejected as unfair. Instead, the writers after 1840 painted a new picture of the republic.[4] Gone were the differences between the United States and Great Britain; the similarities were stressed. Much emphasis had earlier been laid on political institutional divergences between the two lands, but even from the beginning, writers noted that the law, language, and general attitudes and customs (save deference) were nearly identical. Whereas Frances Trollope said the main reason to visit the United States was to be more contented with life in England, scores of writers instead argued that what they saw, in the phrasing of Frederick Jobson, was "so substantially English." Edward Freeman commented in

1883 that "the United States did not seem a foreign country; it was simply England with a difference." James Dixon in 1849 admitted that the whole British dialogue about the United States revolved around the "vexed question of republicanism," but he ignored that aspect to generalize that the United States contained "*in substance,* the institutions of England."[5]

Part of the ongoing reconciliation was abandoning the emphasis on the institutional differences between universal manhood suffrage and a constitutional monarchy. Many came to the conclusion that whatever merits or demerits democracy had, the system oddly suited the Americans best, but in no way could England ever adopt such a mode of politics. Indeed, it was the fixed opinion of the visitors that neither side understood the other politically: "Americans generally, really know as little what British monarchy is, as the people of England know of American republicanism."[6] Some visitors were quite willing to admit the Americans had a case for revolution in 1776. In 1856, Robert Playfair decided it was time for everyone to get over the American Revolution as it was now in a distant past. Lady Stuart-Wortley called the British of the 1770s "stupid" in their treatment of colonial Americans. In 1901, Andrew Iredale told of going to Bunker Hill: "I cannot say that my national pride was offended by these memorials of an event which was brought about by the political stupidity of the English Government." William Hardman discussed his trip to the United States and on the first page expressed sadness that England had lost what became the United States due to "the folly and mismanagement of its rulers a century ago." Interestingly, he decided to view the Declaration of Independence and found out that no one knew where it was. He finally located it at the State Department.[7]

An irritant that often confronted British travelers, certainly one that was frequently commented on, was American boasting. Isabella Bird made an incisive mockery of what she believed was American arrogance: "'We're a great people, the greatest nation on the face of the earth.'"[8] But one of the reasons the British were becoming reconciled to the United States, despite its democratic politics, was American economic growth. By the late 1840s it was undeniable that the economic prospects of the country were as vast as the continent in which it dwelled. John Bristed in 1818 noted how large the United States was and called it a "mighty empire, covering in greater extent of territory than all Europe," while in 1861 Henry Ashworth wrote about the "MAGNITUDE OF THE COUNTRY." Charles MacKay thought the United

States should, like Europe, fragment into numerous separate countries. In 1888 James H. Bridge recounted that Texas was as large as England, France, and Germany combined, while in 1879 George Campbell marveled that the United States was "not one England, but forty Englands." As to resources, Archibald Prentice recalled the fact unearthed by Charles Lyell that the coal field in Illinois and Indiana was not much inferior in size to *"the whole of England."*[9]

Matilda Houstoun in 1850 penned an older fear about the United States and its resources: she did not like the idea of the United States "rising triumphant on our ashes."[10] That perspective was being drowned out by a striking sense of ethnic solidarity. Instead of seeing the growth of the United States in agriculture, manufacturing, and commerce as a competitor to Great Britain, the British travelers felt part of a grand Anglo-Saxon adventure. England was part of America's success. The onward march of American civilization—deadly though it was to Native Americans—was the "onward march of the Anglo-Saxon with the rifle, and steam, and commerce." Charles Weld visited the United States to "see that marvelous Anglo-Saxon offshoot of our little island." W. E. Baxter had doubts about US expansion, and yet the nation was fulfilling the "mission of the Anglo-Saxon race." In 1873, Julius George Medley wrote that the British should be proud of the nation that the United States had become because it had been built "on the basis of English laws, customs, religious and political ideas," so "who does not feel that he too has a share in that goodly heritage?"[11]

One might surmise from some of this praise for the Americans being ancestrally derived from the English that the British visitors considered themselves part of the American economic expansion and that it was still being directed by England. In short, the United States was still a colony but one that had a somewhat bizarre political form and improper social customs. In some ways, such an attitude made sense, as the United States was the investment opportunity, especially the railroads, that many British wealth-holders took advantage of. London was the financial capital of the world, and the greatest consumer of British manufactured goods was the American republic. During the last quarter of the nineteenth century, many American daughters of millionaires married English nobility. Perhaps England could have continued to rule the United States as a colonial outpost economically if it had not committed the folly of entering World War I. After World War I, the financial capital of the world became New

York City, and with that transition, the status of the United States as being a British colony came to an end.

AMERICAN EQUALITY AND INEQUALITY, 1865–1914

In the years after the Civil War, British tourists continued to come to the United States. They found the climate barely sufferable, were appalled by the flatness of the Plains, held the small mountains of the Appalachian chain to be insignificant, continued to marvel at Niagara Falls, but were very interested in California and the Rocky Mountains. The debate over aristocracy and democracy, over equality and inequality, continued on much the same terms that it had in the first half of the nineteenth century, but now the discourse was leavened with recognition of the economic might of the republic.[12]

The ideal of American equality still impressed British visitors in the half-century after the Civil War, even though the growth of the wealthy had become obvious. In 1867, John Walter walked about the palatial homes of New York City: “So much for the equality of condition among the citizens of the Great Republic, about which DeTocqueville descants so eloquently.” Baron Charles Russell decided that “it is clear that in this country of so-called equality, one thing that most strongly recommended the Pullman was the fact that it enabled the rich to create the clearest possible inequality in the conditions of even ordinary travel.” James Bryce, who wrote one of the most noted commentaries on the United States at the end of the nineteenth century, produced an extended commentary on equality. He found Europeans were continuing to believe Tocqueville, and while there was equality of politics and education, there was no equality of material condition. The nation had evolved into one with great fortunes and a poverty class, though the (undefined) middle class was well off and “much larger than in the great countries of Europe.”[13]

While many agreed with the skeptics about American equality, many did not. Joseph Hatton in 1881 decided that though the Americans might deprecate the equality in their society, “it appears to Englishmen very real,“ while Lepel Griffin three years later argued that equality was “the monomania of an entire nation.” Even in 1912, the voyager George Smart held that the “American refuses to think of other men as politically superior,” and that attitude “affects all other fields, and no one is allowed to assume superiority to others in the great mass of American life.” Into the twentieth century,

Americans—the English generalization—continued to sneer at the idea of aristocracy. Foster Zincke detailed how Americans disliked the concept of "privileged classes": Americans conceived of aristocracy as "a ridiculous institution, for it assumes a superiority which . . . is impossible [to] exist; and it is an unjust institution, because it degrades the great bulk of society, by putting them in an inferior position."[14]

The British wayfarers found equality in social customs. Rudyard Kipling was in San Francisco and recorded his annoyance at the lack of service at a hotel; the clerk talked to others and whistled for attention—"These performances, I gather, are to impress upon you that he is a free man and your equal." In the 1880s Lepel Griffin wrote that "equality is a bitter pill to swallow," and he found it outrageous that in farmhouses in the West, the landowners "were compelled to take their meals with the farm labourers . . . all were socially equal." In his account published in 1909, Alexander Francis remarked, as had earlier visitors, on the "genuine" politeness of Americans, and decided that the "distinguishing feature of American life" was "that to every person respect, and to all persons equal respect, is shown"; this made the United States a democracy "in fact as well as in name." Frederic Harrison in 1906 again wrote about how Americans disliked "domestic service" and he noted, with accuracy on the question of race, that Americans overreacted to European society by "this ingrained sense of the absolute equality of all white citizens." William Hardman found American theaters "democratic" because, unlike those in London, there were no private viewing booths (stalls); the theaters in America were the result of the "general equality of station and fortune among Americans." In 1897 George W. Steevens went into a town in the Great Lakes area to the home of a manager of a large dairy supply factory; he lived next to a blacksmith "and upon my life I could see no vital difference between the outward aspect of the two." Foster Zincke even held that "republicanism" had seeped into the family because he thought the children had more independence and equality than England's progeny, and when sons grew up they became more like companions to their fathers than dependents.[15]

Some of the travelers tried to explain the benefits of hereditary aristocracy by reference to the American example. Julius Medley instructed readers that the perspective of family over the centuries taught youth to associate with others in the same rank in a communal bond that brought out the best qualities of human activity. Moreover, the aristocratic elite was above money-making, office-seeking, and other pedestrian activities; its members created an intellectual class that rose above the common and vulgar aspects of life. The real benefit he saw to republicanism in American life was the absence of paupers, which he believed justified American republicanism. Most Americans had little experience with aristocracy and only had an ideological dislike of it, and to some extent could consider it quaint. However, when Americans got a taste of actual aristocracy amongst them in the arrival of several English aristocrats who bought huge tracts of land in the Plains states for hunting purposes, they reacted with disgust.[16]

One of the more interesting writers about the postbellum United States was Lepel Griffin. His purpose was to denounce democracy and to warn the English of its evils, and in his quest he earnestly defended personal servitude. He bewailed the loss of the patriarchal ideal in America, that the lessers had lost respect for the masters. In England, the relations between servant and master were "mutually respectful." The two did not collide but moved in parallel paths. Moreover, the master-and-servant relationship "underlies every social" aspect of a nation; it provides social stability, gives traditions, and rears a cultivated leadership. Griffin's portrayal of servants and masters certainly showed how in England the institution of domestic servitude had evolved into a more gentle and polished condition than the crudities that had marked its past.[17]

If there was one constant in British views of America during the Gilded Age and after, it was the abhorrence of American politics. Universal manhood suffrage was a disaster, now made worse because of the immigration wave sweeping over the United States from central and eastern Europe. Aristocracy made for reasoned debate and polite discourse over turbulent topics. Julius Medley said aristocracy made politics in England "respectable and honourable." James Bryce's lengthy volumes on the United States were largely devoted to recording the horrors of machine politics and political corruption. The archconservative Lepel Griffin recorded his repugnance at the democratic vista when listening to James Russell Lowell, then an ambassador to Great Britain, give a lecture on American democracy. Lowell had said that in a democracy every man has a chance for a higher position and knows it: "a man can climb from a coal pit to the highest position for which he is fitted." Griffin decided that Lowell had just defined democracy as that "form of Government in which a man can climb from a coal pit to the highest position for which he is most unfit."

Others were less contentious, and argued that England and the United States in politics were actually more alike than different. William Archer in 1900 affirmed that the American president was "much more effectively the Ruler of America than the Queen is the Ruler of England"; Americans, he added, needed to be corrected in their belief that they "have a monopoly on democracy." George T. Smart in a book published in 1912 related the differences in the political systems of the United States and Great Britain but then downplayed them. As for the insistence that aristocratic control of government produced wise policy, he related an adage about the House of Lords: "The cure for admiring the House of Lords was to go and look at it." The same applied to American politics. The cure for outrageous praise for democracy was to observe an American political party convention "where mediocrity and philistinism carry the day."[18]

Where was equality in the United States? It was not in the cities. John Walter wrote, "If it exists anywhere, it is in the rural districts, and not in the great towns, where talent and enterprise assert their superiority and find their reward even more quickly than in England." The English transplant editor, E. L. Godkin, noted this in 1887. The classes in the American city were following the "old European model, divided largely into two classes, the one great capitalists, the other day laborers, living from hand to mouth." Emily Faithful wrote that America was supposed to contain "perfect equality," but every city had the equivalent of an aristocracy. In the cities were societal dividing lines that separated people as distinctly as "the aristocrat from the peasant in the Old World." Frederic Harrison in 1906 decided that throughout the Western world, the large cities were ever the same; "for my part I noticed no radical difference between Americans and Englishmen." Even in the countryside, visitors found country mansions.[19]

Historians have not lately written much on agricultural America between 1865 and 1912. They have been entranced with industrialization, urbanization, and labor turmoil.[20] This was not the case with some British wayfarers. Rural America still commanded some attention, and there they found equality.

The hallmark of the United States after the Civil War was its agriculture in the North, and its character remained egalitarian. It was still a land of owner-occupiers, of "yeomen, and those on a magnificent scale." Travelers from their railroad windows saw the landscape dotted with small farms and no castles, no landlord mansions, and no hovels. "Every 100 or

150 acres belong to a separate proprietor (large estates being unknown)," wrote Foster Zincke, "who has his house upon his small farm, which [he] cultivates with his own hands and the assistance of his family." This was where the wealth of the nation lay, Zincke decided. It was in the countryside, determined Edward Freeman, that the United States most differed from England. In a discussion comparing English workers to American workers, James Brydges in 1888 emphasized that by a ratio of three to one American workers were agriculturalists rather than manufacturing laborers. To get a grasp of the actual nature of American life, wrote George Campbell in a sanguinary type of explanation, consider if in Scotland "you were to kill off all the country gentlemen, with all their wives and families, and make the farmers the owners of the land which they till, you would have something which you could hardly distinguish from America." As before, travelers in the post–Civil War era talked about how labor and energy on the land would earn a person independence and competency but not luxury.[21]

Discussion about American farm life, except in the South, did not change much in the postbellum decades. The ideal was the family farm on which the owner did manual labor himself. No class of farmworkers existed because farmworkers continued to climb the ladder to farm ownership. As in the early nineteenth century, writers warned migrants to stay away from cities; if they went to farms they had to possess stamina and physical strength to succeed. Indeed, even Canada resorted to the same appeals Americans made when it came to acquiring migrants for agriculture. In 1880, the Province of Ontario published a handbook for immigrants, and it stressed how, unlike in England, a farmer owned his land, agricultural workers received high wages, there "was no primogeniture to work injustice," and Ontario had free schools, "no State Church," and was "preeminently the land of self-government." The reaction against the huge estate agriculture of England transcended national boundaries in North America.[22]

Even though most foreign travelers reviled political democracy, they nonetheless admitted that their aristocratic homelands had some very real defects in comparison to the nonpolitical aspects of society based on principles of equality. A few rethought the question of leisure and the disdain for manual labor. The belittling of labor explicit in the aristocratic ethos had a chilling effect on a nation's performance. Julius George Medley wondered whether it was not time to give up on that code; too many young aristocratic sons had become useless "by that foolish pride which teaches them that manual labour is degrading." In the newer countries, by which he meant Great Britain's colonies, "there is not the same prejudice against manual occupations that exists with ourselves; there is greater respect paid to the dignity of labor."[23]

British wayfarers continued to note the lack of deference in spite of the developing plutocratic aristocracy in the cities. Alexander Francis in the twentieth century admitted that he at times resented some individuals acting with familiarity when they seemed to be from an "inferior" class; class deference might be acceptable in other countries but not in the United States. Americans operated with a "genuine" and "common politeness" to all. Foster Zincke stated that people in the republic "measure others much more fairly than we do." One displeased with the lack of deference was "Edward Money," who decided that "The maxim in America seems to be that every man is as good as his neighbor, or better." Still, as visitors in the first half of the nineteenth century noticed, the lower class acted civilly: "Though every one spoke without diffidence,"wrote Newman Hall, "there was no rudeness or vulgarity."[24]

A continuing matter of interest was the fate of a land with no established religion. Reverend Newman Hall found it odd that religion remained strong in the United States "without the compulsory interference of the State." In a book published in 1870, "two gentlemen" found the religious question the most interesting to Europeans; the United States had no established church but it had become the most religious of all nations. James Macaulay added that in Europe the belief was that without an established church there was bound to be low religious feeling; but "there could not be a greater mistake." Julius Medley had a prejudice for an established church, but from his visit he saw "no ill consequences resulting from the want of it in the States."[25]

After the Civil War, British sojourners in the republic commented, with apprehension, on the impact of public education. The proportion of literate citizens in the United States far surpassed that in England, and the economic effects began to be frequently noticed. The Reverend Newman Hall, in a trip to St. Louis in 1867, was surprised at the knowledge of American farmers: "Men of the roughest exterior, of the class we might call 'clod-hoppers,' and from whom one would expect no coherent reply to any question on matters beyond the daily toils and necessities of life, were discussing domestic and foreign politics with great astuteness, and were prompt to reply with rough but ready courtesy and intelligence to inquiries respecting, not only the agriculture, but the manufactures and general state of the country." When George Steevens visited Wisconsin and South Dakota, he noted that at "every turn this average farm displayed that combination of ingenuity and desire to avoid trouble which is known as labour-saving, and from which the English farmer might take a useful example." Foster Zincke ascribed the common education of the country to the plentitude of small farms and the equality it produced; he had also made a comparison, common in the post–Civil War period, between "our stolid type [of farmer]" and the "keen American type."[26]

Britishers commented regularly on the extent of education in the United States and the pervasive reading habits of the people.[27] Julius Medley noted the pervasiveness of the schools but doubted they maintained high standards; the education was "too utilitarian and the pupils leave too early." Moreover, they read inferior newspapers. Nonetheless, it was public education, paid for by taxes. Joseph Wright picked up the philosophy behind the public support for education: "If on the one hand, every citizen in a free state of society has a right to a voice in the affairs of government, so on the other hand society has the right to require that each one of its members shall be qualified for an intelligent expression on those affairs." Thus, one got public education funded by taxes. However, it was the economic impact that caught the visitors' eye. In 1851, James F. W. Johnston commented on the need for public education where all were voters, but added that even at that early date, when England was the undisputed leader in agriculture, the ignorance of the farm laborers was hindering English agriculture. The "wild man" of British journalism, William Thomas Stead, wrote in 1901 that the United States was destined to outstrip all the other nations economically because of education. The nation was at least thirty years in advance of the United Kingdom, which had only begun compulsory public education in 1870. Some English people believed that education ruined the worker with inappropriate aspirations for higher positions. Stead believed that in the United States, education was considered "a boon, a necessity of life," and quoted Richard Cobden saying that the United States because of its educational system was destined to become "the most powerful people in the world."[28]

In the contest between equality and inequality, between democracy and aristocracy, one other subject cropped up all the time in the British travelers' accounts of the United States: the subject of "energy." Americans were a "go-ahead" people, the "most enterprising people in the world." The United States was proof that commoners had talent and could earn a fair reward; Americans had a "*natural desire to rise,*" they were an energetic people.[29] It showed up in business hours; in 1906 Frederick Harrison wrote that Americans got to their office by 7:00 a.m.; in European banking, it was 10:00 or 11:00 a.m. So what was the source of this energy that seemingly marked them off so clearly from Europeans? For James Bridge, something happened when Europeans set foot in North America, they became overly competitive and the result was "selfishness is supreme."[30] Others ascribed the energy to a republican form of government that offered equal laws and made no invidious distinctions between people and gave government privileges to all. David McCrae decided that enterprise was "stimulated further by republican institutions," and all avenues were "*open* to the humblest."[31]

But in the understanding of the mainsprings of a people's energy, the emphasis was placed on the hindrances of inequality, which sapped the will of the people to achieve their aspirations. No one put this more strongly than Robert W. Russell in 1848. Aristocracy scorned public education, monopolized local government, and robbed the masses of "all sense of personal dignity, and [they became] cringing and servile." Moreover, the inequality fostered by aristocracy was allied to a monopoly of government offices and a monopoly of landholdings. William Ouseley earlier had pointed out that inequality produced a "disgusting and contemptible vulgarity; . . . an abject worship of rank and wealth that debases the lower orders." Even Lord Brougham admitted that aristocratic preferment had a deadening impact on aspiration. While England did not prevent commoners from achieving wealth, they still "are in this most important particular, worse off than hereditary patricians—they have to make their way—to win their spurs; the others start on a [advantaged] vantage ground—they are born spurred."[32]

In this discussion, one viewpoint was vital. The point of practical difference between equality and inequality was the reward for work, or more specifically, wages. The aristocratic inequality attitude held that people were naturally indolent and did not want to work, and only by pressing commoners close to the point of starvation were they motivated to put forth effort. In short, monetary incentives meant nothing for common people; they only responded, like beasts, to the immediate need for food. Equality demanded high wages. Americans were energetic because of high wages, because they knew they could advance (at least in rural America) to farm ownership via savings, because they knew the fruits of their labors would go to themselves and not be leeched off by a supposedly superior class. The result of egalitarian institutions was energy and movement; the result of inequality—so obvious in the English agricultural laborer—was torpor and inertia.[33]

William T. Stead explained American enterprise and energy not in terms of the market or a strange cultural trait of the Americans; he found it in the embrace of democratic, egalitarian ideals and the rejection of the inegalitarian premises of aristocracy. He gave his 1901 book the frightening title of *The Americanization of the World,* but probably meant by it the triumph of equality over inequality rather than an American economic takeover of the planet. First, the ideal of equality in a democracy might not give excellent government, but it "energizes a people," makes them all active. He wrote that aristocracies, because of their class bias, did not really develop the human potential of citizenship: "They effectively paralyze that consciousness of individual power which gives so great and constant a stimulus to the energy and self-respect of the citizens of the Republic."[34] In economic terms, equality drew forth the best efforts of everyone, whereas inequality suppressed a commoner's belief in his or her ability to achieve.[35]

Another powerful appeal of equality was the suppression of class animosities. Aristocracy was supposed to inspire people to imitate their superiors, to give people a model to emulate. For some it probably did; for the majority it evoked resentment, envy, and class hatred. In all the nineteenth-century depictions British travelers made of the United States, a constant observation was the civility and good conduct of the American lower class, especially when compared to the British lower class. The reason for that civil behavior was ascribed to equality. In fact, the turn of the British Isles away from aristocratic governance to democratic governance was probably due to the problem of civility more than any other. Inequality was producing in Great Britain a divided society in which people loathed one another and did not cooperate. Such a society was slowly descending into class war.[36]

In the midst of finding positive qualities of American democracy and the Declaration's creed of equality, British travelers were not blind to fundamental changes in American society and its economy. Americans suffered immense strikes during these years (the Great Railroad strike of 1877, the Haymarket Square riot, the Pullman strike, the Homestead strike, and western mining strikes). Concurrently, American business was organizing into a new corporate structure of immense size, as in the Standard Oil Corporation. Agriculture continued to be a dominant force in the economy, but in terms of wealth, investment, income, and employment, manufacturing was outstripping the agrarians. Rural America was slowly yielding its preeminence to urban America.[37]

The British wayfarers saw other problems. The fate of the Irish in the United States continued to be a problem, and they noted as well the racism of the republic; it was still indeed the "white" republic, and the equality that resided there was for whites only. Not a few discussed the residual sectional resentment that lingered for years after the Civil War. The British writers also picked up a new theme: the influx of immigrants from non–western European nations. This phenomenon was tied to the dangers of universal manhood suffrage as a threat to the republic. Although they may not have clearly seen this, the new immigration wave of 1885–1914 composed of central and eastern Europeans would fundamentally change the society of the United States by effectively diminishing its Anglo-Saxon character and introducing diversity for the first time (it would later in the 1930s and 1940s be called pluralism).[38]

But the changes associated with corporate industrialism caught their eye, even as they spoke about the egalitarian legacies of the American Revolution. On the eve of the First World War, George T. Smart saw the spreading factory population in America afflicted "with physical and moral weakness," and while George Campbell in 1879 lauded the American yeoman he nonetheless knew that "the plutocrats, the money people, are quite as strong in America as in this country—perhaps stronger." Several mentioned the rise of the "labor" question, and James Bryce summarized that "unrestricted competition has shown its dark side: great corporations have been more powerful than in Britain, and more inclined to abuse their power." Where this was all heading no one was quite willing to say, but in earlier days it had been predicted that pools of wealth were the breeding grounds of aristocracy.[39]

THE ALLURE OF INEQUALITY IN GREAT BRITAIN FADES

Inequality supposedly was so inbred into the British character, said its major statesmen, that no repudiation of it was possible. Lord Brougham stated in 1843, "The notion of equality, or anything approaching to equality, among the different members of any community, is altogether wild and fantastic."

Richard Cobden told an American interviewer that democracy was not the fate of the British Isles: "the British Government was essentially Aristocratic in its character, and the People gloried in it as such." (To which the interviewer, Warren Isham, added that "the conviction was everywhere forced upon me, that the Government of the country was instituted and upheld for the benefit of the few, at the expense of the many.") Walter Bagehot in 1867 defended the British parliamentary system against the American presidential system, and in so doing he defended the House of Lords because they would impose on the people's "quiescent imaginations what would not otherwise be there." William Ewart Gladstone, intermittent prime minister who exchanged the post with Benjamin Disraeli in the years after 1866, explained the difference between the United States and England as the result of a heritage of the Puritans in one, the triumph of the Cavaliers in the other. Because of the triumph of the aristocracy in England by 1660, he wrote, "inequality lies imbedded in the very base of the [English] social structure." By the 1890s Herbert Spencer was warning of the wealth-distribution fantasies of socialism (which was democracy taken to its agrarian law extreme), and, though the private property system created some "immense inequalities of means," nonetheless the system worked better than any other. He added what amounted to be the aristocratic assessment of the worker: "Speaking broadly, every man works that he may avoid suffering. Here, remembrance of the pangs of hunger prompts him." In this vein, various writers admonished Great Britain to abjure democracy; W. E. H. Lecky, the respected late nineteenth-century historian, warned about democracy, specifically American democracy, and its deleterious impact on human liberty—the usual refuge for aristocratic opponents of universal manhood suffrage. "Equality is the idol of democracy," he wrote, but "inequality is certain to ensue."[40]

But the British zenith of popular belief in aristocracy was around 1850. The Crimean War destroyed, it appears, some of its presumed invincibility in wisdom and disinterestedness. However, the particular aristocratic form of society in Great Britain was failing on many fronts, most especially economically.

The existence of great estates led to the conclusion that the British agricultural sector was falling into a monopolistic condition, and by classical economics monopoly produced the few rich and the multitudinous poor. Reformers started grumping. John Bright said the kingdom was owned by 30,000 landlords, and John Stuart Mill was at the head of a Land Tenure

Reform League. In response to these forebodings, Parliament authorized the Registrar's Office to take the 1871 census and determine the land ownership pattern in Great Britain. The results were published in 1873 and referred to as the second Doomsday Book; the numbers have been massaged by economists and historians ever since, but the essential story they told was of a massive concentration of land in a few hands.[41] It was hardly any wonder that Henry George was celebrated by English reformers when he visited England in the 1880s and peddled his panacea of the single tax, a tax designed to break up the monopoly on land.

Many in England and America thought they knew the reason land ownership had become so concentrated in Great Britain: the laws of entail (strict settlement) and primogeniture. Those laws enabled the estates to remain together over time and, when smaller farms ran into financial difficulty, the estates were able to buy them out and thereby to grow continuously. Thus one found the explanation for the disappearance of the peasant and yeoman: they were ruined by the large estate. Independent proprietors and peasants were transformed into wage-earning farmworkers. Americans in the late nineteenth century were certain that the great estates, and therefore great inequality, came from entail and primogeniture.[42]

Most now believe the British aristocracy did not suffer collapse until the second decade of the twentieth century, but its problems multiplied after 1860, most of them tied to landowning and to the economy. The state of rural society became a concern. Many Britons were disturbed about the disappearance of the yeoman farmer. Then, the farmworkers' condition seemed unusually degraded; by parliamentary investigation, the shocking condition of the wage-earning farmworker had become known. In 1872, disgruntled agricultural workers, led by Joseph Arch, formed the National Agricultural Labourer's Union, although it only lasted about four years. Americans were well aware of these agricultural movements in Britain. Arch visited the United States, and the American press continued to detail the inequalities that marred rural England. Because of these social problems, the issues of rent and landownership came under scrutiny.[43]

In the midst of the growing agitation over the concentration of land ownership, the aristocracy and gentry suffered an economic downturn. Beginning in 1874, England entered the "great depression," which lasted over two decades. During those years, Great Britain faced intense agricultural competition from the wheat-producing Baltic nations and the American prairies. The rural areas depopulated; in 1851, Great Britain had 2.1 million people in agriculture; by 1901 the number was down to 1.5 million. For the aristocracy and gentry, however, the key fact was the decline in income from rents. Rental income dropped, it has been estimated, by 25 percent.[44]

At the same time the aristocracy faced economic hardships, the basic premise of their existence was being questioned—the rationale for inequality. The essayist, poet, and literary critic Matthew Arnold wrote in 1878 one of the most insightful nineteenth-century analyses of the demerits of inequality. He was not concerned with "equality before the law" because "we all take [it] as a matter of course"; he was concerned with "social equality." Arnold had no desire to import American standards of equality—he wanted the intellectual refinement that he believed only inequality could bring—but he found the inequality practiced by the English to be so extreme it endangered a civilized life: "our inequality materializes our upper class, vulgarizes our middle, brutalizes our lower." What was wrong was that inequality divided a society and set its classes against each other so that life was characterized by continual conflict instead of harmony. Arnold basically traced British class hostility to the great landed estates that dominated rural Britain, and he singled out primogeniture and strict settlement as the legal devices responsible for the condition. His solution was rather mild: alter the laws of inheritance.[45]

Arnold made a noteworthy argument about the Declaration of Independence. Like most Englishmen, he rejected the doctrine that "all men are created equal" as well as the concept of natural rights. What was interesting was the twist he gave to the idea that individual duties and privileges originated in society, not nature. Opponents of natural rights, such as Edmund Burke in England and John C. Calhoun in the United States, relied on the argument that rights or social liberties were given by a society to its members as needed to secure stability, harmony, and property rights. Thus one justified aristocracy and slavery as the social inequality needed to create a stable society. Arnold took the idea and showed how the idea of privileges given by society could be used to undermine property rights and undo a class structure. "If it is the sound English doctrine that all rights are created by law and are based on expediency," he wrote, "and are alterable as the public advantage may require, certainly that orthodox doctrine is mine. Property is created and maintained by law." And when property concentrated in vast estates became detrimental to national welfare, the doctrine of expediency allowed the state to retract or redefine property rights. True, inequality was inevitable: "But that the power of disposal [i.e., the transfer of property to others as in inheritance] should be practically *unlimited,* that the inequality should be *enormous,* or that the degree of inequality admitted at one time should be admitted *always*—this is by no means certain." Whether the right of inheritance should be limited or not "is one of expediency." Arnold was no wild-eyed reformer, and he retreated from his egalitarian stand in the 1880s as the land question grew more vexing, but it is interesting that he used the social framework of Burkean conservatives and slaveholders to justify essentially a redistribution of property on the grounds that extreme inequality produced a society too rancorous to fulfill the ideals of a civilized life.

Arnold used comic relief to discuss primogeniture and entail/strict settlement by referring to the inheritance customs of the United States. It "is notorious," he wrote, that Americans did not have great landed estates. A British citizen told an American that Americans could do by their laws exactly what the British accomplished by primogeniture and strict settlement; so if a person did try to transmit the entire estate to the eldest male, what could a person do? "The American answered, 'Set aside the will on the ground of insanity.'"[46]

In 1885, an incisive critique of the English aristocracy came from the pen of an American diplomat, Adam Badeau. Badeau simply blasted away all the talk of liberty, all the intellectual pretensions, and all the grace that supporters of aristocracy ascribed to the system. He delineated the absurd attention given at state functions to proper ordering by social rank; the rules that aristocrats and their servants followed were full of "labyrinthine mysteries" that Americans invariably trespassed. The liberty that aristocrats so loudly trumpeted, Badeau found, was merely a license to be rude: "They have no need, they think, to defer, with equals or inferiors. They can gratify their minds, or their whims, be amiable or disagreeable, or indifferent as they please." What mystified Badeau was the deference that the rest of British society gave to the aristocracy; the servility shown to aristocrats was "incomprehensible to an American." Indeed, in one simple phrase he summed up the difference between the two societies: "In England everybody looks up." In the United States, nobody looked up to anyone else.

Badeau detailed the wealth of the English aristocracy, the number of servants employed, the role of inheritance laws, and the condition of life in the countryside. The social cost of maintaining an aristocracy he found in the life of the agricultural laborer: "They [farm laborers] never save; they have insufficient food"; they were "dwarvish, their gait slow and sluggish, like their minds. They have no education. Their only pleasure is drink. Above all, they have no possibility of bettering themselves. But it is upon their poverty, degradation, and misery that the grandeur and luxury of the aristocracy are founded, one is the direct cause of the other."[47]

And of course the aristocratic system was at its most vulnerable on the subject of heredity—it operated by the mechanism of family inheritance. One defender of aristocracy, Sir Henry Maine, tried to argue that people doubted rule by birth when they lost their religious faith—an argument that by 1885 had little resonance with anyone. To say that "rule of the best" should be the standard and not "rule of the worst" is simply commonsensical; but what has rule by the best to do with families over time? Talent is an individual trait, not a family trait. Because equality lets talent rise by a person's ability, it is more likely to bring out the best than family preferment, which by its very nature must exclude a host of talented people. It is for this reason that aristocracy was always connected with "privilege."[48]

As the nineteenth century was closing, many understood that the days of aristocracy were numbered and that democratic forms of government, with their attendant if ambiguous notions of equality, were advancing. Within the British empire itself this fact was becoming obvious. In 1897, Britain held in London the Diamond Jubilee in celebration of Queen Victoria's sixtieth year on the throne; all the colonies sent their premiers and honor guards to the festival. The American special representative was Whitelaw Reid. After observing the statesmen the colonies sent to the imperial center, Reid declared them to be "downright Yankees." When the reporter William Stead asked him to explain, Reid responded:

> What I mean is that these men are not in the least like British Ministers or any of your English politicians. Their point of view is American. Their political ideas are the same as ours. They are loyal to the Queen, no doubt, but that is a thing apart. In their work-a-day politics they are as Republican as ourselves. They start from the same principles, they reason in the same way, and they arrive at the same conclusions. Not one of them would tolerate a House of Lords in his own colony, or an Established Church. . . . In talking to them [colonial representatives] I am never conscious of that break of gauge which I constantly feel in talking to a British statesman.

Stead agreed that the English overseas did not replicate English institutions. The colonists, Stead wrote, gave their allegiances to the descendants of George III, "but all . . . frame their Constitution on the principles of George Washington." The equality principle in the Declaration of Independence was winning.[49]

The final victory over the bastion of hereditary privilege and inequality took decades to consummate. The reform acts of 1832 and 1867 did not much faze the aristocracy and the gentry, but the third reform act of 1884–1885 and the County Councils Act of 1888 took away for the first time their undisputed sway in local government. Parliament also tinkered with the strict settlement laws and rights of tenants. In 1894 under Lord Harcourt, "Death Duties" were introduced in a mild way to fix some budget deficiencies and to equalize taxes on land with taxes on personalty. All this was a prelude to the great constitutional battle of 1909–1911 when Lloyd George produced a budget that increased taxes on land and inheritance; the House of Lords started a confrontation that led to its virtual elimination as a force in British legislation. The political power of the great landowners was falling apart. The final blow came after World War I. Possession of land had lost its charms, and a huge land sale occurred in Great Britain between 1919 and 1925; one-fourth of England's land, between six and eight million acres, was sold. Not all the great estates collapsed, but many of the middling ones (3,000–10,000 acres) did. In place of the peers and gentry came a rising tide of owner-occupiers.[50]

Seemingly, equality had won the one and one-quarter centuries' war between the United States and Great Britain, and the light of equality had evaporated the dark spectre of inequality. But some shadows are impervious to the light of day.

CONCLUSION

The Revival of the Aristocratic Ethos

Great Britain followed a path of enhanced democratization in the twentieth century, the path having its smooth parts and its bumpy ones. The Labour Party added a socialist flavor to the democratic surge, although by the end of the twentieth century the socialist agenda had fairly well been abandoned. Equality may have scored some victories in the realm of public policy, but its advance in personal relations is questionable. The aristocracy, shorn of its political power, remained intact, and the monarchy continued as a symbol of the realm; both became economically important to Great Britain because they became tourist attractions for foreign visitors. Nonetheless, deference still plays a role in British social life.[1]

In the first four decades of the twentieth century, people in the United States had a struggle with the democratic form of governance. Throughout the nineteenth century, there had always been a vocal element in the nation who found universal manhood suffrage distressing and who feared that minority rights could be trampled by the majority. The minority rights they most fretted about were property rights. The uninstructed masses, especially those of immigrant origins, had been improperly trained in observance of property rights and could elect demagogues who might devise agrarian laws, though by 1900 the word *agrarian* in "agrarian laws" had been displaced by the word *socialist.* The last two decades of the nineteenth century had seen a surge in the fortunes of the richest Americans as well as the rise of gigantic corporations such as the United States Steel Corporation and Standard Oil Trust Company. Those who found themselves with riches that European monarchs could only envy had no truck with a political system that could disturb their piles of wealth. Paul Elmer More wrote *Aristocracy and Justice* at this time and commented, "To the civilized man *the rights of property are more important than the right to life.*" The prominent public figure Nicholas Murray Butler in 1915 attacked equality because it meant that the inefficient deserved the same reward as the efficient. Historian Roland Stromberg, in discussing the ideal of democracy, noted that most intellectuals since the Enlightenment could not favor such a system because "the test of truth cannot be popularity," and later added, "Nobody who is sure of the truth will think it sensible to leave it to an election." In the early republic, liberty and equality marched together hand in hand; after 1880, various American writers saw liberty and equality as totally antagonistic. Edward Bellamy, a novelist denouncing the rise of American fortunes, described correctly how the wealthy won the public forum: "It was in the name of individual liberty, industrial freedom, and individual initiative that the economic government of the country was surrendered to the capitalists."[2]

The democratic ideal of equality was not abandoned, especially not by historians. They recognized the achievement of creating self-government without an aristocracy and the equality that seemed to characterize the northern states. They celebrated the history of the United States for taking a distinct turn away from the old European practices of governance and class separation. Much of what they wrote could be tied to the recognition that the North was the land of small farms. There had indeed been established a yeoman democracy. For the historians between 1900 and 1950, the American record was the triumph of democracy and equality. Thus one got Charles Wiltse writing about Thomas Jefferson and American democracy, and Merle Curti discussing the rise of egalitarianism. Carl Fish labeled his 1927 book *The Rise of the Common Man,* while Henry Steele Commager put "the sense of equality" at the center of the "American Mind."[3]

Such scholars saw the Progressive Era and the New Deal as periods that sought to combat the new inequality of urban industrialism and reestablish the equality that had characterized the nineteenth-century rural North. These writers had no problem in locating the challenge to the democratic ideal: it was industrialism and the factory system, but not necessarily urbanization. By means of regulation and taxation, the progressives and New Dealers hoped to tame the industrial beast and reestablish equality in American life.[4]

But agriculture was losing its social, economic, and intellectual position to urban centers. The Populist crusade of the 1890s had shocked many middle-class urban dwellers for its embrace of unorthodox economic doctrines. At the same time it revealed distress on the farm. The isolation and crushing burden of manual labor in rural life came through in works like Hamlin Garland's *Main Traveled Roads.* It was not long before rural America came under the withering attack of writers like H. L. Mencken and Sinclair Lewis. Lewis, the first American to win a Nobel Prize for Literature, wrote the novel *Main Street,* in which he depicted the intellectual barrenness and even mendacity of the rural towns of the Midwest. Then in the 1920s the conflict between the urban and rural areas broke into the open. The cities were multiethnic, immigrant, and non-Protestant; they contained museums, libraries, zoos, and universities; they had professional sports and amusements galore; they allowed people more personal independence. The rural areas were Protestant, often Anglo-Saxon, frequently intolerant, and boring. Whereas visitors in the nineteenth century were enthralled by the American rural landscape of small farms and small towns lacking castles and run-down hovels, American writers in the twentieth century were disgusted with its uniformity, conformity, and intellectual deadness. While nineteenth-century visitors saw the egalitarian qualities of rural life, people in the twentieth saw only unrelenting labor, stifling mental orthodoxy, and intolerance. The twentieth-century writers had simply lost the wonderment of finding equality in an unequal world, a wonderment that had overwhelmed European visitors decades before.

The battle lines for cultural supremacy were drawn, and by 1932 the urban areas had won. They also won in the historical arena. Arthur M. Schlesinger Sr. wrote one of the first forays into urban history, deserting what had been the emphasis on rural America. Afterward, Richard Hofstadter pilloried the idea of the "yeoman farmer," and termed the being in reality a businessman who cared little for the land. Grant McConnell best described the evolution of the country in his book *The Decline of Agrarian Democracy.*[5]

In this transition of attention from rural America to urban America, the ideal of equality got damaged. The cities stood for many social values, but one value was conspicuously absent: equality. As European travelers endlessly repeated in the nineteenth century, American cities were simply copies of European cities, and all European cities were massive conglomerations of poor people, some middling elements, and a small elite at the top. How to create equality in urban areas was a challenge that Americans did not consider in the nineteenth century. Equality in the rural areas was easier to conceptualize: simply stop land monopoly. Nonetheless, it would be an obvious result of the new historical fascination with urban areas that inequality would become the dominant theme, and the equality found in northern farm areas would be simply dismissed, discarded, or discredited.

Thus starting in the 1960s, the wave of the "new" histories came to focus on cities and the factory, thereby emphasizing inequalities among the citizenry and making them the hallmark of American life, utterly ignoring the egalitarianism of northern family farm agriculture. In labor studies the emphasis was on class differentiation between factory owners and factory laborers. In women's studies, authors detailed the limitations women faced in every endeavor of American life, and almost all of the studies were of northern urban women. In ethnic studies, the study of slavery made stark the racism and violence white Americans employed to gain fortunes; Native Americans were deprived of their lands in what could almost be called ethnic cleansing. And then there was the discriminatory treatment of the immigrant Irish. If one took these studies and figured matters out quantitatively, then out of an adult population of about 15 million in 1860, American democracy and equality at best only affected about 6.5 million, and that does not include the impact of class, which then probably would have reduced the number down to less than 3 million. Certainly this was not much of an economic or a political democracy, and the equality was tightly circumscribed.[6]

This evolution of historical writing had the effect of erasing equality from the American experience. It went further. American equality became the great hypocrisy because so much of the nation never had equality. Thus the American egalitarian tradition was ignored and left to rot in historical cellars. The critics of American equality are absolutely correct in its limitations and the failure of the founders and their ancestors to live up to the universalisms they so eagerly gave voice to; they and their successors in the nineteenth century were guilty of a murderous ethnocentrism. But the critics are incorrect to ignore what was accomplished: even if restricted to northern family farms and the harshness of life thereon, the equality was an important part of the experiment, one that enabled dozens of foreigners to find a reality that was a practical alternative to aristocracy, inequality, and mass poverty. And this difference between a social system of equality versus one based on inequality was not an intellectual debate; the comparison was between two societies that actually existed.

RISE OF MODERN AMERICAN CONSERVATISM

I have extensively quoted nineteenth-century British travelers and some American historians to drive home the point that foreigners described the United States as an experiment in egalitarianism, often portraying it with admiration and approval. The use of the extensive quoting is to impress upon the reader that this depiction was commonly used in regard to the United States after the Revolution and lasted until late in the nineteenth century. Many historians at this point would end their book and leave the reader to extrapolate the ideas presented about the nineteenth-century debate over equality to the current situation of the United States in the twenty-first century. *I will not* leave the extrapolations to the reader's imagination but will draw them out explicitly. This means that this section is distinctly enmeshed in current politics, and my political message is that the conservatism spawned in the last three decades of the twentieth century and which remains prominent in 2017 is the aristocratic principle reborn. And its new home is the United States.

Modern American conservatism comes from a number of sources, most of which were covered in the introduction of this book. Numerous wealthy businessmen and lawyers were outraged at the New Deal and have battled it ever since, funding a host of "research" institutions to trumpet their message of the glory of their fortunes being left alone. Another group entering the fray were southerners who could not let go of the heritage of slavery and race segregation; they used the cry of states' rights to keep in place the elites who control state politics so they might browbeat ethnic minorities without fear of federal intervention. Some became conservatives because they were upset at the peddling of immoral scenes by the publishing and movie industries. The immigration of intellectuals from central and eastern Europe also brought numerous individuals who distrusted the masses (that is, were hostile to democratic principles) and favored elite rule. Added to this was the development of microeconomics, an academic endeavor that attempted to demonstrate by mathematical theorems that uncoerced choices by individuals produced better economic outcomes than government interventions. Indeed, for a subset of these economists, government was the enemy, a position eagerly seconded and then advocated by various political philosophers.[7]

The post–World War II conservatives called for a return to the unregulated free market, known in the nineteenth century as the ideal of laissez-faire. The historical oddity of the advocates of laissez-faire becoming the architects of the new aristocracy deserves a note. In nineteenth-century Great Britain, the advocates of laissez-faire (John Bright, Richard Cobden, John Stuart Mill) were considered the enemies of aristocracy because the inequality that the aristocracy prized had a political foundation—people were aristocrats by law, by order of the state. What has come to pass, however, is that aristocracy does not need the exercise of a brutal power of the state, only a subtle one—basically it is the right of extraordinarily rich people to be left alone, and they justify their position by the alleged inviolability of the right to private property. The right to private property that sustains an aristocracy now, as has been argued throughout the ages, is that an individual's right to his or her property, no matter its extent or nature, is (and was) absolute and never to be invaded by the society or government without the property holder's consent. The right to private property is fundamental to market economics, and it is widely admitted that such a right necessitates inequality. To advocate laissez-faire economics, therefore, is equivalent to advocating inequality. Thus, when it comes to the question of equality and inequality, modern advocates of laissez-faire are distinctly on the aristocratic side of the fence. The famed progenitors that the current denouncers of equality agree with are not Thomas Jefferson and George Mason, but John C. Calhoun and George Fitzhugh—the defenders of slavery—as well as Edmund Burke and Lord Acton—the defenders of aristocracy.[8]

The second icon among the current conservative movement is Edmund Burke, who was largely absent in American writing and oratory in the nineteenth century. The conservatives who have championed him are not necessarily free marketeers; they believe elitists ought to run the country so that the right morality gets propagated. The person most known for resuscitating Burke's philosophy, especially the centrality of worshipping God, was Russell Kirk. Likewise, Melvin E. Bradford went to lengths to show that the American Revolution was about upholding Burke's ideas about the rights of Englishmen, not about equality. Yet these authors keep their writing focused on Burke's abstractions and never look at the society he was defending. One may search through all the modern writings on Burke and never encounter the social misery on the great estates that his philosophy justified. Burke wrote in the 1790s when the great estates had formed and the misery of the farm laborer became more plentiful than the wheat harvest. But in the present renditions of Burke's philosophy, the fate of the farm laborer is ignored, which is to say that such writers elide the fate of the majority of the British citizenry.[9]

CONCLUSIONS

I offer these conclusions from the debate between Americans and the British over which social system produced better results, equality or inequality.

First: Why Is Equality A Desirable Goal? Equality Reduces Conflict and Provides For Liberty

The arguments for and against equality in the nineteenth century lead only to one conclusion, one derived from experience: equality produced a more harmonious society in which people learned to respect other individuals' humanity. This reduced the conflict between income classes. Moreover, equality evoked a more vigorous, active society because the general sense that no group existed to squash individual talents led people to be more optimistic about their chances to achieve their goals. In other words, equality gave meaning to the word *liberty*—it became not merely a slogan used to justify class stratification but imparted to individuals the belief that they could act, could exercise their liberty. Equality produced a social environment that made liberty meaningful to the bulk of the (white, rural) population.

Modern conservatism dismisses the social environment in favor of dwelling entirely on the rights of the individual. Philosopher John Hospers wrote: "'Society' has no rights; only the individual has rights . . . there *is* no such entity as 'society'; there are only individual human beings."[10] However one wants to define society or the community in which one lives, the condition or status of that community will determine what individuals can achieve or not achieve. At the very least, community provides an overall social, political, and economic environment in which the individual acts, and the health of the environment will either aid or retard the individual's pursuit of his or her own goals. In this regard, the history of the equality-inequality debate between Britons and Americans speaks so loudly as to drown out the current scribbling of libertarians and conservatives on the subject of society and social rights. This is not an exercise in theoretical possibilities—trying to imagine life under egalitarian or inegalitarian assumptions—but a revelation of how the experience of humankind, that is, its history, actually played out: the egalitarian American northern rural community versus the inegalitarian British rural community. The result is absolutely clear and uncontestable: an inegalitarian community produced (and produces) incivility, disobedience to laws, and class hatred. An egalitarian community produced (and produces) a society of civility, obedience to laws, and a tolerance of income differences.

Indeed, the question of the social environment—whether society exists or not and has rights or duties—can be reduced to very practical terms. A harmonious society is one of uncoerced law obedience—people obey the law not because they fear punishments from a legal system but because they believe in the justness of their society and its laws. But if the nineteenth-century discussion of inequality and equality has any contribution to make to this subject, it is that equality produces bonds that hold people together without force, while inequality requires a powerful government to keep people in their place. It was admitted on all sides in aristocratic Europe in the nineteenth century: poor people would not obey the laws that the wealthy had laid down (all, of course, in the name of civilization), and so government force had to be used against them. Conservatives and libertarians are adamant that their strictures for a properly run society are universally true and no rational person should ever transgress them. When they find out that starving people will not obey their strictures, they demand a powerful state to coerce the lower class into submission. Conservatives cannot argue for civility and inequality at the same time, and given the history of conservatism and its resort to governmental force to keep the dispossessed in their place, they are far more likely to surrender their desires for limited, small government than to take measures to lessen the inequality that threatens societal dissolution.[11]

Second: Inequality's Foundation Is Wealth and Inheritance

This topic divides into three distinct parts. First, aristocracy in the nineteenth century stood for inequality as the natural and essential element of the human community, and its defenders left no doubt that the existence of aristocracy depended on vast accumulations of wealth and, as a by-product, the immiseration of the multitude. While the infant United States lacked the pools of capital and the population necessary to erect an aristocracy and an impoverished populace, British travelers had little trouble foreseeing the future and predicting that an aristocracy would arise because of wealth accumulation. "Many point to the accumulation of wealth," wrote Alexander Mackay in 1850, "as that which will work the change. It is quite true that some of the millionaires of America would have no objection to the establishment of a different order of things [like monarchy]." Mackay, however, thought the democratic sentiments of the people were too strong to be easily overcome. Others were not so convinced. All it took was great property being passed from generation to generation in the family line, for as Thomas Grattan said, "Aristocracies are built on the indestructible rights of property." Patrick Shirreff had some doubts about writers on the future of the American republic, but even he foretold the time when wealth would push the "natural aristocracy" of talent into creating a different government and society: "There cannot be a doubt that aristocracy, which is already deep-rooted and flourishing among the people, will, when aided by wealth and luxury, and their inseparable evils, destroy the Union."[12]

In the guise of microeconomics and the free market, all hailed under the name of liberty, modern conservativism is enabling an aristocracy to take shape. It is doing so by allowing massive pools of capital to arise, be left alone, and then be transmitted to progeny. Because of their sensitivity to possible attacks on their hoards, the aristocrats are drawn into politics and seek to steer public policy in a direction favorable to their interests—the same rationale, in fact, that the British aristocracy had for their role in politics. Eventually, the new American aristocracy, with or without titles, will manage to exclude the rest of society from lawmaking. This aristocratic tendency in the United States is being promoted and funded by the economic elite of the country, and they reveal their aristocracy in the multitude of behaviors, programs, and publications that mirror the ideals of the British aristocracy in the eighteenth and nineteenth centuries. At the heart of it all is the belief that inequality is good and must triumph over equality in every area of human life.

The second part connected to the topic of wealth and inheritance is the conservative ideal of property rights. Invading an individual's private property was tantamount to destroying an individual's liberty, as conservatives virtually equate the right to property with the existence of human liberty. In economic terms, government exactions on a person's property or income (i.e., taxes) amount to an act of redistribution of wealth and income, and the mere mention of the word redistribution elicits from conservatives a fierce cry of injustice.[13]

Either by invoking natural rights or conventional rights, modern conservatism claims that property rights are absolute and unconditional; the size of the holding does not matter. But there is a counter to the claim, and it involves the actual nature of the universe. The principle is that when extremes are encountered, the laws governing the universe change. In the physical world, the principle operates in this fashion. For human life, the gravitational laws of Isaac Newton predict everyday life almost perfectly. But when one goes to the extremes of physical existence, to the level of the electron on the one hand, and to stars having a mass ten times that of our sun on the other, reality simply changes. At the subatomic level, the laws of quantum physics take over and Newton's laws are totally inapplicable (one cannot predict the orbit of an electron using Newtonian laws as one can predict the movements of the planets); at the quantum level it is surmised that existence is wholly random. At the stellar level, large massive stars collapse into black holes in which the laws of Newton fail completely, and scientists cannot even imagine what exists within such phenomena.

In economics, extreme poverty and extreme wealth are like physics at the subatomic and stellar levels; reality changes. The particular reality that changes is the individual's outlook on the world. In the case of extreme poverty, the individual's only outlook is finding a means to survive. With survival at stake, all other rules of human interaction (i.e., morality) die. Incivility is the result and law disobedience becomes the rule, not the exception. If one wants a civil society, one will have to ensure that extreme poverty is eliminated. At the other end, extreme wealth will have the effect of magnifying a person's personality—all parts of it, the noble and the ignoble as well. Such people will tend to tyranny because they expect their orders to be obeyed, and opposition will evoke retaliation. Moreover, they become obsessed—possessed might be a better word—that their hoards might be invaded and taken from them, and therefore all other subjects, such as justice, equity, and reciprocity, have to be abandoned in order to protect their wealth from any hint of public duty or social obligation, let alone outright attack. As is becoming increasingly clear in the United States, people of extreme wealth can buy the political situation they want.

The inviolability of property rights might be appropriate for some limited amounts of property, but the doctrine if left unconditional is obviously capable of extraordinary abuse. One example: according to a report in the union newspaper *The Carpenter,* the Duke of "Southerland" in 1914 ejected 15,000 peasants from his land so he could construct a "hunting reserve." He could of course do so because the land was his private property. Political philosophers and economists stress the constructive use of property rights to advance material welfare, but we should not be blind to the other side of the coin.[14]

Moreover, extreme wealth defies the original rationales for low taxes, private property, and economic freedom. Most of these propositions came into existence to allow individuals to have a solid opportunity at living a comfortable existence; historically, even a low level of taxation could plunge many people into poverty. After all, the complaints about taxation originally came from peasants, tenant farmers, and yeoman farmers (such as the participants in Shays' Rebellion), and not from the wealthy. It is one thing in present terms to complain about a taxation rate of 20 percent when one earns $50,000 a year, and quite another to complain about it when one earns $10 million per year. The taxation rate in the first case plunges the person into a significantly lower standard of living; in the second case it does no such thing.

In justification of seeking a limit to great incomes by means of taxation, I will rely on the advice of the first Republican president, Abraham Lincoln. When Reverend Newman Hall of England traveled to the United States he visited Springfield, Illinois. There he was told that Abraham Lincoln once said that if he became a vice president, with William H. Seward as president, he would get a salary of $20,000, "and that is as much as any man ought to want."[15]

The third part of the topic of wealth producing inequality in aristocratic societies was the practice of inheritance. By keeping fortunes in their families over the centuries, those families became entrenched in politics, society, and the economy. Thomas Piketty's research has demonstrated how important inheritance was in the nineteenth century to the top 1 percent of British and French society. Moreover, he describes the means by which the exceedingly rich manage almost never to lose their hoards but instead augment them: they can afford to hire the ablest money managers available and take advantage of situations that people with less wealth never hear of, let alone are able to act upon.[16]

Within the present conservative movement are distinct trends toward establishing a pseudoaristocracy—an actual but untitled aristocracy. Among the George W. Bush tax cuts of 2002 was the elimination of the federal inheritance tax. The inheritance tax seems to be one of the policies in the crosshairs of conservative weaponry. To make the comparison between the British aristocracy and twenty-first-century American conservativism complete, the American conservatives have even used the British name for inheritance taxes—"death taxes" or "death duties." It was precisely the possibility of imposing an inheritance tax that led the aristocrats in the House of Lords to rebel in 1909–1911 because they knew that taxation was a means of breaking up the great estates—in reality, of destroying their monopoly of the land. Now the Americans have created exactly the same conditions that allow wealth to accumulate in families and to let those families through their wealth control the politics of the nation.

Inheritance represents a thorny issue for the libertarians, but not for cultural conservatives who see the family as the cornerstone of society anyway and have a disposition to favor elitism.[17] If one takes the dictum of Milton Friedman seriously, then the justification of capitalism is, "Payment in accordance with product has been, and, in large measure, still is, one of these accepted value judgments or institutions." How then can inheritance be justified, as it is the transmission of payment to a person who has produced no product? From the vantage point of European history, the danger of unlimited inheritance in a family over time should be clear enough: it will produce monopoly and political favoritism.[18]

Third: A High Wage Is the Path to Equality and Social Harmony

Two aspects of this question may be considered. In the nineteenth-century comparison between the rural equality of the United States versus the rural inequality of Great Britain, visitors made constant reference to the one condition that enabled equality to become a reality. It was high wages. High wages enabled social mobility in North America and reinforced the idea that common people could obtain property (farms) and enjoy a competence, if not luxury. The commentary was explicit: high wages enabled individuals to think a comfortable existence was a likely outcome and that society's rules benefited them. As the testimony of European travelers to the United States in the nineteenth century showed, low wages shrunk the human mind and extinguished the human spirit. The effect of low wages on the human psyche—on economic incentive—has evidently been as forgotten as the impact of high wages.[19] For equality to operate successfully, high wages are a necessity.[20]

Second, the fate of the poor is another topic that reminds one of the aristocratic outlook of today's conservative movement. The attitude that the poor deserved their fate was frequently expressed in the nineteenth century. Poverty, in the aristocratic worldview, was part of the natural order of things, a condition ordered by divinity, and no human intervention could change the divine ordinance. More bluntly, people on the top of the social order simply did not care. The only concern that the aristocracy then had was that the poor have no ability to disturb the social order.

Because of the Great Depression, poverty in the twentieth century was early understood as a crucial problem that required some solution. At the founding of the Mont Pelerin society it was agreed that "if unemployment and poverty, however, were the inevitable consequences of the competitive order, what should be the liberal [i.e., laissez-faire] response to poverty and to those who argued for greater equality of income?" While levels of income for all were not decided, "it was agreed; no democratic government would tolerate people starving, it was not politically realistic not to make some provision for the poor." The conservatives and libertarians at this meeting argued about this topic without coming to a consensus, some even approving some form of a welfare state.[21] However, the general mood of present conservatives seems to be that each person deserves his or her own fate; if a person is poor, that is that person's fault. In its more dreamlike state, social order for the conservative/libertarian camp comes when people in the bottom half of society realize that they belong in the bottom half and peacefully accept their fate.

The justification of poverty by insistence on the principle of inequality, however, and reference to the alleged moral/mental shortcomings of the impoverished, should be tempered and revised by the US northern family farm experience. The rural American North had people move with regularity from poverty (usually youthful) to farm ownership. It was a common experience. What accounted for this movement was not an individual's moral faculties; it was an environment that enabled people to become property holders via the path of high wages. High wages taught people the right behaviors for becoming productive citizens. The constant reference to poor people's bad habits of one kind or another is an aristocratic smokescreen to obscure the mechanism that enabled people to participate meaningfully in the economy and rise above poverty.

Fourth: Liberty without Equality Equals Tyranny

The cry of liberty has always been an aristocratic cry and at the same time a declaration for inequality. When the British aristocrats denounced the United States and warned about democracy and leveling, they based their claims on the threats to individual liberty that democracy (and hence equality) entailed.

But what exactly did the aristocratic banner of liberty mean for the population that was to live under aristocratic liberty? What did the aristocrats do with that liberty? Let us return to the comment of Adam Badeau in his 1885 assessment of the British nobility: The liberty that aristocrats so loudly trumpeted was merely a license to be rude: "They have no need, they think, to defer, with equals or inferiors. They can gratify their minds, or their whims, be amiable or disagreeable, or indifferent as they please." So it is upon this behavioral base that one can obtain Pareto optimality, fairness in bargaining, and the win-win scenario?[22]

To go into the writings of all types of modern conservatives, one becomes immersed in an ocean of screams for individual liberty. The culprits who reduce liberty are democrats with their doctrines of equality. Liberty was "the absence from our society of overwhelming concentrations of power," and the obvious concentration of power—the monopoly of armed force—was government. Libertarianism is based on the idea of individual liberty; David Bergland, a libertarian, emphasized "YOU OWN YOURSELF" and thus had freedom to act without anyone's permission, and David Boaz chimed in, "Libertarianism is the view that each person has the right to live his life in any way he chooses so long as he respects the equal rights of others." Whether they recognize it or not, modern-day libertarians are simply reiterating the aristocratic denunciation of democracy and equality by elevating the ideal of liberty above all others.[23]

The guiding principle of libertarianism is basically a rewrite of the New Testament's Golden Rule of doing unto others as you would have them do unto you. Just as people flagrantly violate the Golden Rule of the New Testament, so they flagrantly violate the principle of recognizing the rights of others that libertarianism/conservatism calls for—their principle in many ways is as idealistic about human nature as the communist's belief that people want to share their goods with others ("to each according to their needs"). Moreover, the historical record is filled with such transgressions against the freedom principle. Who along with abolitionists were the greatest "liberty shriekers" in the antebellum United States? They were southern slaveholders. When American citizens and British colonists wanted Indian land, they stole it in the name of their liberty. When slavery ended in the United States, in a few decades race relations were governed by Jim Crow segregation. And the defense of Jim Crow was white individualism: a white person had the right to deny people of different skin colors equal treatment.

Without the word *equality,* liberty is a synonym for tyranny. One person's liberty to do whatever he or she wants without regard for others is equivalent to saying the others live under a tyranny. There are clear examples of this ongoing paradox. Friedrich von Hayek is a lion among conservative economists, a winner of the Nobel Prize, and an opponent of government interference with the marketplace. The part of his name "von" indicates a connection to an aristocratic family in Austria, and the resemblance between him and aristocracy does not stop there. He decided that his favorite idea of liberty was lodged in the works of Edmund Burke and Lord Acton, the would-be aristocrat and the actual aristocrat. Lord Acton decried democracy and praised liberty, and in 1866 he wrote a public letter to Confederate General Robert E. Lee thanking him for fighting the battle for liberty, and at the same time justified African slavery. He only retracted his defense of slavery when he found out that southerners did not give their slaves routine religious instruction, not because the slaves deserved liberty. In the aristocratic camp, liberty belonged to the few, not the many.[24]

Fifth: Education

It is impossible to read the travel accounts of British wayfarers to the United States in the nineteenth century without acknowledging the awe they had of tax-funded public education. Not only did they marvel at the widespread reading public, but also they realized that education was a silent but mighty force stimulating the American economy. Included within the commentary is the fact that those who favored inequality believed in education only for the elite; that the mass of humankind deserved their fate as hewers of wood and drawers of water, and for that they needed no education. The inegalitarians of the nineteenth century paid the price for their worship of public ignorance as economic development in the United States raced ahead of western Europe's.[25]

The aristocratic contempt for public education has now been revived by the modern libertarian/conservative movement. Once again American conservativism is mimicking aristocratic inequality. Milton Friedman has written, "Our school system is centralized and bureaucratic, because it's a governmental, socialist school system."[26] Since the conservative movement began vigorously around 1978 or so, the attack on the public school system has been relentless. Public funding has been cut mercilessly. The public universities have become nearly privatized. They survive only by raising tuition and student fees, cutting out the bottom half of American society. Increasingly the universities are becoming the preserves of rich children. All of this is wholly characteristic of the aristocratic impulse. University education is only for the leisured elite so they can become gentlemen; aristocrats hold that public money, which comes from taxes, is wasted on the common person. Moreover, just as the aristocrats of the eighteenth and nineteenth centuries did, rich Americans resort to private education and so have no real interest, they think, in educating other people's youth.

One cannot find a more shocking repudiation of the legacy of the nineteenth century than the current conservative rejection of public education. Even the aristocrats came to recognize that the economic power of the United States was coming from an educated society, and they realized as well that education had something to do with the civility they found in America. Aristocratic critics of American education pointed to a lack of refinement and an overemphasis on utilitarian purposes, but they were forced to acknowledge its success. On no other topic did the United States in the nineteenth century receive as much praise as it did for its public education. And the modern conservative movement has decided not to preserve this legacy but to squander it away in pursuit of private luxury.

Sixth Religion

Libertarianism has no intention of restitching the ties between church and state, but cultural conservatives do. Again, this is an aristocratic desire motivated by religion's usefulness in placating the populace and making them accept the status quo, the status quo of inequality. Advocates of establishing ties between churches and government should return to the commentary that British wayfarers made about the state of religion in their homeland—its torpor and political abuses.

Seventh The Failure of the Microeconomics Model

The old aristocracy of the eighteenth and nineteenth centuries did not worship the free market, did not lionize Adam Smith, and did not hold up businesspeople as models of heroism. The life of leisure that aristocrats pursued did not include absorption in business details. The modern conservative/libertarian reliance upon the free market economic model—the microeconomists' model—is a new addition to conservatism, even as it is used for aristocratic, inegalitarian ends. Although this book has little to offer in the way of commentary about free markets by aristocrats in the nineteenth century, still it is worthwhile to point out the deficiency in the model and how those who celebrate inequality can nonetheless declare a "win-win scenario" for all participants in a free market.

Conservatives and libertarians offer as an alternative to government decree—that is, the employment of force behind taxes and regulations—the operation of the market mechanism by which individuals choose without coercion (i.e., the condition of freedom) the goods and actions that most satisfy them. Because bargains are made without coercion in the marketplace, so the model predicts, all the participants always advance from their initial position because no one chooses an action that would result in a reduction of their happiness; thus one obtains Pareto optimality or the win-win scenario. Governments use the police power, or coercion; and the individual must buckle under no matter his or her preferences. In democracies, therefore, the majority forces the minorities into accepting outcomes they would never accept in a marketplace. This analysis is then extended to how democracy actually works. Because democracies allow the unpropertied access to political power, democracies necessarily must plunder the successful. The latter claim dates back to Cicero, and in the nineteenth century it was the major aristocratic argument against letting the mass of people vote.[27]

Among numerous problems with the exhortations against democracy and egalitarianism, a single one is the total dismissal of the social environment. First, if one takes a close look at microeconomics and its theoretical foundation, one finds what is missing is the social environment. It is not even made an assumption. The hidden assumptions are that people will not steal, will not kill, will confine their self-interest to the point where they will not damage others, will believe opportunity exists for them, and will not resent bargains that produce outrageously unbalanced outcomes (even if both sides improve their initial positions). One assumes that any modern society will have to have rule by law and a government strong enough to enforce rules. That condition is nowhere to be found in the microeconomists' models using marginal utility analysis (such as the work-leisure decision, effect of minimum wages, rent controls, and the like). Equality provides the social environment that makes the assumptions of the free marketeers work; inequality does not. Inequality instead invokes attitudes and behaviors that are the opposite of those assumed as "universal" qualities of humankind and upon which microeconomists build their models.[28]

The second problem confronting this denunciation of democracy is the one Abraham Lincoln posed: if the many do not rule, then the only alternative is that the few do. We are back to the aristocratic principle that only the leisured (i.e., wealthy) can conduct the affairs of state in accord with universal truths and individual justice. The short answer to that claim is the one the Americans gave in the early nineteenth century: the few always ruled in favor of themselves and never for the generality of the citizenry; the self-interest assumption of the economists will not be displaced by "virtue," virtue being the ideal descended from antiquity that political leaders should possess—the intellectual quality of being able to rise above self-interest and to rule for the general welfare. Finally, it might be added that government is about policies at a specific time that produce a healthy society, not about transcendent universal truths. Whether the effective rate of taxation should be 15 percent or 40 percent has no relation to natural law or the way the universe was designed.[29]

When these points are added up, we find the modern libertarian/conservative movement on the side of aristocracy and inequality. But as one observer after another flatly stated, the United States after the Revolution, with obvious blatant violations, was based on democracy and equality. That fact can only lead to the conclusion that the modern libertarian/conservative movement is a betrayal of the principles of the American Revolution.

FUZZY MATH AND THE AMERICAN PARADOX OF DEFINING EQUALITY

It is only fair that the author offer some conclusions about the meaning of equality after extended bouts with the historical and philosophical literature. The debate always has had a nebulous quality to it because definitions of equality have either been ludicrously extreme or ludicrously ambiguous. Indeed, one is impressed with how far apart on the issue authors are ideologically. The libertarians on the one hand find no good in government at all—calling for, in the extreme, privatization of police forces and road ownership—versus those who hail from a socialist position denouncing any economic inequality at all. One can hardly find more opposite views on the market than those of Milton Friedman, who saw the market producing religious and ethnic toleration and improvement in everything, and philosopher John Dunn who wrote that "The market economy is the most powerful mechanism for dismantling equality that humans have ever fashioned"; and he then added, the global free market is creating "the World Order of Egoism."[30]

None can doubt that the revolutions of central and eastern Europe in 1989 and the fall of the Soviet Union in 1991 have tarnished the political Left and have raised important questions about the type of structures that could promote equality without producing tyranny over all other aspects of life (that is, the extinguishment of civil liberties as well as economic ones). Whereas before, economic equality meant a narrow range of incomes for all citizens, and for a few absolute equality in incomes with no deviations at all, the collapse of communism caused a rethinking of what constituted equality. The result has been a journey into a mental wilderness (see introduction of this book). The Russian/Soviet historian Roy Medvedev offered this redefinition of equality for the socialist Left:

> Socialism, even the ideal conception of it, does not guarantee full equality of material possibilities or an equal position in society to everyone, because people differ individually. But socialism must, however, ensure substantial progress toward equality in the most important sense—equality of rights and obligations, just treatment of all, and equal opportunity for all to discover and develop their talents and abilities.

This definition of equality under socialism hardly differs from that of the Locofoco Democrats of Jacksonian America. All Medvedev could say of capitalism was that it produced "flagrant material inequality" and that excessive wealth and poverty had to be eliminated.[31]

I would offer the following summation about what "equality" has meant in the American past. First, equality meant equal treatment of others in social interaction, in political power, and in the rules of society: i.e., no privileged groups. Its major constraint was that such equality was limited to the male gender and descent from western Europeans. The late twentieth-century version has added that this idea of equality has to cut across gender, religious, and ethnic lines, an addition to the ideal that early Euro-Americans violated consistently.

As for economic equality, the nineteenth-century white majoritarian view of it was that equality did not have a mathematical definition; economic equality did not mean an absolute material equality among all citizens. Back then, Americans pioneered in the development of fuzzy math. There would be a spread of incomes, a range. What equality meant was that people were rewarded adequately for their work and talent, and the income range allowed people to develop the talents they had to the extent their talents would allow, and that such conditions produced a harmonious, civil society. However, the income had to be munificent enough to enable the individual to find citizenship worthwhile.

For almost all Americans, regardless of gender, ethnic, and religious division, an absolute equality in material life was unjust. For American society then, as well as now, the place between the hammer and the anvil for anyone arguing for absolute material equality is that virtually no person then or now would agree to the proposition that people with great talents and industriousness should obtain the same rewards as people with lesser talents and less industriousness.

The enduring American paradox in the definition of equality is this: Americans insist upon a general equality so they can develop to the fullest extent possible their unequal talents. This paradox is beyond resolution.

But people deserving great rewards for their talents and industry does not mean that people with few talents and less industry have to be economically punished, which is what the free market system does. The American idea of economic equality rests on the belief that an adequately formed economy not only allows the talented to rise, but enables common people to achieve a "good" standard of living, as defined by the conditions of the time period, by a common standard of dutiful labor, decent personal habits, and observance of citizenship rules. To put this another way, no person should have to live up to heroic standards of talent and industry to achieve a decent standard of living. It should be obvious to anyone that any nation's economy that only awards heroes means only a few achieve economic fulfillment while the many suffer deprivation; this outcome derives immediately from the fact that heroes are rare individuals, and nations are composed of masses of nonheroes. If one wants a civil society, then one has to have a better reward system than one that only bestows material plentitude on the few. The means of rewarding the many is through high wages.

To achieve the ends of a fair distribution of income, I would offer the following program: Social Security for the Young. It is based on the nineteenth-century practice that youth starting out in life required a patrimony and practical education. In northern farming communities, this consisted of high wages, family aid in starting a farm (in some states nearly a legal requirement), and basic education acquired from public schools and on-the-job training on the family farm. Because the United States is now so urban and this type of aid to youth is now impossible, I offer a substitute based on giving young people a "patrimony," that is, income, and demanding that the income be earned by attending school. Its basics consist of providing income to youth beginning at age 12, which reaches the sum of $2,000 per month by age 16. In return, the youth must attend school and achieve passing grades; they cannot until age 18 accept work outside of school. The income received ($24,000 per year per individual) would continue to age 24, at which time the stipends would end. Society thereby requires its youth to become educated and to learn the pathways of society; society gives youth an endowment (in nineteenth-century terms, a patrimony) to start adult life. Such a program would require that only two children per woman would be included and that immigrants would be excluded. Once the children reach age 24, they should be prepared economically to engage in a free market and be left to their own talents and abilities until age 66, when Social Security for the aged would kick in. The program thus has a symmetry to it; aiding people when they begin the life of freedom, and aiding people when the body starts to fail. As for cost, it could largely be financed by an inheritance tax, allowing an inheritor to receive a maximum of, say, $5 or $10 million, the rest to be turned over to the government. The government then would sell whatever assets the deceased had and use the funds to finance the program.[32]

In the course of researching and writing this book, and over the course of my academic career, I have come across two quotes which are favorites of mine and are applicable to this topic. The first comes from William Henry Seward, a political Whig, governor of New York in the 1840s, a US senator given to making inflammatory phrases that disguised his somewhat conservative nature, and secretary of state under Lincoln and then Andrew Johnson. Seward, an indefatigable schemer in politics, nonetheless had an intellectual quality that on occasion shone brightly. He lived at the time when slaves were property, and his battle against slavery and slave masters took the form of fighting the propertied class of the nation. To those libertarians and conservatives who are obsessed with property rights, his words serve as a stern but wise warning:

> Property is an essential element of civil society. So is liberty, which, properly understood, is only the equal security of all citizens against oppression. How to adjust the balance between property and liberty in States, is the great problem of government. Property is always jealous of enlarged liberty, and especially so when it is based on relations subversive of natural justice, which is nothing more than equality among men. Property, therefore, has always a bias towards oppression, and it derives power to oppress from its own nature, the watchfulness of its possessors, and the ease with which they can combine. Liberty is exposed to the danger of such oppression by the means of the inconsiderateness and the jealousies which habitually prevail among subjects or citizens. In every State, all the property classes sympathize with each other through the force of common instincts of fear, cupidity, and ambition, and are easily marshaled under the lead of one which becomes dominant, and represents the whole. Wherever the rights and duties of the property classes are defined and regulated, with sufficient constraints to prevent oppression, and liberty is at the same time so bounded as to secure property against social or individual aggression, there the people are free and the State is republican. Where this balance is not accurately adjusted, liberty is abridged, and a property class administers the Government, in the form of an aristocracy, or a monarchy, or a despotism.[33]

The second quote is from Henry A. Myers, a philosopher who took up the subject of equality after World War II. He gave a history of equality and then justified its existence, especially denouncing inequality because it ultimately relied on force to achieve its preeminence. But he wrote this striking line about Jefferson, the Revolution, and the meaning of the United States: “A nation established in the name of equality must keep the faith or lose its best excuse for being.”[34] Amen.

NOTES

ABBREVIATIONS

AER	*American Economic Review*
AgH	*Agricultural History*
AHR	*American Historical Review*
EHR	*Economic History Review*
JAH	*Journal of American History*
JEH	*Journal of Economic History*
JER	*Journal of the Early Republic*
JSH	*Journal of Southern History*
WMQ	*William and Mary Quarterly*

PREFACE

1. See remarks of David Cannadine, *Rise and Fall of Class in Britain,* 55.
2. I made this comment in Huston, *Securing the Fruits of Labor,* appendix, 394–406.

INTRODUCTION

1. Piketty, *Capital in the Twenty-First Century,* trans. Goldhammer, 257, 265, quotes 443.
2. Maxwell, *Income Inequality in the United States;* Levy, *Dollars and Dreams;* Osberg, *Economic Inequality in the United States;* Danziger and Gottschalk, eds., *Uneven Tides.* For examples of very recent work, Dorling, *Injustice;* Taibbi, *The Divide: American Injustice in the Age of the Wealth Gap;* Noah, *Great Divergence;* Stiglitz, *Price of Inequality.* See story of Piketty in *Bloomberg Business Week,* June 2–8, 2014, 42–47.
3. Jacobs and Skocpol, eds., *Inequality and American Democracy;* Phillips, *Politics of Rich and Poor;* Milne, *Politics, Wellbeing, and the Market;* Marshall, *Class, Citizenship, and Social Development;* Dahl, *On Political Equality.*

4. Rawls, *Theory of Justice.* For a short tour of Rawls's detailed presentation, which many see as a form of liberalism and social contract theory, consult Stanford Encyclopedia of Philosophy at www.plato.stanford.edu/entries/rawls/, accessed June 23, 2016. See Newman, *Liberalism at Wit's End,* and Daniel S. Jones, *Masters of the Universe,* for the histories of the rise of American libertarianism.

5. Nozick, *Anarchy, State, and Utopia,* ch. 7, 8; the Chamberlain illustration is on 161–63. On the Chamberlain example, Cohen, *Self-Ownership,* 4; Cohen, *On the Currency of* Egalitarian *Justice,* 126–27; Barbara Fried, "Wilt Chamberlain Revisited," 226–28. For an example of the exchanges, see Okun, *Equality and Efficiency;* and the selections in Colin D. Campbell, ed., *Income Redistribution.*

6. Knock, *Our Enemy, the State;* Stigler, *Economist as Preacher and Other Essays,* ch. 2, 3; Stigler, *Intellectual and the Market Place and Other Essays,* 85–89; Stigler, *Economist as Preacher and Other Essays,* 10–13; Friedman, *Capitalism and Freedom,* 161–76.

7. Barry, *Hayek's Social and Economic Philosophy,* 149. In general, see Waligorski, *Political Theory of Conservative Economics.*

8. Machan, *Capitalism and Individualism,* 20 (quote), 8–31–52; see also his *Moral Case for the Free Market Economy.* Norman Barry has written, "In twentieth-century liberalism and libertarianism the predominant intellectual tradition has been undoubtedly economics," and he also describes their attack on other disciplines as "economic imperialism"; Barry, *On Classical Liberalism and Libertarianism,* 44 (quote), 53 (quote), and 2–17. For an attack on the economic model now overriding all other considerations from a person on the Left, see Wendy Brown, *Undoing the Demos,* 9, 18–28, 31.

9. See Hospers, *Libertarianism;* Murray, *What It Means to Be a Libertarian;* Boaz, *Politics of Freedom;* Bergland, *Libertarianism in One Lesson.* Other political philosophers who emphasize personal freedom rather than economic efficiency would include Oakeshott, *Rationalism in Politics and Other Essays,* 40–55; Flathman, *Willful Liberalism,* 2; Machan, *Capitalism and Individualism,* ix–xiii.

10. On the implication of equality in democracy, Christano, *Constitution of Equality,* 1–2. For the attack on democracy, see Bovard, *Freedom in Chains,* 102–107, 129–36; Hayek, *Individualism and Economic Order,* 29–30; Gwartney and Wagner, "Public Choice and Constitutional Order," 50; Hospers, *Libertarianism;* Buchanan and Tullock, *Calculus of Consent;* Waligorski, *Political Theory of Conservative Economists,* 36–43.

11. Miller, *Market, State and Community,* 6; Berry, *Culture and Equality,* 3–4; Roemer, *General Theory of Exploitation and Class,* 2–6.

12. Nagel, *Equality and Partiality,* 99; Cohen, *Self-Ownership, Freedom, and Equality,* 2–7; Roemer, *Analytical Foundations of Marxian Economic Theory,* 12, 52, 158.

13. Dworkin, *Sovereign Virtue,* 1.

14. There is a considerable body of work done on the advantages of some over the disadvantages of others in a free market. For current examples, Haworth, *Anti-Libertarianism;* Miller, *Market, State, and Community;* Sunnstein, *Free Markets and Social Justice.* Piketty would add to the list the ability of the rich to get better investment advice than anyone else and the current manifestation of excessive salaries to "super-managers" of US corporations. Piketty, *Capital in the Twenty-First Century,* ch. 9, 12.

15. Sen, *Inequality Reexamined,* ix–x.

16. For these positions, see Roemer, "A Pragmatic Theory of Responsibility for the Egalitarian Planner," 146–48; Cohen, *On the Currency of Egalitarian Justice,* 13; Arneson, "Equality and Equal Opportunity for Welfare," 229–41; Dworkin, *Sovereign Virtue,* ch. 1; Scheffler, *Equality and Tradition,* 113–19. On "Luck Egalitarianism," see S. L. Hurley, *Justice, Luck, and Knowledge;* Elizabeth S. Anderson, "Against Luck Egalitarianism: What is the Point of Equality?" 154–85; Van Parijs, *Real Freedom for All;* essays in Reeve and Williams, eds., *Real Libertarianism Assessed.*

17. Sen, *Inequality Reexamined,* ix–x; Dworkin, *Sovereign Virtue,* 1; Devins and Douglas, "Introduction: The Pursuit of Equality," in Devins and Douglas, eds., *Redefining Equality,* 3; Verba and Orren, *Equality in America,* viii, 1.

18. Bradford was criticizing the work of Harry Jaffa, who praised Lincoln for his belief in equality through the concept of equal natural rights; Bradford, "Heresy of Equality," 62; see also Michael Walzer's comment in *Radical Principles,* 237–39.

19. Piketty, *Capital in the Twenty-First Century,* 347, 350.

20. Gawalt, "Drafting the Declaration," in Gerber, ed., *Declaration of Independence,* 6.

21. Maier, *American Scripture,* 135. For a recent interpretation stressing that the equality in the Declaration was meant to be taken literally, see Danielle Allen, *Our Declaration.* Patrick Griffin has also tried to recapture the sense that equality in the American founding, though limited to landed white men, nonetheless was a major change from the English setting; Griffin, *America's Revolution,* 218–19, 276–77. Michal Jan Rozbicki finds equality seeping into American life through the elite's need to delegitimize Great Britain and recruit allies on North American soil; it took time for the culture of deference of the eighteenth century to accept the ideal of equality. Rozbicki, *Culture and Liberty in the Age of the American Revolution,* 98–102, 119–30.

22. De Tocqueville, *Democracy in America,* ed. Goldhammer, vol. 1, introduction, 3, in general 3–15.

23. Berry, *Culture and Equality,* 3–14; Sterba, ed., *Ethics: The Big Questions,* part 4; Duggan, *Twilight of Equality,* xi–xvi; Schwartz, *Future of Democratic Equality,* viii–x. For an example of Marxist reaction to poststructuralism, see Wood and Fosters, ed., *In Defense of History.*

24. For examples, which are nearly infinite, see Wallerstein, *Modern World-System,* III: 234–36; Pole, *Pursuit of Equality;* Young and Nobles, *Whose American Revolution Was It,* 92–131, 156–66, 192–246; Weeks, *Farewell My Nation;* Drinnon, *Facing West;* Saxton, *Rise and Fall of the White Republic;* the various articles in Zakim and Kornblith, eds., *Capitalism Takes Command;* Allan Kulikoff, "Progress of Inequality," 375–412; Pessen, *Jacksonian America;* Pessen, *Riches, Class, and Power;* Nash, *Unknown American Revolution;* Johnson, *Shopkeeper's Millennium,* 5–33; Katz, Doucet, and Stern, *Social Organization of Early Industrial Capitalism;* Williamson and Lindert, *American Inequality,* 5, 21–57. Virtually all labor history written after 1962 stressed inequality; for just one example, Dawley, *Class and Community,* 1–6, 55. For a critique of this approach, Rozbicki, *Culture and Liberty,* 1–34.

25. Lovejoy, "Rights Imply Equality," 459; Temkin, *Inequality,* 3.

26. Walzer, *Spheres of Justice,* xiii; Scheffler, *Equality and Tradition,* 227; Lovett, *General Theory of Domination and Justice,* 119, 130 (quote), 195–99. See Christiano, "Argument for Democratic Equality," 39–68;. See Gaitlin and Jennings, *Perversion of Autonomy,* 85–87; Milne, *Politics, Wellbeing, and the Market,* xiii–xiv; Marshall, *Class, Citizenship, and Social Develop-*

ment, 77–106; Russell, *Authority and the Individual,* 1, 2, 12, 19–20, 54–57. On inequality, see Temkin, *Inequality,* 292–93. This is a version of the "cement of society" idea, which is examination of what forces hold a society together. Conservatives argue for tradition and the example of social superiors—and in dire times, the police state—while left-interventionist writers argue for equality or practices that minimize the alienation that citizens may have for others. See Elster, *Cement of Society,* 248–87.

27. G. A. Cohen wrote in 1995 that his idea of moral and political philosophy is "a standard academic one: they are ahistorical disciplines which use abstract philosophical reflection to study the nature and truth of normative judgements." Cohen, *Self-Ownership,* 1.

28. This point will be explored later. The actual point of discussion that dominated in the nineteenth century was the existence of inequality in one ethnic group. The idea that all ethnic groups were equal—modern-day notions of diversity—was practically nonexistent. Thus the discussion from twenty-first-century eyes was damaged because of the inability of white male Americans to include Native Americans, African Americans, Mexican-Americans, immigrant groups, women, and others in their ideal of equality, let alone allowing anything like cultural diversity.

CHAPTER ONE

1. Generally, I have followed the researches of the following scholars: on the Stoics, Peter Gay, *Enlightenment,* II: 407; on slavery in Aristotle and Plato, David Brion Davis, *Problem of Slavery in Western Culture,* 66–72, 89, 93–98, 292; Quentin Skinner, "Political Philosophy," 389–99, 403–407; Ellen Wood, *Liberty and Property,* 42–44, 260–61; Ellen Wood, *Citizens to Lords,* 14–60; Bendix, *Kings or People,* 3–10, 57, 96–105, 218–19, 229, and ch. 3; Walzer, *Revolution of the Saints;* Skinner, *Foundations of Modern Political Thought,* II: 12–19, 192–212; Zoll, *Reason or Rebellion,* 65–66. On the humanists, Israel, *Enlightenment Contested,* 5; Gay, *Enlightenment,* II: 455. The community ideals of liberty and equality can be found in Pocock, *Machiavellian Moment;* Gordon Wood, "History of Rights in Early America," 233–39. On Locke, Hutson, "Emergence of the Modern Concept of a Right in America," 40–41.

2. The debate over the Enlightenment will not be treated extensively here; only a few of the major arguments will be noted. Intellectual historians prior to 1960 tended to outline the major ideas of the thinkers and at times to ascribe large social movements to them. After 1960 came an attack on this interpretation of the Enlightenment because it was so exclusive; for example, the attack on slavery probably came more from religion than from the Enlightenment; David Brion Davis, *Problem of Slavery in Western Culture,* ch. 10, 11, 13, 14. In the hands of poststructuralists, especially the French school under Foucault, the universalisms produced by the Enlightenment were seen as masking its capitalist, imperialist, racist, and sexist assumptions. Others questioned where one could see the results of the Enlightenment at all. In the last decade, Jonathan Israel has attempted to rescue the Enlightenment from its defamers and to posit that it alone was responsible for the French Revolution. Ellen Wood has questioned a number of Israel's interpretations, though she agrees that the poststructuralists exaggerated the negative features of the Enlightenment. She has approached the subject from

the vantage point of describing the social conditions under which various philosophers wrote (to wit, economic arrangements and the structure of political power), and she extracts meanings for their literary expressions from those conditions. For a discussion of these matters, see Ellen Wood, *Liberty and Property,* 17–19, 26–28, 304; Israel, *Democratic Enlightenment,* 15–26; Outram, *Enlightenment,* 4–11.

3. The basic argument of both authors can be gleaned from their introductions; Israel, *Democratic Enlightenment,* 1–35; Ellen Wood, *Liberty and Property,* 11–29.

4. See Hirschman, *Passions and the Interests,* 9–11, 43, 63; Bendix, *Kings or People,* 3–5, 7, 218–34. On the masses, Gay, *Enlightenment,* II: 497–99, 517–18; Himmelfarb, *Roads to Modernity,* 154–60.

5. Israel, *Enlightenment Contested,* 33–49, 226–33, 261, 546; Schlatter, *Private Property,* 133–45; Ellen Wood, *Liberty and Property,* 211–55. On the Levellers and the English Revolution, Ashton, *English Civil War,* 298–310, 349–51; Brailsford, *Levellers and the English Revolution;* Coward, *Stuart Age,* 160–208; Edwards, *Making of the Modern English State,* ch. 10.

6. According to Jonathan Israel, the egalitarian element in the Enlightenment was essentially French and much less English; among the French it included such authors as Buffon, d'Alembert, and Mably. Franciscus Van den Enden (1602–1674) had not only argued for men being everywhere equal, but for women as well. Israel, *Enlightenment Contested,* 43, 242; on Hobbes and Locke, ibid., 551–53; on Diderot, Israel, *Democratic Enlightenment,* 414–20. For Hutcheson, Winch, *Adam Smith's Politics,* 49–51; on Helve'tius, Gay, *Enlightenment,* II: 513; on Helve'tius and d'Holbach, Hampson, *Cultural History of the Enlightenment,* 110; on Condorcet, Ellen Wood, *Liberty and Property,* 302, 304–306.

7. Rousseau, "Discourse Upon the Origin and the Foundation of the Inequality among Mankind" (1755), 202–13. Rousseau now is seen as being out of step with the Enlightenment in his concept of the general will. Most Enlightenment writers were persecuted for being intellectual deviants from the standard justifications of society offered by church and state, and so they probably were not attracted to a potentially new form of censorship. On Rousseau, see Israel, *Democratic Enlightenment,* 550–51, 563; Ellen Wood, *Liberty and Property,* 189–207, 302–304, 308.

8. Israel, *Enlightenment Contested,* ch. 21, "The Problem of Equality," 545–71, esp. 554–55, 560–63; *Democratic Enlightenment,* 14. Ellen Wood also discusses equality generally, not as a separate topic, but weaves the subject into the various philosophers she investigates; overall, her work seems motivated by linking capitalism to various groups of philosophers. Ellen Wood, *Liberty and Property,* ch. 7, 8.

9. Tomaselli, "Equality," 156–57. For a recent author who distinctly attaches Enlightenment ideas, especially equality, to Jefferson and the Declaration, see Jayne, *Lincoln and the American Manifesto,* 13–18.

10. See Porter, *English Society in the Eighteenth Century;* Plumb, *Men and Centuries,* 69–76; Plumb, *England in the Eighteenth Century,* 18–19; Ellen Wood, *Liberty and Property,* 147–209; Palmer, *Age of Democratic Revolution,* I, ch. 2, 3; Huston, *Securing the Fruits of Labor,* 31; Kilbride, *Being American in Europe,* 19–37.

11. It is sometimes asserted that members of the Continental Congress intended the Declaration for purposes of gaining international recognition and aid. Actually, it is difficult to see

the Declaration in this light precisely because of the second paragraph. The nations that could aid the American revolutionaries were all run by monarchs and aristocrats; they could have only been repulsed by the egalitarian sentiments in the Declaration.

12. For example, see the articles in Pestana and Salinger, eds., *Inequality in Early America.* Also testifying to early inequality are Beeman, "Deference, Republicanism and the Emergence of Popular Politics in Eighteenth-Century America," 401–30; Bouton, *Taming Democracy,* 33–66; Cornell, "Aristocracy Assailed," 1148–72; Isaac, *Transformation of Virginia,* 265–79; Shalhope, *Roots of Democracy,* 10–19; Gary Nash, *Unknown American Revolution,* 443–49; Pole, *Pursuit of Equality in American History,* 36; McDonnell, "Popular Mobilization and Political Culture in Revolutionary Virginia," 946–81; Gordon Wood, *Radicalism of the American Revolution,* 19–38; Young and Nobles, *Whose American Revolution Was It,* 156–92. For one who comes from the conservative camp but disputes the idea that the Founders were badly flawed with inegalitarianism, West, *Vindicating the Founders,* ix–xiv.

13. Burns, *Fire and Light,* 83–84; Tsesis, *For Equality and Liberty,* 20–21; White, *Philosophy of the American Revolution,* 66–74; Hawke, *A Transaction of Free Men,* 187; Cunningham, *In Pursuit of Reason,* 48–50; Maier, *American Scripture,* 136; Griffin, *America's Revolution,* 240, 135–37; Rozbicki, *Culture and Liberty,* 36–53, 132. Allen Jayne argues that the intention of Jefferson was not exclusive but inclusive; Jayne, *Lincoln and the American Manifesto,* 49–54. Henry F. May is unenlightening about the Declaration; May, *Enlightenment in America,* 163.

14. Mancke, "The Languages of Liberty in British North America," 26; Reid, *Concept of Liberty in the Age of the American Revolution,* 112–13; Rossiter, *American Quest,* 215–25; Laski, *American Democracy,* 7. The English writer David Cannadine sees the contradictions of the revolutionary leaders but he nonetheless understands the break they made with the European past, and one surmises that he can understand it because the aristocratic heritage was part of his mental inheritance: Cannadine, *Rise and Fall of Class,* 28–37, 54–56.

15. For the modernist, capitalist John Locke, consult Macpherson, *Political Theory of Possessive Individualism,* ch. 5, 6; Ellen Wood, *Liberty and Property,* 250–87. For factoring Locke out of his role as the primary philosopher on whom the American revolutionaries depended, Pocock, *Machiavellian Moment,* 423–36, 506–27; on republicanism and the country ideology, Bernard Bailyn, *Ideological Origins of the American Revolution;* Banning, *Jeffersonian Persuasion,* 25–69. For the Scottish common sense philosophy absorbed by Jefferson, see White, *Philosophy of American Revolution,* ch. 3; Wills, *Inventing America,* 175–208, 211–15; Taylor, *Young Charles Sumner and the Legacy of the American Enlightenment,* 5–6. As to confusion about individualism versus community, see Hutson, "Emergence of the Modern Concept of a Right in America," 27–53; Shain, "Rights Natural and Civil in the Declaration of Independence," 119–29.

16. Rozbicki, *Complete Colonial Gentleman,* 181–90; Rozbicki, *Culture and Liberty,* ch. 5.

17. Douglas speech in Sheahan, *Life of* Stephen A. *Douglas* (1860), 519; Shain, "Rights Natural and Civil in the Declaration of Independence," 116–44.

18. Quote from *Cato's Letters,* January 20, 1721, no. 62, in Jacobson, ed., *English Libertarian Heritage,* 128; for other examples, see the letters in ibid., 177–82, 133–34, 245–47, 172–76. For American utterances of these ideas about property, see Huston, *Securing the Fruits of Labor,* ch. 1.

19. Quote from Jefferson in his draft of the Declaration, found at www.ushistory.org/Declaration/document/rought.htm, accessed 08/29/2014. His Original Rough Draft is also in Boyd, ed., *Papers of Thomas Jefferson,* I: 25–31. This comparison of Jefferson's language about Africans in his rough draft with the final Declaration, to see whether he intended to include Africans in his egalitarian sentiments, was performed by Jayne, *Lincoln and the American Manifesto,* 51–54. For Jefferson's dour comments on Africans in the revolutionary era, see Jefferson, *Notes on the State of Virginia,* in Lipscomb, ed., *Writings of Thomas Jefferson,* II: 194. Interestingly, in the Declaration, Native Americans are reduced to "savages" and virtually expelled from the human family, but in the *Notes on the State of Virginia,* Jefferson sees them as the freest people on the planet; ibid., 84–87. On Jefferson and race, see Finkelman, *Slavery and the Founders,* ch. 5, 6; Miller, *Wolf by the Ears.*

20. On natural aristocracy, Morgan, *Inventing the People,* 249–50, and Rozbicki, *Culture and Liberty,* 214; on the elite being undemocratic, Curti, *Growth of American Thought,* 40, 113–20; Wiebe, *Self-Rule,* 18–20; on the Constitution, Morone, *Democratic Wish,* 63–64; Nedelsky, *Private Property and Limits of American Constitutionalism,* 1–2, 16–66; Hobson, "Republicanism, Commerce, and Private Rights," 89–97; Appleby, "American Heritage," 801–805; overall moderate to skeptical views of the American Revolution found in Israel, *Democratic Enlightenment,* 443–79; on limitations due to republicanism, Dowd, "Declarations of Dependence," 47–61; on limiting democracy, Onuf, "Federalism, Democracy, and Liberty in the New American Nation," 196–203.

21. Gordon Wood, *Radicalism of the American Revolution,* 232–81; Greene, *Intellectual Construction of America,* 178–89; Greene, *Imperatives, Behaviors, and Identities,* 274–86.

22. Maier, *American Scripture,* 160–67, 176–77, 200–212; Wills, *Inventing America,* xvi–xxiv; Kendall and Carey, *Basic Symbols of the American Political Tradition,* 88–92; Detweiler, "The Changing Reputation of the Declaration of Independence," 557–74. For an author who believes the Declaration and its affirmation of equality were celebrated from the beginning, see Alexander Tsesis, *For Equality and Liberty,* 4.

23. Wood, *Radicalism of the American Revolution,* 229–43; see also Greene, *Imperatives, Behaviors, and Identities,* 274–86; Tsesis, *For Equality and Liberty,* 25–36; Matthews, *Toward a New Society,* 10–15. Maier agrees that equality was generally talked about after the Revolution, but not in the Jeffersonian phrasing; *American Scripture,* 208.

24. Maier, *American Scripture,* 162–65, 192–93; Armitage, *Declaration of Independence,* 90–92; Eastman, "The Declaration of Independence as Viewed from the States," in Gerber, ed., *Declaration of Independence,* 96–104.

25. On the battle over democracy, see Wiebe, *Self-Rule,* 4–22; Stromberg, *Democracy,* 3–28. For the pairing of equality with democracy, Roper, *Democracy and Its Critics,* 6–7.

26. For a prime example of how conservatives see the American Revolution as primarily about liberty and not equality, consult M. E. Bradford, "Heresy of Equality," and Bradford, *Remembering Who We Are,* 21–44. For individualism and the American Revolution, see also Laski, *American Democracy;* Rossiter, *American Quest,* 215–25; Reid, *Concept of Liberty,* 109–119. For a rejection of individualism in the Revolution, see Shain, *Myth of American Individualism,* xv–xviii. An example of the early battle between equality and liberty is in Onuf, "Federalism, Democracy, and Liberty in the New American Nation," 132–59. On the political split between conservatives and left-liberals over liberty and equality, see Walzer, *Spheres of Justice,* 29, 65;

Walzer, *Radical Principles,* 237; Dworkin, "Liberalism," 125–27; Dworkin, *Sovereign Virtue,* 1–2. The recent work of Danielle Allen tries to argue that Americans meant both equality and liberty, an argument that this monograph agrees with; Allen, *Our Declaration,* 21–22, 275–81.

27. For the economic inequality brought by the rice industry, see Coclanis, *Shadow of a Dream,* 68–90; on the sugar islands, Curtin, *Rise and Fall of the Plantation Complex,* ch. 2; Richard Dunn, *Sugar and Slaves;* Betty Wood, *Origins of American Slavery,* 40–66; for tobacco plantations, Fischer and Kelly, *Bound Away,* 28–45; Parent, *Foul Means,* 30–32, 36–39. For the British gentry, see Huston, *British Gentry, the Southern Planter, and the Northern Family Farmer,* ch. 1–3; for the French, Ellen Wood, *Liberty and Property,* 15–17, ch. 6.

28. Huston, *Securing the Fruits of Labor,* ch. 1, 2.

29. Jefferson to James Madison, January 30, 1787, in Boyd, ed., *Papers of Thomas Jefferson,* XI: 92–93; Jefferson to Charles Bellini, September 30, 1785, ibid., VIII: 568; Jefferson to Madison, October 28, 1785, ibid., VIII: 681–82. The antiaristocracy of the American Revolution is the theme of Huston, *Securing the Fruits of Labor,* ch. 1–3.

30. James Madison to Jefferson, June 19, 1786, in Boyd, ed., *Papers of Jefferson,* IX: 659; John Adams to Jefferson, July 16, 1814, in Lipscomb, ed., *Writings of Jefferson,* XIV: 157–58. Adams is one of the oddest characters on the subject as he sees the need for an equitable distribution of wealth, yet intellectually he cannot grope his way to a solution. In many ways, though, he and Jefferson had similar ideas on the economy and rural society. See Adams, *Discourses of Davila,* in Charles F. Adams, ed., *Works of John Adams,* VI: 276, 285–86, 392–98; Adams, *Defense of the Constitutions,* in ibid., VI: 8–9; Adams to Jefferson, December 18, 1819, in ibid, X: 386; and Adams to Thomas Brand-Hillis, June 11, 1790, in ibid., IX: 570; Ellis, *Passionate Sage,* 128–38; Staloff, *Hamilton, Adams, Jefferson,* 180–87; Peterson, *Adams and Jefferson,* 35–51, 56–57.

31. This is a standard interpretation. Gordon Wood, *Creation of the American Republic,* 393–429; Nedelsky, *Private Property and the Limits of American Constitutionalism,* 1–7, 16–66. For more moderate assessments of Madison, see Banning, *Sacred Fire of Liberty,* 64–65, 98, 120, 182–83, 204–11; generally, see Cunliffe, *Right to Property,* 5–14.

32. Paine, *Common Sense,* in *Complete Writings of Thomas Paine,* ed. Philip S. Foner, I: 11–13; Paine, *Rights of Man,* in ibid., I: 364. See Gordon Wood, *Radicalism of the American Revolution,* 181–82.

33. William Vans Murray, "Political Sketches," *American Museum* II (September 1787), 235; Morse, *Annals of the American Revolution,* 385–86.

34. Noah Webster, "Sketches of American Policy," in *On Being American,* ed. Babbidge, 37; see Ramsey, *History of the American Revolution,* I: 31; Richard Price, "Observations on the Impact of the American Revolution," in Peach, ed., *Richard Price and the Ethical Foundations of the American Revolution,* 208–210; James Sullivan, *Path to Riches* (1792), 8.

35. Federalist № 43, in James Madison, *Papers of James Madison,* ed. Hutchinson et al., X: 413–14.

36. On the Federalist side, see Webster, *On Being American,* 30–39; William Vans Murray, "Political Sketches," *American Museum* II (September 1787), 233–34; Sullivan, *Path to Riches,* 6, 8–9.

37. John F. Mercer (presumed author), "Essays by a Farmer," in Storing, ed., *Complete Anti-Federalist,* V: 19; "Letter of Cato," in ibid., II: 122. The fear of the rich running government for

their own benefit suffuses Antifederalist writing; see Storing, "What the Antifederalists Stood For," in Storing, ed., *Complete Anti-Federalist,* I: 38–40, 44, 48–51. On the rejection of hereditary principles, see Jack P. Greene, *Intellectual Construction of America,* 107–109, 178–80. Michal Jan Rozbicki argues that the American elite had more of a mercantile basis than did the English, who based their power on landownership. Thus the American elite was not as wedded to inheritance as the English; moreover, by focusing on inheritance, the Americans found a way to discredit British rule while at the same time arguing for a "natural" aristocracy to run America because of talent. Rozbicki, *Culture and Liberty,* 98–102, 214. For the struggle within the Revolution between the would-be gentry and common folk, see McDonnell, *Politics of War,* 1–15; Saul Cornell, "Aristocracy Assailed," 1148–72; Bouton, "A Road Closed," 855–87; Bouton, *Taming Democracy,* 33–34. It might be mentioned, as the gentry versus the people has become a commonplace in writing about the Revolution, that a silent but prominent current in the Revolution had to be the retreat of the American gentry from the English model. The reason is forthright and simple. Who would be the allies of the, say, Virginia gentry, when the leaders of the colonies decided to revolt? They simply had to give away some of their advantages to the common folk to create a coalition of Americans to fight the British because they lacked the numbers among themselves to be militarily successful. Thus a silent negotiation went on throughout the Revolution whereby the American upper class retreated in their social and political pretensions in order not to face the British noose for being traitors. What the American upper class would not give away was property rights in land, slaves, and commerce. But they did give up distinctions, special access to legislation, and government restricted only to their own class.

38. John Adams, *Defense of the Constitutions,* in *Works of Adams,* ed. Charles F. Adams, IV: 392–98; John Adams to Samuel Adams, October 18, 1790, and Samuel Adams to John Adams, November 20, 1790, in ibid., VI: 418, 421–22; Jefferson, "Bill to Enable Tenants in Fee Tail to Convey Their Lands in Fee Simple," October 14, 1776, in *Papers of Jefferson,* ed. Boyd, I: 560; see Ellis, *Passionate Sage,* 128–29, 133–39; Howe, *Changing Political Thought of John Adams,* 137–38; Dauer, *Adams Federalists,* 46–49.

39. Ramsey, *History of American Revolution,* I: 32; Adams, *Defense of Constitutions,* in *Works of Adams,* ed. Charles F. Adams, IV: 361, 66.

40. For example, son of George Bryan, "Letters of Centinel," in Storing, ed., *Complete Anti-Federalist,* II: 139; John Warren, *An Oration, Delivered July 4th, 1783, . . . Boston,* 6; see Van Doren, *Franklin,* 707. For the standard treatment of virtue and luxury, see Pocock, "Virtue and Commerce in the Eighteenth Century," 119–34.

41. Thomas Jefferson to James Madison, December 20, 1787, *Papers of Jefferson,* ed. Boyd, XII: 440; RUSSEL, "On banking companies in the United States," *American Museum* XII (September 1792), 144–45; RUSSEL, "On Monopolies," ibid., 188–89; P. W. on monopolies, in Commager and Morris, eds., *Spirit of 'Seventy-Six,'* II: 802; James Wilson, *Works of James Wilson,* ed. McCloskey, II: 570; John Adams to John Taylor, April 15, 1814, in *Works of Adams,* ed. Charles F. Adams, VI: 510; see James Madison, "Money, 1779–1780," *Papers of Madison,* ed. Hutchinson, I: 460. For a description of the economic effect of monopoly that anticipates modern analysis, see George Mason to Richard Henry Lee, May 18, 1776, in Robert Rutland, ed., *Papers of George Mason,* I: 272.

42. Benjamin Franklin to Count de Campomanes, June 5, 1784, in Bigelow, ed., *Life of Benjamin Franklin,* III: 268; Van Doren, *Franklin,* 707; John Adams to sons, August 21, 1809, in John Quincy Adams, *Memoirs,* II: 13; George Logan, "Five Letters addressed to the Yeomanry . . . ," *American Museum* XII (September 1792), 159; Thomas Jefferson to Thomas Cooper, September 10, 1814, in Jefferson, *Writings of Jefferson,* ed. Lipscomb, XIV: 182. See Gordon Wood, *Radicalism of the American Revolution,* 277–84.

43. John Adams to Dr. Morse, December 2, 1815, in Morse, *Annals of the American Revolution,* 198; see Thomas Jefferson, "Rough Draft of Jefferson's Resolutions for Disestablishing the Church of England," before November 19, 1776, in *Papers of Jefferson,* ed. Boyd, I: 530; Governor Livingston, "Observations on the Support of the Clergy," *American Museum* VIII (December 1790), 254; John Taylor, *An Enquiry Into the Principles,* 1794, 53. See Kramnick and Moore, *The Godless Constitution;* Barry Shain, "Rights Natural and Civil in the Declaration of Independence," 119–21; see Isaac, *Transformation of Virginia,* 187–97.

44. On entail and primogeniture, see Young and Nobles, *Whose American Revolution Was It,* 92–93; Brewer, "Entailing Aristocracy," 307–46; Nisbet, *Social Impact of the Revolution,* 8–12; Malone, *Jefferson and His Time,* vol. 1, *Jefferson the Virginian,* 251–57; Dangerfield, *Chancellor Robert R. Livingston of New York,* 192–93. On the difference in natural thought between the Americans and John Locke on inheritance (Americans believed it a positive act of government, Locke saw it as a natural right), see Chester, "Inheritance in American Legal Thought," in Miller and McNamee, eds., *Inheritance and Wealth in America,* 23–26. See Huston, *Securing the Fruits of Labor,* 46–50; Gordon Wood, *Radicalism of the American Revolution,* 46–47. On strict settlement, Habakkuk, *Marriage, Debt, and the Estates System,* 1–51; Mingay, *English Landed Society in the Eighteenth Century,* 32–34.

45. Cato's Letters, #16, February 18, 1720, in Jacobson, ed., *English Libertarian Heritage,* 53.

46. Ibid., #71, March 31, 1722, 189.

47. Jefferson to John Banister Jr., October 15, 1786, in *Papers of Jefferson,* ed. Boyd, VIII: 636; Jefferson to John Adams, October 28, 1813, in *Writings of Jefferson,* ed. Lipscomb, XIII: 399–400; see also Jefferson to Charles Bellini, September 30, 1785, in *Papers of Jefferson,* ed. Boyd, VIII: 569.

48. James Madison to W. T. Barry, August 4, 1822, in *Writings of Madison,* ed. Hunt, IX: 105–108; John Adams, "Twenty-Six Letters Upon Interesting Subjects Respecting the Revolution of America" [1780], in *Works of John Adams,* ed. Charles F. Adams, VII: 283; John Adams, *Defense of the Constitutions,* in ibid., VI: 185.

49. See Curti, *Growth of American Thought,* 136; Hunt, "Sectionalism, Slavery, and Schooling in Antebellum Virginia," 125–29; Burns, *Fire and Light,* 81–82. Michal Jan Rozbicki underlines that the idea of equality for the people among the leaders of the Revolution was a future projection based on the people acquiring education and property; Rozbicki, *Culture and Liberty,* 119–30.

50. Samuel Bryan, "Letters of Sentinel," in Storing, ed., *Complete Anti-Federalist,* II: 176. For other examples, see Elias Boudinot, "Oration Before the Society of the Cincinnati" [1787], in Boudinot, *Life, Public Services, Addresses, and Letters,* ed. Boudinot, II: 373; David Ramsey, "Oration, 1778," 276, in Frank Moore, ed., *American Eloquence,* I: 311; William Drayton speech, 1776, in Dabney and Dargan, *William Drayton and the American Revolution,* 190; "The Politician," *American Museum* VII (February 1790), 82; Belknap, *History of New-Hampshire* (1792), I:

256–59; Banner, *To the Hartford Convention,* 9–10; Gordon Wood, *Radicalism of the American Revolution,* 232–34; on the leaders being upset with upcoming people, Gordon Wood, *Creation of the American Republic,* 476–83.

51. For example, see this distinction clearly made by St. George Tucker, *A Dissertation on Slavery* (1796), 18–22.

52. Modern commentators note as well the exclusion of women and native Americans generally from the ideals of equality, but for contemporaries and for many scholars, the blatant inconsistency centered on the practice of slaveholding. For the process of making the Declaration effective in American life after the Revolution, see Rozbicki, *Culture and Liberty,* 1–34; Griffin, *America's Revolution,* x, 135–37; Tsesis, *For Equality and Liberty;* Young and Nobles, *Whose American Revolution Was It,* 156–69.

53. St. George Tucker, *Dissertation on Slavery,* 48; Othello, "Essay on Negro Slavery," *American Museum* IV (November 1788), 415; Thomas Paine, "African Slavery in America," 1774, in Foner, ed., *Complete Writings,* II: 16–19; for Abigail Adams, see Ferling, *John Adams,* 172–73. Jeremy Belknap wrote in 1792, "Slavery was thought so inconsistent with the natural rights of mankind, and detrimental to society, that an express law was made, prohibiting the buying or selling of slaves" in New Hampshire; Belknap, *History of New-Hampshire,* I: 74. For others, Buchanan, *Oration Upon the Moral and Political Evil of Slavery* (1793); [Rush], *An Address . . . Upon Slave-keeping* (1773).

54. James Madison, "Notes for the National Gazette Essays," c. December 1791–March 1792, in Hutchinson, ed., *Papers of Madison,* XIV: 163; John Adams to Joseph Hawley, November 25, 1775, in Charles F. Adams, ed., *Works of Adams,* IX: 367; Agrippa [James Winthrop], January 11, 1788, in Storing, ed., *Complete Anti-Federalist,* IV: 94; Cato, September 1797–1788, in ibid., II: 112; Warren, *History of the Rise, Progress, and Termination of the American Revolution* (1805), I: 21–22. Both Madison and Jefferson had troubles conceiving of emancipation, but both continued to see slavery as a stain on the American emblem; Jefferson in 1823, while saying some of the vituperation against the institution was lessening, still admitted that "it is a hideous blot." Jefferson to William Short, September 8, 1823, in Lipscomb, ed., *Writings of Jefferson,* XV: 469; Robert Rutland, *James Madison,* 239–41.

55. Beyond this, Trollope found that slavery was too divisive for the United States to continue as a nation divided into half slave states and half free states; Anthony Trollope, *North America* (1862), I: 8–9.

56. Tocqueville, *Democracy in America,* trans. Goldhammer (1835), I: 394, 394–95.

57. *American Museum* XII (November 1792), 256–57.

CHAPTER TWO

1. I am accepting the conclusions of Ellen Meiksins Wood, *Citizens to Lords,* 28–143. Wood is a Marxist historian/philosopher of political thought and thereby has an interpretation of Plato, Aristotle, Cicero, and others that is at variance with others, and her interpretation is specifically on the ideals of aristocracy and democracy; for comparison, see Leo Strauss, "Plato," 7–63, and James E. Holton, "Marcus Tullius Cicero," 130–150.

2. Ellen Wood, *Citizens to Lords,* 154–63; Ellen Wood, *Liberty and Property,* 59–79; Skinner, "Political Philosophy," 390–92, 396–402, 413–14; Skinner, *Foundations of Modern Political Thought,* II: 191–212; Schlatter, *Private Property,* 90–92, 106, 113–15; J. C. D. Clark, *English Society,* 76; Doyle, *Aristocracy and Its Enemies in the Age of Revolution,* 37; Curti, *Growth of American Thought,* 113.

3. Point made by Ellen Wood, *Citizens to Lords,* 137–54.

4. Ibid., 55–74, 82–98; see Huston, *British Gentry, Southern Planters, and the Northern Family Farmer,* ch. 2.

5. Cannon, *Aristocratic Century,* 2–3; Palmer, *Age of Democratic Revolution,* I: 59; Israel, *Enlightenment Contested,* 291; Ellen Wood, *Liberty and Property,* 173–89; Gordon Wood, *Creation of the American Republic,* 11, 29, 34–35, 152, 153, 160, 356, 449, 450, 451, 499.

6. Ellen Wood, *Citizens to Lords,* 120–26, 129–37. On the development of property doctrines, Schlatter, *Private Property,* 12–26; Stockton, *Gracchi,* 6–18.

7. Ellen Wood, *Citizens to Lords,* 95–96, 114–126.

8. The Levellers during the English Civil War, the republican theorists of the Italian City-States, and English republicans did address the problem of excessive wealth accumulation in the form of a bad distribution of wealth, but these people were not advocates of aristocracy; they generally argued for citizen equality, not inequality. Schlatter, *Private Property,* 133–48; Skinner, *Foundations of Modern Political Thought,* I: 162–64, 179.

9. Tocqueville, *Democracy in America,* trans. Goldhammer (1835), I: 56.

10. Skinner, "Political Philosophy," 422.

11. Ibid., 423; Skinner, *Foundations Modern Political Thought,* I: 236.

12. Mingay, *English Landed Society in the Eighteenth Century,* 15, 19–22; Porter, *English Society in the Eighteenth Century,* 13–14, 68–84; Beckett, *Aristocracy in England,* 40.

13. Cannadine, *Decline and Fall of the British Aristocracy;* Beckett, *Aristocracy in England,* 2–4.

14. Beckett, *Aristocracy in England,* 22–27, 40; Doyle, *Aristocracy and Its Enemies,* 9–22; Palmer, *Age of Democratic Revolution,* I: 29–47, 73–79; Cannon, *Aristocratic Century,* 1–3, 54–57.

15. Porter, *English Society,* 2. Those stressing the domination of English society by the aristocracy and its demand for deference include Porter, *English Society,* 49–50; Baugh, "Introduction," in Baugh, ed., *Aristocratic Government and Society in Eighteenth-Century England,* 2–9, 17–18; Beckett, *Aristocracy in England,* 2–5; Plumb, *England in the Eighteenth Century,* 17–19; Stone and Stone, *An Open Elite,* 416–25. For a softer depiction of the dominance of the aristocracy, Mingay, *English Landed Society,* 279–87; Gordon Wood, *Radicalism of the American Revolution,* 14–19.

16. Stone, *Crisis of the Aristocracy,* 41; Thompson, *English Landed Society in the Nineteenth Century,* 5–6; Mingay, *English Landed Society,* 3, 283–84; Mingay, *Gentry,* 2–3, 17; Habakkuk, *Marriage, Debt, and the Estates System,* 403.

17. Mingay, *English Landed* Society, 78–79; Garnier, *History of the English Landed Interest,* 395; see also Mingay, *English Landed* Society, 32; Fordham, *Short History of English Rural Life,* 96; Willcox, *Age of Aristocracy,* 38; Stone, *Crisis of Aristocracy,* 178–82; Habakkuk, *Marriage, Debt, and the Estates System,* 1–35; F. M. L. Thompson, *English Landed Society,* 6. George Brodrick dated the origin of primogeniture at the time of the Norman conquest; *English Land and English Landlords,* 89–99.

18. Schochet, *Patriarchalism in Political Thought,* 7–14, 137–45; Stone, *Family, Sex and Marriage in England,* 28–29; Stone and Stone, *Open Elite,* 412–13; Clark, *English Society,* 69–80, 93–94. On servants, Edmund Morgan, *American Slavery American Freedom,* 123–27, 319–25; Hecht, *Domestic Servant Class in Eighteenth-Century England,* 74–81.

19. Plumb, *Men and Centuries,* 23–24; Thompson, *English Landed Society,* 48; J. C. D. Clark, *English Society,* 36–41; Beckett, *Aristocracy in England,* 10–12; Schlatter, *Private Property,* 136–43; Eastwood, *Governing Rural England,* 9–11.

20. Eastwood, *Governing Rural England,* 16–21, 28–67; Stater, *Noble Government: Stuart Lord Lieutenancy,* 8–31; Fordham, *Short History of English Rural Life,* 69–70, 108–111.

21. Cannon, *Aristocratic Century,* 149–53; Thompson, *English Landed Society,* 71 and ch. 7; Clark, *English Society,* 80, 89, 93–94; McGarvie, *One Nation Under Law,* 5, 8, 21; Curti, *Growth of American Thought,* 113.

22. Thompson, *English Landed Society,* 71–72; Doyle, *Aristocracy and Its Enemies,* 21–22; Stone and Stone, *Open Elite,* 416.

23. On the game laws, Fordham, *Short History of English Rural Life,* 131–32; Stone, *Crisis of the Aristocracy,* 224–28; Thompson, *English Landed Society,* 96–97, 136–45.

24. Stone, *Crisis of the Aristocracy,* 39–40; Wood, *Radicalism of the American Revolution,* 36–38; Levy, *Large and Small Holdings,* 20; Brodrick, *English Land and English Landlords,* 216; Cannon, *Aristocratic Century,* 2; Mingay, *English Landed Society,* 247–49; Doyle, *Aristocracy and Its Enemies,* 32–33; Thompson, *English Landed Society,* 82–86; Hecht, *Domestic Servant Class in Eighteenth-Century England,* 21–22; Orwin and Whetham, *History of British Agriculture,* 90.

25. Doyle, *Aristocracy and Its Enemies,* 48–49; Hirschman, *Passions and the Interests,* 60–63, 70–74. It seems that the virtue aristocrats were supposed to cultivate was approximately the same virtue that republicans were supposed to possess.

26. See discussion in ch. 4 and consult Rozbicki, *Culture and Liberty,* 1–34.

27. Plumb, *Men and Centuries,* 2–3; Gordon Wood, *Radicalism of the Revolution,* 14; Mingay, *English Landed Society,* 11; Edmund Morgan, *American Slavery, American Freedom,* 381–83.

28. Hecht, *Domestic Servant Class in Eighteenth-Century England,* 3–7, 19, 22, 35 72–73 (quotes), 85, 117, 177–85; Hobsbawm and Rudé, *Captain Swing,* 38–41; Stone, *Crisis of Aristocracy,* 547; Clark, *English Society,* 104; Porter, *English Society,* 15–16; see Schwarz, "English Servants and Their Employers during the Eighteenth and Nineteenth Centuries," 231–56; Thompson, *English Landed Society,* 95. See comments of master-servant relations in Tocqueville, *Democracy in America,* trans. Goldhammer (1840), II: 671–72, and ch. 4 of this book.

29. The behaviors that deference in England demanded will become clearer in succeeding chapters. On English deference generally, Beckett, *Aristocracy in England,* 9–11; Cannon, *Aristocratic Century,* viii; Porter, *English Society,* 16.

30. Lillibridge, *Beacon of Freedom,* 1.

31. Plumb, *Men and Centuries,* 78; Thompson, *English Landed Society,* 96–102, 136–45; Doyle, *Aristocracy and Its Enemies,* 38. On wealth, Garnier, *History of the English Landed Interest,* 46–49; Plumb, *Men and Centuries,* 69–75; Plumb, *England in the Eighteenth Century,* 18–19; Stone and Stone, *Open Elite,* 416–17; Cannadine, *Decline and Fall of the English Aristocracy,* ch. 1.

32. The assessment of the English aristocracy is somewhat interesting. They have their defenders, partly because compared to the continental aristocracy, the British were more open

and constitutional. Yet, as F. M. L. Thompson wrote, they had "an obsession with the degrees of the peerage" and they formed a "loosely-knit club"; Lawrence Stone and Jeanne C. F. Stone remarked after denouncing the wealth inequality caused by aristocratic/gentry land ownership that at no time were the English elite "wholly irresponsible," a rather backhanded compliment. An interesting assessment was made by H. J. Habakkuk; although he was from a "Welsh non-conformist radical tradition," he admitted "the extraordinarily high level of ability" the elite had. Thompson, *English Landed Society,* 12, 15; Stone and Stone, *Open Elite,* 415; Habakkuk, *Marriage, Debt, and the Estates System,* x.

33. See Huston. *British Gentry, Southern Planter, and the Northern Family Farmer,* ch. 1–2; Beckett, *Aristocracy in England,* 44–52; Mingay, *English Landed Society,* 3–25; Lindert, "Who Owned Victorian England," 25–51.

34. Mingay, *English Landed Society,* 11; Orwin and Whetham, *History of British Agriculture,* 79–82; Hobsbawm and Rudé, *Captain Swing;* E. P. Thompson, *Making of the English Working Class,* ch. 14.

35. Stone and Stone, *Open Elite,* 408; Clark, *English Society,* 88, 94–99; Morgan, *Inventing the People,* 13; Beckett, *Aristocracy in England,* 5, 9; Porter, *English Society,* 63–65; Cannon, *Aristocratic Century,* 148–54, 170–72.

36. Great Britain, Registrar-General, *Census of Great Britain in 1851,* 60, 72; Peter Mathias, *First Industrial Nation,* 57 (quote), table VII, p. 239; Cannadine, *Decline and Fall of the British Aristocracy,* 8–9; O'Brien and Heath, "English and French Landowners," 24–56; George W. Grantham, "Scale and Organization in French Farming, 1840–1880," 293–326.

37. Allen, *Enclosure and the Yeoman,* 1; Garnier, *History of the English Landed Interest,* 527; Lindert, "Who Owned Victorian England," 36–44; Lindert, "Unequal Living Standards," 378–80; Orwin and Whetham, *History of British Agriculture,* ch. 3, 8.

38. Stone, *Crisis of the Aristocracy,* 9; Cecil Frances Alexander, quoted in Lindert, "Who Owned Victorian England," 25; John Wesley, quoted in Porter, *English Society,* 14–15. See Eastwood, *Governing Rural England,* ch. 8, 9; E. L. Jones, *Agriculture and the Industrial Revolution,* 222–23.

39. Porter, *English Society,* 15–16; Eastwood, *Governing Rural England,* 16–21; Cannon, *Aristocratic Century,* 151, 170; Doyle, *Aristocracy and Its Enemies,* ch. 2. On the embrace of inequality and rejection of equality by important nineteenth-century writers, see Roper, *Democracy and Its Critics;* Prochaska, *Eminent Victorians on American Democracy;* Lippincott, *Victorian Critics of Democracy.*

40. On American conservatives in the eighteenth century generally, see Guttman, *Conservative Tradition in America,* 14–37; Labaree, *Conservatism in Early American History.* For some treatments on individuals, see Bernhard, *Fisher Ames,* 47–51; Turner, *William Plumer of New Hampshire,* 25, 92–93; Peterson, *Adams and Jefferson,* 6, 10, 31; Pole, *Pursuit of Equality,* 4, 46; McDonnell, *Politics of War,* 1–15; Cornell, "Aristocracy Assailed," 1142–72; Bouton, *Taming Democracy;* Mintz, *Gouverneur Morris and the American Revolution,* 44–46, 73; Alexander, *Revolutionary Conservative,* 26, 97–98; Dunbar, *Study of "Monarchical" Tendencies in the United States;* Rozbicki, *Culture and Liberty,* 214. On deference, see Gilsdorf and Gilsdorf, "Elites and Electorates," 207–44. For those stressing less conservatism in American society and more difference between the Americans and the British, Greene, *Intellectual Construction of America,* 106–109, 178–89; Gordon Wood, *Radicalism of the American Revolution.*

41. For the French Revolution and its problems, Schama, *Citizens,* 785–91; the now somewhat dated description of the French Revolution by R. R. Palmer is still a good summary; Palmer and Colton, *History of the Modern World,* 341–51, 355–75. For the American reaction, now well documented, consult Elkins and McKitrick, *Age of Federalism;* Stromberg, *Democracy,* 22–24; Banner, *To the Hartford Convention,* 18–24; John C. Miller, *Federalist Era,* 126–32.

42. Palmer and Colton, *History of the Modern World,* 370–75, 388–95; Doyle, *Aristocracy and Its Enemies,* ch. 6–7 and 321–39.

43. On Burke and the United States, see Guttman, *Conservative Tradition in America,* 6–11; Kirk, *Conservative Mind,* 3–10; Brian Berry, *Culture and Equality,* 9–11; Norman, *Edmund Burke,* 245–54, 283; Kramnick, *Rage of Edmund Burke,* 39–51. A good illustration of the differences between Americans and Burke is the comparison that Drew Maciag did between Burke and John Adams; Adams was and is considered a conservative of the American Revolution, but he did not have Burkean principles; Maciag, *Edmund Burke in America,* ch. 3. On Burke's background and his being spokesman of the landed gentry, Thompson, *English Landed Society,* 6; Kramnick, *Rage of Edmund Burke,* 21–30, 60–63; C. B. Macpherson, *Burke,* 42–43; Fasel, *Edmund Burke,* 55–57, ch. 4; Norman, *Edmund Burke,* 187–90.

44. This is a standard description; e.g., Norman, *Edmund Burke,* 199–203.

45. On his relation to the aristocracy, Kramnick, *Rage of Burke,* 60, 164; Fasel, *Edmund Burke,* 83; Norman, *Edmund Burke,* 206, 208; Maciag, *Edmund Burke in America,* 20–21. Burke's desire to be a member of the gentry, and perhaps begin a landed ownership that over time would place future members of his family in the nobility, is in Kramnick, *Rage of Edmund Burke,* 174–80.

46. Macpherson, *Burke,* 4; Norman, *Edmund Burke,* 202–210, 245–54; Jedediah Purdy, "Introduction," to Purdy, ed., *Democratic Vistas,* 2–4; Kramnick, *Rage of Burke,* 21, 30, 32, 161–65; Fasel, *Edmund Burke,* 41, 51–57, 83–86, 97–99. On Burke and his ideas of liberty and restraint, Kammen, *Spheres of Liberty,* 84; Guttman, *Conservative Tradition in America,* 7–8.

CHAPTER THREE

1. E.g., Brooke, *Columbia Rising;* Bruegel, *Farm, Shop, Landing.*

2. Fladeland, *Men and Brothers;* McDaniel, *Problem of Democracy in the Age of Slavery;* Stange, *British Unitarians Against American Slavery;* Blackett, *Building an Antislavery Wall;* Blackett, *Divided Hearts;* Turley, *Culture of English Antislavery.*

3. Boesche, *Strange Liberalism of Alexis de Tocqueville;* Welch, *De Tocqueville;* Mancini, *Alexis de Toqueville.*

4. Nevins, *American Social History as Recorded by British Travellers;* Mesick, *English Traveller in America;* Berger, *British Traveller in America.* More recent writers include Rapson, *Britons View America;* Burk, *Old World, New World;* Pachter, ed., *Abroad in America.*

5. For the years 1800–1825, see especially Eaton, *Anglo-American Paper War.*

6. Nevins, ed., *American Social History,* 10–25, 114–26, 283–304.

7. Both Berger and Mesick are excellent in detailing the subjects that the travelers focused on. David P. Crook has interesting comments on how little the American experiment influenced

domestic British politics, but he reveals opinions clearly; *American Democracy in English Politics.* Both Chris Mulvey and Richard L. Rapson take the story beyond 1865, which early writers often failed to do; Mulvey, *Transatlantic Manners;* and Rapson, *Britons View America;* a brief history is Howard Temperley, *Britain and America Since Independence.* Kathleen Burk is one of the few recent authors to stress difference; *Old World, New World.* An older and less reliable work is Lillibridge, *Beacon of Democracy.* For the view of Americans on Europe, see Daniel Kilbride, *Being American in Europe.* Vignettes about British travelers can be found in Pachter, ed., *Abroad in America.*

8. Maier, *American Scripture,* 194–208; Wills, *Inventing* America, xvi–xxi, 324–25.

9. Palmer, *Journal of Travels* (1818), 80; Blowe, *Geographical, Historical, Commercial* (1820), 66; Blane, *Excursion Through the United States* (1824), 59–60; Wilson, *Wanderer in America* (1822), 86; Charles Dickens, *American Notes* (1842) I: 288; Welby, *Visit to North America* (1821), vii. The Declaration had little commentary in England up to 1783; Conway, "From Fellow-Nationals to Foreigners: British Perceptions of the Americans," 86–96.

10. Martineau, *Society in America* (1839), I: 3–4; Maury, *Englishwoman in America* (1848), lxxxiii; Prentice, *Tour in the United States* (1850), 111; D. R. Thomason, *Hints to Emigrants* (1848), 123; Jobson, *America and American Methodism* (1857), 27.

11. Weld, *Vacation Tour of the United States and Canada* (1855), 266.

12. Marshall Hall, *Two-Fold Slavery of the United States* (1854), 18; Sullivan, *Rambles and Scrambles in North and South America* (1852), 21–22; William Brown, *America* (1849), 51; Reid, *Sketches in North America* (1861), 27.

13. D. Mitchell, *Ten Years Residence in the United States* (1862), 253. See Berger, *British Traveller in America,* 108.

14. Featherstonhaugh, *Excursions Through the Slave States* (1844), I: 115–16, quote 120; Shirreff, *Tour Through North America* (1835), 311–12; Stuart, *Three Years in North America* (1833), II: 147; William Ouseley, *Remarks on the Statistics and Political Institutions of the United States* (1832), 159; Dickens, *American Notes,* I: 288. Other writers commented on the paradox of the Declaration and the existence of slavery, but it might be noted that most travelers considered the United States a republic that honored freedom, and slavery was the exception. The course of modern historiography seems to be that slavery was the main current of the nation's life, and that freedom was the exception. For example, Baptist, *The Half Has Never Been Told;* Van Cleve, *Slaveholder's Union.*

15. Mrs. Felton, *Life in America* (1838), 65.

16. For example, Fibbleton, *Travels in America* (1833), 9–10; Sullivan, *Rambles and Scrambles* (1852), 227; Mitchell, *Ten Years Residence in the United States* (1861), 75–76; Wilson, *Wanderer in America* (1822), 5–7.

17. Stirling, *Letters from the Slave States* (1857), 104; Hamilton, *Men and Manners in America* (1834), I: 107, 108. Frederic Marryat related that he talked to an individual named Vaugh[a?]n who found Jefferson's first draft of the Declaration with the paragraph on slavery; Marryat, *Diary in America,* 188.

18. Chevalier, *Society, Manners and Politics in the United States* (1839), 96. Almost all travelers noted the antagonism between slavery and equality, and most saw that poverty in the United States bore the characteristic of race, most commonly African and Native American, but in the

1850s the Irish bore the stigma as well. See, for example, Flower, *Errors of Emigrants* (1841), 15–17; Mitchell, *Ten Years Residence in the United States* (1861), 147–52. The most emphatic rejection of the United States being an egalitarian society is Pessen, *Jacksonian America*, 9–57.

19. Thomas Cooper, *Some Information Respecting America* (1794), 53; Ruffin's son quoted in Betty Mitchell, *Edmund Ruffin*, 62.

20. Maury, *Englishwoman in America* (1848), 214; Maxwell, *Run Through the United States* (1841), I: 258. See Mrs. Houstoun, *Hesperos* (1850), I: 97; Chevalier, *Society, Manners and Politics* (1839), 97; Daubeny, *Journal of a Tour Through the United States* (1843), 57–58; Dalton, *Travels in the United States of America* (1821), 4, 57–58; Lewis, *Impressions of America and the American Churches* (1845), 42.

21. Lyell, *Travels in North America* (1845), I: 102; Charles Johnson, *Letters from the British Settlement in Pennsylvania* (1819), 97; see William Ferguson, *America By River and Rail* (1856), 81–82; Bird, *Englishwoman in America* (1856), 382–384; Vigne, *Six Months in America* (1833), 91. On beggars, see Nevins, comp. and ed., *America Through British Eyes*, 13.

22. Chevalier, *Society, Manners and Politics* (1839), 110; Martineau, *Retrospect of Western Travel* (1838), I: 87; Arfwedson, *United States and Canada* (1834), I: 111; Baxter, *America and the Americans* (1855), 211; Robert Russell, *North America* (1857), 15; Shirreff, *Tour Through North America* (1835), 340. The character of American agriculture as opposed to Great Britain's was caught by E. J. Hobsbawm, *Age of Revolution*, 29–34. Travelers going to Niagara often visited the Van Rensselaer manor, but they considered it an anomaly in the republic; Christopher Clark, *Social Change in America*, 241–44.

23. Tocqueville, *Democracy in America*, trans. Goldhammer (1840), II: 642. See Chevalier, *Society, Manners and Politics* (1839), 418; Gurowski, *America and Europe* (1857), 68–70; Martineau, *Society In America* (1839), II: 295, 302–305. Older writers, like Henry Fearon and William Faux, said Americans were lazy because they had too much land and were willing to live at subsistence levels; Fearon, *Sketches of America* (1818), 173, 224; Faux, *Faux's Memorable Days in America* (1823), 118, 128–29, 232–39.

24. Tocqueville, *Democracy in America*, trans. Goldhammer (1840), II: 682–84. For others, A. Thomason, *Men and Things in America* (1838), 113, 124, 279; Rich, *General View of the United States of America* (1833), 86; Melish, *Travels Through the United States of America* (1818), 438; Maury, *Englishwoman in America* (1848), 216. For examples of those stressing the density of population argument, see Hamilton, *Men and Manners in America* (1834), I: 296–97; Melish, *Travels Through the United States* (1818), 438. Labor historians have rejected the high-wage observations of Tocqueville and others: e.g., Rockman, *Scraping By*, 141–42, 158, 241–43; Wilentz, *Chants Democratic*, 285–86, 300–306. For class analysis, see examples in Paul Johnson, *Shopkeeper's Millennium*, 5–10; Dawley, *Class and Community*, 1–6; Blumin, *Emergence of the Middle Class*, 1–12.

25. Palmer, *Journal of Travels* (1818), 91; Bird, *Englishwoman in America* (1856), 367–69; Chambers, *Things As They Are in America* (1854), 196–97.

26. Tocqueville, *Democracy in America*, trans. Goldhammer (1835), I: 34, 57–58; Mackay, *Western World* (1850), III: quote 326–28, generally 329–41; Phillippo, *United States and Cuba* (1857), 90. Chevalier, *Society, Manners and Politics* (1839), 418–19; Lyell, *Travels in North America* (1845), I: 70.

27. Vigne, *Six Months in America* (1833), 197; Mackay, *Western World* (1850), III: 333; Houstoun, *Hesperos* (1850), I: 176; Hugh Murray, *United States of America* (1844), III: 43; Buckingham, *America Historical, Statistic, and Descriptive* (1841), I: 118–19.

28. For example, Kent, *Memoirs and Letters of James Kent,* 218, 220–21; Nicholas Wainwright, ed., *A Philadelphia Perspective: The Diary of Sidney George Fisher,* entries of December 25, 1836, p. 16; January 15, 1837, p. 18; June 30, 1844, p. 171; "A Word to Southern Democrats by a Northern Conservative," *American* [Whig] *Review* X (August 1849), 194; Noah Webster to Daniel Webster, 1837, in Warfel, ed., *Letters of Noah Webster,* 489–502; entry of December 17, 1835, in Nevins, ed., *Diary of Philip Hone,* 187. See Baltzell, *Puritan Boston and Quaker Philadelphia,* 199–200, 207; Brown, *American Conservatives,* 64–84; Sheidley, *Sectional Nationalism,* 3, 22, 34. An excellent example of aristocratic longings among some Americans is the case of Elizabeth Patterson Bonaparte of Baltimore; see Lewis, *Elizabeth Patterson Bonaparte,* 65–70, 98–109.

29. Sullivan, *Rambles and Scrambles* (1852), 179; Mackay, *Western World* (1850), III: 339; William Thomson, *Tradesman's Travels* (1842), 225; Thomason, *Hints to Emigrants* (1848), 56; see Pulszky and Pulszky, *White, Red, Black* (1853), I: 113–16.

30. Beaufoy, *Tour Through Parts of the United States and Canada* (1828), 75, 139; see discussion in Tocqueville, *Democracy in America,* trans. Goldhammer (1835), I: 8–11.

31. Grattan, *Civilized America* (1859), 98; Basil Hall, *Travels in North America* (1830), II: 305; Pulszky and Pulszky, *White, Red, Black* (1853), I: 118.

32. Tocqueville, *Democracy in America,* trans. Goldhammer (1835), I: 9, 58–59; Hamilton, *Men and Manners in America* (1834), I: 301; Basil Hall, *Travels in North America* (1830), I: 305.

33. Robert W. Russell, *America Compared with England* (1848), 27; London *Atlas* related in George Combe, *Notes on the United States of North America* (1841), I: 212; Featherstonhaugh, *Excursion through the Slave States* (1844), xv.

34. Houstoun, *Hesperos* (1850), I: 221–22; Robert W. Russell, *America Compared with England* (1848), 122; Ouseley, *Remarks on the Statistics and Political Institutions of the United States* (1832), 51; Martineau, *Society in America* (1839), I: 163; see Gurowski, *America and Europe* (1857), 68–71.

35. Pulszky and Pulszky, *White, Red, Black* (1853), I: 113.

36. Grattan, *Civilized America* (1859), 471–72.

37. James Johnston, *Notes on North America* (1851), I: 254.

38. Chevalier, *Society, Manners and Politics* (1839), 62–63; Gurowski, *America and Europe* (1857), 109–116; Robert W. Russell, *America Compared with England* (1848), xvi, xxi.

39. On attitudes to labor and how desperation was the only way to get the masses to work, see Amphlett, *Emigrant's Directory to the Western States of North America* (1819), 84; Kendall, *Travels Through the Northern Parts of the United States* (1809), III: 74; Ferrall, *Ramble of Six Thousand Miles Through the United States of America* (1832), 202; Phillippo, *United States and Cuba* (1857), 94; Maury, *Englishwoman in America* (1848), cx–cxi.

40. Mackenzie, *Sketches of Canada and the United States* (1833), 356; Tocqueville, *Democracy in America,* trans. Goldhammer (1835), I: 53–57; O'Bryan, *Narrative of Travels in the United States of America* (1836), 345; see Melish, *Travels Through the United States* (1818), 100; Holmes, *An Account of the United States of America* (1823), 102.

41. Charles Murray, *Travels in North America* (1854), I: 141, 142; Mackay, *Western World* (1850), II: 136; Robert Russell, *North America* (1857), 138–39; most believed that the practice of inheritance to a family member continued after the ending of entail and primogeniture; Stirling, *Letters from the Slave States* (1857), 63.

42. Vigne, *Six Months in America* (1833), 94–95. The same explanation was given by Richard Cobden, in "Warren Isham, 'Interview with Cobden,'" *Michigan Farmer* IX (November 1, 1851), 329. Sir Charles Lyell indicated that entail and primogeniture were "an integral portion of a great political system, wholly different from their own," Lyell, *Second Visit to the United States of North America* (1849), I: 59–65. See also Hamilton, *Men and Manners in America* (1834), 61–62.

43. "Observations on Obscurity of Birth," *New York Farmer,* VIII (December 1835), 17; Martineau, *Society in America* (1839), II: 295, 302–305; Grund, *Aristocracy in America* (1839), 108. For the defense of inheritance, see Basil Hall, *Travels in America* (1830), 322–23.

44. Pulszky and Pulszky, *White, Red, Black* (1853), II: 249.

45. Henry, Lord Brougham, *Political Philosophy, Part II: Aristocracy* (1843), quote 23, and 23–28; Holmes, *An Account of the United States* (1823), 125; Lewis, *Impressions of America and the American Churches* (1845), 395–96. See Prochaska, *Eminent Victorians on American Democracy,* 137; Roper, *Democracy and Its Critics,* 6–7, 200.

46. Vigne, *Six Months in America* (1833), 92–94; Tocqueville, *Democracy in America,* trans. Goldhammer (1840), vol. 2, part 2, ch. 20; Marryat, *Diary in America* (1839), 468–72.

47. "A Yankee Among the Aristocrats," *Cincinnati Weekly Herald and Philanthropist,* April 2, 1845, vol. 9, p. 2. Same story related in *Atkinson's Saturday Evening Post,* 7 September 1833, vol. 13, no. 632, p. 1.

48. County convention, Vandalia, Illinois, "Address to the Democratic Republicans to the State of Illinois," in *Illinois State Register* (Vandalia), November 4, 1837. See "Necessity of Organization—and Its Objects," Democratic Members of the New York Legislature, in *Illinois State Register* (Springfield), June 19, 1840; Stephen A. Douglas to Gehazi Granger, November 9, 1835, in Johannsen, ed., *Letters of Stephen A. Douglas,* 21; resolutions of National Democratic Convention, in *Illinois State Register* (Springfield), May 29, 1840; Stephen A. Douglas toast at Democratic Celebration, in *Illinois State Register* (Vandalia), January 29, 1839.

49. Martin Van Buren to Convention of New York City, June 20, 1848, in Van Buren Papers, LC, reel 31; July 4, 1849 speech of J. Glancy Jones, in Jones, ed., *Life of J. Glancy Jones,* I: 145; Bangor, Maine, Independent Democrats in (Augusta, Maine) *Kennebec Journal,* September 11, 1846; *Milwaukee Weekly Wisconsin,* March 8, 1848. On Jefferson's first inaugural, *Kenosha (Wisc.) Democrat,* September 8, 1854.

50. Speech at Buffalo, New York, October 20, 1859, in John Dickinson, ed., *Speeches, Correspondence, etc., of the Late Daniel S. Dickinson,* 655. This should be compared to Lincoln's distinction between the Declaration and the Constitution in his speech about the apples of gold in a picture of silver; Guelzo, *Abraham Lincoln as a Man of Ideas,* ch. 6.

51. Edwin M. Stanton to Salmon P. Chase, January 5, 1847, in Niven, ed., *Salmon P. Chase Papers,* 2: 139–40.

52. Abraham Lincoln speech, July 6, 1852, in Basler, ed., *Collected Works of Abraham Lincoln,* II: 130–31; *Toledo Blade,* March 12, 1857; on the Pettit incident, see Tewell, *A Self-Evident Lie;* for resolutions, Minnesota State resolutions, *New York Tribune,* September 18, 1857, p. 5;

speech of Charles Case in Ridgefield, Conn., in *New York Times,* March 28, 1860, p. 2; Republican national nominating convention at Chicago, *New York Tribune,* May 18, 1860, p. 5; New Jersey convention in *Newark Daily Advertiser,* February 3, 1860. The abolitionist use of the Declaration's statement on equality is well known; see Maier, *American Scripture.* 197–99.

53. *Milwaukee Weekly Wisconsin,* March 15, 1848; "Industrial Reform," *United States and Democratic Review* 23 (December 1848), 516; "Wealth of the Aristocracy," *Saturday Evening Post,* October 4, 1856, p. 4; "British Incomes," *Niles Weekly Register,* March 2, 1816, p. 13; "Mr. Coke of Norfolk, England," (Baltimore) *Farmer and Gardener* 4 (October 31, 1837), 210; R. Wheateley, "English Land Tenure: The Aristocracy," *Christian Advocate and Journal* 39 (March 3, 1864), 65; "European Agriculture and Rural Economy," (Albany) *Cultivator* 1 (June 1844), 178. For an American enjoying the wealth displayed by the aristocracy, see Washington Irving, *Voyage and Other English Essays from the Sketch Book,* 13–21.

54. Theodore Parker to Rev. S. J. May [1853?], in *Life and Correspondence of Theodore Parker,* ed. Weiss, II: 118; Coffin, *Drum-Beat of the Nation* (1888), 2; Boardman, *America, and the Americans* (1833), 328; Lang, *Religion and Education in America* (1840), 43.

55. Cooper, *American Democrat* (1839), viii–ix, 36–41, 41 (quote), 46 (quote).

56. James K. Paulding to John C. Calhoun, April 5, 1848, in *Papers of John Calhoun,* ed. Meriwether, XXV: 296.

CHAPTER FOUR

1. The comparison has often been missed because authors have either emphasized the question of democracy, focused entirely on Tocqueville, or have been so taken by the transportation/market revolution, that they have lost the aristocratic comparison. Most of the literature on American manners and behaviors stresses class differences or semiotics, not the impact of equality, in particular the attempt to escape aristocratic pretensions. On behaviors and exchanges, see Kasson, *Rudeness and Civility;* Bushman, *Refinement of America;* Persons, *Decline of American Gentility;* Zakim and Kornblith, eds., *Capitalism Takes Command;* Sellers, *Market Revolution.* Unlike the presentation given in this chapter, Christopher Mulvey sees commonalities between the British and the Americans; Mulvey, *Transatlantic Manners.* Most of the labor and urban histories deal with class formation in American cities, not a comparison of class actions in Europe and the United States, e.g., Johnson, *Shopkeeper's Dilemma;* Ryan, *Cradle of the Middle Class;* Wilentz, *Chants Democratic;* Pessen, *Jacksonian America,* esp. ch. 2, 3; Laurie, *Artisans into Workers;* Blumin, *Emergence of the Middle Class;* Dawley, *Class and Community.*

2. Edward Pessen gave a decidedly negative reading of foreign visitors' claims about American equality; Pessen used a strictly economic idea of equality as meaning no deviation from an average. He did not, however, go very deeply into arguments the visitors created, nor did he look closely at the comparisons between the United States and Europe that these wayfarers were making. Pessen, *Jacksonian America,* 27–30, 42–57.

3. Oldmixon, *Transatlantic Wanderings* (1855), iv, 1–2; Godley, *Letters from America* (1844), I: vii–xiv.

4. Tocqueville, *Democracy in America,* trans. Goldhammer (1840), II: 655–59, quotes on 660, 661. On deference, see Zuckerman, "Tocqueville, Turner, and Turds," 13–42, and the ensuing roundtable discussion with discussants Aaron S. Fogelman, Kathleen M. Brown, John M. Murrin, and Robert A. Gross, 43–97. There is an immense literature on Tocqueville. For an attack on Tocqueville's belief that Americans had egalitarian social structures, see Pessen, *Jacksonian America,* ch. 3. An author who underscores Tocqueville's reluctance to see the withering away of aristocracy is Boesche, *Strange Liberalism of Alexis de Tocqueville.* For the tension between the new world of equality and the old world of aristocracy in Tocqueville, see Mancini, *Alexis de Tocqueville.* See also Welch, *De Tocqueville;* Harvey Mitchell, *America After Tocqueville.*

5. Parkinson, *Tour in America* (1805), I: 30–31; Blowe, *Geographical, Historical, Commercial, and Agricultural View* (1820), 61; Davies, *American Scenes, and Christian Slavery* (1849), 148 (quote), 310; Gurney, *Journey in North America* (1841), 12.

6. Mitchell, *Ten Years Residence in the United States* (1862), 187; Stirling, *Letters from the Slave States* (1857), 34.

7. Bristed, *Resources of the United States of America* (1818), 444; Warren Isham, "Interview with Cobden," *Michigan Farmer* IX (November 1, 1851), 329.

8. Phillippo, *United States and Cuba* (1857), 94; Oldmixon, *Transatlantic Wanderings* (1855), 3; see also Mitchell, *Ten Years Residence* (1862), 163–64.

9. The two classic delineations of English landed society are Mingay, *English Landed Society;* and Thompson, *English Landed Society.* For servants, see Kussmaul, *Servants in Husbandry in Early Modern England;* Hecht, *Domestic Servant Class.*

10. Fordham, *Personal Narrative of Travels* (1818), 168 (quote), 135, 210; Faux, *Faux's Memorable Days in America* (1823), quote 31, 148; Robert W. Russell, *America Compared with England* (1848), 81; Oldmixon, *Transatlantic Wanderings* (1855), 3–4; see Flower, *Letters from the Illinois* (1822), 103–106; Fearon, *Sketches of America* (1818), 69–71, 224; Parkinson, *Tour in America* (1805), I: 170.

11. Robert Russell, *North America* (1857), 15; Baxter, *America and the Americans* (1855), 211; Shirreff, *Tour Through North America* (1835), 340, 347–48; Tocqueville, *Democracy in America,* trans. Goldhammer (1840), II: 679. The character of American agriculture as opposed to Great Britain's was caught by Hobsbawm, *Age of Revolution,* 29–34. Travelers going to Niagara often visited the Van Rensselaer manor, but they considered it an anomaly in the republic; Clark, *Social Change in America,* 241–44. On the agricultural ladder and the historiography behind it, see Atack, "The Agricultural Ladder Revisited," 1–26. The basic work on farm labor remains Schob, *Hired Hands and Plowboys.* On egalitarianism in northern farming, see Atack and Bateman, *To Their Own Soil,* 86–101.

12. Hancock, *Emigrant's Five Years in the Free States of America* (1860), 86-87; Thomson, *Tradesman's Travels* (1842), 77; Ferrall, *Ramble of Six Thousand Miles* (1832), 66 . On the celebration of labor, see Mackay, *Western World* (1850), III: 342; Gerhard, *Illinois As It Is* (1857), 451; Chevalier, *Society, Manners and Politics* (1839), 333, 344–45; Martineau, *Society in America* (1839), II: 302; Power, *Impressions of America* (1836), I: 333–34.

13. D. Griffiths, *Two Years in the New Settlements of Ohio* (1835), 80; Stuart, *Three Years in North America* (1833), II: 421; Hodgson, *Remarks during a Journey Through North America* (1823), 203–204; Flower, *Letters from the Illinois* (1822), 105–106; see also W. M. Stewart, *Eleven Years' Experience in the Western States of America* (1870), 83–94.

14. Tocqueville, *Democracy in America*, trans. Goldhammer (1840), II: 669, 671 (quote).

15. Elkanah Watson in *Men and Times of the Revolution* (1856), ed. Watson, 170; Basil Hall, *Travels in North America* (1830), I: 300.

16. Priest, *Travels in the United States of America* (1802), 24.

17. Holmes, *An Account of the United States* (1823), 125; Bernhard, Duke of Saxe-Weimar Eisenach, *Travels Through North America* (1828), I: 126; Gurney, *Journey in North America* (1841), 22, 24. On Irish and African American slaves, Boardman, *America, and the Americans* (1833), 35–36; Fowler, *Journal of a Tour in the State of New York* (1831), 218. See also Pulszky and Pulszky, *White, Red, Black* (1853), I: 63; Bromley, *A Woman's Wanderings in the Western World* (1861), 34, 40.

18. Kingdom, *America and the British Colonies* (1820), 16.

19. Frances Trollope, *Domestic Manners of the Americans* (1832), I: 61, 106–107. Frances Trollope was the person who penned the famous line that egalitarians would change their minds about equality "when it presents itself in the shape of a hard, greasy paw." Ibid., 109. On Trollope, see Wheeler, *O My America*, ch. 1.

20. Blowe, *Geographical, Historical, Commercial, and Agricultural View* (1820), 74; Fordham, *Personal Narrative of Travels* (1818), 195; Griffiths, *Two Years in the New Settlements of Ohio* (1835), 81–82; Houstoun, *Hesperos* (1850), I: 109; Hancock, *Emigrant's Five Years in the Free States* (1860), 41, 85; Combe, *Notes on the United States* (1841), I: 93; Trollope, *Domestic Manners* (1832), I: 61.

21. Adam Hodgson, William Amphlett, and Adlard Welby mentioned that they took servants with them; others probably did as well. Hodgson, *Remarks during a Journey* (1823), 21; Amphlett, *Emigrant's Directory to the Western States* (1819), 71; Welby, *Visit to North America and the English Settlements in Illinois* (1821), 59.

22. Vigne, *Six Months in America* (1833), 9; Welby, *Visit to North America and the English Settlements in Illinois* (1821), 37; Trollope, *Domestic Manners of the Americans* (1832). Many of these acerbic statements were collected in a book, [unknown ed.], *Domestic Manners of the Americans* (1836).

23. Tocqueville, *Democracy in America*, trans. Goldhammer (1840), II: 661 (quote), 660–62, 673–78; Blane, *Excursion Through the United States and Canada* (1824), 146; Fordham, *Personal Narrative of Travels* (1818), 145; Charles B. Johnson, *Letters from the British Settlement in Pennsylvania* (1819), 111; John Palmer, *Journal of Travels in the United States* (1818), 13.

24. Carlisle, *Travels in America* (1851), 76; Bird, *Englishwoman in America* (1856), 311; Reid, *Sketches in North America* (1861), 46–47; Stuart-Wortley, *Travels in the United States* (1851), 32. On Isabella Bird, see Wheeler, *O My America*, ch. 5.

25. Dalton, *Travels in the United States* (1821), 52–53; Shirreff, *Tour Through North America* (1835), 405–406; Palmer, *Journal of Travels* (1818), 241.

26. Griffiths, *Two Years in the New Settlements of Ohio* (1835), 78; Prentice, *Tour in the United States* (1850), 22; Dalton, *Travels in the United States* (1821), 53; Mattson, *Story of an Emigrant* (1891), 12; O'Hanlon, *Irish Emigrant's Guide for the United States* (1851), 160, 161; see John Howe, *Emigrants' New Guide* (1822), 46.

27. Marryat, *Diary in America* (1839), 460–61; Ferrall, *Ramble of Six Thousand Miles* (1832), 179–80; Robert Russell, *North America* (1857), 5; Ranken, *Canada and the Crimea* (1863), 4.

28. Holmes, *Account of the United States* (1823), 202; Prentice, *Tour in the United States* (1850), 22; Reid, *Sketches in North America* (1861), 44–45. For an opposite view that having a distant upper class raised the lower class, see Washington Irving, "Rural Life in England [1822]," in *Voyage and Other English* Essays (1891), 17–19.

29. An American, *American Husbandry* (1775), I: 71; Bristed, *Resources of the United States* (1818), 290; see also Tremenheere, *Notes on Public Subjects* (1852), 13; Edward Augustus Kendall, *Travels Through the Northern Parts of the United States* (1809), III: 74; for lower classes reacting to incentives, see Crèvecoeur, *Letters from an American Farmer* (1782), 83–84. On the difference in police protection, Kilbride, *Being American in Europe,* 114. The frank admission of classes is in Hancock, *Emigrant's Five Years in the Free States* (1860), 86–87.

30. Lyell, *Travels in North America* (1845), I: 49; *Maine Farmer,* VI (July 31, 1838), 195. See An Englishman [Frances Wright], *Views of Society and Manners in America* (1821), 460. On American gentility, the basic work, somewhat at variance with the view given here, is Persons, *Decline of American Gentility.*

31. Tudor, *Narrative of a Tour in North America* (1834), I: 448; Hugh Murray, *United States of America* (1844), III: 29; Robert Russell, *North America* (1857), 133; see Francis Hall, *Travels in Canada and the United States* (1818), 59; Pairpoint, *Uncle Sam and His Country* (1857), 36.

32. Reid, *Sketches in North America* (1861), 23; Moore, *Journal of a Voyage Across the Atlantic* (1845), 71; Davies, *American Scenes, and Christian Slavery* (1849), 202.

33. Houstoun, *Hesperos* (1850), I: 168; James Stuart, *Three Years in North America* (1833), I: 32; Ferrall, *Ramble of Six Thousand Miles* (1832), 179–80; Robert Baird, *Impressions and Experiences of the West Indies and North America* (1850), II: 56.

34. Vigne, *Six Months in America* (1833), 9; Pairpoint, *Uncle Sam and His Country* (1857), 336; Tudor, *Narrative of a Tour* (1834), I: 317. See Jobson, *America and American Methodism* (1857), 27; Trollope, *Domestic Manners* (1832), I: 60; Parkinson, *Tour in America* (1805), 30–31; H, "Agriculture and Rural Economy of Europe," *Cultivator* IV (August 1847), 251.

35. Johnston, *Notes on North America* (1851), I: 425.

36. Bunn, *Old England and New England* (1853), II, 304; Flower, *Letters from the Illinois* (1822), 94, 96 ; Murray, *United States of America* (1844), III: 30; Houstoun, *Hesperos* (1850), I: 177; Rochefoucault Liancourt, *Travels Through the United States of America,* 422–23.

37. Blane, *Excursion Through the United States and Canada* (1824), 49; Robertson, *A Few Months in America* (1855), 38; see Weld, *Vacation Tour of the United States and Canada* (1855), 273; Tocqueville, *Democracy in America,* trans. Goldhammer (1835), I: 232–33.

38. Incident in Willson, *America's Ambassadors to England,* 281–85, 284 (quote).

CHAPTER FIVE

1. Education during the colonial era was conceived to have two major tasks: to induce young people to accept hierarchy and authority, and to entrench Protestant beliefs and behaviors. By the 1820s, change drifted into education as some working-class radicals felt education was a way to dethrone the financial aristocracy and establish democracy, while others, in the

1840s and 1850s, found public schooling a necessity for creating an educated public who could maintain representative government. Carl Kaestle acknowledges that some authors are correct in seeing schools as mechanisms of social control that elicited consent to the existing social and economic order, yet antebellum education in Kaestle's view was primarily about teaching republicanism to children. Jean Baker finds that common schools in practice were excellent in fostering egalitarian attitudes among youth. Curti, *Social Ideas of American Educators,* 4–10, 57–61, 76–92; Welter, *Popular Education and Democratic Thought in America,* 1–4, 17–19, 35–36, 45–56, 68–72, 103–116; Kaestle, *Pillars of the Republic,* 75–100, 219; Baker, *Affairs of Party,* ch. 2.

2. Ashworth, *Tour in the United States, Cuba, and Canada* (1861), 13; Carlisle, *Travels in America* (1851), 76; Pairpoint, *Uncle Sam and His Country* (1857), 334; Bird, *Englishwoman in America* (1856), 434; Bristed, *Resources of the United States* (1818), 229; Wilson, *Wanderer in America* (1822), 94–95; Dickens, *American Notes* (1842), I: 170; Baird, *Impressions and Experiences of the West Indies and North America* (1850), II: 56–57; Davies, *American Scenes, and Christian Slavery* (1849), 310.

3. Houstoun, *Hesperos* (1850), I: 47–48; Priest, *Travels in the United States* (1802), 208–209; Chambers, *Things as They Are in America* (1854), 159–60, 233; Buckingham, *America Historical, Statistic, and Descriptive* (1841), II: 320–21; see Combe, *Notes on the United States* (1841), I: 56; Griffiths, *Two Years in the New Settlements of Ohio* (1835), 83–84; Chevalier, *Society, Manners and Politics in the United States* (1839), 335; O'Hanlon, *Irish Emigrant's Guide* (1851), 162; Stewart, *Eleven Years' Experience* (1870), 115; Dickens, *American Notes* (1842), 208.

4. Hamilton, *Men and Manners in America* (1834), I: 354–55; Tremenheere, *Notes on Public Subjects* (1852), 3, 6, 8, 13–15, 32–36; Gurney, *Journey in North America* (1841), 139; Godley, *Letters from America* (1844), II: 31–33.

5. Bristed, *Resources of the United States* (1818), 422–23; Chevalier, *Society, Manners and Politics* (1839), 347; Finch, *Englishwoman's Experience in America* (1853), 271. However, it may have been that southerners were about to address this deficiency; for example, the fire-eating extremist John A. Quitman called for the creation of a public school system in Mississippi in his 1849 gubernatorial inaugural address; Claiborne, *Life and Correspondence of John A. Quitman* (1860), II: 22–24.

6. Rich, *General View of the United States* (1833), 76; Johnston, *Notes on North America* (1851), I: 248; Cobden, *Political Writings* (1867), I: 121, 123; Mackay, *Western World* (1850), III: 331; Hancock, *Emigrant's Five Years* (1860), 260.

7. James Stirling, *Letters from the Slave States* (1857), 130, 354 (quote); Robert Russell, *North America* (1857), 94–95. See Chambers, *Things As They Are in America* (1854), 237–38.

8. See Soltow and Stevens, *Rise of Literacy and the Common School in the United States,* ch. 3.

9. Shirreff, *Tour Through North America* (1835), 26, 53; for an overview of education in the nineteenth century, see Kaestle, *Pillars of the Republic.* A good summary of the expectations of educated reform-minded New Englanders on education can be found in Robert Rantoul, "The Education of a Free People" (1839), in Rantoul, *Memoirs, Speeches and Writings,* ed. Hamilton (1854), 119–38.

10. Pairpoint, *Uncle Sam and His Country* (1857), 59; Reid, *Sketches in North America* (1861), 44; Prentice, *Tour in the United States* (1850), 123–24; Henry Ashworth, *Tour in the United*

States, Cuba, and Canada (1861), 19; Pulszky and Pulszky, *White, Red, Black* (1853), III: 44–45; Robert Russell, *North America* (1857), 5; James D. Lang, *Religion and Education in America* (1840), 40.

11. Clarke, *Autobiography, Diary and Correspondence* (1891), ed. Hale, 28; see Baker, *Affairs of Party,* ch. 2.

12. Robert W. Russell, *America Compared with England* (1848), 43, 121–23; Martineau, *Society in America* (1839), I: 163; Shirreff, *Tour Through North America* (1835), 54–55; Chambers, *Things as They Are in America* (1854), 236–37, see 346; Lang, *Religion and Education in America* (1840), 40–41. See comment of Brodrick, *English Land and English Landlords* (1881), 216; Doyle, *Aristocracy and Its Enemies,* 32–33. For an assessment of the impact of inequality on public funding for education, based on South America versus North America, see Engerman, Mariscal, and Sokoloff, "Evolution of Schooling in the Americas, 1800–1925," 94–128.

13. "Extract from an Address delivered at the close of the Winter Session of Western Agricultural School, Parke County, Indiana, 1853," in *Indiana Farmer* 2 (July 15, 1853), 332–33; Olmsted, *Walks and Talks* (1859), 241; Hetty Lee, "A Few Thoughts on the Duties of Women," *Indiana Farmer* 2 (April 15, 1853), 254; see A Laborer, "Elevate the Laboring Man," *Colman's Rural World* 34 (November 24, 1881), 1.

14. Salter, *Life of James W. Grimes,* 26, 57 (quote); Gerritt Smith at Cooper Institute, October 6, 1858, in *New York Tribune,* October 7, 1858, p. 5.

15. Cunynghame, *Glimpse at the Great Western Republic* (1851), 62–63. For comments about reading, Buckingham, *America Historical, Statistic, and Descriptive* (1841), II: 91; Anthony Trollope, *North America* (1862), I: 203–204; Ouseley, *Remarks on the Statistics and Political Institutions of the United States* (1832), 56. On how education was attached to the ideology of free labor, Martineau, *Society in America* (1839), II: 295, 302–305; Blowe, *Geographical, Historical, Commercial, and Agricultural View of the United States* (1820), 73; *Ohio State Journal* (Columbus), May 18, 1854, p. 2. For a modern assessment of the importance of education in the twentieth century, thereby creating the century of "human capital," see Goldin, "The Human-Capital Century and American Leadership," 263–92.

16. Cobden, *Political Writings* (1867), I: 98–99; Duhring, *Remarks on the United States of America* (1833), ch. 2; Wyse, *America, Its Realities and Resources* (1846), ch. 9; Sullivan, *Rambles and Scrambles* (1852), 32; see Lewis, *Impressions of America and the American Churches* (1845), 397; Logan, *Notes of a Journey Through Canada, the United States of America, and the West Indies* (1838), 194. For the problems of George Lewis, see Aladsdair Pettinger, "George Lewis and the American Churches," 145–62.

17. Davies, *American Scenes, and Christian Slavery* (1849), 118; Lyell, *Second Visit to the United States* (1849), I: 46; Kingdom, *America and the British Colonies* (1820), 14; Houstoun, *Hesperos* (1850), I: 82; Carlisle, *Travels in America* (1851), 29–30, 77.

18. Thomason, *Hints to Emigrants* (1848), 13–14, 28; Ashworth, *Tour in the United States* (1861), 181.

19. Bristed, *Resources of the United States* (1818), 122–23; Stirling, *Letters from the Slave States* (1857), 355.

20. Tremenheere, *Notes on Public Subjects* (1852), 6, 8, 13, 15, 35–36; see also Gurney, *Journey in North America* (1841), 139; Robert Russell, *North America* (1857), 99.

21. Cobbett, *Emigrant's Guide* (1830), 7, 92, 93; Cobbett, *Rural Rides . . . during the Years 1821 to 1832* (1909), II: 1; Cobbett, *Year's Residence in the United States* (1819), 194, 227–32; Cobbett, *Cottage Economy* (1833), 4; Holmes, *Account of the United States* (1823), 2–3; Buckingham, *America Historical, Statistic, and Descriptive* (1841), II: 90.

22. Bunn, *Old England and New England* (1853), I: 21.

23. Godley, *Letters from America* (1844), I: 43–46; Jobson, *America and American Methodism* (1857), 113; Combe, *Notes on the United States* (1841), I: xiv; Cawley, ed., *American Diaries of Richard Cobden,* 194; Goldwin Smith, *Civil War In America* (1866), quotes 4, 13, and generally 2–27.

24. Buckingham, *America Historical, Statistic, and Descriptive* (1841), I: 118; Bristed, *Resources of the United States* (1818), 422–23; MacKay, *Life and Liberty in America* (1859), I: 312–14; Marshall Hall, *Two-Fold Slavery of the United States* (1854), 89; Davies, *American Scenes, and Christian Slavery* (1849), 26, 72.

25. Lewis, *Impressions of America and the American Churches* (1845), 54; O'Bryan, *Narrative of Travels* (1836), 293; Davies, *American Scenes, and Christian Slavery* (1849), 224; John Godley, *Letters from America* (1844), II: 89; Vigne, *Six Months in America* (1833), 192.

26. O'Bryan, *Narrative of Travels* (1836), 293. The *United States Democratic Review* in 1848 reported that England had 10,190 clergy paid £10,600,000, which works out to be £1,040 per person (about $5,200). William Ouseley arrives at an average for clergy of about £200 ($1,000), but the numbers may be doubted. G. W. Quinby reported in 1860 that there were two archbishops and twenty-five bishops, earning probably over $50,000 per year; Queen Victoria was given $2,000,000 per year by Parliament; the US president's salary was $50,000. "Industrial Reform," *United States Democratic Review* 23 (December 1848), 516; Ouseley, *Remarks on the Statistics and Political Institutions of the United States* (1832), 120–22; Quinby, *Plea for Humanity* (1860), 313. A listing of the gross incomes of the English sees is given in *Bankers' Magazine* 1 (April 1847), 561. The total was £3,151, 681.

27. Dalton, *Travels in the United States* (1821), 253–54; Stephen Davis, *Notes of a Tour in America in 1832 and 1833* (1833), 23; Francis Hall, *Travels in Canada and the United States* (1818), 293. Compare this to the modern analysis of Finke, Guest, and Stark, "Mobilizing Local Religious Markets," 203–218.

28. Francis Hall, *Travels in Canada and the United States* (1818), 470–72; Johnston, *Notes on North America* (1851), I: 412; Combe, *Notes on the United States* (1841), I: 214; see also Chevalier, *Society, Manners and Politics* (1839), 394–95.

29. On the idea of religion being important primarily to obtain social order, not merely to save souls, see Isaac, *Transformation of Virginia,* 291; McGarvie, *One Nation Under Law,* 21–23; Doyle, *Aristocracy and Its Enemies,* 37–39. For Jefferson's denunciation of religious leaders being the dupes of tyrants, see Kramnick and Moore, *Godless Constitution,* 98–99.

30. Playfair, *Recollections of a Visit to the United States* (1856), 145; Ferrall, *Ramble of Six Thousand Miles* (1832), 70; Robert W.. Russell, *America Compared with England* (1848), 84; Maury, *Englishwoman in America* (1848), 97; Fidler, *Observations on Professions, Literature, Manners, and Emigration in the United States and Canada* (1833), 31–32.

31. Playfair, *Recollections of a Visit to the United States* (1856), 146; O'Bryan, *Narrative of Travels in the United States* (1836), 293–94.

32. Combe, *Notes on the United States* (1841), I: 214; Lang, *Religion and Education in America* (1840), iv–vi, 40–41; Chambers, *Things as They Are in America* (1854), 235; see also Olmsted, *Walks and Talks* (1859), 114–16, 238–39, 241; see Doyle, *Aristocracy and Its Enemies,* 21.

33. Robert W. Russell, *America Compared with England* (1848), 124 (quote), 43.

CHAPTER SIX

1. Fibbleton, *Travels in America* (1833), 9; Lewis, *Impressions of America and the American Churches* (1845), 397; Sullivan, *Rambles and Scrambles* (1852), vi.

2. For examples, Boesche, *Strange Liberalism of Alexis de Tocqueville;* Mitchell, *America After Tocqueville;* Cheryl Welch, *De Tocqueville.* For a good summary, Mancini, *Alexis de Tocqueville.* For the British attack on democracy and equality in the nineteenth century, see Roper, *Democracy and Its Critics;* Prochaska, *Eminent Victorians on American Democracy;* Lippincott, *Victorian Critics of Democracy.*

3. Bristed, *Resources of the United States* (1818), 220 (quote), 227–28.

4. Henry, Lord Brougham, *Political Philosophy, Part II: Of Aristocracy* (1843), 23–28. Isaac Holmes added to this an analogy to the human body; for centuries, government required a head to direct the community in the same fashion a head directs the motions of the body; Holmes, *Account of the United States* (1823), 4.

5. Williams, *Rise and Fall of the 'The Model Republic,'* (1863), 155–56; Mitchell, *Ten Years Residence in the United States* (1862), 252; Bristed, *Resources of the United States* (1818), 243–44.

6. Palmer, *Journal of Travels in the United States* (1818), 91; Ferrall, *Ramble of Six Thousand Miles* (1832), 243; Dickens, *American Notes* (1842), I: 130–31; see Wilson, *Wanderer in America,* 16.

7. William Dalton, *Travels in the United* States (1821), 53–54.

8. Fearon, *Sketches of America* (1818), 11; Palmer, *Journal of Travels in the United States* (1818), 76; Holmes, *Account of the United States* (1823), 104; Johnson, *Letters from the British Settlement in Pennsylvania* (1819), 113.

9. Blane, *Excursion through the United States and Canada* (1824), 69; Stirling, *Letters from the Slave States* (1857), 146; Chevalier, *Society, Manners and Politics* (1839), 322; Tocqueville, *Democracy in America,* trans. Goldhammer (1835), I: 99–100, 276–77.

10. Holmes, *Account of the United States* (1823), 102–103.

11. Mitchell, *Ten Years Residence in the United States* (1862), 163–64. See "Civilization: American and European," *American [Whig] Review* III (June 1846), 622.

12. Tocqueville, *Democracy in America,* trans. Goldhammer (1835), I: 224–27, 232–34, 238–45, 264–68.

13. Robert W. Russell, *America Compared with England* (1848), 59; Rhode Island governor's salary in Chambers, *Things as They Are in America* (1854), 233; presidential salary in Kingdom, *America and the British Colonies* (1820), 14–15; New York governor salary in Mackenzie, *Sketches of Canada and the United States* (1833), 357; Queen Victoria income in Quinby, *Plea for Humanity* (1860), 313; comparison of president with English minister, Blane, *Excursion Through the United States and Canada* (1818), 64; revenue from Erie Canal, Gurney, *Journey in North America* (1841), 138.

14. William Brown, *America* (1849), 34–35; Johnston, *Notes on North America* (1851), I: 246–48.

15. Palmer, *Journal of Travels in the United States* (1818), 263; Holmes, *Account of the United States* (1823), 121 (quote), 116–22; "Salaries," *Niles Weekly Register,* January 20, 1816, p. 350; "Industrial Reform," *United States Democratic Review* XXIII (December 1848), 513–24, numbers on p. 518.

16. Actually, few foreign writers ever said "white" manhood suffrage; they just left it at universal manhood suffrage.

17. Featherstonhaugh, *Excursion Through the Slave States* (1844), I: xxv–xxvi; Stirling, *Letters from the Slave States* (1857), 104, 190–91; Mitchell, *Ten Years Residence in the United States* (1862), 76.

18. Basil Hall, *Travels in North America* (1830), II: 278–84, 300–301; Hamilton, *Men and Manners in America* (1834), I: 362–66; Lyell, *Second Visit to the United States* (1849), I: 82–85; Bird, *Englishwoman in America* (1856), 412–14.

19. Vigne, *Six Months in America* (1833), 71.

20. Lyell, *Second Visit to the United States* (1849), I: 85–86; Hamilton, *Men and Manners in America* (1834), 313–16; Stirling, *Letters from the Slave States* (1857), 167.

21. Ashworth, *Tour in the United States, Cuba, and Canada* (1861), 182; see also Hancock, *Emigrant's Five Years* (1860), 126, 171.

22. Baird, *Impressions and Experiences of the West Indies and North America* (1860), II: 75; Dickens, *American Notes* (1842), I: 290–91; Logan, *Notes of a Journey Through Canada, the United States of America, and the West Indies* (1838), 188; Tocqueville, *Democracy in America,* trans. Goldhammer (1835), I: 225–27; Mitchell, *Ten Years Residence in the United States* (1862), 168–70; Lyell, *Second Visit to the United States* (1849), I: 82–85; Bird, *Englishwoman in Canada* (1856), 416–18; Bristed, *Resources of the United States* (1818), 117–21; Baxter, *America and the Americans* (1855), 56. Harriet Martineau remarked on how wealth was the element that divided American parties; Martineau, *Society in America* (1839), I: 11–14.

23. Tocqueville, *Democracy in America,* trans. Goldhammer (1835), I: 225, 258, 265–66, 271, 279; Johnson, *Letters from the British Settlement in Pennsylvania* (1819), 125; Ferrall, *Ramble of Six Thousand Miles* (1832), 295–96; also, Blane, *An Excursion Through the United States and Canada* (1824), 67–68.

24. Stockton, *Gracchi,* 6–18; [George Bancroft?], "Slavery in Rome," *North American Review* 39 (October 1834), 415–19.

25. Hamilton, *Men and Manners in America* (1834), I: 295–300; Basil Hall, *Travels in North America* (1830), II: 309–321; Beaufoy, *Tour Through Parts of the United States and Canada* (1828), 139; Vigne, *Six Months in America* (1833), 91; also included in this group would be Shirreff, *Tour Through North America* (1835), 292–301.

26. Tocqueville, *Democracy in America,* trans. Goldhammer (1835), I: 240–42, 275–76, 319–30; Martineau, *Society in America* (1839), I: 16–17, 22–29; Ouseley, *Remarks on the Statistics and Political Institutions of the United States* (1832), 74; Robert W. Russell, *America Compared with England* (1849), 19–24; "Radicalism," *United States Democratic Review* III (October 1838), 106–109.

27. Tocqueville, *Democracy in America,* trans. Goldhammer (1835), I: 283–300, the phrase "tyranny of the majority," pp. 288, 301.

28. Sullivan, *Rambles and Scrambles in North and South America* (1852), 205; Logan, *Notes of a Journey Through Canada, the United States of America, and the West Indies* (1838), 188;

Frances Trollope, *Domestic Manners of the Americans* (1832), II: 299; Daubeny, *Journal of a Tour Through the United States and In Canada* (1843), 70; Carlisle, *Travels in America* (1851), 79; Bunn, *Old England and New England* (1853), I: 65; see also Hugh Murray, *United States of America* (1844), III: 15; Featherstonhaugh, *Excursion Through the Slave States* (1844), I: xxvii; Baird, *Impressions and Experiences of the West Indies and North America* (1860), II: 75.

29. Bristed, *Resources of the United States* (1818), 110–13; Shirreff, *Tour Through North America* (1835), 299; Wansey, *Excursion to the United States of North America* (1798), 236; Carlisle, *Travels in America* (1851), 78–79.

30. Taken from Currin V. Shields, "Introduction" to John Stuart Mill, *Considerations on Representative Government,* vii–xxv.

31. Phillippo, *United States and Cuba* (1857), 318–19.

32. Stirling, *Letters from the Slave States* (1857), 28–33.

33. Chevalier, *Society, Manners and Politics in the United States* (1839), 327–29.

34. For examples of repression in the eighteenth century, see Israel, *Enlightenment Contested.*

35. Chevalier, *Society, Manners and Politics* (1839), 96; "The Duke of Newcastle," *Niles Weekly Register* 44, August 10, 1833, p. 388.

36. "Notes from England," *Michigan Farmer* X (December 1, 1852), 354.

37. Elizur Wright to wife, April 17, 1844, in Elizur Wright Papers, LC. As a reader of this manuscript informed me, one of the "most famous" verifications of the need of aristocratic approval or patronage to gain access to publishers was Samuel Johnson's letter to Lord Chesterfield (February 8, 1755), when Johnson complained that for years Chesterfield had ignored him and only reentered Johnson's life when his *Dictionary* got published. Wain, *Samuel Johnson,* 74–79.

38. "Republicanism vs. Monarchy," *Boston Cultivator* II (October 17, 1840), 4.

39. Vigne, *Six Months in America* (1833), 92; Blane, *An Excursion Through the United States and Canada* (1824), 69.

40. Gurowski, *America and Europe* (1857), 109; "Civilization: American and European," *American [Whig] Review* III (June 1846), 612, 613 (quote); "The Condition of England," *Massachusetts Ploughman* IV (April 12, 1845), 1; Wendell Phillips, "Letter from Naples," April 12, 1841, in Phillips, *Speeches, Lectures, and Letters,* II: 219, 221. The American celebration of democracy, though many denounced it, can be found in Baker, *Affairs of Party,* 147–65; on equality in the Jackson period, Gabriel, *Course of American Democratic Thought,* 12–19; Curti, *Growth of American Thought,* 301–302; Hanson, *Democratic Imagination in America,* ch. 4; Rodgers, *Contested Truths,* 73–74; Tsesis, *For Equality and Liberty,* 47–48; Matthews, *Toward a New Society,* 6–9; Wilentz, *Rise of American Democracy,* 511–13; Welter, *Mind of America,* 77–86, 116–21; Watson, *Liberty and Power,* 221–22; Benson, *Concept of Jacksonian Democracy,* 330–37. For the mechanics of party, see, for example, Remini, *Martin Van Buren and the Making of the Democratic Party;* Silbey, *American Political Nation;* McCormick, *Second American Party System.*

41. "Democracy—What is It?" *United States Democratic Review* 33 (July 1853), 3–4.

CHAPTER SEVEN

1. For modern examples, Douglas Miller, *Birth of Modern America,* 103–123, 154; Dawley, *Class and Community,* 1–10; Pessen, *Jacksonian America,* ch. 3; Johnson, *Shopkeeper's Mil-*

lennium, 5–10; Weeks, *Farewell My Nation;* Richard Drinnon, *Facing West;* Roediger, *Wages of Whiteness;* Saxton, *Rise and Fall of the White Republic;* Hartnett, *Democratic Dissent and the Cultural Fictions of Antebellum America;* Clinton, *Other Civil War;* Hersh, *Slavery of Sex.*

2. E.g., Hugh Murray, *United States of America* (1844), III: 32–34; Frances Trollope, *Domestic Manners of the Americans* (1832), 105–106; Francis Hall, *Travels in Canada and the United States* (1818), 296–97; Reid, *Sketches in North America* (1861), 37; Butler, *Journal* (1835), I: 87–88. Charles Murray, *Travels in North America* (1854), I: 108 (Scot Irish). A different view on women is found in Chevalier, *Society, Manners and Politics* (1839), 330–31; on Germans, Featherstonhaugh, *Excursion Through the Slave States* (1844), I: 18; for women reformers, Finch, *Englishwoman's Experience in America* (1853); Bunn, *Old England and New England* (1853), I: 65–78.

3. Palmer, *Journal of Travels in the United States* (1818), 101; Boardman, *America, and the Americans* (1833), 163; Gurney, *Journey in North America* (1841), 100–101; Ferrall, *Ramble of Six Thousand Miles* (1832), 46–49; Charles Murray, *Travels in North America* (1854), I: 1–2. For others, Marryat, *Diary in America* (1839), 109–29; Jobson, *America and American Methodism* (1857), 285–86; Martineau, *Society in America* (1839), II: 70–71; Flower, *Errors of Emigrants* (1841), 15; Tocqueville, *Democracy in America,* trans. Goldhammer (1835), I: 365–370, and section II, ch. 10 generally; Adam Hodgson had an appendix detailing his journey among the Creeks, Choctaws, Chickasaws, and Cherokees; Hodgson, *Remarks during a Journey Through North America* (1823), appendix.

4. For American abolitionism, see James B. Stewart, *Holy Warriors;* Sinha, *Slave's Cause.* For British abolitionism, consult Walvin, *England, Slaves and Freedom;* Oldfield, *Popular Politics and British Anti-Slavery;* David Brion Davis, *Problem of Slavery in the Age of Revolution;* David Brion Davis, *Problem of Slavery in the Age of Emancipation.* A useful discussion of the historiography of British comment on American slavery is contained in Tim Youngs, "Strategies of Travel: Charles Dickens and William Wells Brown," 163–77.

5. Robert W. Russell, *America Compared with England* (1848), xv.

6. Tocqueville, *Democracy in America,* trans. Goldhammer (1835), I: 366–68, 393–97, and generally 392–419; Mackay, *Western World* (1850), II: 137–38; Pairpoint, *Uncle Sam and His Country* (1857), 343; Fearon, *Sketches of America* (1818), 271; see Ouseley, *Remarks on the Statistics and Political Institutions of the United States* (1832), 162; Sullivan, *Rambles and Scrambles* (1852), 209; Hamilton, *Men and Manners in America* (1834), I: 89–90, 94.

7. Quotes from Holmes, *Account of the United States* (1823), 328, also 323–28; and Featherstonhaugh, *Excursion Through the Slave States* (1844), I: 120; Chambers, *Things As They Are in America* (1854), 266, 273–85; Felton, *Life in America* (1838), 101; Buckingham, *Slave States of America* (1842), II: 213–14; Francis Hall, *Travels in Canada and the United States* (1818), 318–19; Martineau, *Society in America* (1839), II: 307–43; Ferrall, *Ramble of Six Thousand Miles* (1832), 193–96; Basil Hall, *Travels in North America* (1830), III: 35–42; Boardman, *America, and the Americans* (1833), 245–46; Bristed, *Resources of the United States* (1818), 152–55; Hamilton, *Men and Manners in America* (1834), II: 216–21. On the economics of slavery, see Robert Russell, *North America* (1857), 136–39; Faux, *Faux's Memorable Days* (1823), 118; Hugh Murray, *United States of America* (1844), III: 52–60; Gurney, *Journey in North America* (1841), 49–89; Mackay, *Western World* (1850), II: 146–50. Adam Hodgson, however, said he saw blacks and whites

working in the fields together; Hodgson, *Remarks during a Journey Through North America* (1823), 211.

8. Lyell, *Travels in North America* (1849), I: 135, 169, 182–87; MacKay, *Life and Liberty in America* (1859), I: 311; Playfair, *Recollections of a Visit to the United States* (1856), 169; Holmes, *Account of the United States* (1823), 325–26, 327 (quote); Palmer, *Journal of Travels in the United States* (1818), 127, 142; Harris, *Remarks Made during a Tour Through the United States* (1821), 49; Ferguson, *America by River and Rail* (1856), 62.

9. Flower, *Letters from the Illinois* (1819), 106–107; Stirling, *Letters from the Slave States* (1857), 111–18, 118 (quote); Martineau, *Society in America* (1839), II: 115–16; Grattan, *Civilized America* (1859), 433.

10. Chevalier, *Society, Manners and Politics* (1839), 315; Woods, *Two Years' Residence* (1822), 316; Mattson, *Story of an Emigrant* (1891), 24; Godley, *Letters from America* (1844), I: 152; Shirreff, *Tour Through North America* (1835), 242. See also Marshall Hall, *Two-Fold Slavery of the United States* (1854), 11; Grattan, *Civilized America* (1859), 419–20; Davis, *Notes of a Tour in America* (1833), 97–98. The "beast analogy" is highly important for the moral denunciation of slavery; not only for the secular reason that people should not be subjected to the same floggings as work animals, but in terms of the bible, because God created humans with a soul but not animals. See Huston, "Abolitionists, Political Economists, and Capitalists," 487–521; and the recent work of David Brion Davis, *Problem of Slavery in the Age of Emancipation,* ch. 1.

11. Although I generally find the work of W. Caleb McDaniel admirable, I believe he has not quite represented accurately British abolitionists on democracy and aristocracy; McDaniel, *Problem of Democracy in the Age of Slavery,* ch. 6.

12. Lyell, *Second Visit to the United States* (1856), I: 262; Finch, *Englishwoman's Experience in America* (1853), 294–95; Harris, *Remarks Made during a Tour Through the United States* (1821), 49; Marshall Hall, *Two-Fold Slavery of the United States* (1854), 7. This also coincided with the belief of some that slaves were not treated as badly as the abolitionists claimed, Charles Murray, *Travels in North America* (1854), I: 136–37; Maury, *Englishwoman in America* (1848), 239–40; Henry Murray, *Lands of the Slave and the* Free (1855), II: 200–204; Featherstonhaugh, *Excursion Through the Slave States* (1844), I: 127–29. For one who claimed British workers lived better lives than American slaves, see Buckingham, *Slave States of America* (1842), I: 399–400.

13. Flower, *Errors of Emigrants* (1841), 16; Shirreff, *Tour Through North America* (1835), 313.

14. For example, Marshall Hall, *Two-Fold Slavery of the United States* (1854), 8–9; Stirling, *Letters from the Slave States* (1857), 112. On the deprecation of physical violence, which is almost in all the tourist books, see as well Jobson, *America and American Methodism* (1857), 262–63; Blane, *Excursion Through the United States* (1824), 150–51; Bristed, *Resources of the United States* (1818), 150–55.

15. Wheeler, *O My America,* 41. The idea of equality in the Declaration was, of course, important to the American abolitionists and antislavery politicians; see McInerney, *Fortunate Heirs of Freedom,* 127–48; and Maier, *American Scripture,* 197–212.

16. Mackay, *Western World* (1850), I: 208; Carlisle, *Travels in America* (1851), 52, 54; Chevalier, *Society, Manners and Politics* (1839), 100; William Russell, *Pictures of Southern Life* (1861), 3; see also Ferguson, *America by River and Rail* (1856), 133.

17. Ferrall, *Ramble of Six Thousand Miles* (1832), 230; Mackay, *Western World* (1850), I: 209; William Russell, *Pictures of Southern Life* (1861), 7–8, 33; Grattan, *Civilized America* (1859), 181, 223, 230, 246–47.

18. Lyell, *Travels in North America* (1845), I: 85, 102; Francis Hall, *Travels in Canada and the United States* (1818), 318–19; Davies, *American Scenes, and Christian Slavery* (1849), 175–76; Davis, *Notes of a Tour in America* (1833), 97–98. For a work that sees more similarities in the cultures north and south of the Ohio River rather than differences, see Salafia, *Slavery's Borderland.*

19. Tocqueville, *Democracy in America,* trans. Goldhammer (1835), I: 35–46, 53, 69–78, 90–96; William Russell, *Pictures of Southern Life* (1861), 4–6. Thomas Piketty in his study of wealth and income distribution over time wrote that the wealth imbalance between the free and slave states of the United States exposed "two diametrically opposed realities." Piketty, *Capital in the Twenty-First Century,* 161.

20. Hamilton, *Men and Manners in America* (1834), I: 225; Frances Trollope, *Domestic Manners of the Americans* (1832), II: 240; Sullivan, *Rambles and Scrambles in North and South America* (1852), 27; Chevalier, *Society, Manners and Politics* (1839), 391–92.

21. Bunn, *Old England and New England* (1853), I: 13, 15–16; Daubeny, *Journal of a Tour Through the United States* (1843), 57; Dickens, *American Notes* (1842), I: 169–70.

22. Bristed, *Resources of the United States* (1818), 420; Hamilton, *Men and Manners in America* (1834), I: 225–26; Bird, *Englishwoman in America* (1856), 95; Houstoun, *Hesperos* (1850), I: 97.

23. Holmes, *Account of the United States* (1823), 373; Martineau, *Society in America* (1839), II: 302, 307–308; Chevalier, *Society, Manners and Politics* (1839), 341, 344–45; Stirling, *Letters from the Slave States* (1857), 65. See also Rochefoucault Liancourt, *Travels Through the United States of North America* (1800), 227–32, 422–23; Flower, *Errors of Emigrants* (1841), 17–18; Pulszky and Pulszky, *White Red Black* (1853), I: 119–22.

24. Atack and Bateman, "The 'Egalitarian Ideal' and the Distribution of Wealth in the Northern Agricultural Community," 129–32; and Atack and Bateman, *To Their Own Soil,* 3–6.

25. Tocqueville, *Democracy in America,* trans. Goldhammer (1835), I: 3.

26. Martineau, *Retrospect of Western Travel* (1838), I: 87; Mackay, *Western World* (1850), III: 65; Robert W. Russell, *America Compared with England* (1848), 81; Shirreff, *Tour Through North America* (1835), 349; Prentice, *Tour in the United States* (1850), 84. The colonial goal of "competency" is in Alan Taylor, *American Colonies,* 172; Huston, *British Gentry, the Southern Planter, and the Northern Family Farmer,* ch. 1, 5. On the agricultural quality of the United States, consult Phillippo, *United States and Cuba* (1857), 83; Blowe, *Geographical, Historical, Commercial, and Agricultural View of the United States of America* (1820), 98; de Warville, *New Travels in the United States of America* (1792), 20–21; Fordham, *Personal Narrative of Travels* (1818), 105. Various historians tend to emphasize industrialism by 1860, not agriculture: James A. Henretta, *Evolution of American Society,* 193–225; Larson, *Market Revolution in America,* 88–90, 101–103, 155–66. Jeremy Atack and Fred Bateman correctly emphasize that the northern states were dominated in 1860 by agriculture; Atack and Bateman, *To Their Own Soil,* 3–6.

27. On the agricultural ladder and the historiography behind it, see Jeremy Atack, "Agricultural Ladder Revisited," 1–26. The basic work on farm labor remains David E. Schob, *Hired Hands and Plowboys;* for an example of a questioning of social mobility for farmworkers, see

Larkin, "'Labor is the Great Thing in Farming,'" 217–26. For a fuller depiction of these themes of egalitarianism in northern agriculture, see Huston, *British Gentry, the Southern Planter, and the Northern Family Farmer,* ch. 4, 5, 8.

28. Thomson, *Tradesman's Travels* (1842), 77; Ferrall, *Ramble of Six Thousand Miles* (1832), 66; Holmes, *Account of the United States* (1823), 3; Hancock, *Emigrant's Five Years in the Free States of America* (1860), 86–87. On the celebration of labor, see Benjamin Franklin, "Information To Those Who Would Remove to America," in Cooper, *Some Information Respecting America* (1794), 232; Mackay, *Western World* (1850), III: 342; Chevalier, *Society, Manners and Politics in the United States* (1839), 333, 344–45; Martineau, *Society in America* (1839), II: 302; Power, *Impressions of America* (1836), I: 333–34. Quote on cutting forests, Baxter, *America and the Americans* (1855), 125; Oldmixon, *Transatlantic Wanderings* (1855), 3; quote on white hands in Webb, *Manual for Emigrants* (1849), 10. The advice for only manual laborers to migrate to North American can be found in Hamilton, *Men and Manners in America* (1834), I: 80; Beaufoy, *Tour Through Parts of the United States and Canada* (1828), 140–41; Robert W. Russell, *America Compared with England* (1848), 81; Ashe, *Travels in America* (1808), I: 63; Baso; Hall, *Travels in North America* (1830), 305, 323–24. On advice to English artisans telling them to avoid East Coast cities and recommendations that clerks and shopmen stay in England, see *Wiley and Putnam's Emigrant's Guide* (1845), 136–37; O'Hanlon, *Irish Emigrant's Guide for the United States* (1851), 48–49; Howe, *Emigrants' New Guide* (1822), 42–43; Cassell, *Cassell's Emigrants' Handbook: Being a Guide to the Various Fields of Emigration in all Parts of the Globe* (London, 1852), 9, 21, 23; Holmes, *Account of the United States of America* (1823), 126–28; Pairpoint, *Uncle Sam and His Country* (1857), 327–32; Thomason, *Hints to Emigrants* (1848), 29–30; Mesick, *English Traveller in America,* 30, 178.

29. U.S. Bureau of the Interior, *Population of the United States in 1860* [Eighth Census] (1864), 662–63; Great Britain, Registrar-General, *Census of Great Britain in 1851 . . .* (1854), 60, 72. The calculation of British tenants and owner-occupiers is invariably fuzzy because one person could have several different tenures of land—be a tenant of one farm and an owner of another. The figure also varies according to whether plots of land under 5 acres are included. Mathias argues for about 95,000 in 1831; Porter, about 100,000; Beckett, about 31,000 in 1861—all authors agreeing that the number of owner-occupiers is confusing. Almost all accept a figure of 75 percent tenancy by 1851, and probably as early as 1790. Mathias, *First Industrial Nation,* 57, 311; Porter, *English Society in the Eighteenth Century,* 68, 70; Chambers and Mingay, *Agricultural Revolution,* 93; Clapham, *Economic History of Modern Britain,* 264; Orwin and Whetham, *History of British Agriculture,* 307; Beckett, "The Decline of the Small Landowner in England and Wales, 1660–1900," 86, 90, 100. Attempts have also been made to refine the figures for British farm laborers: Wrigley, *Poverty, Progress, and Population,* table 4.12, p. 124, table 4.4, p. 97; Edward Higgs, "Occupational Censuses and the Agricultural Workforce in Victorian England and Wales," 700–716. In terms of occupations for the country, the United States had about 58 percent in agriculture in 1860, Great Britain 19 percent in 1861; Huston, *Securing the Fruits of Labor,* 89; Mathias, *First Industrial Nation,* 224.

30. "Farm Laborers, East and West," *New England Farmer and Horticultural Register* 59 (October 30, 1880), 1; Mathias, *First Industrial Nation,* 197; Allen, *Enclosure and the Yeoman,* 1; Orwin and Whetham, *History of British Agriculture,* ch. 8; Dewey, "Farm Labour," 810–62;

Armstrong, "Labour I: Rural Population Growth, Systems of Employment, and Incomes," 649–728. One of the few scholars to note the American-British discussion of the status of the farm worker was Crook, *American Democracy in English Politics,* 35. The mobility of and therefore the constant disappearance of the American farmworker from the farmworking class can be found in Crèvecoeur, *Letters from an American Farmer* (1782), 52–54; Chambers, *Things As They Are in America* (1854), 344; Shirriff, *A Tour Through North America* (1835), 16, 347–48, 450–51; Phillippo, *United States and Cuba* (1857), 328; Martineau, *Society in America* (1839), II: 93–102; Ashe, *Travels in America* (1808), I: 63; Basil Hall, *Travels in North America* (1830), I: 302–305.

31. Olmsted, *Walks and Talks* (1859), 236–38, quotes on 238–39 and 250. See also "The English Peasantry," *Boston Review* II (July 1862), 411–21. For a different version of Olmsted, see Bushman, *Refinement of America,* 393–94, 421.

32. Colman, *European Agriculture and Rural Economy* (1849), quotes I: 14, 39, 43, and generally 39–43; Chambers, *Things As They Are in America* (1854), 344; Brodrick, *English Land and English Landlords* (1881), 231–40.

33. Olmsted, *Walks and Talks* (1859), 239; Colman, *European Agriculture and Rural Economy* (1849), I: 63.

34. Anthony Trollope, *North America* (1862), I: 203–204; see Nevins, *American Social History as Recorded by British Travellers,* 301–304.

35. Cooper, *Some Information Respecting America* (1794), 48; Harrison, *Memories and Thoughts* (1906), 174. See Dixon, *Personal Narrative of a Tour Through the United States and Canada* (1849), 70; Dickens, *American Notes* (1842), I: 191, 206–207; "Sam Slick" [Thomas Haliburton], *Americans At Home* (1854), I: vi–vii; Mitchell, *Ten Years Residence in the United States* (1862), 142–51; Bird, *Englishwoman in America* (1856), 346–55, 367–69; Mulvey, *Transatlantic Manners,* 181.

36. John Palmer, *Journal of Travels in the United States* (1818), 289; Thomason, *Men and Things in America* (1838), 229; Holmes, *Account of the United States* (1823), 125, 356; see Phillippo, *United States and Cuba* (1857), 89–91; Reid, *Sketches in North America* (1861), 42–43. The American Elkanah Watson wrote of 1780s England and France that Paris was civil but London was "brutal" and filled with pickpockets; Watson, ed., *Men and Times of the Revolution* (1856), 221.

37. Dixon, *Personal Narrative of a Tour Through a Part of the United States and Canada* (1849), 70; Robert Russell, *North America* (1857), 128, 133; Hancock, *Emigrant's Five Years in the Free States of America* (1860), 314; Marryat, *Diary in America* (1839), 129; Hamilton, *Men and Manners in America* (1834), I: 330.

38. MacKay, *Life and Liberty in America* (1859), I: 190; Faux, *Faux's Memorable Days in America* (1823), 74; Chambers, *Things as they Are in America* (1854), 217; Palmer, *Journal of Travels in the United States* (1818), 182–86; Frances Trollope, *Domestic Manners of the Americans* (1832), II: 240; Godley, *Letters from America* (1841), I: 5, 14, II: 136; Hodgson, *Remarks during a Journey Through North America* (1823), 239–48; Holmes, *Account of the United States* (1823), 338; Bird, *Englishwoman in America* (1856), 95; Bunn, *Old England and New England* (1853), I: 15–19; Wakefield, *Excursions in North America* (1806), 174–90; Daubeny, *Journal of a Tour Through the United States and In Canada* (1843), 37, 58; Pairpoint, *Uncle Sam and His Country* (1857), 38, 50; Buckingham, *America Historical, Statistic, and Descriptive* (1841), II: 400; Vigne, *Six Months in America* (1833), 188–89, 196.

39. Bird, *Englishwoman in America* (1856), 321.

40. A standard place to find descriptions of New York is Dickens, *American Notes* (1842), I: 191–206; the use of coal is in Sullivan, *Rambles and Scrambles* (1852), 24; on prostitution, Robert W. Russell, *America Compared with England* (1848), 83–84; on paupers, Chambers, *Things As They Are in America* (1854), 342; Jobson, *America and American Methodism* (1857), 27; George Lewis, *Impressions of America and American Churches* (1845), 42; Dalton, *Travels in the United States* (1821), 4; D. W. Mitchell, *Ten Years Residence in the United States* (1862), 142–51.

41. Bunn, *Old England and New England* (1853), I: 79–81, 109; Stirling, *Letters from the Slave States* (1857), 104–105; Houstoun, *Hesperos* (1850), I: 172–76; Bird, *Englishwoman in America* (1856), 355, 367–70.

42. Lyell, *Second Visit to the United States* (1849), I: 85; Stirling, *Letters from the Slave States* (1857), 167.

43. Hamilton, *Men and Manners in America* (1834), I: 295–301; Johnston, *Notes on America* (1851), I: 422–23; Marryat, *Diary in America* (1839), 467–68; Mitchell, *Ten Years Residence in the United States* (1862), 154–63; Godley, *Letters from America* (1841), I: 8–14. For those not envisioning an American future ruled by aristocrats, see Mackay, *Western World* (1850), III: 326–42; Combe, *Notes on the United States* (1841), I: 94–96.

CHAPTER EIGHT

1. For example, Maude, *Visit to the Falls of Niagara in 1800* (1826); MacKay, *Life and Liberty in America* (1859), I: 72; Beaufoy, *Tour Through Parts of the United States and Canada* (1828), 51, 74–75; Basil Hall, *Travels in North America* (1830), I: 179–220; Sturge, *A Visit to the United States in 1841* (1842), 111; Bromley, *Woman's Wanderings in the Western World* (1861), 40; Bird, *Englishwoman in America* (1856), 202; Fowler, *Journal of a Tour in the State of New York* (1831), 127; MacGregor, *Our Brothers and Cousins* (1859), 39–58.

2. Quote from Baxter, *America and the Americans* (1859), 6; Ferrall, *Ramble of Six Thousand Miles* (1832), vi–vii; see Jobson, *American and American Methodism* (1857), 19–21.

3. For example, William Smith, *Yorkshireman's Trip to the United States* (1892); Medley, *An Autumn Tour in the United States and Canada* (1873), 1–2; Money, *Truth About America* (1886), 9; Iredale, *Autumn Tour in the United States and Canada* (1901); Hardman, *Trip to America* (1884); Hardy, *Through Cities and Prairie Lands* (1881); Lindley-Cowen, *West Australian Settler's Guide and Farmer's Handbook* (1897). See Nevins, *America Through British Eyes*, 305–41; Rapson, *Britons View America*, 4–23; Temperley, *Britain and America*, ch. 4; Burk, *Old World, New World*, 277–78, 296–300, 361–62; Mulvey, *Transatlantic Manners*, 203–204; Wheeler, *O My America*, ch. 5, 6; Rose, *Unspeakable Awfulness*, 20–21.

4. Ouseley, *Remarks on the Statistics and Political Institutions of the United States* (1832), 44; Reid, *Sketches in North America* (1861), 46–47; Brown, *America* (1849), iv; Oldmixon, *Transatlantic Wanderings* (1855), iii–iv.

5. Frances Trollope, *Domestic Manners of the Americans* (1832), I: 58; Jobson, *America and American Methodism* (1857), 27; Freeman, *Some Impressions of the United States* (1883), 10;

Dixon, *Personal Narrative of a Tour Through the United States and Canada* (1849), 5. Earlier commentary making England and the United States similar can be found in Holmes, *Account of the United States* (1823), 102; Howe, *Emigrants' New Guide* (1822), 41; Shirreff, *Tour Through North America* (1835), 347; Melish, *Travels Through the United States of America* (1818), iii; Maude, *Visit to the Falls of Niagara in 1800* (1826), iii–iv; Oldmixon, *Transatlantic Wanderings* (1855), 2; Hodgson, *Remarks during a Journey Through North America* (1823), 258–59.

6. D. R. Thomason, *Hints to Emigrants* (1848), 56; Mackay, *Western World* (1850), III: 24, 35; Baird, *Impressions and Experiences of the West Indies and North America* (1860), II: 76–78; Thomson, *Tradesman's Travels* (1842), 225; Sullivan, *Rambles and Scrambles in North and South America* (1852), vi–vii; Hancock, *Emigrant's Five Years in the Free States of America* (1860), 87–88; Pairpoint, *Uncle Sam and His Country* (1857), 341.

7. Robert Playfair, *Recollections of a Visit to the United States* (1856), 235; Stuart-Wortley, *Travels in the United States* (1851), 40; Iredale, *Autumn Tour of the United States and* Canada (1901), 66; Hardman, *Trip to America* (1884), 1 (quote), Declaration discussion on pp. 200–201. Frank Prochaska has written that the reconciliation of Great Britain and the United States was based on the recognition of a common ethnicity; he also interpreted it as a rejection of American "exceptionalism." Prochaska, *Eminent Victorians on American Democracy,* 100–110, 123–27.

8. Bird, *Englishwoman in America* (1856), 90. Charles Dickens noted, as a counterpoint, that Englishmen misbehaved in America with their "insolent conceit and cool assumption of superiority," and to some extent brought out the boastfulness of Americans. Dickens, *American Notes* (1842), I: 271–72.

9. Bristed, *Resources of the United States* (1818), 15, 35; Ashworth, *Tour in the United States, Cuba, and Canada* (1861), 15; Mackay, *Western World* (1850), II: 50; Brydges, *Uncle Sam at Home* (1888), 11, 15; Campbell, *White and Black* (1879), 8–9; Prentice, *Tour in the United States* (1850), 181. See also Hole, *Little Tour in America* (1895), 5; William Smith, *Yorkshireman's Trip to the United States* (1892), 5.

10. Houstoun, *Hesperos* (1850), I: 234–35.

11. Charles Murray, *Travels in North America* (1854), I: 1–2; Weld, *Vacation Tour of the United States and Canada* (1855), 2; Baxter, *America and the Americans* (1855), 66; Medley, *An Autumn Tour in the United States and Canada* (1873), 105–106. Zincke, *Last Winter in the United States* (1868), 26–30; Archer, *America To-Day* (1900), 82, 138–40; Prentice, *Tour in the United States* (1850), vi; James, *Rambles in the United States and Canada* (1846), 198; Dixon, *Personal Narrative of a Tour Through the United States and Canada* (1849), 5; Mackay, *Western World* (1850), III: 6; Godley, *Letters from America* (1844), I: 19. See Mulvey, *Transatlantic Manners,* 204; Rapson, *Britons View America,* 181; Temperley, *Britain and America,* 66–67, 82–85.

12. There was considerable commentary on the American Civil War, but the subject will not be attended to here. For British opinion during the war, see Temperley, *Britain and America,* 56–58; Blackett, *Divided Hearts.*

13. Walter, *First Impressions of America* (1867), 70; Baron Charles Russell, *Diary of a Visit to the United States* (1883), 46; Bryce, *American Commonwealth* (1908), II: 810–11. For criticisms of American equality, Baron Charles Russell, *Diary of a Visit to the United States* (1883), 46. Rapson, *Britons View America,* 56–59, 189; Burk, *Old World, New World,* 298–99; Rose, *Unspeakable Awfulness,* 15–16, 18, 39.

14. Hatton, *To-Day in America* (1881), 3; Griffin, *The Great Republic* (1884), 69; Smart, *Temper of the American People* (1912), 51; Zincke, *Last Winter in the United States* (1868), 199. Observers finding the antiaristocratic sentiment still alive include Bryce, *American Commonwealth* (1908), II: 813, 819–20; Alex Harris, *Reminiscences of America* (1870), x–xi; Wagner, *My Impressions of America* (1906), 147–48; Francis, *Americans* (1909), 3–4.

15. Kipling, *American Notes* (1899), 15; Griffin, *Great Republic* (1884), 73; Francis, *Americans* (1909), 26–27; Harrison, *Memories and Thoughts* (1906), 186; Hardman, *Trip to America* (1884), 48, see 42–43; Steevens, *Land of the Dollar* (1898), 160; Zincke, *Last Winter in the United States* (1868), 70, 174–75, 198–99. For one expression that railroads' seating continued to be democratic, see Fergus Ferguson, *From Glascow to Missouri and Back* (1878), 68. For examples of seeing equality, Hardman, *Trip to America* (1884), 42, 48; Stewart, *Eleven Years' Experience in the Western States of America* (1870), 92; Harrison, *Memories and Thoughts* (1906), 186–87; Stead, *Americanization of the World* (1901), 393–94; Faithful, *Three Visits to the United States* (1884), 33–34; Rapson, *Britons View America*, 53, 56, 70. James Bryce did note that the idea of hereditary position and titles brought out sneers among Americans; Bryce, *American Commonwealth* (1908), II: 819–20.

16. Medley, *Autumn Tour in the United States and Canada* (1873), 30, 53–56; see also Zincke, *Last Winter in the United States* (1868), 175–77. On aristocrats on the prairies, see Pagmenta, *Prairie Fever*, xii–xv.

17. Griffin, *Great Republic* (1884), 70–72. The continued problem with independent servants is in Faithful, *Three Visits to the United States* (1884), 278. However, the ideal of servitude died in the twentieth century, as it was beginning to be seen as an example of masculine degeneracy; Leonard Schwarz, "English Servants and Their Employers during the Eighteenth and Nineteenth Centuries," 232–56; Wheeler, *O My America*, ch. 6.

18. Medley, *Autumn Tour in the United States and Canada* (1873), 53; Griffin, *Great Republic* (1884), viii (quote), ix–xiii, 7, ch. 7; Bryce, *American Commonwealth* (1908), II: 53–75, and ch. 84; Archer, *America To-Day* (1900), 166–67; Smart, *Temper of the American People* (1912), 56–58; see Francis, *Americans* (1900), 19–23; Rose, *Great Country* (1868), vii–xv; Macaulay, *Across the Ferry* (1872), 418–19. For the general British description of American politics, see Rapson, *Britons View America*, ch. 8; on Lord Bryce, see Prochaska, *Eminent Victorians on American Democracy*, ch. 5.

19. Walter, *First Impressions of America* (1867), 70; Ogden Rollo, ed., *Life and Letters of Edwin Lawrence Godkin*, II: 186; Faithful, *Three Visits to the United States* (1884), 33, 34 (quote); Harrison, *Memories and Thoughts* (1906), 174; Wagner, *My Impressions of America* (1906), 45–47. Godkin blamed the class division on the effects of the protective tariff.

20. Laurie, *Artisans into Workers;* Licht, *Working for the Railroad;* Licht, *Industrializing America;* Chandler, *Visible Hand.*

21. Freeman, *Some Impressions of the United States* (1883), 215 (quote); Walter, *First Impressions of America* (1867), 57; Zincke, *Last Winter in the United States* (1868), 31; Brydges, *Uncle Sam At Home* (1888), 206; Campbell, *White and Black* (1879), 27 (quote), 97–102; see also Steevens, *Land of the Dollar* (1898), 157, 160; Newman Hall, *From Liverpool to St. Louis* (1870), 121–22; Freeman, *Some Impressions of the United States* (1883), 11, 215; Macaulay, *Across the Ferry* (1872), 396, 398; Stewart, *Eleven Years' Experience in the Western States of America* (1870), 57–66.

22. Goddard, *Where to Emigrate, and Why* (1869), 557–60; Stewart, *Eleven Years' Experience in the Western States of America* (1870), 45–46, 54–57; Steevens, *Land of the Dollar* (1898), 159; Campbell, *White and Black* (1879), 99–107; Macaulay, *Across the Ferry* (1872), 398–402. Ontario Provincial Government, *Emigration* (1880), 2, 4, 5, 6, 54–56; see also Easton, *Travels in America* (1871), 81–91, 98. By 1920, some were admitting that the era of easy farm acquisition was over; Butterfield, *Farmer and the New Day* (1919), 8–12.

23. Medley, *Autumn Tour in the United States and Canada* (1873), 97–98, 100 (quote).

24. Francis, *Americans* (1909), 26–27; Zincke, *Last Winter in the United States* (1868), 230; Money, *Truth About America* (1886), 9; Newman Hall, *From Liverpool to St. Louis* (1870), 125–26. On lower-class behavior, also see Medley, *Autumn Tour in the United States and Canada* (1873), 40.

25. Newman Hall, *Liverpool to St. Louis* (1870), 161; Alexander Rivington and Harris, *Reminiscences of America* (1870), xii; Macaulay, *Across the Ferry* (1872), 369–70; Medley, *Autumn Tour in the United States and Canada* (1873), 44. See also Vivian, *Notes of a Tour in America* (1878), 247; Edward Freeman, *Some Impressions of the United States* (1883), 158; Rapson, *Britons View America,* ch. 9.

26. Newman Hall, *Liverpool to St. Louis* (1870), 121–22; Steevens, *Land of the Dollar* (1898), 156; Zincke, *Last Winter in the United States* (1868), quote 40, 301–302; Rapson, *Britons View America,* ch. 5.

27. Campbell, *White and Black* (1879), 35–36; Macaulay, *Across the Ferry* (1872), 398, 416; Vivian, *Notes of a Tour in America* (1878), 240–41.

28. Medley, *Autumn Tour in the United States and Canada* (1873), 38–39; Johnston, *Notes on America* (1851), I: 248; Joseph Wright, *Centennial Tour in the United States and Canada* (1877), 42; Stead, *Americanization of the World* (1901), 384, 385, 387–88. On Stead and journalism, see Heindel, *American Impact on Great Britain,* 27. See discussion of American education in Goldin and Katz, "Why the United States Led in Education, 1910–1940," 143–47.

29. Pairpoint, *Uncle Sam and His Country* (1857), 333; Dalton, *Travels in the United States* (1821), 226; D. R. Thomason, *Hints to Emigrants* (1848), 123; Jobson, *America and American Methodism* (1857), 393; Cunynghame, *Glimpse at the Great Western Republic* (1851), 49.

30. Brydges, *Uncle Sam at Home* (1888), 21; Harrison, *Memories and Thoughts* (1906), 179.

31. David Macrae, *Americans at Home* (1870), I: 18, 19; Wagner, *My Impressions of America* (1906), 144–51.

32. Robert W. Russell, *America Compared With England* (1848), 122 (quote) and 121–23; Ouseley, *Remarks on the Statistics and Political Institutions of the United States* (1832), 51; Tompkins and Lord Brougham, *Thoughts Upon the Aristocracy of England* (1835), 7; Brydges, *Uncle Sam at Home* (1888), 242.

33. On idea of wages and reward motivating workers, see Bristed, *Resources of the United States* (1818), 290; Kendall, *Travels Through the Northern Parts of the United States* (1809), III: 74; Faux, *Faux's Memorable Days* (1823), 232–39; for workers responding to incentives and being depressed by low wages, see, for example, Shirreff, *Tour Through North America* (1835), 345; Oldmixon, *Transatlantic Wanderings* (1855), 3; Howe, *Emigrants' New Guide* (1822), 46.

34. Stead, *Americanization of the World* (1901), 393–94, 395; Zincke, *Last Winter in the United States* (1868), 174–75.

35. Smart, *Temper of the American People* (1912), 48; Medley, *Autumn Tour in the United States and Canada* (1873), 40–41; Temperley, *Britain and America Since Independence,* 58.

36. In some ways, the problem was personified in the way French peasants contrasted with English farmworkers in their social interactions with superiors. The French aristocrats exhibited an ease in speaking to commoners while the British aristocracy acted with rigid aloofness. See Tocqueville, *Democracy in America,* trans. Goldhammer (1835), II: 669; Matthew Arnold, "Equality" (1878), in Arnold, *Essays, Religious and Mixed,* ed. Super, 485–87, 491; Brodrick, *English Land and English Landlords* (1881), 231; Lippincott, *Victorian Critics of Democracy,* 130; Beales, *From Castlereagh to Gladstone,* 206–208, 268–73. The idea of class warfare destroying British society was portrayed, with exaggeration, in Dangerfield, *Strange Death of Liberal England.*

37. For example, Painter, *Standing at Armageddon;* Sklar, *Corporate Reconstruction of American Capitalism;* Laurie, *Artisans into Workers;* Licht, *Industrializing America;* Pole, *Pursuit of Equality,* 205–208; Rodgers, *Atlantic Crossings,* 42–43, 58–59. The carpenter union paper at Indianapolis, *The Carpenter,* reported in 1916 that land monopoly was finally becoming a problem; in California, one estate contained 14 million acres; *Carpenter* 36 (April 1916), 44.

38. For example, Harrison, *Memories and Thoughts* (1906), 186, 198; Zincke, *Last Winter in the United States* (1868), 57–58, 68–70, 291–92; Griffin, *Great Republic* (1884), 14; Francis, *Americans* (1909), socialism in chapters 17, 18; Freeman, *Some Impressions of the United States* (1883), 137–58; Joseph Wright, *Centennial Tour in the United States and Canada* (1877), 72–73; Iredale, *Autumn Tour in the United States and Canada* (1901), 101; Rose, *Great Country* (1868), vii–xv, 68–69.

39. Smart, *Temper of the American People* (1912), 79; Campbell, *White and Black* (1879), 28; Bryce, *American Commonwealth* (1908), II: 593; Bryce on p. 926 did not see an aristocracy forming in the United States. Rivington and Harris, *Reminiscences of America in 1869* (1870), 322; Alexander Francis had two chapters on socialism; *Americans* (1909). For predictions that wealth in America would produce an aristocracy, see Hamilton, *Men and Manners in America* (1834), I: 293–300; Marryat, *Diary in America* (1839), 468; Butler, *Journal* (1835), I: 56.

40. Henry Lord Brougham, *Political Philosophy* (1843), 23; Cobden in Warren Isham, "Young and Old England—Interview with Mr. Cobden," July 4, 1851, *Michigan Farmer* IX (November 1, 1851), 329; Bagehot, *English Constitution* (1867), 121; Gladstone, "Kin Beyond the Sea" (1875), 355; Herbert Spencer, *Man Versus the State* (1892), 41–58, quotes 57, 58; Lecky, *Democracy and Liberty* (1896), I: 63–100, 256 (quote), 257–60. On Lecky, see Prochaska, *Eminent Victorians on American Democracy,* 139; Lippincott, *Victorian Critics of Democracy,* 208, 216.

41. Orwin and Whetham, *History of British Agriculture,* 306–307; Lindert, "Who Owned Victorian England," 28–30; Thompson, *English Landed Society in the Nineteenth Century,* 27–28; Clapham, *Economic History of Modern Britain,* 264–65; "British Land Monopoly," *The Independent* 21, October 7, 1869, p. 4; R. Wheateley, "English Land Tenure: The Aristocracy," *Christian Advocate and Journal* 39, March 3, 1864, p. 65. John Stuart Mill's attack on aristocratic landholding and inheritance laws can be found in his *Principles of Political Economy* (1871), 156–83; Habakkuk, *Marriage, Debt, and the Estates System,* 628–29. David Cannadine figures that the 4,736 English in 1870 who owned 1,000 acres or more held 12,825,643 acres or 56.1 percent of the land of England. J. V. Beckett believes that some 7,000 landowners held 80 percent of English land; see Cannadine, *Decline and Fall of the British Aristocracy,* table 1.1, pp. 9, 14; see also Beckett, *Aristocracy in England,* p. 40 and ch. 2; Stone and Stone, *An Open Elite,* 417.

42. "The British Landowners," *Bankers' Magazine* 8 (February 1879), 595–98; Arthur Pember, "The Coming Revolution in England," *Lippincott's* 5 (March 1870), 279; Brodrick, *English Land and Landlords* (1881), 89–127; Marquis of Blandford, "Reform of Feudal Laws," *Nineteenth Century* 9 (April 1881), 664–80; Kay, *Free Trade in Land* (1885), 18, 28–33; William Miller, "Primogeniture, Entail, and Endowment in English Classical Economics," 558–81; Habakkuk, *Marriage, Debt, and the Estates System,* 629–38; Thompson, *English Landed Society,* 65–68. For a modern assessment, see Julia A. Smith, "Land Ownership and Social Change in Late Nineteenth-Century Britain," 767–76; skepticism about entail and primogeniture from the American historical perspective in Young and Nobles, *Whose American Revolution Was It,* 92–93. By all accounts, yeomen in England had declined in the eighteenth century, but whether they continued to lose ground in the nineteenth century remains a contested question; see discussion in Overton, *Agricultural Revolution in England,* 168–84; Grigg, *English Agriculture,* 140–47; Allen, *Enclosure and the Yeoman,* 1–21.

43. Olmsted, *Walks and Talks* (1859), 93; Heath, *English Peasantry* (1874), 1–6, 203–228; "Land Reform in England," (New York) *Evangelist,* January 1, 1874, p. 8; "Editor's Table," *Appleton's Journal of Literature, Science, and Art* 10 (November 12, 1873), 663; "Joseph Arch and His Mission," *Prairie Farmer* 34 (August 23, 1873), 265; Marquis of Blandford, "Reform of the Feudal Laws," *Nineteenth Century* 9 (April 1881), 664–80; "Farm Laborers in Europe," *Massachusetts Ploughman* 29 (March 19, 1870), 2; "British Agriculture," ibid., 45 (December 18, 1886), 1; "British Land Monopoly," *Independent* 21 (October 7, 1869), 4; "The British Landowners," *Bankers' Magazine* (February 1879), 595–98; "Editor's Table," *Appleton's Journal of Literature, Science, and Art* 10 (November 12, 1873), 663; Badeau, *Aristocracy in England* (1885), 234–37; Grigg, *English Agriculture,* 141; Daunton, *Progress and Poverty,* ch. 3; Beckett, "Decline of the Small Landowner in England and Wales," 89–111.

44. Mathias, *First Industrial Nation,* 224 (table); Havighurst, *Twentieth-Century Britain,* 16–17; Grigg, *English Agriculture,* 137–40; Cormac Ó. Gráda, "British Agriculture, 1860–1914," in Floud and McCloskey, eds., *Economic History of Britain Since 1700,* II: 159–63; (rents fall 29 percent); Grigg, *English Agriculture,* 103; Clapham, *Economic History of Modern Britain,* 279–96; Prothero, *English Farming Past and Present* (1912), 393–99. On the impact of railroads, Orwin and Whetham, *History of British Agriculture,* 94; E. L. Jones, *Agriculture and the Industrial Revolution,* 218.

45. Matthew Arnold, "Equality" (1878), in *Essays Religious and Mixed,* ed. Super, 278, 298–99, 305. Arnold did visit the United States in the 1880s to give lectures, and neither he nor his American audience were particularly pleased with the results. Arnold was a superb writer but evidently a lackluster speaker; in any event, he found the United States a land still lacking in refinement and intellectual acuity. Some of his views on the United States can be gleaned from his *Civilization in the United States* (1888), 69–86, 115, 173–77; views on English aristocracy and ending primogeniture and entail, 142–48; McCarthy, *Matthew Arnold and the Three Classes,* 134–52; Raleigh, *Matthew Arnold and American Culture,* 10, 55–66.

46. Arnold, "Equality" (1878), 284–85. See Read, *Majority Rule versus Consensus,* 18–19, 35, 41–48; O'Brien, *Conjectures of Order,* II: 804–807, 832, 856–71; Poole, *Never Surrender,* 4.

47. Badeau, *Aristocracy in England* (1885), quotes on pp. 56, 149, 155, 156, 234; see also 19–20, 42–56, 104, 173, 230–54.

48. Maine, *Popular Government* (1885), vi and ch. 1; Brydges, *Uncle Sam At Home* (1888), 243–44; William Fowler quoted in Habakkuk, *Marriage, Debt, and the Estates System,* 629. Plato supported inequality but not by inheritance; Myers, *Are Men Equal,* 12.

49. Stead, *Americanization of the World* (1901), 22.

50. Alfred Havighurst adds that land taxes after World War II ultimately crushed the landed aristocracy; *Twentieth-Century Britain,* 144. A contemporary, Joseph Kay, argued that in 1886, 292 people owned one-third of Ireland, and 744 owned one-half; Kay, *Free Trade in Land,* 17. Beckett, *Aristocracy in England,* 13, land sales figures on 474–78; Habakkuk, *Marriage, Debt, and the Estates System,* 631–32, 638, 645–46, 660–97; Cannadine, *Decline and Fall of the British Aristocracy,* 27–28; Clarke, "Hodge's Politics, 119–36; Daunton, "Political Economy of Death Duties," 137–71; Stone and Stone, *Open Elite,* 425–26; Orwin and Whetham, *History of British Agriculture,* 308, 314–16; Grigg, *English Agriculture,* 103–105; Dangerfield, *Strange Death of Liberal England,* ch. 3; Arnstein, *Britain Yesterday and Today,* 209–13; Rodgers, *Atlantic Crossings,* 34–36, 44–59. For a brief history of democracy in Great Britain, consult Ian Machin, *Rise of Democracy in Britain.*

CONCLUSION

1. On the evolution of the British economy, see Avner Offer, "Farm Tenure and Land Values in England, c. 1750–1950," 1–20; Booth, *British Economy in the Twentieth Century,* table 4.1, p. 90; Grigg, *English Agriculture,* 9, 103–107; Beckett, *Aristocracy in England,* 468–78; Machin, *Rise of Democracy in Britain;* Cannadine, *Rise and Fall of Class in Britain.*

2. Guttman, *Conservative Tradition in America,* 139 (Paul Elmer More quote), 134–44; Nicholas Butler, *True and False Democracy* (1915), 9–11; Stromberg, *Democracy,* 18–20, 27; Bellamy, *Equality* (1897), 9; see Dunn, *Setting the People Free,* 133–37; Stromberg, *Democracy,* 9. On politics and the turn from democracy, McGerr, *Decline of Popular Politics,* 45–52; Sproat, *"Best Men,"* ch. 8, 9.

3. Wiltse, *Jeffersonian Tradition in American Democracy,* 82–87; Curti, *Growth of American Thought,* 295–306; Fish, *Rise of the Common Man;* Commager, *American Mind,* 13; see also Paxson, *Recent History of the United States,* 127; Nichols and Randall, eds., *Democracy in the Middle West;* Hicks, Mowry, and Burke, *American Nation;* Craven, *Democracy in American Life.* For philosophers of equality, see T. V. Smith, *American Philosophy of Equality;* Myers, *Are Men Equal?*

4. The impact of industrialization on American politics and life is a common theme; for example, Stromberg, *Democracy,* 57–74; Destler, *American Radicalism,* 11–31; Kirkland, *Industry Comes of Age,* 195–217; Craven, *American Democracy,* ch. 4; Richard Franklin Bensel, *Political Economy of American Industrialization,* 5–11; Hicks, Mowry, and Burke, *American Nation,* 135–140, 218; Ralph Gabriel, *Course of American Democratic Thought,* 151–83; Paxson, *Recent History of the United States,* 151–52; Commager, *American Mind,* 41, 410–16; Elizabeth Sanders, *Roots of Reform,* 1–4; Doan, *La Follettes and the Wisconsin Idea,* 288. In a way, Arthur M. Schlesinger Jr. offered a transition point in the writing, as he put the urban working class as a fundamental force in shaping the democratic impulses; Schlesinger, *Age of Jackson,* 8–9, 79, 126.

5. Hamlin Garland, *Main-Travelled Roads* (1899); Hofstadter, *Age of Reform,* ch. 1; Grant McConnell, *Decline of Agrarian Democracy.* On the rural-urban split, see David Birner, *Politics of Provincialism;* Glad, *McKinley, Bryan, and the People,* 14, 34; Commager, *American Mind,* 34, 41–46. The question of democracy after World War II being at a low ebb was an interpretation of Stromberg, *Democracy,* ch. 7. On literary developments, see Leuchtenberg, *Perils of Prosperity,* ch. 8; and Cowley, *Exile's Return.*

6. Number based on a population of 30 million in 1860, with one-half being adult; subtracting 2 million black adult males and females, and then taking the remainder and dividing by one-half to get the white males. Given the extent of poverty in the cities and the age profile of Americans, one might consider one-half of the males to have had no property. For examples of the writing of the 1960s and afterward, Laurie, *Artisans into Workers;* Dawley, *Class and Community;* Clinton, *Other Civil War;* Pestana and Salinger, eds., *Inequality in Early America;* Woloch, *Women and the American Experience;* Kolchin, *American Slavery;* Genovese, *Roll, Jordan, Roll;* Saxton, *Rise and Fall of the White Republic;* Weeks, *Farewell My Nation;* Griffin, *American Leviathan;* Hartnett, *Democratic Dissent and the Cultural Fictions of Antebellum America.*

7. Kirk, *Conservative Mind,* ch. 1; George Nash, *Conservative* Intellectual *Movement in America,* 77–81. For the New Deal, Schlesinger Jr., *Crisis of the Old Order;* Leuchtenberg, *Roosevelt and the New Deal;* Biles, *A New Deal for the American People.* For microeconomists and political philosophers advocating the negative state, see Hartwell, *History of the Mont Pelerin Society,* 7–18; Newman, *Liberalism at Wit's End,* 26–31; Machan, *Capitalism and Individualism,* x–xii, 17–31; Daniel Stedman Jones, *Masters of the Universe;* for a political scientist's rebuke to the microeconomists, see Waligorski, *Political Theory of Conservative Economists.*

8. Indeed, Richard M. Weaver in an article on politics made this incredible claim: "It took the study of John Calhoun to wake me up to a realization that a constitution is and should be primarily a negative document," and then after citing Calhoun as his source of wisdom, went on to claim that conservatism was tolerant toward other people. If possible, he should have consulted Calhoun's slaves about Calhoun's toleration. Richard M. Weaver, "Conservatism "Conservativism and Libertarianism," in Carey, ed., *Freedom and Virtue,* 73, 76. See also, Friedman, *Capitalism and Freedom,* 5.

9. Kirk, *Conservative Mind,* 4–9; Bradford, *Remembering Who We Are,* 21–44; George Nash, *Conservative Intellectual Movement in America,* 68–81; Kendall and Carey, *Basic Symbols of the American Political Tradition,* 15; Willmoore Kendall, *Contra Mundumn,* 250–62.

10. Hospers, *Libertarianism,* 81; see T. Patrick Burke, *No Harm,* 172–73; Michael J. Thompson, *Politics of Inequality,* 147–59.

11. On the matter of what holds people in communities together, see Lears, "Concept of Cultural Hegemony," 567–93; Elster, *Cement of Society,* 1–13, 248–87; J. C. D. Clark, *English Society,* 79–81. On the libertarian ideal of the negative state, Douglass C. North's comment should be remembered: "Indeed, a neoclassical world would be a jungle and no society would be viable." North, *Structure and Change in Economic History,* 11. The "liberal" view can be found in Galbraith, *Good Society,* 23–28, 59. For the difference between cultural conservatives and libertarians on government power, see M. Morton Auerbach, "Do-It-Yourself Conservatism," in Carey, ed., *Freedom and Virtue,* 1–12; Meyer, "Twisted Tree of Liberty," ibid., 13–19; Nisbet, "Dreary Cousins," ibid., 38–47; Boaz, *Libertarianism,* 21–22.

12. Mackay, *Western World* (1850), III: 333; Grattan, *Civilized America* (1859), 472; Shirreff, *Tour Through North America* (1835), 301. See also Thomas Hamilton, *Men and Manners in America* (1834), I: 295–300; Basil Hall, *Travels in North America* (1830), I: 309–310. Most found the source to be wealth piling up in the cities, not paying great attention to its actual source. Tocqueville wrote that industrialization might produce an aristocracy, but actually most foreign visitors had a wider view of the process than he did. Tocqueville, *Democracy in America,* trans. Goldhammer (1840), II, ch. 20.

13. Nozick, *Anarchy, State, and Utopia;* Irving Kristol, "Thoughts on Equality and Egalitariansim," in Colin Campbell, ed., *Income Redistribution,* 35–36; G. Warren Nutter, "Commentaries," in ibid., 43–45; Robert Nozick, "Commentaries," ibid., 50–54; Finis Welch, "In Defense of Inequality," 1–17; J. R. Lucas, "Against Equality," in Pojman and Westmoreland, eds., *Equality,* 104–108; Lal, *Reviving the Invisible Hand,* 50; Knapp, "Introduction," in Knapp, et al., *Assault on Equality,* ix; T. Patrick Burke, *No Harm,* 100–101, 103; Barry, *Hayek's Social and Economic Philosophy,* 148–49.

14. (Indianapolis) *The Carpenter* 36 (April 1916), 44, taken from *Successful Farming Magazine.* On the constructive uses of property, see North, *Institutions, Structure and Change in Economic History;* and Olson Olson, "Dictatorship, Democracy, and Development," 567–76.

15. Newman Hall, *From Liverpool to St. Louis* (1870), 181.

16. Piketty, *Capital in the Twenty-First Century,* ch. 8, 11, 12.

17. It is somewhat awkward to find the family as the solution to society's problems since libertarians are supposedly advocates of individualism and self-interest. Family structure is dictatorial, socialist, or some combination of both; and the more democratic the family is, the less likely the children will grow up to be sociopaths, as sociopaths typically come from dictatorial, patriarchal families. However, the stress on the family for teaching children proper behavior and norms is strikingly reminiscent of aristocratic ideals. Once again, Fredrich von Hayek betrays his aristocratic economics by stressing family; Hayek, *Individualism and Economic Order,* 31; see Lal, *Reviving the Invisible Hand,* 161–80.

18. Friedman, *Capitalism and Freedom,* 167; Friedman is indeterminate on whether inheritance is justifiable or not, ibid., 164–65. Friedman also offered as a rule, "To each according to what he and the instruments he owns produces," ibid., 162. See Lester Thurow's criticism of the neoclassical economists' position; Thurow, *Generating Inequality,* 130, 149–54.

19. In fact, we probably have returned to the old aristocratic idea that the way to make people work—as they all wanted to do as little as possible—was to push them into near-starvation so they had to become employed in order to survive. Incentives only exist for upper management people, not for workers.

20. For example, Huston, "A Political Response to Industrialism," 35–57; Huston, *Securing the Fruits of Labor,* ch. 5, 10.

21. Quotes from Hartwell, *History of Mont Pelerin Society,* 37; Barry, *Hayek's Social and Economic Philosophy,* 105, 111–14; Hospers, *Libertarianism,* 89, 115, 144; Friedman, *Capitalism and Freedom,* 190–95.

22. Badeau, *Aristocracy in England* (1885), quote on p. 149.

23. Oakeshott, *Rationalism in Politics,* 40; Bergland, *Libertarianism in One Lesson,* 5; Hospers, *Libertarianism,* 10, 50; Boaz, *Libertarianism,* 2; Tinder, *Liberty;* Flathman, *Willful*

Liberalism, 123; Murray, *What It Means to Be a Libertarian,* 4; Lal, *Reviving the Invisible Hand,* 50. In this shriek of liberty, certainly from libertarians but from the conservative movement generally, there are several grievous problems. The first is the standard that such writers raise and how it conflicts with individualism. Individualism is primarily self-interest unbounded and without rules; one does whatever is in one's self-interest regardless of how such actions might affect others. That is not the rule paraded in conservative and libertarian literature. Lansing Pollock called it the "Freedom Principle": one should not use others self-interestedly to gain one's ends unless the other person's consent was obtained. "According to the freedom principle, each person ought to grant other persons an equal right to be free"; it requires "reciprocal respect for autonomy." In other words, people are expected to take into consideration how their actions affect others; they are to be considerate of the rights and freedom of others.

Individualism does not follow this path; individuals can focus solely on themselves no matter what happens to others. People are supposed to consider the rights of others, but libertarians offer no mechanism to make them behave that way. Here is the contradiction: for their system to produce justice and social harmony, people have to respect the rights of others as much as they insist on such rights for themselves, but their insistence on taking away legal power (i.e., the state) to make people behave correctly means they release the trait of individualism without any constraints. So if it is to the benefit of a rugged individualist to ignore the rights of others, that is exactly what that person does. And when such rugged individualists have wealth behind them, then they can trample the rights of others. This is where the "tyranny of capital" comes from; the insistence of rich rugged individualists that they can do whatever they want and treat others any way they wish because they own property and property rights overrule consideration of others. Pollock, *Freedom Principle,* 10, 13; see also Boaz, *Libertarianism,* 2. On individualism, consult Lukes, *Individualism,* 51–65; L. Susan Brown, *Politics of Individualism,* viii–ix, 1–5; Gaitlin and Jennings, *Perversion of Autonomy,* ch. 5, 8, 9; Gamble, *Hayek,* 184–88. For a different rendition of economic individualism, see Olson and Kähkönen, *Not-So-Dismal Science,* 6–7. For the attack of libertarians and conservatives on democracy, see Bovard, *Freedom in Chains,* quotes 3, 134, ch. 4; Hospers, *Libertarianism,* 42–43; Thomas E. Hall, *Rotten Fruits of Economic Controls,* 1–2; Friedman, *Free to Choose,* 8; T. Patrick Burke, *No Harm,* 160, 172; Knock, *Our Enemy, the State,* 18–20; Nozick, "Commentaries," in Campbell, ed., *Income Redistribution,* 54; Gwartney and Wagner, "Public Choice and the Conduct of Representative Government," 3–28; see Buchanan and Tullock, *Calculus of Consent;* Olson and Kähkönen, *Not-So-Dismal Science,* 4–5, 19; Rahe, *Soft Despotism,* 235–63.

24. Lukes, *Individualism,* 41; Hill, *Lord Acton,* 387; Himmelfarb, *Lord Acton,*79–82. On the idea of restricting liberty only to those who can employ it correctly, see Bernard, *Retrospections of America* (1887), 91. The libertarian/conservative attack on democracy and egalitarian ideals because they damage liberty has a ridiculous quality to it. Outside of property and income, what other liberties are even mentioned? As Stephen Newman observed decades ago, the only liberty libertarians acknowledged was the right to property. One assumes the rights of individuals includes the rights to speech, press, movement, association, no unfair confiscation of private property, religion, petitioning government, trial by jury, protection from excessive punishment, bearing arms, and access to courts for damages. Except for the right to bear arms, a contentious issue, conservatives and libertarians never mention these other

rights of individuals—they only talk about property rights. One can make the argument that popular disgust at the old Soviet Union, Nazi Germany, and all other dictatorships was not their economic institutions but their transgressions against civil liberties. While conservatives and libertarians talk about the federal government oppressing them, there is no reference at all to the civil liberties obliterated by the Stalinist USSR or Hitlerian Germany. No American conservative or libertarian has ever been hunted down by the federal government for associating with other conservatives, for writing tracts, for speaking at conventions, or for hunting in approved areas; they have not been denied access to jury trials and have not been handed out inhumane punishments. (On the other hand, those who can complain of such treatment are communists, socialists, and reformers of various stripes; the Red Scares of A. Mitchell Palmer and Joe McCarthy did not seek to incarcerate conservatives.) Their almost sole complaint is the income tax, which they see as "punitive taxation." Punitive? Whatever one may say about the excesses or insufficiencies of federal taxation, it has never made any rich person poor—it has only made them less rich. This is not the place to go into a defense of progressive taxation, but let it be remembered that the leading financiers of libertarianism today are Charles Koch and David Koch, formerly of Wichita, Kansas, and now residents, evidently, of New York City. They are billionaires. If the taxation system of the federal government (and states) was so punitive, how did they ever become billionaires? Newman, *Liberalism at Wit's* End, 10; Becker, *Economic Theory,* 53–54; Gamble, *Hayek,* 174; de Jasay, *Against Politics,* 33; Hospers, *Libertarianism,* 47, 207–209; Friedman, *Capitalism and Freedom,* 172–76. On the Koch brothers, see Nancy Benac, Associated Press, "Meet the Kochs: 4 Brothers Go in 4 Directions," from *Tulsa World,* August 24, 2014, p. A12.

25. See Gallman, "Economic Growth and Structural Change in the Long Nineteenth Century," 2–6; Goldin, "The Human-Capital Century and American Leadership: Virtues of the Past," 263–92; Goldin and Katz, "Why the United States Led in Education: Lessons from Secondary School Expansion, 1910 to 1940," 143–78.

26. Friedman, *Politics and Tyranny,* 32. For a different view, Barro, *Getting It Right,* xiii.

27. On the elevation of the market mechanism, Hospers, *Libertarianism,* 13–16, 115–16; Friedman, *Capitalism and Freedom,* 13–15; Machan, *Capitalism and Individualism,* ch. 6, 7; on rent-seeking, Libcap, *Contracting for Property Rights,* 10–21; and Gwartney and Wagner, "Public Choice and the Conduct of Representative Government," 3–28; on Pareto optimality, Zajac, *Political Economy of Fairness,* 21, 69–77.

28. On the potential problems with the win-win scenario, see Zajac, *Political Economy of Fairness,* 76–77; on advantages of democracy, see comments of Olson and Kähkönen, *Not-So-Dismal Science,* 13–18, 38.

29. On Jefferson, see Kaminski, ed., *Citizen Jefferson,* 14–15, 22–23, 53, 63; on virtue among conservatives, Bandow, *Politics of Envy,* ch. 1; Oakeshott, *Rationalism in Politics,* 40–46; Flathman, *Willful Liberalism,* 2–5; Franco, *Political Philosophy of Michael Oakeshott,* 2, 157–81; see quote of George Will in Lind, *Up From Conservatism,* 6.

30. Friedman, *Capitalism and Freedom,* 7–21; Dunn, *Setting the People Free,* 137, 171.

31. Medvedev, *Let History Judge,* 836. On the others: Parijs, *Real Freedom for All;* Cohen, *On the Currency of Egalitarian Justice;* Dworkin, *Sovereign Virtue;* Sen, *Inequality Reexamined;* Roemer, *Theories of Distributive Justice,* 3–10.

32. Just to point out some consequences of this program: first, it would remove teenagers from the labor pool, and that would immediately hike wage rates. Second, if people aged 18 to 24 went into the labor market, they would have for a number of years a bargaining position with employers; they could refuse employment conditions dictated to them. This would have the effect of dampening the "tyranny of capital." Third, the program makes no invidious discriminations based on gender or ethnicity; it would be a general application and therefore not subject to complaints of some groups being favored over others. Fourth, its implementation should reduce poverty considerably and particularly the poverty of single mothers. It should as well bring children entirely out of poverty. Some recommendations of Piketty should also be observed: making higher education accessible to all, and instituting a much more powerful income tax on the upper 1 percent of the income spectrum. Piketty, *Capital in the Twenty-First Century,* ch. 14, 15.

33. William H. Seward, "The Slaveholding Class Dominant in the Republic," speech at Detroit, October 2, 1856, in Seward, *Speech of William H. Seward, at Detroit* (1856), 5. Also found in George E. Baker, ed., *Works of William H. Seward,* IV: 254–55.

34. Henry A. Myers, *Are Men Equal?,* 153.

SOURCES

PUBLISHER ABBREVIATIONS

CamUP	Cambridge and New York: Cambridge University Press
ColumUP	New York: Columbia University Press
CorUP	Ithaca: Cornell University Press
DukeUP	Durham: Duke University Press
HUP	Cambridge, MA: Harvard University Press
IndUP	Bloomington: Indiana University Press
JHUP	Baltimore: Johns Hopkins University Press
KSUP	Kent, OH: Kent State University Press
LSUP	Baton Rouge: Louisiana State University Press
OUP	Oxford and New York: Oxford University Press
PrinceUP	Princeton: Princeton University Press
UChiP	Chicago: University of Chicago Press
UGaP	Athens: University of Georgia Press
UIllP	Urbana: University of Illinois Press
UMichP	Ann Arbor: University of Michigan Press
UNCP	Chapel Hill: University of North Carolina Press
UPKan	Lawrence: University Press of Kansas
UPennP	Philadelphia: University of Pennsylvania Press
UTnP	Knoxville: University of Tennessee Press
UPVa	Charlottesville: University Press of Virginia
YUP	New Haven: Yale University Press

MANUSCRIPTS

Martin Van Buren Papers. Library of Congress, Washington, DC (microfilm)
Elizur Wright Papers. Library of Congress, Washington, DC

PERIODICALS AND FARM JOURNALS

American Museum
American [Whig] *Review*
Appleton's Journal of Literature, Science, and Art
Bankers' Magazine
Boston Review
The Carpenter (Indianapolis)
Christian Advocate and Journal
Colman's Rural World
Cultivator (Albany, NY)
Evangelist (New York)
Farmer and Gardener (Baltimore)
Independent (New York)
Indiana Farmer
Lippincott's
Massachusetts' Ploughman [and New England Journal of Agriculture]
Michigan Farmer (Jackson, MI)
New Englander
Niles Weekly Register
The Nineteenth Century: A Monthly Review
North American Review
Prairie Farmer (Chicago)
Saturday Evening Post
United States and Democratic Review

NEWSPAPERS

Atkinson's Saturday Evening Post
Boston Cultivator
Cincinnati Weekly Herald and Philanthropist
Illinois State Register (Springfield)
Illinois State Register (Vandalia)
Kennebec Journal (Augusta, ME)
Kenosha (WI) Democrat
Milwaukee Weekly Wisconsin
Newark Daily Advertiser
New York Times
New York Tribune
Niles Weekly Reporter (Baltimore)

Ohio State Journal (Columbus)
Toledo Blade
Tulsa World

PUBLISHED MEMOIRS, TRAVEL ACCOUNTS, AND LETTERS

An American. *American Husbandry: Containing an Account of the Soil . . .* 2 vols. London: J. Bew, 1775.

Amphlett, W[illiam]. *The Emigrant's Directory to the Western States of North America. . . .* London: Longman, Hurst, Rees, Orme, and Brown, 1819.

Archer, William. *America To-Day: Observations and Reflections.* London: William Heinemann, 1900.

Arfwedson, Carl David. *The United States and Canada in 1832, 1833, and 1834.* 2 vols. London: Richard Bentley, 1834.

Arnold, Matthew. *Civilization in the United States: First and Last Impressions of America.* 2nd ed. Boston: Cupples and Hurd, 1888.

———. *Essays, Religious and Mixed.* Edited by R. H. Super. UMichP, 1972.

Ashe, Thomas. *Travels in America: Performed in 1806, For the Purpose of Exploring the Rivers Allegheny, Monongahela, Ohio, and Mississippi.* 3 vols. London: Richard Phillips, 1808.

Ashworth, Henry. *A Tour in the United States, Cuba, and Canada.* London: A. W. Bennett, 1861.

Badeau, Adam. *Aristocracy in England.* New York: Harper and Brothers, 1885.

Bagehot, Walter. *The English Constitution.* 1867. Repr., CorUP, 1966.

Baird, Robert. *Impressions and Experiences of the West Indies and North America in 1849.* 2 vols. Edinburgh: William Blackwood and Sons, 1860.

Baxter, W. E. *America and the Americans.* London: George Routledge & Co., 1855.

[Beaufoy] A British Subject. *Tour Through Parts of the United States and Canada.* London: Longman, Rees, Orme, Brown, and Green, 1828.

Belknap, Jeremy. *The History of New-Hampshire.* 3 vols. Boston: Belknap and Young, 1792.

Bellamy, Edward. *Equality.* New York: D. Appleton, 1897.

Bernard, John. *Retrospections of America, 1797–1811.* New York: Harper and Brothers, 1887.

Bernhard, Duke of Saxe-Weimar Eisenach. *Travels Through North America, during the Years 1825 and 1826.* 2 vols. Philadelphia: Carey, Lea and Carey, 1828.

Bird, Isabella. *The Englishwoman in America.* 2nd ed. London: John Murray, 1856.

[Blane, William Newnham] An English Gentleman. *An Excursion Through the United States and Canada during the Years 1822–23.* London: Baldwin, Cradock, and Joy, 1824.

[Blowe, Daniel]. *A Geographical, Historical, Commercial, and Agricultural View of the United States of America; Forming a Complete Emigrant's Directory Through Every Part of the Republic.* London: Edwards & Knobb, 1820.

[Boardman, James] A Citizen of the World. *America, and the Americans.* 1833. Repr., New York: Arno Press, 1974.

Bridge, James Howard [Brydges, Harold]. *Uncle Sam at Home.* New York: Henry Holt, 1888.

Bristed, John. *The Resources of the United States of America; or, a View of the Agricultural, Commercial, Manufacturing, Financial, Political, Literary, Moral and Religious Capacity and Charter of the American People.* New York: James Eastburn and Co., 1818.

Brodrick, George C. *English Land and English Landlords: An Enquiry into the Origin and Character of the English Land System, with Proposals for its Reform.* London: Cassell, Pitgter, Galpin & Co., 1881.

Bromley, Mrs. Clara Fitzroy Kelly. *A Woman's Wanderings in the Western World: A Series of Letters Addressed to Sir Fitzroy Kelly, M.P. by his Daughter.* London: Saunders, Otley, and Co., 1861.

Brown, William. *America: A Four Years' Residence in the United States and Canada.* . . . Leeds: Kemplay and Bolland, 1849.

Bryce, James. *The American Commonwealth.* 2 vols. 3rd ed. New York: Macmillan Co., 1908.

Buchanan, George. *An Oration Upon the Moral and Political Evil of Slavery.* Baltimore: Philip Edwards, 1793.

Buckingham, James Silk. *America Historical, Statistic, and Descriptive.* 3 vols. New York: Harper and Brothers, 1841.

———. *The Slave States of America.* 2 vols. London: Fisher, Son & Co., 1842.

Bunn, Alfred. *Old England and New England. In a Series of Views Taken on the Spot.* 2 vols. Repr., Philadelphia: A. Hart, 1853.

Butler, Frances Anne. *Journal.* 2 vols. Philadelphia: Carey, Lea and Blanchard, 1835.

Butler, Nicholas Murray. *True and False Democracy.* New York: Charles Scribner's Sons, 1915.

Butterfield, Kenyon Lerch. *The Farmer and the New Day.* New York: Macmillan Co., 1919.

Campbell, George. *White and Black: The Outcome of a Visit to the United States.* London: Chatto and Windus, 1879.

Carlisle, Earl [George William Frederick Howard Carlisle]. *Travels in America: The Poetry of Pope: Two Lectures Delivered to the Leeds Mechanics' Institution and Literary Society, December 5th and 6th, 1850.* New York: G. P. Putnam, 1851.

Cassell, John. *Cassell's Emigrants' Handbook: Being a Guide to the Various Fields of Emigration in All Parts of the Globe with an Introductory Essay. . . .* London: John Cassell, 1852.

Chambers, William. *Things As They Are in America.* London: William and Robert Chambers, 1854.

Chevalier, Michael. *Society, Manners and Politics in the United States: Being a Series of Letters on North America.* 3rd ed., trans. Boston: Weeks, Jordan & Co., 1839.

Claiborne, J. F. H. *Life and Correspondence of John A. Quitman.* 2 vols. New York: Harper and Brothers, 1860.

Cobbett, William. *Cottage Economy. . . .* New York: John Doyle, 1833.

———. *The Emigrant's Guide: in Ten Letters, Addressed to the Tax-Payers of England.* New ed. London: Mills, Jowett, and Mills, 1830.

———. *Rural Rides in the Counties of Surrey, Kent, Sussex, Hants, Berks, Oxford, Bucks. . . . during the Years 1821 to 1832: With Economical and Political Observations.* 2 vols. New ed. London: Reeves and Turner, 1908.

———. *A Year's Residence in the United States of America.* London: Sherwood, Neely, and Jones, 1819.

Cobden, Richard. *The Political Writings of Richard Cobden.* 2 vols. New York: D. Appleton and Co., 1867.

Coffin, Charles Carleton. *Drum-Beat of the Nation: The First Period of the War of the Rebellion from Its Outbreak to the Close of 1862.* New York: Harper and Brothers, 1888.

Colman, Henry. *European Agriculture and Rural Economy. From Personal Observation.* 2nd ed. 2 vols. Boston: Charles C. Little and James Brown, 1850.

Combe, George. *Notes on the United States of North America during a Phrenological Visit in 1838–1840.* 2 vols. Philadelphia: Carey and Hart, 1841.

Cooper, James Fenimore. *The American Democrat: A Treatise on Jacksonian Democracy.* 1838. Repr., New York: Funk and Wagnalls, 1969.

Cooper, Thomas. *Some Information Respecting America.* London: J. Johnson, 1794.

De Crèvecoeur, J. Hector St. John. *Letters from an American Farmer.* 1782; repr., New York: Fox, Duffield & Co., 1904.

Cunynghame, Sir Arthur Augustus Thurlow. *A Glimpse at the Great Western Republic.* London: Richard Bentley, 1851.

Dalton, William. *Travels in the United States of America, and part of Upper Canada.* B. Bateman, 1821.

Daubeny, Charles. *Journal of a Tour Through the United States and In Canada made during the Years 1837–38.* Oxford, Eng.: T. Combe, 1843.

Davies, Ebenezer. *American Scenes, and Christian Slavery: A Recent Tour of Four Thousand Miles in the United States.* London: John Snow, 1849.

Davis, Stephen. *Notes of a Tour in America in 1832 and 1833.* Edinburgh: Waugh & Innes, 1833.

Dickens, Charles. *American Notes for General Circulation.* Edited by John S. Whitley and Arnold Goldman. 1842. Repr., New York: Penguin Books, 1972.

Dixon, James. *Personal Narrative of a Tour Through a Part of the United States and Canada. . . .* New York: Lane and Scott, 1849.

Duhring, Henry. *Remarks on the United States of America, with Regard to the Actual State of Europe.* London: W. Simpkin and R. Marshall, 1833.

Duncan, John M. *Travels Through Part of the United States and Canada in 1818 and 1819.* 2 vols. New York: Howe and Spalding, 1823.

Easton, George. *Travels in America: With Special Reference to the Province of Ontario as a Home for Working Men.* Glasgow: John S. Marr and Sons, 1871.

Faithful, Emily. *Three Visits to the United States.* Edinburgh: David Douglas, 1884.

Faux, William. *Faux's Memorable Days in America. . . .* London: W. Simplkin and R. Marshall, 1823.

Fearon, Henry Bradshaw. *Sketches of America: A Narrative of a Journey of Five Thousand Miles Through the Eastern and Western States of America. . . .* London: Longman, Hurst, Rees, Orme, and Brown, 1818.

Featherstonhaugh, G[eorge]. *Excursion Through the Slave States, From Washington on the Potomac to the Frontier of Mexico. . . .* 2 vols. London: John Murray, 1844.

Felton, Mrs. *Life in America: A Narrative of Two Years City and Country Residence in the United States.* London: Simpkin and Marshall, 1838.

Ferguson, Fergus. *From Glasgow to Missouri and Back.* Glasgow: Thomas D. Morison, 1878.

Ferguson, William. *America by River and Rail, or, Notes by the Way on the New World and Its People.* London: James Nisbet & Co., 1856.

Ferrall, S[imon] A. *A Ramble of Six Thousand Miles Through the United States of America.* London: Effingham Wilson, 1832.

Fibbleton, George [Greene, Asa]. *Travels in America.* New York: William Pearson, 1833.

Fidler, Isaac. *Observations on Professions, Literature, Manners, and Emigration in the United States and Canada Made During a Residence There in 1832.* New York: J. & J. Harper, 1833.

Finch, I. [John]. *Travels in the United States of America and Canada. . . .* London: Longman, Rees, Orme, Brown, Green and Longman, 1833.

Finch, Marianne. *An Englishwoman's Experience in America.* London: Richard Bentley, 1853.

Flower, George. *The Errors of Emigrants: Pointing Out Many Popular Errors Hitherto Unnoticed; . . .* 1841; repr., New York: Arno Press, 1975.

———. *Letters from the Illinois, 1820, 1821.* London: J. Ridgway by C. Teulon, 1822.

Fordham, Elias Pym. *Personal Narrative of Travels in Virginia, Maryland, Pennsylvania, Ohio, Indiana, Kentucky; . . . 1817–1818.* Edited by Frederic Austin Ogg. Cleveland: Arthur H. Clark, 1906.

Fowler, John. *Journal of a Tour in the State of New York in the Year 1830.* London: Whittaker, Treacher, and Arnoit, 1831.

Francis, Alexander. *Americans: An Impression.* New York: D. Appleton and Co., 1909.

Freeman, Edward Augustus. *Some Impressions of the United States.* London: Longman, Green, and Co., 1883.

Garland, Hamlin. *Main-Travelled Roads.* New York: Macmillan, 1899.

Gerhard, Fred. *Illinois As It Is; its History, Geography, Statistics. . . .* Chicago: Keen and Lee, 1857.

Gladstone, William Ewart. "Kin Beyond the Sea" (1878). In *Representative Essays Selected from the Series of "Prose Masterpieces from the Modern Essayists,"* 349–95. Edited by George Haven Putnam. New York: G. P. Putnam's Sons, 1885.

Goddard, Frederick B. *Where to Emigrate, and Why.* New York: Frederick B. Goddard, 1869.

Godley, John Robert. *Letters from America.* 2 vols. London: John Murray, 1844.

Grattan, Thomas Colley. *Civilized America.* 2 vols. London: Bradbury & Evans, 1859.

Great Britain, Registrar-General. *The Census of Great Britain in 1851. . . .* London: Longman, Brown, Green, and Longmans, 1854.

Griffin, Lepel Henry. *The Great Republic.* 2nd ed. London: Chapman and Hall, 1884.

Griffiths, D., Jr. *Two Years in the New Settlements of Ohio.* 1835; repr., Ann Arbor: University Microfilms, 1966.

Grund, Francis J. *Aristocracy in America: From the Sketch-Book of a German Nobleman.* 1839; repr., New York: Harper and Row, 1959.

Gurney, Joseph John. *A Journey in North America, described in Familiar Letters to Amelia Opie.* Norwich, Eng.: Josiah Fletcher, 1841.

Gurowski, Adam G., de. *America and Europe.* New York: D. Appleton, 1857.

[Haliburton, Thomas C.] "Sam Slick." *The Americans at Home: Or, Byeways, Backwoods, and Prairies.* 3 vols. London: Hurst & Blackett, 1854.

Hall, Basil. *Travels in North America, in the Years 1827 and 1828.* 3rd ed. 3 vols. Edinburgh: Robert Cadell, 1830.

Hall, Francis. *Travels in Canada and the United States in 1816 and 1817.* London: Longman, Hurst, Rees, Orme, & Brown, 1818.

Hall, Marshall. *The Two-Fold Slavery of the United States; with a Project of Self-Emancipation.* London: Adam, Scott, 1854.

Hall, Newman. *From Liverpool to St. Louis.* London: George Routledge & Sons, 1870.

Hamilton, Thomas. *Men and Manners in America.* 2nd ed. 2 vols. Edinburgh: William Blackwood, 1834.

Hancock, William. *An Emigrant's Five Years in the Free States of America.* London: T. Cautley Newby, 1860.

Hardman, William. *A Trip to America.* London: T. Vickers, 1884.

Hardy, Lady Duffus. *Through Cities and Prairie Lands: Sketches of an American Tour.* New York: R. Worthington, 1881.

Harris, William Tell. *Remarks Made during a Tour Through the United States of America, in the Years 1817, 1818, and 1819.* London: Sherwood, Neely, & Jones, 1821.

Harrison, Frederic. *Memories and Thoughts: Men-Book-Cities-Art.* New York: Macmillan, 1906.

Hatton, Joseph. *To-Day in America: Studies for the Old World and the New.* New York: Harper and Brothers, 1881.

Heath, Francis George. *The English Peasantry.* London: Frederick Warne & Co., 1874.

Henry, Lord Brougham. *Political Philosophy, Part II: Of Aristocracy.* London: Chapman and Hall, 1843.

Hodgson, Adam. *Remarks during a Journey Through North America in the Years 1819, 1820, and 1821, in a Series of Letters. . . .* New York: Samuel Whiting, 1823.

Hole, Samuel Reynolds. *A Little Tour in America.* London: Edward Arnold, 1895.

Holmes, Isaac. *An Account of the United States of America, derived from Actual Observation, During a Residence of Four Years in that Republic. . . .* London: Canton Press, 1823.

Mrs. Houstoun [Matilda Charlotte]. *Hesperos: Or, Travels in the West.* 2 vols. London: John W. Parker, 1850.

Howe, John. *The Emigrants' New Guide: Shewing a Description of the United States, and the British Possessions in Canada. . . .* Leeds: John Howe, 1822.

Iredale, Andrew. *An Autumn Tour in the United States and Canada.* Torquay: George H. Iredale, 1901.

Irving, Washington. *The Voyage and Other English Essays from the Sketch Book.* Boston: Houghton Mifflin and Co., 1891.

Jobson, Frederick J. *America and American Methodism.* New York: Virtue, Emmins, & Co., 1857.

Johnson, Charles Britten. *Letters from the British Settlement in Pennsylvania, . . .* Philadelphia: H. Hall, 1819.

Johnston, James F. W. *Notes on North America: Agricultural, Economical, and Social.* 2 vols. Boston: Charles C. Little and James Brown, 1851.

Kay, Joseph. *Free Trade In Land.* Edited by his Widow. 8th ed. London: Kegan Paul, Trench, and Co., 1885.

Kendall, Edward Augustus. *Travels Through the Northern Parts of the United States in 1806–08.* 3 vols. New York: I. Riley, 1809.

Kent, William. *Memoirs and Letters of James Kent, LL.D.: Late Chancellor of the State of New York.* Boston: Little, Brown and Co., 1898.

Kingdom, William Jr. *America and the British Colonies: An Abstract of All the Most Useful Information Relative to the United States of America, and the British Colonies. . . .* London: G. and W. B. Whittaker, 1820.

Kipling, Rudyard. *American Notes.* Boston: Brown and Co., 1899.

Lang, John Dunmore. *Religion and Education in America: With Notices of the State and Prospects of American Unitarianism, Property, and African Colonization.* London: Thomas Ward & Co., 1840.

Lecky, Willliam Edward Hartpole. *Democracy and Liberty.* 2 vols. New York: Longmans, Green, and Co., 1896.

Lewis, Rev. G[eorge]. *Impressions of America and the American Churches. . . .* Edinburgh: W. P. Kennedy, 1845.

Lindley-Cowen, L. *The West Australian Settler's Guide and Farmer's Handbook.* 2 vols. Perth, Australia: E. S. Wigg and Son, 1897.

Logan, James. *Notes of a Journey Through Canada, the United States of America, and the West Indies.* Edinburgh: Fraser and Co., 1838.

Lyell, Charles. *A Second Visit to the United States of North America.* 2nd ed. 2 vols. New York: Harper & Bros., 1849.

———. *Travels in North America.* 2 vols. London: 1845.

Macaulay, James. *Across the Ferry: First Impressions of America and its People.* 2nd ed. London: Hodder and Stoughton, 1872.

Macrae, David. *The Americans at Home: Pen-and-Ink Sketches of American Men and Manners and Institutions.* 2 vols. Edinburgh: Edmon, Stone and Douglas, 1870.

MacGregor, John. *Our Brothers and Cousins: A Summer Tour in Canada and the United States.* London: Seeley, Jackson, and Halliday, 1859.

Mackay, A[lexander]. *The Western World; or, Travels in the United States in 1846–47. . . .* 3rd ed. 3 vols. London: Richard Bentley, 1850.

MacKay, Charles. *Life and Liberty in America: Or, Sketches of a Tour in the United States and Canada, in 1857–8.* 2 vols. London: Smith, Elder & Co., 1859.

MacKenzie, William L[yon]. *Sketches of Canada and the United States.* London: Effingham Wilson, 1833.

Maine, Sir Henry Summer. *Popular Government: Four Essays.* London: John Murray, 1885.

Marryat, Capt. Frederick. *A Diary in America, With Remarks on Its Institutions.* New York: William H. Colyer, 1839.

Martineau, Harriet. *Retrospect of Western Travel.* 2 vols. London: Saunders & Otley, 1838.

———. *Society In America.* 2nd ed. 3 vols. London: Saunders and Otley, 1839.

Mattson, Hans. *The Story of an Emigrant.* Saint Paul: D. D. Merrill Co., 1891.

Maude, John. *Visit to the Falls of Niagara in 1800.* London: Longman, Rees, Orme, Brown and Green, 1826.

Maury, Sarah Mytton. *An Englishwoman in America.* London: Thomas Richardson and Son, 1848.

Maxwell, A[rchibald] M[ontgomery]. *A Run Through the United States, during the Autumn of 1840.* 2 vols. London: Henry Colburn, 1841.

Medley, Julius George. *An Autumn Tour in the United States and Canada.* London: Henry S. King and Co., 1873.

Melish, John. *Travels Through the United States of America, in the Years 1806 & 1807, and 1809, 1810, & 1811. . . .* Philadelphia: John Melish, 1818.

Mill, John Stuart. *Considerations on Representative Government.* Edited by Currin V. Shields. New York: Liberal Arts Press, 1958.

———. *Principles of Political Economy with Some of Their Applications to Social Philosophy.* 1871; repr., London: Longmans, Green and Co., 1926.

Mitchell, D[avid] W. *Ten Years Residence in the United States.* London: Smith, Elder & Co., 1862.

Money, Edward. *The Truth About America.* London: Sampson, Low, Marston, Searle, and Rivington, 1886.

Moore, George. *Journal of a Voyage Across the Atlantic: With Notes on Canada & the United States; and Return to Great Britain in 1844.* London: private printing, 1845.

Morse, Jedidiah. *Annals of the American Revolution.* 1824. Repr., Port Washington, NY: Kennikat Press, 1968.

Murray, Charles Augustus. *Travels in North America. Including a Summer Residence with the Pawnee Tribe of Indians. . . .* 3rd ed. 2 vols. London: Richard Bentley, 1854.

Murray, Henry A. *Lands of the Slave and the Free: Or, Cuba, the United States, and Canada.* 2 vols. London: John W. Parker and Son, 1855.

Murray, Hugh. *The United States of America; Their History from the Earliest Period. . . .* 3 vols. Edinburgh: Oliver & Boyd, 1844.

O'Bryan, W[illiam]. *A Narrative of Travels in the United States of America. . . .* London: S. Thorne, Shebbear, Hatherleigh, Devon, Gilbert & Co., 1836.

O'Hanlon, Rev. J[ohn]. *The Irish Emigrant's Guide for the United States.* Boston: Patrick Donahoe, 1851.

Oldmixon, [John W.] *Transatlantic Wanderings: Or, A Last Look at the United States.* London: Geo. Routledge, 1855.

Olmsted, Frederick Law. *Walks and Talks of an American Farmer in England.* 1859; repr., UMichP, 1967.

Ontario, Provincial Government. *Emigration: The British Farmer's and Farm Labourer's Guide to Ontario, the Premier Province of the Dominion of Canada.* Toronto: C. Blackett Robinson, 1880.

Ouseley, William Gore. *Remarks on the Statistics and Political Institutions of the United States, with Some Observations on the Ecclesiastical System of America, Her Sources of Revenue, &c.* London: J. Rodwell, 1832.

Pairpoint, Alfred. *Uncle Sam and His Country; or, Sketches of America, in 1854–55–56.* London: Simpkin, Marshall, and Co., 1857.

Palmer, John. *Journal of Travels in the United States of North America and in Lower Canada, Performed in the Year 1817. . . .* London: Sherwood, Neely and Jones, 1818.

Parker, Theodore. *The Collected Works of Theodore Parker.* Edited by Francis Power Cobbe, et al. 14 vols. London: Trubner & Co., 1864–1871.

Parkinson, Richard. *George Washington: Statement of Richard Parkinson.* Baltimore [?]: Lord Baltimore Press, 1909.

———. *A Tour in America in 1798, 1799, and 1800.* 2 vols. London: J. Harding, 1805.

Phillippo, James M[ursell]. *The United States and Cuba.* London: Petress & Co., 1857.

Phillips, Wendell. *Speeches, Lectures, and Letters.* 2 vols. 1884–1891; repr., New York: Negro Universities Press, 1968.

Playfair, Hugo. *Brother Jonathan, the Smartest Nation in all Creation.* 3 vols. London: Saunders & Otley, 1844.

Playfair, Robert. *Recollections of a Visit to the United States and British Provinces of North America, in the Years 1847, 1848, and 1849.* Edinburgh: Thomas Constable & Co., 1856.

Power, Tyrone. *Impressions of America, during the Years 1833, 1834, and 1835.* 2 vols. London: Richard Bentley, 1836.

Prentice, Archibald. *A Tour in the United States with Two Lectures on Emigration, delivered in the Mechanics' Institution Manchester.* 6th ed. London: John Johnston, 1850.

Priest, William. *Travels in the United States of America, Commencing in the Year 1793 and Ending in 1797, with the Author's Journals of His Two Voyages Across the Atlantic.* London: J. Johnson, 1802.

Prothero, Rowland E. *English Farming Past and Present.* London: Longmans, Green, and Co., 1912.

Pulszky, Francis, and Theresa Pulszky. *White, Red, Black: Sketches of American Society in the United States.* 2 vols. New York: Redfield, 1853.

Quinby, G. W. *A Plea for Humanity; Showing the Demands of Christianity on Behalf of the Criminal and Perishing Classes.* Cincinnati: G. W. Quinby, 1860.

Ramsey, David. *The History of the American Revolution.* 2 vols. Philadelphia: A. Aitken and Son, 1789.

Ranken, Major [George]. *Canada and the Crimea or Sketches of a Soldier's Life from the Journal and Correspondence of the Late Major Ranken, , R. E.* 2nd ed. Edited by W. Bayne Ranken. London: Longman, Green, Longman, Roberts, and Green, 1863.

Rantoul, Robert, Jr. *Memoirs, Speeches and Writings of Robert Rantoul, Jr.* Edited by Luther Hamilton. Boston: John P. Jewett and Co., 1854.

Reid, H[ugo]. *Sketches in North America; with Some Account of Congress and of the Slavery Question.* London: Longman, Green, Longman, and Roberts, 1861.

Rich, Obadiah. *A General View of the United States of America. . . .* London: O. Rich, 1833.

[Rivington, W. J., and W. A. Harris]. Two Gentlemen. *Reminiscences of America in 1869.* London: Gilbert and Rivington, 1870.

Robertson, James. *A Few Months in America: Containing Remarks on Some of its Industrial and Commercial Interests.* London: Longman and Co., 1855.

De La Rochefoucault Liancourt, Duke. *Travels Through the United States of North America, the Country of the Iroquois, and Upper Canada, in the Years 1795, 1796, and 1797.* 2nd ed. 2 vols. London: R. Phillips, 1800.

Rose, George. *The Great Country; or, Impressions of America.* London: Tinsley Brothers, 1868.

Rousseau, Jean Jacques. "A Discourse Upon the Origin and the Foundation of the Inequality among Mankind" (1755). In *The Harvard Classics.* Edited by Charles W. Eliot. Vol. 34, *French and English Philosophers,* 171–202. New York: P. F. Collier, 1910.

Rubio [Thomas Horton James]. *Rambles in the United States and Canada during the Year 1845, with a Short Account of Oregon.* London: John Oliver, 1846.

[Rush, Benjamin]. *An Address to the Inhabitants of the British Settlements in America Upon Slave-Keeping.* Philadelphia: John Dunlap, 1773.

Russell, Baron Charles. *Diary of a Visit to the United States of America in the Year 1883.* New York: United States Catholic Historical Society, 1910.

Russell, Robert. *North America: Its Agriculture and Climate: Containing Observations on the Agriculture and Climate of Canada, the United States, and the Island of Cuba.* Edinburgh: Adam & Charles Black, 1857.

[Russell, Robert W.] *America Compared with England: Respective Social Effects of the American and English Systems of Government and Legislation: and the Mission of Democracy.* London: Effingham Wilson, 1848.

Russell, William Howard. *Pictures of Southern Life, Social, Political, and Military.* New York: James G. Gregg, 1861.

Salter, William. *The Life of James W. Grimes: Governor of Iowa, 1854–1858, a Senator of the United States, 1859–1869.* New York: D. Appleton, 1876.

Seward, William H. "The Slaveholding Class Dominant in the Republic." *Speech of William H. Seward, at Detroit, October 20, 1856.* Washington, DC: Republican Association of Washington, 1857.

Sheahan, James W. *The Life of Stephen A. Douglas.* New York: Harper and Brothers, 1860.

Shirreff, Patrick. *A Tour Through North America; Together with a Comprehensive View of the Canadas and United States as Adapted for Agricultural Emigration.* Edinburgh: Oliver & Boyd, 1835.

Smart, George Thomas. *The Temper of the American People.* Boston: 1912.

Smith, Goldwin. *The Civil War in America: An Address Read at the Last Meeting of the Manchester Union and Emancipation Society.* London: Simpkin, Marshall, and Co., 1866.

Smith, William. *A Yorkshireman's Trip to the United States.* London: Longman's, Green & Co., 1892.

Spencer, Herbert. *The Man Versus the State.* 1892; repr., Caldwell, ID: Caxton Printers, 1965.

Stead, William Thomas. *The Americanization of the World: or, The Trend of the Twentieth Century.* New York: Horace Markley, 1901.

Steevens, G[eorge] W. *The Land of the Dollar.* New York: Dodd, Mead & Co., 1898.

Stewart, W. M. *Eleven Years' Experience in the Western States of America.* London: Houlston and Sons, 1870.

Stirling, James. *Letters from the Slave States.* London: John W. Parker, 1857.

Stuart, James. *Three Years in North America.* 2 vols. Edinburgh: Robert Cadell, 1833.

Stuart-Wortley, Lady Emmeline. *Travels in the United States, etc., During 1849 and 1850.* New York: Harper and Brothers, 1851.

Sturge, Joseph. *A Visit to the United States in 1841.* London: Hamilton, Adams, and Co., 1842.

Sullivan, Sir Edward [Robert]. *Rambles and Scrambles in North and South America.* London: Richard Bentley, 1852.

[Sullivan, James]. A Citizen of Massachusetts. *The Path to Riches. An Inquiry into the Origin and Use of Money, and into the Principles of Stocks and Banks.* Boston: P. Edes, 1792.

Taylor, John. *An Enquiry into the Principles and Tendency of Certain Public Measures.* Philadelphia: Thomas Dobson, 1794.

Thomason, A. [Bell, Andrew]. *Men and Things in America; Being the Experience of a Year's Residence in the United States.* London: William Smith, 1838.

Thomason, D. R. *Hints to Emigrants, or to Those Who May Contemplate Emigrating to the United States of America.* Philadelphia: Isaac Ashmead, 1848.

Thomson, William. *A Tradesman's Travels, in the United States and Canada, in the Years 1840, 41, & 42.* Edinburgh: Oliver & Boyd, 1842.

de Tocqueville, Alexis. *Democracy in America.* 2 vols. Translated by Arthur Goldhammer. 1835, 1840; repr., New York: Library of America, 2004.

Tompkins, Isaac, and Lord Brougham. *Thoughts Upon the Aristocracy of England.* 6th ed. London: Henry Hooper, 1835.

Tremenheere, Hugh Seymour. *Notes on Public Subjects, made during a Tour in the United States and In Canada.* London: John Murray, 1852.

Trollope, Anthony. *North America.* 3 vols. Leipzig: Bernhard Tauchnitz, 1862.

Trollope, Mrs. [Frances]. *Domestic Manners of the Americans.* 4th ed. 2 vols. London: Whittaker, Treacher & Co., 1832.

Tucker, St. George. *A Dissertation on Slavery with a Proposal for the Gradual Abolition of It, in the State of Virginia.* Philadelphia: Mathew Carey, 1796.

Tudor, Henry. *Narrative of a Tour in North America.* 2 vols. London: James Duncan, 1834.

United States Bureau of the Interior. *Population of the United States in 1860.* [Eighth Census.] Washington, DC: Government Printing Office, 1864.

[Unknown editor. "Recent Travellers."] *Domestic Manners of the American; or, Characteristic Sketches of the People of the United States.* Glasgow: Richard Griffin, 1836.

Vigne, Godfrey T. *Six Months in America.* Philadelphia: Thomas T. Ash, 1833.

Vivian, H. Hussey. *Notes of a Tour in America. From August 7th to November 17th, 1877.* London: Edward Stanford, 1878.

Wagner, Charles. *My Impressions of America.* Translated from the French by Mary Louise Hendee. New York: McClure, Phillips and Co., 1906.

Wakefield, Priscilla. *Excursions in North America, Described in Letters from a Gentleman and his Young Companion to Their Friends in England.* London: Darton and Harvey, 1806.

Walter, John. *First Impressions of America.* London: Private Circulation, 1867.

Wansey, Henry. *An Excursion to the United States of North America in the Summer of 1794.* 2nd ed. Salisburg, Eng.: J. Easton, 1798.

Warren, John. *An Oration, Delivered July 4th, 1783, . . . Boston.* Boston: John Gill, 1783.

Warren, Mrs. Mercy. *History of the Rise, Progress and Termination of the American Revolution.* 3 vols. 1805; repr., New York: Ams Press, 1970.

de Warville, J. P. Brissot. *New Travels in the United States of America.* 1792; repr., Bowling Green, OH: Historical Publications Co., 1919.

Watson, Winslow C., ed. *Men and Times of the Revolution: or, Memoirs of Elkanah Watson, including his Journals of Travels in Europe and America, from the Year 1777 to 1842.* 2nd ed. New York: Dana and Company, 1856.

Webb, C[harles] H[enry]. *A Manual for Emigrants, Suggested by Circumstances, Proved by Personal Experience and Intended to be Placed in the Hands of All Foreigners, Especially from the "British Isles," . . .* New York: William Osborn, 1849.

Welby, Adlard. *A Visit to North America and the English Settlements in Illinois, with a Winter Residence in Philadelphia.* London: J. Drury, 1821.

Weld, Charles Richard. *A Vacation Tour of the United States and Canada.* London: Longman, Brown, Green, and Longmans, 1855.

Wiley and Putnam. *Wiley & Putnam's Emigrant's Guide. Comprising Advise and Instruction in Every State of the Voyage to America.* London: Wiley & Putnam, 1845.

Williams, James. *The Rise and Fall of the 'The Model Republic.'* London: Richard Bentley, 1863.

Wilson, C[harles] H[enry]. *The Wanderer in America, or Truth at Home. . . .* Thirsk, Eng.: Henry Masterson, 1822.

Woods, John. *Two Years' Residence in the Settlement on the English Prairie, in the Illinois County, United States.* London: Longman, Hurst, Reessa, Orme, and Brown, 1822.

[Wright, Frances D'Arusmont]. An English Woman. *Views of Society and Manners in America; . . .* London: Longman, Hurst, Rees, Orme, & Brown, 1821.

Wright, Joseph. *A Centennial Tour in the United States and Canada.* Macclesfield, Eng.: Swinnerton and Brown, 1877.

Wyse, Francis. *America, Its Realities and Resources. . . .* 3 vols. London: T. C. Newby, 1846.

Zincke, Foster Barham. *Last Winter in the United States being Table Talk Collected during a Tour Through the Late Southern Confederation, the Far West, the Kocky Mountains, &c.* London: John Murray, 1868.

PUBLISHED COLLECTIONS OF DOCUMENTS

Adams, John. *The Works of John Adams, Second President of the United States.* 10 vols. Edited by Charles Francis Adams. Boston: Little Brown and Co., 1856.

Adams, John Quincy. *Memoirs of John Quincy Adams.* 12 vols. Edited by Charles Francis Adams. Philadelphia: J. B. Lippincott, 1874–1877.

Boudinot, Elias. *The Life, Public Services, Addresses, and Letters of Elias Boudinot.* 2 vols. Edited by J. J. Boudinot. 1896; repr., New York: Da Capo Press, 1971.

Calhoun, John C. *The Papers of John Calhoun.* 25 vols. to date. Edited by Robert L. Meriwether, et al. Columbia: University of South Carolina Press, 1959–.

Cawley, Elizabeth Hoon, ed. *The American Diaries of Richard Cobden.* PrinceUP, 1952.

Chase, Salmon P. *The Salmon P. Chase Papers.* Vol. 2, *Correspondence, 1823–1857.* Edited by John Niven. KSUP, 1994.

Clarke, James Freeman. *Autobiography, Diary and Correspondence.* Edited by Edward Everett Hale. 1891; repr., New York: Negro Universities Press, 1968.

Commager, Henry Steele, and Richard B. Morris, eds. *The Spirit of 'Seventy-Six': The Story of the American Revolution as Told by Participants.* 2 vols. Indianapolis: Bobbs-Merrill, 1958.

Dickinson, John R., ed. *Speeches, Correspondence, etc., of the Late Daniel Dickinson, of New York.* 2 vols. New York: G. P. Putnam and Son, 1867.

Franklin, Benjamin. *The Life of Benjamin Franklin, Written By Himself.* 3rd ed. 3 vols. Edited by John Bigelow. Philadelphia: J. B. Lippincott, 1893.

Jacobson, David L., ed. *The English Libertarian Heritage: From the Writings of John Trenchard and Thomas Gordon in The Independent Whig and Cato's Letters.* Indianapolis: Bobbs-Merrill, 1965.

Jefferson, Thomas. *The Papers of Thomas Jefferson.* Edited by Julian P. Boyd et al. 24 vols. to date. PrinceUP, 1950–.

———. *The Writings of Thomas Jefferson.* Edited by Andrew A. Lipscomb. 20 vols. Washington, DC: Thomas Jefferson Memorial Association, 1904.

Johannsen, Robert W., ed. *The Letters of Stephen A. Douglas.* UIllP, 1961.

Lincoln, Abraham. *The Collected Works of Abraham Lincoln.* Edited by Roy P. Basler, Marion Dolores Pratt, and Lloyd A. Dunlap. 9 vols. New Brunswick, NJ: Rutgers University Press, 1953–1955.

Madison, James. *The Papers of James Madison.* Edited by William T. Hutchinson, M. E. Rachal, and Robert Allen Rutland.. 15 vols. to date. UChiP, 1962–.

——. *The Writings of James Madison.* 9 vols. Edited by Gaillard Hunt. New York: G. P. Putnam's Sons, 1900–1910.

Mason, George. *The Papers of George Mason, 1725–1792.* Edited by Robert A. Rutland. 3 vols. UNCP, 1970.

Moore, Frank, ed. *American Eloquence: A Collection of Speeches and Addresses, by the Most Eminent Orators of America.* 2 vols. New York: D. Appleton, 1895.

Nevins, Allan, ed. *The Diary of Philip Hone, 1828–1851.* New York: Dodd, Mead and Co., 1936.

Paine, Thomas. *The Complete Writings of Thomas Paine.* Edited by Philip S. Foner. 2 vols. New York: Citadel Press, 1945.

Parker, Theodore. *Life and Correspondence of Theodore Parker.* Edited by John Weiss. 2 vols. New York: D. Appleton and Co., 1864.

Phillips, Wendell. *Speeches, Lectures, and Letters.* 2 vols. Boston: Lee and Shepard, 1884–1891.

Price, Richard. *Richard Price and the Ethical Foundations of the American Revolution.* Edited by Bernard Peach. DukeUP, 1970.

Rollo, Ogden, ed. *The Life and Letters of Edwin Lawrence Godkin.* 2 vols. New York: Macmillan, 1907.

Seward, William H. *The Works of William H. Seward.* Edited by George E. Baker. 2nd ed. 5 vols. Boston: Houghton, Mifflin and Co., 1887.

Storing, Herbert J., ed. *The Complete Anti-Federalist.* 7 vols. UChiP, 1981.

Wainwright, Nicholas B., ed. *A Philadelphia Perspective: The Diary of Sidney George Fisher Covering the Years 1834–1871.* Philadelphia: Historical Society of Pennsylvania, 1967.

Webster, Noah. *Letters of Noah Webster.* Edited by Harry R. Warfel. New York: Library Publishers, 1953.

——. *On Being American: Selected Writings, 1783–1828.* Edited by Homer D. Babbidge Jr. New York: Frederick A. Praeger, 1967.

Wilson, James. *The Works of James Wilson.* 2 vols. Edited by Robert Green McCloskey. Cambridge, MA: Belknap Press, 1967.

SECONDARY SOURCES

Alchian, Armen A., and Reuben A. Kessel. "Competitive Monopoly, and the Pursuit of Money." In National Bureau of Economic Research. *Aspects of Labor Economics,* 157–83. PrinceUP, 1962.

Alexander, Edward P. *A Revolutionary Conservative: James Duane of New York.* ColumUP, 1938.

Allen, Danielle. *Our Declaration: A Reading of the Declaration of Independence in Defense of Equality.* New York: W. W. Norton, 2014.

Allen, H. C. *Great Britain and the United States: A History of Anglo-American Relations (1783–1952).* New York: St. Martin's Press, 1955.

Allen, Robert. *Enclosure and the Yeoman.* OUP, 1992.

Anderson, Elizabeth S. "Against Luck Egalitarianism: What is the Point of Equality?" In *Social Justice,* 154–85. Edited by Matthew Clayton and Andrew Williams. Cambridge, MA: Belknap Press, 2010.

Appleby, Joyce. "The American Heritage: The Heirs and the Disinherited." *JAH* 74 (December 1987): 798–813.

Armitage, David. *The Declaration of Independence: A Global History.* HUP, 2007.

Armstrong, W. A. "Labour I: Rural Population Growth, Systems of Employment, and Incomes." In *The Agrarian History of England and Wales.* Vol. 6, *1750–1850,* pp. 641–728. Edited by Joan Thirsk and G. E. Mingay. CamUP, 1989.

Arneson, Richard J. "Equality and Equal Opportunity for Welfare." In *Equality: Selected Readings,* 229–41. Edited by Louis Pojman and Robert Westmoreland. OUP, 1997.

Arnstein, Walter. *Britain Yesterday and Today, 1830 to the Present.* Lexington, MA: D. C. Heath & Co., 1964.

Ashcraft, Richard. *Revolutionary Politics and Locke's Two Treatises of Government.* PrinceUP, 1986.

Ashton, Robert. *The English Civil War: Conservatism and Revolution, 1603–1649.* New York: W. W. Norton, 1978.

Atack, Jeremy. "The Agricultural Ladder Revisited: A New Look at an Old Question with Some Data for 1860." *AgH* 63 (Winter 1989): 1–25.

Atack, Jeremy, and Fred Bateman. "The 'Egalitarian Ideal' and the Distribution of Wealth in the Northern Agricultural Community: A Backward Look." *Review of Economics and Statistics* 63 (February 1981): 129–32.

———. *To Their Own Soil: Agriculture in the Antebellum North.* Ames: Iowa State University Press, 1987.

Auerbach, M. Morton. "Do-It-Yourself Conservatism." In *Freedom and Virtue: The Conservative/Libertarian Debate,* 1–12. Edited by George W. Carey. Wilmington, DE: Intercollegiate Studies Institute, 1998.

Bailyn, Bernard. *Ideological Origins of the American Revolution.* 1967; repr., HUP, 1992.

Baker, Jean. *Affairs of Party: The Political Culture of Northern Democrats in the Mid-Nineteenth Century.* CorUP, 1983.

Baltzell, E. Digby. *Puritan Boston and Quaker Philadelphia: Two Protestant Ethics and the Spirit of Class Authority and Leadership.* New York: Free Press, 1979.

Bandow, Doug. *The Politics of Envy: Statism as Envy.* New Brunswick, NJ: Transaction Press, 1994.

Banner, James M., Jr. *To the Hartford Convention: The Federalists and the Origins of Party Politics in Massachusetts, 1789–1815.* New York: Alfred A. Knopf, 1970.

Banning, Lance. *The Jeffersonian Persuasion: Evolution of a Party Ideology.* CorUP, 1978.

———. *The Sacred Fire of Liberty: James Madison and the Founding of the Federal Republic.* CorUP, 1995.

Baptist, Edward E. *The Half Has Never Been Told: Slavery and the Making of American Capitalism.* New York: Basic Books, 2014.

Barro, Robert J. *Getting It Right: Markets and Choices in a Free Society.* Cambridge, MA: MIT Press, 1996.

Barry, Norman P. *Hayek's Social and Economic Philosophy.* London: Macmillan Press, 1979.

———. *On Classical Liberalism and Libertarianism.* Houndmills, UK: Macmillan Press, 1986.

Baugh, Daniel A., ed. *Aristocratic Government and Society in Eighteenth-Century England: The Foundations of Stability.* New York: New Viewpoints, 1975.

Beales, Derek. *From Castlereagh to Gladstone, 1815–1885.* New York: W. W. Norton, 1969.

Becker, Gary S. *Economic Theory.* New York: Alfred A. Knopf, 1971.

Beckett, J. V. "Agricultural Landownership and Estate Management." In *The Agrarian History of England and Wales.* Edited by Joan Thirsk and E. J. T. Collins. Vol. 7, part 1, *1850–1914,* pp. 693–758. CamUP, 2000.

———. *The Aristocracy in England.* Oxford: Basil Blackwell, 1986.

———. "The Decline of the Small Landowner in England and Wales, 1660–1900." In *Landowners, Capitalists, and Entrepreneurs: Essays for Sir John Habakkuk.* Edited by F. M. L. Thompson. 89–112. OUP, 1991.

Beeman, Richard R. "Deference, Republicanism and the Emergence of Popular Politics in Eighteenth-Century America." *WMQ* 49 (July 1992): 401–30.

Bendix, Reinhard. *Kings or People: Power and the Mandate to Rule.* Berkeley: University of California Press, 1978.

Bensel, Richard Franklin. *The Political Economy of American Industrialization, 1877–1900.* CamUP, 2000.

Benson, Lee. *The Concept of Jacksonian Democracy: New York as a Test Case.* PrinceUP, 1961.

Berger, Max. *The British Traveller in America, 1836–1860.* Gloucester, MA: Peter Smith, 1964.

Bergland, David. *Libertarianism in One Lesson.* 8th ed. Huntington Beach, CA: Orpheus Publications, 2000.

Bernhard, Winfred E. A. *Fisher Ames: Federalist and Statesman, 1758–1808*. UNCP, 1965.

Berry, Brian M. *Culture and Equality: An Egalitarian Critique of Multiculturalism*. HUP, 2001.

Biles, W. Roger. *A New Deal for the American People*. DeKalb: Northern Illinois University Press, 1991.

Billington, Ray Allen. *Westward Expansion: A History of the American Frontier*. 4th ed. New York: Macmillan, 1974.

Birner, David. *The Politics of Provincialism: The Democratic Party in Transition, 1918–1932*. 1967; repr., New York: W. W. Norton, 1975.

Blackett, R. J. M. *Building an Antislavery Wall: Black Americans in the Atlantic Abolitionist Movement, 1830–1860*. LSUP, 1983.

———. *Divided Hearts: Britain and the American Civil War*. LSUP, 2001.

Blumin, Stuart M. *The Emergence of the Middle Class: Social Experience in the American City, 1760–1900*. CamUP, 1989.

Boaz, David. *Libertarianism: A Primer*. New York: Free Press, 1997.

———. *The Politics of Freedom: Taking on the Left, the Right, and Threats to Our Liberties*. Washington, DC: Cato Institute, 2008.

Boesche, Roger. *The Strange Liberalism of Alexis de Tocqueville*. CorUP, 1987; repr., LSUP, 1997.

Booth, Alan. *The British Economy in the Twentieth Century*. Houndmills, UK: Palgrave, 2001.

Bouton, Terry. "A Road Closed: Rural Insurgency in Post-Independence Pennsylvania." *JAH* 87 (December 2000): 855–87.

———. *Taming Democracy: "The People," the Founders, and the Troubled Ending of the American Revolution*. OUP, 2007.

Bovard, James. *Freedom in Chains: The Rise of the State and the Demise of the Citizen*. New York: St. Martin's Press, 1999.

Bowman, Scott R. *The Modern Corporation and American Political Thought: Law, Power, and Ideology*. University Park: Penn State University Press, 1996.

Bradford, M. E. "The Heresy of Equality: Bradford Replies to Jaffa." *Modern Age* 20 (Winter 1976): 62–77.

———. *Remembering Who We Are: Observations of a Southern Conservative*. UGaP, 1985.

Brailsford, H. N. *The Levellers and the English Revolution*. Edited by Christopher Hill. Stanford, CA: Stanford University Press, 1961.

Brewer, Holly. "Entailing Aristocracy." *WMQ* 54 (April 1997): 307–46.

Brinkley, Alan. "The Antimonopoly Ideal and the Liberal State: The Case of Thurman Arnold." *JAH* 80 (September 1993): 557–79.

Brooke, John L. *Columbia Rising: Civil Life on the Upper Hudson from the Revolution to the Age of Jackson*. UNCP, 2010.

Brown, Bernard Edward. *American Conservatives: The Political Thought of Francis Lieber and John W. Burgess*. ColumUP, 1951.

Brown, Christopher Leslie. *Moral Capital: Foundations of British Abolitionism*. UNCP, 2006.

Brown, L. Susan. *The Politics of Individualism: Liberalism, Liberal Feminism and Anarchism*. Montreal: Black Rose Books, 1993.

Brown, Wendy. *Undoing the Demos: Neoliberalism's Stealth Revolution*. Brooklyn, NY: Zone Books, 2015.

Bruegel, Martin. *Farm, Shop, Landing: The Rise of a Market Society in the Hudson Valley, 1780–1860*. DukeUP, 2002.

Buchanan, James M., and Gordon Tullock. *The Calculus of Consent: Logical Foundations of Constitutional Democracy*. UMichP, 1962.

Burk, Kathleen. *Old World, New World: The Story of Britain and America*. London: Little, Brown, 2007.

Burke, T. Patrick. *No Harm: Ethical Principles for a Free Market*. New York: Paragon House, 1994.

Burns, James MacGregor. *Fire and Light: How the Enlightenment Transformed Our World*. New York: St. Martin's Press, 2013.

Bushman, Richard L. *The Refinement of America: Persons, Houses, Cities*. New York: Alfred A. Knopf, 1992.

Campbell, Colin D., ed. *Income Redistribution*. Washington, DC: American Enterprise Institute, 1977.

Cannadine, David. *The Decline and Fall of the British Aristocracy*. YUP, 1990.

———. *The Rise and Fall of Class in Britain*. YUP, 1999.

Cannon, John. *Aristocratic Century: The Peerage of Eighteenth-Century England*. CamUP, 1984.

Chambers, J. D., and G. E. Mingay. *The Agricultural Revolution, 1750–1880*. New York: Schocken Books, 1966.

Chandler, Alfred D., Jr. *The Visible Hand: The Managerial Revolution in American Business*. HUP, 1977.

Chester, Ronald. "Inheritance in American Legal Thought." In *Inheritance and Wealth in America*, 23–43. Edited by Robert K. Miller Jr. and Stephen J. McNamee. New York: Plenum Press, 1988.

Christiano, Thomas. "An Argument for Democratic Equality." In *Philosophy and Democracy: An Anthology*, 39–68. Edited by Thomas Christiano. OUP, 2003.

———. *The Constitution of Equality: Democratic Authority and its Limits*. OUP, 2008.

Clapham, J. H. *An Economic History of Modern Britain: Free Trade and Steel, 1850–1886*. CamUP, 1932.

Clark, Christopher. *Social Change in America: From the Revolution Through the Civil War*. Chicago: Ivan R. Dee, 2006.

Clark, J. C. D. *English Society, 1688–1832: Ideology, Social Structure and Political Practice During the Ancien Regime.* CamUP, 1985.

Clarke, Peter. "Hodge's Politics: The Agricultural Labourers and the Third Reform Act in Suffolk." Assisted by Kevin Langford. Edited by Negley Harte and Roland Quinault. In *Land and Society in Britain, 1700–1914: Essays in Honor of F. M. L. Thompson,* 119–36. Manchester: Manchester University Press, 1996.

Clinton, Catherine. *The Other Civil War: American Women in the Nineteenth Century.* New York: Hill and Wang, 1984.

Coclanis, Peter A. *The Shadow of a Dream: Economic Life and Death in the South Carolina Low Country, 1670–1920.* OUP, 1989.

Cohen, G. A. *On the Currency of Egalitarian Justice, and other Essays in Political Philosophy.* Edited by Michael Otsuka. PrinceUP, 2011.

———. *Self-Ownership, Freedom, and Equality.* CamUP, 1995.

Commager, Henry Steele. *The American Mind: An Interpretation of American Thought and Character Since the 1880s.* 1950; repr., YUP, 1971.

Conway, Stephen. "From Fellow-Nationals to Foreigners: British Perceptions of the Americans, circa 1739–1783." *WMQ* 59 (January 2002): 686–96.

Cornell, Saul. "Aristocracy Assailed: The Ideology of Backcountry Anti-Federalism." *JAH* 76 (March 1990): 1148–72.

Coward, Barry. *The Stuart Age: A History of England, 1603–1714.* London: Longman, 1980.

Cowley, Malcom. *Exile's Return: A Literary Odyssey of the 1920s.* 1934; repr., New York: Viking Press, 1969.

Craven, Avery. *Democracy in American Life: A Historical View.* UChiP, 1941.

Crook, David Paul. *American Democracy in English Politics, 1815–1850.* OUP, 1965.

Cunliffe, Marcus. *The Right to Property: A Theme in American History.* Leicester: Leicester University Press, 1974.

Cunningham, Noble E. Jr. *In Pursuit of Reason: The Life of Thomas Jefferson.* LSUP, 1987.

Curti, Merle. *The Growth of American Thought.* 2nd ed. New York: Harper and Brothers, 1951.

———. *The Social Ideas of American Educators.* New York: Charles Scribner's Sons, 1935.

Curtin, Philip D. *The Rise and Fall of the Plantation Complex: Essays in Atlantic History.* 2nd ed. CamUP, 1998.

Dabney, William M., and Marion Dargan. *William Henry Drayton and the American Revolution.* Albuquerque: University of New Mexico Press, 1962.

Dahl, Robert A. *On Political Equality.* YUP, 2006.

Dangerfield, George. *Chancellor Robert R. Livingston of New York, 1746–1813.* New York: Harcourt, Brace and Co., 1960.

———. *The Strange Death of Liberal England.* 1935; repr., New York: Capricorn Books, 1961.

Danziger, Sheldon, and Peter Gottschalk, eds. *Uneven Tides: Rising Inequality in America.* New York: Russell Sage Foundation, 1993.

Dauer, Manning J. *The Adams Federalists.* JHUP, 1953.

Daunton, M. J. "The Political Economy of Death Duties: Harcourt's Budget of 1894." In *Land and Society in Britain, 1700–1914: Essays in Honor of F. M. L. Thompson,* 137–71. Edited by Negley Harte and Roland Quinault. Manchester: Manchester University Press, 1996.

———. *Progress and Poverty: An Economic and Social History of Britain, 1700–1850.* OUP, 1995.

Davis, David Brion. *The Problem of Slavery in the Age of Emancipation.* New York: Alfred A. Knopf, 2014.

———. *The Problem of Slavery in the Age of Revolution, 1770–1823.* CorUP, 1975.

———. *The Problem of Slavery in Western Culture.* CorUP, 1966.

Dawley, Alan. *Class and Community: The Industrial Revolution in Lynn.* HUP, 1976.

Destler, Chester Arthur. *American Radicalism, 1865–1901: Essays and Documents.* 1946, Rpr. New York: Octagon Books, 1963.

Detweiler, Philip F. "The Changing Reputation of the Declaration of Independence: The First Fifty Years." *WMQ* 19 (October 1962): 557–74.

Devins, Neal, and Davison M. Douglas. "Introduction: The Pursuit of Equality." In *Redefining Equality,* 3–12. Edited by Neal Devins and Davison M. Douglas. OUP, 1998.

Dewey, Peter. "Farm Labour." In *The Agrarian History of England and Wales.* Vol. 7, part 1, *1850–1914,* pp. 810–62. Edited by Joan Thirsk and E. J. T. Collins. CamUP, 2000.

Doan, Edward N. *The La Follettes and the Wisconsin Idea.* New York: Rinehart and Co., 1947.

Dorling, Daniel. *Injustice: Why Social Inequality Persists.* Bristol, UK: Policy Press, University of Bristol, 2010.

Dowd, Gregory Evans. "Declarations of Dependence: War and Inequality in Revolutionary New Jersey, 1776–1815." *New Jersey History* 103 (Spring/Summer 1985): 42–67.

Doyle, William. *Aristocracy and Its Enemies in the Age of Revolution.* OUP, 2009.

Drinnon, Richard. *Facing West: The Metaphysics of Indian-Hating and Empire-Building.* 2nd ed. Norman: University of Oklahoma Press, 1997.

Duggan, Lisa. *The Twilight of Equality? Neoliberalism, Cultural Politics, and the Attack on Democracy.* Boston: Beacon Press, 2003.

Dunbar, Louise Burnham. *A Study of "Monarchical" Tendencies in the United States from 1776 to 1801.* 1922, 1923; repr., New York: Johnson Reprint Corp., 1970.

Dunn, John. *Setting the People Free: The Story of Democracy.* London: Atlantic Books, 2005.

Dunn, Richard S. *Sugar and Slaves: The Rise of the Planter Class in the English West Indies, 1624–1713.* UNCP, 1972.
Dworkin, Ronald. "Liberalism." In *Public and Private Morality,* 113–43. Edited by Stuart Hampshire. CamUP, 1978.
——. *Sovereign Virtue: The Theory and Practice of Equality.* HUP, 2000.
Eastman, John C. "The Declaration of independence as Viewed from the States." In *The Declaration of Independence: Origins and Impact,* 96–104. Edited by Scott Douglas Gerber. Washington, DC: Congressional Quarterly Press, 2002.
Eastwood, David. *Governing Rural England: Tradition and Transformation in Local Development, 1780–1840.* Oxford, Eng.: Clarendon Press, 1994.
Eaton, Joseph. *The Anglo-American Paper War: Debates about the New Republic, 1800–1825.* Houndmills, UK: Palgrave Macmillan, 2012.
Edwards, Philip. *The Making of the Modern English State, 1460–1660.* Houndmills, UK: Palgrave, 2001.
Eichner, Alfred S. *The Emergence of Oligopoly: Sugar Refining as a Case Study.* JHUP, 1969.
Elkins, Stanley, and Eric McKitrick. *The Age of Federalism: The Early American Republic, 1788–1800.* OUP, 1993.
Ellis, Joseph J. *Passionate Sage: The Character and Legacy of John Adams.* New York: W. W. Norton, 1993.
Elster, Jon. *The Cement of Society: A Study of Social Order.* CamUP, 1995.
Engerman, Stanley L., Elisa V. Mariscal, and Kenneth L. Sokoloff. "The Evolution of Schooling in the Americas, 1800–1925." In *Human Capital and Institutions: A Long Run View,* 93–142. Edited by David Eltis, Frank D. Lewis, and Kenneth L. Sokoloff. CamUP, 2009.
Fasel, George. *Edmund Burke.* Boston: Twayne, 1983.
Febrero, Ramón, and Pedro S. Schwartz, "Introduction." In *The Essence of Becker.* Edited by Ramón Febrero and Pedro S. Schwartz. Stanford, CA: Hoover Institution Press, 1995.
Ferling, John. *John Adams: A Life.* Knoxville: UTennP, 1992.
Fine, Sidney. *Laissez Faire and the General-Welfare State: A Study of Conflict in American Thought, 1865–1901.* Ann Arbor: UMichP, 1969.
Finke, Roger, Avery M. Guest, and Rodney Stark. "Mobilizing Local Religious Markets: Religious Pluralism in the Empire State, 1855 to 1865." *American Sociological Review* 61 (April 1996): 203–18.
Finkelman, Paul. *Slavery and the Founders: Race and Liberty in the Age of Jefferson.* Armonk, NY: M. E. Sharpe, 1996.
Fischer, David Hackett, and James C. Kelly. *Bound Away: Virginia and the Westward Movement.* UPVa, 2000.
Fish, Carl Russell. *The Rise of the Common Man.* New York: Macmillan Co., 1927.

Fladeland, Betty. *Men and Brothers: Anglo-American Antislavery Cooperation.* UIllP, 1972.

Flathman, Richard E. *Willful Liberalism: Voluntarism and Individuality in Political Theory and Practice.* CorUP, 1992.

Fordham, Montagu [Edward]. *A Short History of English Rural Life from the Anglo-Saxon Invasion to the Present Time.* London: George Allen and Unwin, 1916.

Franco, Paul. *The Political Philosophy of Michael Oakeshott.* YUP, 1990.

Fried, Barbara. "Wilt Chamberlain Revisited: Nozick's 'Justice in Transfer' and the Problem of Market-Based Distribution." *Philosophy and Public Affairs* 24 (Summer 1995), 226–45.

Friedman, Milton. *Capitalism and Freedom.* With the assistance of Rose D. Friedman. UChiP, 1962.

Friedman, Milton, et al. *Free to Choose: A Personal Statement.* New York: Avon Books, 1981.

———. *Politics and Tyranny: Lessons in Pursuit of Freedom.* Edited by David J. Theroux. San Francisco: Pacific Institute for Public Policy Research, 1984.

Gabriel, Ralph Henry. *The Course of American Democratic Thought.* With Robert H. Walker. 3rd ed. Westport, CT: Greenwood Press, 1986.

Gaitlin, William, and Bruce Jennings. *Perversion of Autonomy: Coercion and Constraints in a Liberal Society.* Rev. ed. Washington, DC: Georgetown University Press, 2003.

Galbraith, John Kenneth. *The Good Society: The Humane Agenda.* Boston: Houghton Mifflin Company, 1996.

Gallman, Robert E. "Economic Growth and Structural Change in the Long Nineteenth Century." In *The Cambridge Economic History of the United States.* Vol. 2, *The Long Nineteenth Century.* Edited by Stanley L. Engerman and Robert E. Gallman. CamUP, 2000.

Gamble, Andrew. *Hayek: The Iron Cage of Liberty.* Boulder, CO: Westview Press, 1996.

Garnier, Russell M[ontagu]. *History of the English Landed Interest: Its Customs, Laws and Agriculture (Modern Period).* London: Swan Sonnenschein, 1893.

Gawalt, Gerard W. "Drafting the Declaration." In *The Declaration of Independence: Origins and Impact,* 1–15. Edited by Scott Douglas Gerber. Washington, DC: Congressional Quarterly Press, 2002.

Gay, Peter. *The Enlightenment.* Vol. 2, *The Science of Freedom.* New York: Alfred A. Knopf, 1969.

Genovese, Eugene D. *Roll, Jordan, Roll: The World the Slaves Made.* New York: Random House, 1972.

Gilsdorf, Joy, and Robert Gilsdorf. "Elites and Electorates." In *Saints and Revolutionaries,* 207–44. Edited by David D. Hall, John Murrin, and Thad Tate. New York: W. W. Norton, 1984.

Glad, Paul W. *McKinley, Bryan, and the People.* Philadelphia: J. B. Lippincott Co., 1964.

Goldin, Claudia. "The Human-Capital Century and American Leadership: Virtues of the Past." *JEH* 61 (June 2001): 263–92.

Goldin, Claudia, and Lawrence F. Katz. "Why the United States Led in Education: Lessons from Secondary School Expansion, 1910 to 1940." In *Human Capital and Institutions: A Long Run View,* 143–78. Edited by David Eltis, Frank D. Lewis, and Kenneth L. Solokoff. CamUP, 2009.

Gráda, Cormac Ó. "British Agriculture, 1860–1914." In *The Economic History of Britain Since 1700.* Vol. 2, *1700–1860,* pp. 145–72. Edited by Roderick Floud and Donald N. McCloskey. 2nd ed. CamUP, 1994.

Grantham, George W. "Scale and Organization in French Farming, 1840–1880." In *European Peasants and their Markets: Essays in Agrarian Economic History,* 293–326. Edited by William N. Parker and E. L. Jones. JHUP, 1985.

Greene, Jack P. *Imperatives, Behaviors, and Identities: Early American Cultural History.* UPVa, 1992.

———. *The Intellectual Construction of America: Exceptionalism and Identity from 1492 to 1800.* UNCP, 1993.

Gregg, Pauline. *A Social and Economic History of Britain, 1760–1970.* 6th ed. London: George G. Harrap, 1971.

Griffin, Patrick. *American Leviathan: Empire, Nation, and Revolutionary Frontier.* New York: Hill and Wang, 2007.

———. *America's Revolution.* OUP, 2013.

Grigg, David. *English Agriculture: An Historical Perspective.* Oxford: Basil Blackwell, 1989.

Guelzo, Allen C. *Abraham Lincoln as a Man of Ideas.* Carbondale: Southern Illinois University Press, 2009.

Guttman, Allen. *The Conservative Tradition in America.* OUP, 1967.

Gwartney, James D., and Richard E. Wagner. "Public Choice and Constitutional Order." In *Public Choice and Constitutional Economics,* 29–56. Edited by James D. Gwartney and Richard E. Wagner. Greenwich, CT: Jai Press, 1988.

———. "Public Choice and the Conduct of Representative Government." In *Public Choice and Constitutional Economics,* 3–28. Edited by James D. Gwartney and Richard E. Wagner. Greenwich, CT: Jai Press, 1988.

Habakkuk, John. *Marriage, Debt, and the Estates System: England Landownership 1650–1950.* OUP, 1994.

Hall, Thomas E. *Rotten Fruits of Economic Controls, and the Rise from the Ashes, 1965–1989.* Lanham, MD: University Press of America, 2003.

Hampson, Norman. *A Cultural History of the Enlightenment.* New York: Pantheon Books, 1968.

Hanson, Russell L. *The Democratic Imagination in America: Conversations With Our Past.* PrinceUP, 1985.

Hartnett, Stephen John. *Democratic Dissent and the Cultural Fictions of Antebellum America.* UIllP, 2002.

Hartwell, R. M. *A History of the Mont Pelerin Society.* Indianapolis: Liberty Fund, 1995.

Havighurst, Alfred F. *Twentieth-Century Britain.* 2nd ed. New York: Harper and Row, 1966.

Hawke, David. *A Transaction of Free Men: The Birth and Course of the Declaration of Independence.* New York: Charles Scribner's Sons, 1964.

Haworth, Alan. *Anti-Libertarianism: Markets, Philosophy and Myth.* London: Routledge, 1994.

Hayek, Friedrich A. *Individualism and Economic Order.* UChiP, 1948.

Hecht, J. Jean. *The Domestic Servant Class in Eighteenth-Century England.* London: Routledge & Kegan Paul, 1956.

Heindel, Richard Heathcote. *The American Impact on Great Britain, 1898–1914: A Study of the United States in World History.* UPennP, 1940.

Henretta, James A. *The Evolution of American Society, 1700–1815.* Lexington, Mass.: D. C. Heath & Co., 1973.

Hersh, Blanche Glassman. *The Slavery of Sex: Feminist-Abolitionists in America.* UIllP, 1978.

Hicks, John D., George E. Mowry, and Robert E. Burke. *The American Nation: A History of the United States from 1865 to the Present.* 1933; repr., Boston: Houghton Mifflin Co., 1963.

Higgs, Edward. "Occupational Censuses and the Agricultural Workforce in Victorian England and Wales." *EHR* 48 (November 1995): 700–716.

Hill, Roland. *Lord Acton.* YUP, 2000.

Himmelfarb, Gertrude. *Lord Acton: A Study in Conscience and Politics.* UChiP, 1962.

———. *The Roads to Modernity: The British, French, and American Enlightenments.* New York: Alfred A. Knopf, 2005.

Hirschman, Albert O. *The Passions and the Interests: Political Arguments for Capitalism Before Its Triumph.* PrinceUP, 1977.

Hobsbawm, E. J. *The Age of Revolution, 1789–1848.* New York: New American Library, 1962.

Hobsbawm, E. J., and George Rudé. *Captain Swing.* New York: Random House, 1968.

Hobson, Charles F. "Republicanism, Commerce, and Private Rights: James Madison's Path to the Constitutional Convention of 1787." In *Liberty, Property, and the Foundations of the American Constitution,* 89–97. Edited by Ellen Paul and H. Dickman. Albany: State University of New York Press, 1989.

Hofstadter, Richard. *The Age of Reform: From Bryan to F. D. R.* New York: Random House, 1955.

Holton, James E. "Marcus Tullius Cicero." In *History of Political* Philosophy, 130–150. Edited by Leo Strauss and Joseph Cropsey. Chicago: Rand McNally, 1963.

Hospers, John. *Libertarianism: A Political Philosophy for Tomorrow.* Los Angeles: Nash Publishing, 1971.

Howe, John R., Jr. *The Changing Political Thought of John Adams.* PrinceUP, 1966.

Hunt, Thomas C. "Sectionalism, Slavery, and Schooling in Antebellum Virginia." *West Virginia History* 46 (1985–1986): 125–36.

Hurley, S. L. *Justice, Luck, and Knowledge.* HUP, 2003.

Huston, James L. "Abolitionists, Political Economists, and Capitalists." *JER* 20 (Fall 2000): 487–521.

——. *The British Gentry, the Southern Planter, and the Northern Family Farmer: Agriculture and Sectional Antagonism in North America.* LSUP, 2015.

——. "A Political Response to Industrialism: The Republic Embrace of Protectionist Labor Doctrines." *JAH* 70 (June 1983): 35–57.

——. *Securing the Fruits of Labor: The American Concept of Wealth Distribution, 1765–1900.* LSUP, 1998.

Huston, Reeve. *Land and Reform: Rural Society, Popular Protest, and Party Politics in Antebellum New York.* OUP, 2000.

Hutson, James. "Emergence of the Modern Concept of a Right in America: The Contribution of Michel Villey." In *The Nature of Rights at the American Founding and Beyond,* 25–63. Edited by Barry Alan Shain. UVaP, 2007.

Isaac, Rhys. *The Transformation of Virginia, 1740–1790.* 1982; repr., New York: W. W. Norton, 1988.

Israel, Jonathan. *Democratic Enlightenment: Philosophy, Revolution, and Human Rights, 1750–1790.* OUP, 2011.

——. *Enlightenment Contested: Philosophy, Modernity, and the Emancipation of Man, 1670–1752.* OUP, 2006.

Jacobs, Lawrence R., and Theda Skocpol, eds. *Inequality and American Democracy: What We Know and What We Need to Learn.* New York: Russell Sage Foundation, 2005.

De Jasay, Anthony. *Against Politics: On Government, Anarachy, and Order.* London: Routledge, 1997.

Jayne, Allen. *Lincoln and the American Manifesto.* Amherst, NY: Prometheus Books, 2007.

Johnson, Paul E. *A Shopkeeper's Millennium: Society and Revivals in Rochester, New York, 1815–1837.* New York: Hill and Wang, 1978.

Jones, Charles Henry. *The Life and Public Services of J. Glancy Jones.* 2 vols. Philadelphia: J. B. Lippincott, 1910.

Jones, Daniel Stedman. *Masters of the Universe: Hayek, Friedman, and the Birth of Neoliberal Politics.* PrinceUP, 2012.

Jones, E. L. *Agriculture and the Industrial Revolution.* New York: Wiley and Sons, 1974.

Kaestle, Carl F. *Pillars of the Republic: Common Schools and American Society, 1780–1860.* New York: Hill and Wang, 1983.

Kaminski, John P., ed. *Citizen Jefferson: The Wit and Wisdom of an American Sage.* Madison, WI: Madison House, 1994.

Kammen, Michael. *Spheres of Liberty: Changing Perceptions of Liberty in American Culture.* 1986; repr., Jackson: University Press of Mississippi, 2001.

Kasson, John F. *Rudeness and Civility: Manners in Nineteenth-Century Urban America.* New York: Hill and Wang, 1990.

Katz, Michael B., Michael J. Doucet, and Mark J. Stern. *The Social Organization of Early Industrial Capitalism.* HUP, 1982.

Kelley, John L. *Bringing the Market Back In: The Political Revitalization of Market Liberalism.* Washington Square: New York University Press, 1997.

Kendall, Willmoore. *Willmoore Kendall: Contra Mundum.* Edited by Nellie D. Kendall. New Rochelle, NY: Arlington House, 1971.

Kendall, Willmoore, and George W. Carey. *The Basic Symbols of the American Political Tradition.* LSUP, 1970.

Kilbride, Daniel. *Being American in Europe, 1750–1860.* JHUP, 2013.

Kirk, Russell. *The Conservative Mind from Burke to Santayana.* Chicago: Henry Regnery Co., 1953.

Kirkland, Edward Chase. *Industry Comes of Age: Business, Labor and Public Policy, 1860–1897.* 1961; repr., Chicago Quadrangle Paperbacks, 1967.

Knapp, Peter. "Introduction." In Peter Knapp, Jane C. Kroniek, R. William Markes, and Miriam G. Vosburgh. *The Assault on Equality.* Westport, CT: Praeger, 1996.

Knock, Albert J. *Our Enemy, the State.* New York: W. Morrows and Co., 1935.

Kolchin, Peter. *American Slavery, 1619–1877.* 1993; repr., New York: Hill and Wang, 2003.

Kramnick, Issac. *The Rage of Edmund Burke: Portrait of an Ambivalent Conservative.* New York: Basic Books, 1977.

Kramnick, Isaac, and Laurence Moore. *The Godless Constitution: The Case Against Religious Correctness.* New York: W. W. Norton, 1996.

Kristol, Irving. "Thoughts on Equality and Egalitariansim." In *Income Redistribution,* 35–42. Edited by Colin Campbell. Washington, DC: American Enterprise Institute, 1977.

Kulikoff, Allan. "The Progress of Inequality in Revolutionary Boston." *WMQ* 28 (July 1971): 375–412.

Kussmaul, Ann. *Servants in Husbandry in Early Modern England.* CamUP, 1981.

Labaree, Leonard Woods. *Conservatism in Early American History.* New York: New York University Press, 1948.

Lal, Deepak. *Reviving the Invisible Hand: The Case for Classical Liberalism in the Twenty-First Century.* PrinceUP, 2006.

Larkin, Jack. "'Labor is the Great Thing in Farming': The Farm Laborers of the Ward Family of Shrewsbury, Massachusetts, 1787–1860." In *Proceedings of the American Antiquarian Society* 99, part 1 (1989): 217–26.

Larson, John Lauritz. *The Market Revolution in America: Liberty, Ambition, and the Eclipse of the Common Good.* CamUP, 2010.

Laski, Harold J. *The American Democracy: A Commentary and an Interpretation.* New York: Viking, 1948.

Laurie, Bruce. *Artisans into Workers: Labor in Nineteenth-Century America.* New York: Hill and Wang, 1988

Lears, T. Jackson. "The Concept of Cultural Hegemony: Problems and Possibilities." *AHR* 90 (June 1985): 567–93.

Leuchtenburg, William E. *Franklin D. Roosevelt and the New Deal, 1932–1940.* New York: Harper and Row, 1963.

———. *The Perils of Prosperity, 1914–32.* UChiP, 1958.

Levy, Frank. *Dollars and Dreams: The Changing American Income Distribution.* New York: Russell Sage Foundation, 1987.

Levy, Hermann. *Large and Small Holdings: A Study of English Agricultural Economics.* Translated by Ruth Kenyon. CamUP, 1911.

Lewis, Charlene M. Boyer. *Elizabeth Patterson Bonaparte: An American Aristocrat in the Early Republic.* UPennP, 2012.

Libcap, Gary D. *Contracting for Property Rights.* CamUP, 1989.

Licht, Walter. *Industrializing America: The Nineteenth Century.* JHUP, 1995.

———. *Working for the Railroad: The Organization of Work in the Nineteenth Century.* PrinceUP, 1983.

Lillibridge, G. D. *Beacon of Freedom: The Impact of American Democracy Upon Great Britain, 1830–1870.* UPennP, 1955.

Lind, Michael. *Up From Conservatism: Why the Right is Wrong for America.* New York: Free Press, 1996.

Lindert, Peter H. "Unequal Living Standards." In *The Economic History of Britain Since 1700.* Vol. 1, *1700–1860*, pp. 357–86. Edited by Roderick Floud and Donald N. McCloskey. 2nd ed. CamUP, 1994.

———. "Who Owned Victorian England? The Debate Over Landed Wealth and Inequality." *AgH* 61 (Fall 1987): 25–51.

Lippincott, Benjamin Evans. *Victorian Critics of Democracy: Carlyle, Ruskin, Arnold, Stephen, Maine, Lecky.* Minneapolis: University of Minnesota Press, 1938.

Lovejoy, David S. "Rights Imply Equality: The Case Against Admiralty Jurisdiction in America, 1764–1776." *WMQ* 16 (October 1959): 459–84.

Lovett, Frank. *A General Theory of Domination and Justice.* OUP, 2010.

Lucas, J. R. "Against Equality." In *Equality: Selected Readings*, 104–108. Edited by Louis Pojman and Robert Westmoreland. OUP, 1997.

Lukes, Steven. *Individualism.* New York: Harper and Row, 1973.

Lustig, R. Jeffrey. *Corporate Liberalism: The Origins of Modern American Political Theory, 1890–1920.* Berkeley: University of California Press, 1982.

Machan, Tibor R. *Capitalism and Individualism: Reframing the Argument for the Free Society.* New York: St. Martin's Press, 1990.

_______. *The Moral Case for the Free Market Economy : A Philosophical Argument.* Lewiston, NY: E. Mellen Press, 1988.

Machin, Ian. *The Rise of Democracy in Britain, 1830–1918.* Houndmills, UK: Macmillan, 2001.

Maciag, Drew. *Edmund Burke in America: The Contested Career of the Father of Modern Conservatism.* CorUP, 2013.

Macpherson, C. B. *Burke.* New York: Hill and Wang, 1980.

———. *The Political Theory of Possessive Individualism: Hobbes to Locke.* OUP, 1962.

McCarthy, Patrick J. *Matthew Arnold and the Three Classes.* ColumUP, 1964.

McConnell, Grant. *The Decline of Agrarian Democracy.* Berkeley: University of California Press, 1955.

McCormick, Richard P. *The Second American Party System: Party Formation in the Jacksonian Era.* New York: W. W. Norton, 1966.

McDaniel, W. Caleb. *The Problem of Democracy in the Age of Slavery: Garrisonian Abolitionists and Transatlantic Reform.* LSUP, 2013.

McDonnell, Michael A. *The Politics of War: Race, Class, and Conflict in Revolutionary Virginia.* UNCP, 2007.

———. "Popular Mobilization and Political Culture in Revolutionary Virginia: The Failure of the Minutemen and the Revolution from Below." *JAH* 85 (December 1998): 946–81.

McGarvie, Mark Douglas. *One Nation Under Law: America's Early National Struggles to Separate Church and State.* DeKalb: Northern Illinois University Press, 2004.

McGerr, Michael E. *The Decline of Popular Politics: The American North, 1865–1929.* OUP, 1986.

McInerney, Daniel J. *The Fortunate Heirs of Freedom: Abolition and Republican Thought.* Lincoln.: University of Nebraska Press, 1994.

Maier, Pauline. *American Scripture: Making the Declaration of Independence.* New York: Alfred A. Knopf, 1997.

Malone, Dumas. *Jefferson and His Time.* Vol. 1, *Jefferson the Virginian.* Boston: Little, Brown and Co., 1948.

Mancini, Matthew. *Alexis de Tocqueville.* New York: Twayne, 1990.

Mancke, Elizabeth. "The Languages of Liberty in British North America, 1607–1776." In *Exclusionary Empire: English Liberty Overseas, 1600–1900,* 25–49. Edited by Jack P. Greene. CamUP, 2010.

Marshall, T. H. *Class, Citizenship, and Social Development: Essays*. Garden City, NY: Doubleday and Co., 1964.

Mathias, Peter. *The First Industrial Nation: An Economic History of Britain, 1700–1914*. 2nd ed. London: Methuen, 1983.

Matthews, Jean V. *Toward a New Society: American Thought and Culture, 1800–1830*. Boston: Twayne, 1991.

Maxwell, Nan L. *Income Inequality in the United States, 1947–1985*. New York: Greenwood Press, 1980.

May, Henry F. *The Enlightenment in America*. OUP, 1976.

Mayer, Jane. *Dark Money: The Hidden History of the Billionaires behind the Rise of the Radical Right*. New York: Doubleday, 2016.

Medvedev, Roy. *Let History Judge: The Origins and Consequences of Stalinism*. Translated by George Shriver. 2nd ed. ColumUP, 1989.

Mesick, Jane Louise. *The English Traveller in America, 1785–1835*. 1922; repr., Westport, CT: Greenwood Press, 1970.

Meyer, Frank S. "The Twisted Tree of Liberty." In *Freedom and Virtue: The Conservative/Libertarian Debate*, 12–19. Edited by George W. Carey. Wilmington, DE: Intercollegiate Studies Institute, 1998.

Miller, David. *Market, State, and Community: Theoretical Foundations of Market Socialism*. Oxford, UK: Clarendon Press, 1989.

Miller, Douglas T. *The Birth of Modern America, 1820–1850*. New York: Pegasus, 1970.

Miller, John Chester. *The Federalist Era, 1789–1801*. New York: Harper & Brothers, 1960.

———. *The Wolf by the Ears. Thomas Jefferson and Slavery*. New York: Free Press, 1977.

Miller, William L. "Primogeniture, Entail, and Endowment in English Classical Economics." *History of Political Economy* 12 (Winter 1980): 558–81.

Milne, A. J. M. *Politics, Wellbeing and the Market*. Edited by Roger Crisp and Alistair Milne. Houndmills, UK: Palgrave, 2001.

Mingay, G. E. *English Landed Society in the Eighteenth Century*. London: Routledge and Kegan Paul, 1963.

———. *The Gentry: The Rise and Fall of a Ruling Class*. London: Longman, 1976.

Mintz, Max M. *Gouverneur Morris and the American Revolution*. Norman: University of Oklahoma Press, 1970.

Mitchell, Betty L. *Edmund Ruffin: A Biography*. IndUP, 1981.

Mitchell, Harvey. *America After Tocqueville: Democracy Against Difference*. CamUP, 2002.

Morgan, Edmund S. *American Slavery, American Freedom: The Ordeal of Colonial Virginia*. New York: W. W. Norton, 1975.

——. *Inventing the People: The Rise of Popular Sovereignty in England and America.* New York: W. W. Norton, 1988.

Morone, James A. *The Democratic Wish: Popular Participation and the Limits of American Government.* New York: Basic Books, 1990.

Mulvey, Christopher. *Transatlantic Manners: Social Patterns in Nineteenth-Century Anglo-American Travel Literature.* CamUP, 1990.

Murray, Charles. *What It Means to Be a Libertarian: A Personal Interpretation.* New York: Broadway Books, 1997.

Myers, Henry Alonzo. *Are Men Equal? An Inquiry into the Meaning of American Democracy.* New York: G. P. Putnam's Sons, 1945.

Nagel, Thomas. *Equality and Partiality.* OUP, 1991.

——. "Equality and Partiality." In *Equality: Selected Readings,* 250–61. Edited by Louis P. Pojman and Robert Westmoreland. OUP, 1997.

——. *The Unknown American Revolution: The Unruly Birth of Democracy and the Struggle to Create America.* New York: Viking Penguin, 2005.

Nash, George. *The Conservative Intellectual Movement in America Since 1945.* New York: Basic Books, 1976.

Nedelsky, Jennifer. *Private Property and the Limits of American Constitutionalism: The Madisonian Framework and Its Legacy.* UChiP, 1990.

Nevins, Allan, ed. and comp. *American Social History As Recorded by British Travellers.* New York: Henry Holt and Co., 1923.

——, ed. and comp. *America Through British Eyes.* OUP, 1948.

Newman, Stephen L. *Liberalism at Wit's End: The Libertarian Revolt Against the Modern State.* CorUP, 1984.

Nichols, Jeanette, and James G. Randall, eds. *Democracy in the Middle West, 1840–1940.* New York: D. Appleton-Century, 1941.

Nielsen, Kai. *Equality and Liberty: A Defense of Radical Egalitarianism.* Totowa, NJ: Rowman and Allanheld, 1985.

Nisbet, Robert. "Dreary Cousins." In *Freedom and Virtue: The Conservative/Libertarian Debate,* 38–47. Edited by George W. Carey. Wilmington, DE: Intercollegiate Studies Institute, 1998.

——. *The Social Impact of the Revolution.* Washington, DC: American Enterprise Institute, 1973.

Noah, Timothy. *The Great Divergence: America's Growing Inequality Crisis and What We Can Do About It.* New York: Bloomsbury Press, 2013.

Norman, Jesse. *Edmund Burke: Philosopher, Politician, Prophet.* London: William Collins, 2013.

North, Douglass C. *Structure and Change in Economic History.* New York: W. W. Norton, 1981.

Nozick, Robert. *Anarchy, State, and Utopia.* New York: Basic Books, 1974.

——. "Commentaries." In *Income Redistribution,* 50–55. Edited by Colin D. Campbell. Washington, DC: American Enterprise Institute, 1977.

Nutter, G. Warren. "Commentaries." In *Income Redistribution,* 43–46. Edited by Colin D. Campbell. Washington, DC: American Enterprise Institute, 1977.

Nutter, G. Warren, and Henry Adler Einhorn. *Enterprise Monopoly in the United States: 1899–1958.* ColumUP, 1969.

Oakeshott, Michael. *Rationalism in Politics and Other Essays.* New York: Basic Books, 1962.

O'Brien, Michael. *Conjectures of Order: Intellectual Life and the American South, 1810–1860.* 2 vols. UNCP, 2004.

O'Brien, P. K., and D. Heath. "English and French Landowners." In *Landowners, Capitalists, and Entrepreneurs: Essays for Sir John Habakkuk,* 23–62. Edited by F. M. L. Thompson. OUP, 1994.

Offer, Avner. "Farm Tenure and Land Values in England, c. 1750–1950." *EHR* 44 (February 1991), 1–20.

Okun, Arthur M. *Equality and Efficiency: The Big Tradeoff.* Washington, DC: Brookings Institution, 1975.

Oldfield, J. R. *Popular Politics and British Anti-Slavery: The Mobilisation of Public Opinion Against the Slave Trade, 1787–1807.* London: Frank Cass, 1995.

Olson, Mancur. "Dictatorship, Democracy, and Development." *American Political Science Review* 87 (September 1993): 567–76.

Olson, Mancur, and Satu Kähkönen. *A Not-So-Dismal Science: A Broader View of Economies and Societies.* OUP, 2000.

Onuf, Peter S. "Federalism, Democracy, and Liberty in the New American Nation." In *Exclusionary Empire: English Liberty Overseas, 1600–1900,* 132–59 . Edited by Jack P. Greene. CamUP, 2010.

Orwin, Christabel S., and Edith H. Whetham. *History of British Agriculture, 1846–1914.* London: Archon Books, 1964.

Osberg, Lars. *Economic Inequality in the United States.* Armonk, NY: M. E. Sharpe, 1984.

Outram, Dorinda. *The Enlightenment.* CamUP, 1995.

Overton, Mark. *Agricultural Revolution in England: The Transformation of the Agrarian Economy, 1500–1850.* CamUP, 1996.

Pachter, Marc, ed., and Frances Wein, coed. *Abroad in America: Visitors to the New Nation, 1776–1914.* Reading, MA: Addison-Wesley, 1976.

Pagmenta, Peter. *Prairie Fever: British Aristocrats in the American West, 1830–1890.* New York: W. W. Norton, 2012.

Painter, Nell Irvin. *Standing at Armageddon: The United States, 1877–1919.* New York: W. W. Norton, 1987.

Palmer, R. R. *The Age of Democratic Revolution: A Political History of Europe and America, 1760–1800.* 2 vols. PrinceUP, 1959.

Palmer, R. R., and Joel Colton. *A History of the Modern World.* 3rd ed. New York: Alfred A. Knopf, 1965.

Parent, Anthony S., Jr. *Foul Means: The Formation of a Slave Society in Virginia, 1660–1740.* UNCP, 2003.

Parijs, Philippe Van. *Real Freedom For All: What (If Anything) Can Justify Capitalism.* Oxford: Clarendon Press, 1995.

Paxson, Frederic L. *Recent History of the United States.* Boston: Houghton Mifflin, 1921.

Persons, Stow. *The Decline of American Gentility.* ColumUP, 1973.

Pessen, Edward. *Jacksonian America: Society, Personality, and Politics.* Homewood, IL: Dorsey Press, 1969.

———. "On a Recent Cliometric Attempt to Resurrect the Myth of Antebellum Egalitarianism." *Social Science History* 3 (Winter 1979): 208–227.

———. *Riches, Class, and Power Before the Civil War.* Lexington, MA: D. C. Heath, 1973.

———. "Social Structure and Politics in American History." *AHR* 87 (December 1982): 1290–1325.

Pestana, Carla Gardiner, and Sharon V. Salinger, eds. *Inequality in Early America.* Hanover, NH: University Press of New England, 1999.

Peterson, Merrill D. *Adams and Jefferson: A Revolutionary Dialogue.* OUP, 1978.

Pettinger, Aladsdair. "George Lewis and the American Churches." In *Travel Writing in the Nineteenth Century,* 14–62. Edited by Tim Youngs. London: Anthem Press, 2006.

Phillips, Kevin. *The Politics of Rich and Poor: Wealth and the American Electorate in the Reagan Aftermath.* New York: Random House, 1990.

Piketty, Thomas. *Capital in the Twenty-First Century.* Translated by Arthur Goldhammer. HUP, 2014.

Plumb, J. H. *England in the Eighteenth Century.* Middlesex, Eng.: Penguin Books, 1950.

———. *Men and Centuries.* Boston: Houghton Mifflin, 1963.

Pocock, J. G. A. *The Machiavellian Moment: Florentine Political Thought and the Atlantic Republican Tradition.* PrinceUP, 1975.

———. "Virtue and Commerce in the Eighteenth Century." *Journal of Interdisciplinary History* 3 (1972): 119–34.

Pole, J. R. *The Pursuit of Equality in American History.* Berkeley: University of California Press, 1978.

Pollock, Lansing. *The Freedom Principle.* Buffalo: Prometheus Books, 1981.

Poole, W. Scott. *Never Surrender: Confederate Memory and Conservatism in the South Carolina Upcountry.* UGaP, 2004.

Porter, Roy. *English Society in the Eighteenth Century.* Rev. ed. New York: Penguin Books, 1990.

Prochaska, Frank. *Eminent Victorians on American Democracy: The View from Albion.* OUP, 2012.

Prothero, Rowland E. *English Farming Past and Present.* London: Longmans, Green, & Co., 1912.

Purdy, Jedediah, ed. *Democratic Vistas: Reflections on the Life of American Democracy.* YUP, 2004.

Rahe, Paul A. *Soft Despotism, Democracy's Drift: Montesquieu, Rousseau, Tocqueville and the Modern Prospect.* YUP, 2009.

Raleigh, John Henry. *Matthew Arnold and American Culture.* Berkeley: University of California Press, 1957.

Rapson, Richard L. *Britons View America: Travel Commentary, 1860–1935.* Seattle: University of Washington Press, 1971.

Rawls, John. *A Theory of Justice.* 2nd ed. HUP, 1999.

Read, James H. *Majority Rule versus Consensus: The Political Thought of John C. Calhoun.* UPKan, 2009.

Reeve, Andrew, and Andrew Williams, eds. *Real Libertarianism Assessed: Political Theory After Van Parijs.* Houndmills, UK: Palgrave Macmillan, 2003.

Reid, John Phillip. *The Concept of Liberty in the Age of the American Revolution.* UChiP, 1988.

Remini, Robert V. *Martin Van Buren and the Making of the Democratic Party.* ColumUP, 1959.

Rockman, Seth. *Scraping By: Wage Labor, Slavery, and Survival in Early Baltimore.* JHUP, 2009.

Rodgers, Daniel T. *Atlantic Crossings: Social Politics in a Progressive Age.* HUP, 1998.

———. *Contested Truths: Keywords in American Politics Since Independence.* New York: Basic Books, 1987.

Roediger, David R. *The Wages of Whiteness: Race and the Making of the American Working Class.* London: Verso Press, 1991.

Roemer, John E. *Analytical Foundations of Marxian Economic Theory.* CamUP, 1981.

———. *A General Theory of Exploitation and Class.* HUP, 1982.

———. "A Pragmatic Theory of Responsibility for the Egalitarian Planner." *Philosophy and Public Affairs* 212 (Spring 1993): 146–66.

———. *Theories of Distributive Justice.* HUP, 1996.

Roper, Jon. *Democracy and Its Critics: Anglo-American Democratic Thought in the Nineteenth Century.* London: Unwin Hyman, 1989.

Rose, Kenneth D. *Unspeakable Awfulness: America Through the Eyes of European Travelers, 1865–1900.* New York: Routledge, 2014.

Rossiter, Clinton. *The American Quest, 1790–1860: An Emerging Nation in Search of Identity, Unity, and Modernity.* New York: Harcourt Brace Jovanovich, 1971.

Rozbicki, Michal J. *The Complete Colonial Gentleman: Cultural Legitimacy in Plantation America.* UPVa, 1998.

———. *Culture and Liberty in the Age of the American Revolution.* UVaP, 2011.

———. "The Curse of Provincialism: Negative Perceptions of Colonial Plantation Gentry." *JSH* 63 (November 1997): 727–52.

Russell, Bertrand. *Authority and the Individual.* New York: Simon and Schuster, 1949.

Rutland, Robert A. *James Madison: The Founding Father.* New York: Macmillan, 1987.

Ryan, Mary P. *Cradle of the Middle Class: The Family in Oneida County, New York, 1790–1865.* CamUP, 1981.

Salafia, Matthew. *Slavery's Borderland: Freedom and Bondage along the Ohio River.* UPennP, 2013.

Sanders, Elizabeth. *Roots of Reform: Farmers, Workers, and the American State, 1877–1917.* UChiP, 1999.

Saxton, Alexander. *The Rise and Fall of the White Republic: Class Politics and Mass Culture in Nineteenth-Century America.* London: Verso Press, 1990.

Schama, Simon. *Citizens: A Chronicle of the French Revolution.* New York: Alfred A. Knopf, 1989.

Scheffler, Samuel. *Equality and Tradition: Questions of Value in Moral and Political Theory.* OUP, 2010.

Schlatter, Richard. *Private Property: The History of an Idea.* New Brunswick, NJ: Rutgers University Press, 1951.

Schlesinger, Arthur M. Jr. *The Age of Jackson.* Boston: Little, Brown and Co., 1949.

———. *The Crisis of the Old Order, 1919–1933.* Boston: Houghton Mifflin, 1957.

Schlesinger, Arthur Meir Sr. *The Rise of the City, 1878–1898.* New York: Macmillan, 1933.

Schob, David E. *Hired Hands and Plowboys: Farm Labor in the Midwest, 1815–60.* UIllP, 1975.

Schochet, Gordon J. *Patriarchalism in Political Thought: The Authoritarian Family and Political Speculation and Attitudes Especially in Seventeenth-Century England.* New York: Basic Books, 1975.

Schwartz, Joseph M. *The Future of Democratic Equality: Rebuilding Social Solidarity in a Fragmented Society.* New York: Routledge, 2009.

Schwarz, Leonard. "English Servants and Their Employers during the Eighteenth and Nineteenth Centuries." *EHR* 52 (May 1999): 231–56.

Sellers, Charles. *The Market Revolution: Jacksonian America, 1815–1846.* OUP, 1991.

Sen, Amartya. *Inequality Reexamined.* HUP, 1992.

Shain, Barry Alan. *The Myth of American Individualism: The Protestant Origins of American Political Thought.* PrinceUP, 1994.

———. "Rights Natural and Civil in the Declaration of Independence." In *The Nature of Rights in the American Founding and Beyond,* 116–162. Edited by Barry Alan Shain and Rogers M. Smith. UVaP, 2007.

Shalhope, Robert. *The Roots of Democracy: American Thought and Culture, 1760–1800.* Boston: Twayne, 1990.

Sheidley, Harlow W. *Sectional Nationalism: Massachusetts Conservative Leaders and the Transformation of America, 1815–1836.* Boston: Northeastern University Press, 1998.

Shields, Currin V. "Introduction." In John Stuart Mill, *Considerations on Representative Government.* Edited by Currin V. Shields. New York: Liberal Arts Press, 1958.

Silbey, Joel H. *The American Political Nation, 1838–1893.* Stanford, CA: Stanford University Press, 1991.

Sinha, Manisha. *The Slave's Cause: A History of Abolition.* YUP, 2016.

Skinner, Quentin. *The Foundations of Modern Political Thought.* Vol. 2, *The Age of Reformation.* CamUP, 1978.

———. "Political Philosophy." In *The Cambridge History of Renaissance Philosophy,* 387–452. Edited by Charles B. Schmitt. CamUP, 1988.

Sklar, Martin J. *The Corporate Reconstruction of American Capitalism, 1890–1906: The Market, the Law, and Politics.* CamUP, 1988.

Smith, Julia A. "Land Ownership and Social Change in Late Nineteenth-Century Britain." *EHR* 53 (November 2000): 767–76.

Smith, T. V. *The American Philosophy of Equality.* UChiP, 1927.

Soltow, Lee, and Edward Stevens. *The Rise of Literacy and the Common School in the United States: A Socioeconomic Analysis to 1870.* UChiP, 1981.

Sproat, John G. *"The Best Men": Liberal Reformers in the Gilded Age.* OUP, 1968.

Staloff, Darren. *Hamilton, Adams, Jefferson: The Politics of Enlightenment and the American Founding.* New York: Hill and Wang, 2005.

Stange, Douglas C. *British Unitarians Against American Slavery, 1833–65.* Rutherford, NJ: Fairleigh Dickinson University Press, 1984.

Stater, Victor L. *Noble Government: The Stuart Lord Lieutenancy and the Transformation of English Politics.* UGaP, 1994.

Sterba, James P., ed. *Ethics: The Big Questions.* Malden, MA: Blackwell, 1998.

Stewart, James B. *Holy Warriors: The Abolitionists and American Slavery.* 2nd ed. New York: Hill and Wang, 1997.

Stigler, George J. *The Economist as Preacher and Other Essays.* UChiP, 1982.

———. *The Intellectual and the Market Place and Other Essays.* Glencoe, IL: Collier-Macmillan, 1963.

Stiglitz, Joseph E. *The Price of Inequality: How Today's Divided Society Endangers Our Future.* New York: W. W. Norton, 2012.

Stockton, David. *The Gracchi.* Oxford, UK: Clarendon Press, 1979.

Stone, Lawrence. *The Crisis of the Aristocracy, 1558–1641.* OUP, 1965.

———. *The Family, Sex and Marriage in England, 1500–1800.* Abridged. New York: Penguin Books, 1979.

Stone, Lawrence, and Jeanne C. Fawtier Stone. *An Open Elite? England 1540–1880.* OUP, 1984.

Strauss, Leo. "Plato." In *History of Political Philosophy*, 7–63. Edited by Leo Strauss and Joseph Cropsey. Chicago: Rand McNally, 1963.

Stromberg, Roland N. *Democracy: A Short, Analytical Study*. Armonk, NY: M. E. Sharpe, 1996.

Sunnstein, Cass R. *Free Markets and Social Justice*. OUP, 1997.

Taibbi, Matt. *The Divide: American Injustice in the Age of the Wealth Gap*. New York: Spiegel and Grau, 2014.

Taylor, Alan. *American Colonies*. New York: Viking Penguin, 2001.

Taylor, Anne-Marie. *Young Charles Sumner and the Legacy of the American Enlightenment*. Amherst: University of Massachusetts Press, 2001.

Temkin, Larry S. *Inequality*. OUP, 1993.

Temperley, Howard. *Britain and America Since Independence*. Houndmills, UK: Palgrave, 2002.

Tewell, Jeremy. *A Self-Evident Lie: Southern Slavery and the Threat to American Freedom*. KSUP, 2013.

Thompson, E. P. *The Making of the English Working Class*. New York: Random House, 1963.

Thompson, F. M. L. *English Landed Society in the Nineteenth Century*. London: Routledge and Kegan Paul, 1963.

Thompson, Michael J. *The Politics of Inequality: A Political History of the Idea of Economic Inequality in America*. ColumUP, 2007.

Thurow, Lester C. *Generating Inequality: Mechanisms of Distribution in the U.S. Economy*. New York: Basic Books, 1975.

Tinder, Glenn. *Liberty: Rethinking an Imperiled Ideal*. Grand Rapids, MI: Eerdmans, 2007.

Tomaselli, Sylvana. "Equality." In *The Blackwell Companion to the Enlightenment*, 156–57. Edited by John W. Yolton, Roy Porter, Pat Rogers, and Barbara Maria Stafford. Oxford, UK: Blackwell, 1995.

Tsesis, Alexander. *For Equality and Liberty: The Life and Times of the Declaration of Independence*. OUP, 2012.

Turley, David. *The Culture of English Antislavery, 1780–1860*. London: Routledge, 1991.

Turner, Lynn W. *William Plumer of New Hampshire, 1759–1850*. UNCP, 1962.

Van Cleve, George William. *A Slaveholders' Union: Slavery, Politics, and the Constitution in the Early American Republic*. UChiP, 2010.

Van Doren, Carl. *Benjamin Franklin*. New York: Viking Press, 1938.

Verba, Sidney, and Gary R. Orren. *Equality in America: The View from the Top*. HUP, 1985.

Wain, John. *Samuel Johnson*. New York: Viking Press, 1974.

Waligorski, Conrad P. *The Political Theory of Conservative Economists*. UPKan, 1990.

Wallerstein, Immanuel. *The Modern World-System III: The Second Era of Great Expansion of the Capitalist World-Economy, 1730–1840s.* San Diego: Academic Press, 1989.

Walsh, James. *Liberty in Troubled Times: A Libertarian Guide to Laws, Politics and Society in a Troubled World.* Los Angeles: Silver Lake Publications, 2004.

Walvin, James. *England, Slaves and Freedom, 1776–1838.* Houndmills, UK: Macmillan Press, 1986.

Walzer, Michael. *Radical Principles: Reflections of an Unreconstructed Democrat.* New York: Basic Books, 1980.

——. *The Revolution of the Saints: A Study in the Origins of Radical Politics.* HUP, 1965.

——. *Spheres of Justice: A Defense of Pluralism and Equality.* New York: Basic Books, 1983.

Watson, Harry L. *Liberty and Power: The Politics of Jacksonian America.* New York: Noonday Press, 1990.

Weaver, Richard M. "Conservatism and Libertarianism." In George W. Carey, *Freedom and Virtue: The Conservative/Libertarian Debate,* 68–78. Wilmington, DE: Intercollegiate Studies Institute, 1998.

Weeks, Phillip. *Farewell My Nation: The American Indian and the United States, 1820–1890.* Arlington Heights, IL: Harlan Davidson, 1990.

Welch, Cheryl B. *De Tocqueville.* OUP, 2001.

Welch, Finis. "In Defense of Inequality." *AER* 89 (May 1999): 1–17.

Welter, Rush. *The Mind of America, 1820–1860.* ColumUP, 1975.

——. *Popular Education and Democratic Thought in America.* ColumUP, 1962.

West, Thomas G. *Vindicating the Founders: Race, Sex, Class, and Justice in the Origins of America.* Lanham, MD: Rowman and Littlefield, 1997.

Wheeler, Sara. *O My America! Six Women and Their Second Acts in a New World.* New York: Farrar, Strass and Giroux, 2013.

White, Morton. *The Philosophy of the American Revolution.* OUP, 1978.

Wiebe, Robert H. *Self-Rule: A Cultural History of American Democracy.* UChiP, 1995.

Wilentz, Sean. *Chants Democratic: New York City and the Rise of the American Working Class, 1788–1850.* OUP, 1984.

——. *The Rise of American Democracy: Jefferson to Lincoln.* New York: W. W. Norton, 2005.

Willcox, William B. *The Age of Aristocracy, 1688–1830.* 2nd ed. Lexington, MA: D. C. Heath, 1971.

Williamson, Jeffrey G., and Peter H. Lindert. *American Inequality: A Macroeconomic History.* New York: Academic Press, 1980.

Wills, Garry. *Inventing America: Jefferson's Declaration of Independence.* Garden City, NY: Doubleday and Co., 1978.

Willson, Beckles. *America's Ambassadors to England (1785–1928): A Narrative of Anglo-American Diplomatic Relations.* London: John Murray, 1928.

Wiltse, Charles Maurice. *The Jeffersonian Tradition in American Democracy.* 1935; repr., New York: Hill and Wang, 1960.

Winch, Donald. *Adam Smith's Politics: An Essay in Historiographic Revision.* CamUP, 1978.

Woloch, Nancy. *Women and the American Experience: A Concise History.* 2 vols. New York: McGraw-Hill, 1996.

Wood, Betty. *The Origins of American Slavery: Freedom and Bondage in the English Colonies.* New York: Hill and Wang, 1997.

Wood, Ellen Meiksins. *Citizens to Lords: A Social History of Western Political Thought from Antiquity to the Middle Ages.* London: Verso, 2008.

———. *Liberty and Property: A Social History of Western Political Thought from Renaissance to Enlightenment.* London: Verso, 2012.

Wood, Ellen Meiksins, and John Bellamy Foster, eds. *In Defense of History: Marxism and the Postmodern Agenda.* New York: Monthly Review Press, 1997.

Wood, Gordon S. *The Creation of the American Republic, 1776–1787.* UNCP, 1969.

———. "History of Rights in Early America." In *The Nature of Rights at the American Founding and Beyond,* 233–57. Edited by Barry Alan Shain. UVaP, 2007.

———. *The Radicalism of the American Revolution.* New York: Vintage, 1993.

Wrigley, E. A. *Poverty, Progress, and Population.* CamUP, 2004.

Young, Alfred E., and Gregory H. Nobles. *Whose American Revolution Was It?* New York: New York University Press, 2011.

Youngs, Tim. "Strategies of Travel: Charles Dickens and William Wells Brown." In *Travel Writing in the Nineteenth Century,* 163–77. Edited by Tim Youngs. London: Anthem Press, 2006.

Zajac, Edward E. *The Political Economy of Fairness.* Cambridge, MA: MIT University Press, 1995.

Zakim, Michael, and Gary D. Kornblith. "Introduction: An American Revolutionary Tradition." In *Capitalism Takes Command: The Social Transformation of Nineteenth-Century America,* 1–12. Edited by Michael Zakim and Gary D. Kornblith. UChiP, 2012.

Zoll, Donald Atwell. *Reason or Rebellion: An Informal History of Political Ideas.* Englewood Cliffs, NJ: Prentice-Hall, 1963.

Zuckerman, Michael. "Toccqueville, Turner, and Turds: Four Studies of Manners in Early America." *JAH* 85 (June 1988): 13–42.

INDEX